MW00958196

SLAVERY, RELIGION AND REGIME

SLAVERY, RELIGION AND REGIME

The Political Theory of Paul Ricoeur
as a Conceptual Framework for a
Critical Theological Interpretation
of the Modern State

Phillip J. Linden Jr., S.S.J.

Library of Congress Control Number: 2019912546
ISBN: Hardcover   978-1-7960-5489-7
                 Softcover   978-1-7960-5488-0
                 eBook   978-1-7960-5487-3

Print information available on the last page.

Rev. date: 08/26/2019

To order additional copies of this book, contact:
Xlibris
1-888-795-4274
www.Xlibris.com
Orders@Xlibris.com
797306

Mrs. Jewell R. Crawford Mazique committed all her life to the struggle for justice and the clarification of truth as a mother, government servant, intellectual, scholar, theoretician, activist, and freelance writer. It's Mrs. Mazique who has introduced me to the struggle of the Jesuits against the enslavement of natives, especially Fr. Andrew White, SJ, and the significance of his life and work in the Maryland colony (1634–1646). Mrs. Mazique will always be a beacon of light whereby many will pilot their course. To her, I express my sincerest gratitude.

Special gratitude to the Faculty of Theology of the Katholieke Universiteit Leuven, especially Prof. Georges De Schrijver, for the knowledge imparted and the support given. The Leuven method has instilled in me a way of expressing a vision of survival for the poor and oppressed of the world. It provides hope for one who accepts the challenge of the "preferential option for the poor" and who is committed to struggle with and on behalf of the poor. Also, I am grateful to Xavier University of Louisiana. The charism of the founder of Xavier, Saint Katharine Drexel, continues to inspire excellence in both faculty and students.

CONTENTS

CHAPTER THREE
The Struggle for Humanity in the Context of Religious Conflict

INTRODUCTION

THE PURPOSE OF this dissertation is to establish a critical theological interpretation of the interplay among the major political, economic, and religious expressions of modernity in the Atlantic world; namely, a developing political regime (the modern state regulated by reason-based science), merchant-class economics (capitalism and slavery), and adjusted religion (the Protestant revolution).

The critical theological perspective we shall use in this work is in the tradition of Gustavo Gutiérrez in his works *A Theology of Liberation: History, Politics, and Salvation* and *The Power of the Poor in History* and beyond.[1] For Gutiérrez, theology is critical reflection with a perspective from the "underside of history." *Critical reflection* means analysis of the changes in the sociohistorical context with a critical stance on political, economic, and religious issues. The concern is on meaning and particularly on the manner in which those issues affect the lives of those being undermined by various ideologies of oppression.

Taking into account the view of Antonio Gramsci, Gutiérrez depicts the one engaged in critical reflection from the underside of history as an "organic intellectual." For the organic intellectual in the Gramsci-Gutiérrez sense,

---

[1] Gustavo Gutiérrez, *A Theology of Liberation: History, Politics, and Salvation,* trans. and ed. Sr. Caridad Inda and John Eagleson (Maryknoll: Orbis Books, 1973); Gustavo Gutiérrez, *The Power of the Poor in History,* trans. Robert R. Barr (Maryknoll: Orbis Books, 1983). On this topic, Gustavo Gutiérrez cites the study of Antonio Gramsci entitled "La fondazione degli intellettuali."

"theological reasoning is an effort on the part of concrete persons to form and think out their faith in determinate circumstances, to plan activities and make interpretations that play a role in the real-life occurrences and confrontations of a given society. The theologian is not working in some kind of ahistorical limbo."[2]

Gutiérrez then goes on to say that "the true interpretation of the meaning revealed by theology is achieved only in *historical praxis*." He continues, "The *organic intellectual* will be someone personally and vitally engaged in historical realities with specific times and places. The *organic intellectual* will be engaged where nations, social classes, people struggle to free themselves from domination and oppression by other nations, classes, and people."[3] Thus, the sociohistorical context becomes the landscape from which one does theology, and theology as critical reflection becomes a place for the resistance of structural oppression and dominance.

The use of theology as critical reflection by Gutiérrez is a reference point for another component of the methodology in this enterprise; namely, recognizing the study of religion as a "space of confrontation" against the structures of

---

[2] According to this Gustavo Gutiérrez–Antonio Gramsci understanding of the organic intellectual, the theologian who begins by placing theology in its social context by seeking to understand faith by raising questions asked by those who have no history, "those who are oppressed and marginalized," and do so by trying to show "the exact point of historical, political, and social breach" that has taken place between the oppressed and the oppressor is the organic intellectual. "The organic intellectual is organically linked to the popular undertaking of liberation" (Gutiérrez, *The Power of the Poor in History*, 212).

[3] Gutiérrez, *A Theology of Liberation*, 13; Gutiérrez, *The Power of the Poor in History*, 212. The technical term *organic intellectual* refers to the intellectual propagators of modernity. A significant question is whether the term is the most accurate way to describe doing history from the "underside," especially when it is the forces of modernity that have created ideologies of oppression, which keeps its victims subservient.

The interesting point, however, is that Gutiérrez uses the term to describe those involved in liberation, struggling for freedom from domination. He says that the concept of the organic intellectual is used to distinguish liberation theology from those who do theology "created by the intelligentsia, the affluent, the powerful, those on top; it is theology from the bottom, from 'the underside,' created by the victims, the poor, the oppressed. It is not theology spun out in a series of principles or axioms of timeless truth that are then 'applied' to the contemporary scene, but a theology springing up out of poverty, oppression, the heart-rending conditions under which the great majority of Latin Americans live." According to Gutiérrez, the organic intellectual places theology in its social context, thus making theology a response and a challenge to vast historical processes (*The Power of the Poor in History*, vii, 212).

oppression. As a basis for this approach, Ricoeur's interpretation of Kant's *Religion within the Limits of Reason Alone* (1793) is significant.[4] Accordingly, it is in Ricoeur's post-Hegelian return to Kant that he describes the totalization potential of religion when it is limited to the realm of moral action; namely, ethics and ethical statements. This is when religion becomes "rationality." The totalization potential of religion relegates religion to appearances. In this sense, religion becomes one of the defining characteristics of dominance (evil as a rational regulatory tool). Ricoeur suggests that hope (resistance) in the face of this kind of dominance is theology being a context for the confrontation of systems of totalization that sustain ideologies of oppression.

Ricoeur gives insight to the problem of religion as a dominant and totalizing entity when he says that "evil is not the violation of an interdict, the subversion of the law, disobedience, but fraudulency in the work of totalization. In this sense, true evil appears only in the very field where religion is produced."[5]

Confronting the "evil" of totalization (Ricoeur) becomes the role of critical theological reflection of the "organic intellectual" (Gutiérrez). It is in

---

4   Carl J. Friedrich, ed., *Religion within the Limits of Reason Alone*, in *The Philosophy of Kant: Immanuel Kant's Moral and Political Writings* (New York: Modern Library; Random House, Inc.), 365–411.

5   Paul Ricoeur continues by stating that the field where religion is produced is "in the field of contradictions and conflicts determined, on the one hand, by the demand for totalization which constitutes reason (ethics), both theoretical and practical, and, on the other hand, by the illusion which misleads thought, the subtle hedonism which initiates moral motivation, and finally by the malice which corrupts the great human enterprises of totalization. The demand for a complete object of the will is basically antinomic. The evil of evil is born in the area of this antinomy."

Ricoeur asserts that "evil and hope are more closely connected than we ever think of them; if the evil of evil is born on the way of totalization, it would appear only in a pathology of hope, as the inherent perversion in the problematic of fulfillment and of totalization. . . . The true malice of man appears only in the state and in the church, as institutions of gathering together, of recapitulation, of totalization. . . . This culminates not with transgression, but with *flawed synthesis* [italics added] in the political and religious spheres. That is why true religion (theology) is always in a debate with false religion that is for Kant statutory religion." See Paul Ricoeur, "Faith in the Light of Hope," in *Conflict of Interpretation* (Evanston, IL: Northwestern University Press, 1974), 402–24; Paul Ricoeur, "On Biblical Hermeneutics," *Semeia* 4 (1975): 23–148; Diogenes Allen, *Philosophy for Understanding Theology* (Atlanta: John Knox Press, 1985; London: SCM Press Ltd., 1985), 202–19; Immanuel Kant, "Religion within the Limits of Reason Alone" (1793), in *The Philosophy of Kant: Immanuel Kant's Moral and Political Writings*, ed. with an introduction by Carl Friedrich (New York: Random House, Inc. Modern Library, 1949), 365–411.

this sense, though quite summarily expressed, that theology or a history of religion methodology becomes a space of confrontation; it becomes engaged in "debate with false religion." This approach "organically" ties theology itself to a process of resistance of oppression as a way of grounding the process of liberation. The critical reflection approach by Gutiérrez is recognizing the study of religion as a "space of confrontation" against the structures of oppression.

Charles H. Long provides still another reference point that confirms the history of religion methodology to be used in this study. He too confronts the tendency to see the study of religion as nothing more than just an ivory tower construction created by the academy and buoyed up by the human sciences. For Long, perceiving the study of religion as a science in the Enlightenment sense is problematic. This is due to what he describes as the "universality of reason within an Enlightenment orientation."[6]

What Charles Long does is place the study of religion against the background of expansionist merchant theories and practices of modern Europe. Such theories, according to Long, exist within the context of an evolutionary meaning of history. Within this context, "the actions, behaviors, and customs of other cultures could then be seen as embryonic growths of reason or as reason hidden and obscured by its shadows."[7]

The study of religion seen in this light considers that the meaning of religion is rooted in the cultural preconditions of those who study it (hermeneutics). A hermeneutical approach to religion derives understanding within the context of these diverse meanings. Long asserts, though, that "the presence of hermeneutical methods and theories does not automatically rule out the possibility of a systematic human science in the Enlightenment sense but it does set up tensions between the vision of the totality of such a science in relationship to the other disciplines that had to be encompassed and comprehended in the definition of this science." The hermeneutical approach allows for the confrontation of the "antinomies at the heart of the constitution of the Enlightenment meaning of the human sciences."[8]

Thus, the "space of confrontation" (Ricoeur) or the "space of mediation" (Long) seeks to decipher and critique "the reciprocities, relationships, and discourses between the Europeans and their *others* . . . It is my hope that such a procedure will allow for another analysis of the history of colonialism as a reservoir for the data of religion and give specification to the known but unspoken languages of relationship and reciprocities that took place during

---

6   Charles H. Long, "Towards a Post-Colonial Method in the Study of Religion," *Religious Studies News, Spotlight on Teaching* 10, no. 2 (May 1995): 4–5.

7   Long, "Towards a Post-Colonial Method in the Study of Religion," 5.

8   Long, "Towards a Post-Colonial Method in the Study of Religion," 4.

the tragic and ambiguous period of colonialism."[9] Though Long's focus is the colonialism of the nineteenth century, his approach to history also gives insight to the methodological concerns of this study. It is with the approaches to history of Gutiérrez, Ricoeur, and Long in mind that we speak of engaging in a critical theological interpretation of modernity.

The first of three chapters discusses the creation of the modern state, fashioned by political, economic, and religious forces as a legacy for the New World. Our theory is that the development of religion in the New World has accommodated itself to the entrepreneurial interests of the newly rising merchant class, which has outgrown its Mediterranean context and expanded into the Atlantic world. Thus, British America has been the product of modernity, a society (the modern nation-state) whose underlying principles have actually meant freedom from religion with profits at any cost.

The second chapter consists in an extraction of a political theory from the works of the French philosopher Paul Ricoeur, giving us the authority to give a new reading of the history of religious development in the Americas. Beginning with the Ricoeurian theory of imagination, we have derived what is called a hermeneutics of historical consciousness. Significant in this process is the role of productive imagination, which provides the creative dimension at the level of configuration, especially the role and function of sedimented history and paradigm. It is in taking the traditional or sedimented history and creatively adding the temporal dimension that a new understanding can be derived. It serves as a bridge that connects the first chapter to the third one on the Maryland colony.

The third chapter consists in the story of the Maryland colony, which is consistent with and supports the original theory that the forces of modernity. The Maryland colony thus becomes a specific instance of how the seventeenth-century expansion has formed a society whose underlying principles have actually meant freedom from religion and profits at any cost. The story of severe persecution and what is tantamount to "enslavement" of the Catholic founders of the Maryland colony unmasks the cultural clash that stands as the foundation of the modern state as it expresses itself in the New World. The meaning of this clash has deep roots that go back to the rise of the nation-state with its political, economic, and religious expression of modernity.

---

[9]   Long, "Towards a Post-Colonial Method in the Study of Religion," 5; see also Charles H. Long, *Significations: Signs, Symbols, and Images in the Interpretation of Religion* (Philadelphia: Fortress Press, 1986), 9.

CHAPTER ONE

Forgotten Memories: The Creation of the Modern State and its Legacy in the New World

INTRODUCTION

DURING THE LAST five hundred years, the Judeo-Christian world has been dominated by the creation and preservation of the modern state. The modern state is associated with complex ideas, movements, and forces that have their origins in the radical changes that have begun in Europe and are at the heart of the clash of cultures that have characterized the New World since its genesis.

By "New World" is meant European expansion from the burgeoning Mediterranean world into the Atlantic world. This expansion represents the geopolitical grounding of modernity with its political, socioeconomic, and redefined religious forces. With the coming of the Atlantic world, a new era has emerged in which rational schemes of domination have been secured by surveillance (coercion), violence, and technology-based management, along with various imperceptible forms of domination and manipulation.

This chapter is in no way meant to be just an event-by-event chronicling of what has transpired during the rise of the Atlantic world. Using broad strokes, a picture will be painted showing how modernity has been a rational, planned reality, how it has established and has continued to maintain itself. This study entails crawling back through history to the juncture where a radical disruption in Western culture has occurred. The radical changes associated with the disruption form the background for a critical interpretation of the new "religiously" motivated reality of the New World.[10]

The purpose of this chapter is to lay the background for raising critical theological questions regarding the exercise of power and power relationships

---

[10] Although numerous sources are used in this chapter, the following are primary in situating the origins of the modern state as a construction, its political economy, and its religious expression within the European historical context.

We use sources that provide a definition and a general overview of some of the issues associated with the rise of the modern state: James Anderson, ed., *The Rise of the Modern State* (Atlantic Highlands, New Jersey: Humanities Press International, Inc., 1986); R. H. Tawney, *Religion and the Rise of Capitalism: A Historical Study (Holland Memorial Lectures, 1922)* (New York and Toronto: Mentor Books, the New American Library, Inc., 1954); Max Weber, *The Protestant Ethic and the Spirit of Capitalism: A Classic Study of the Fundamental Relationship between Religion and the Economic and Social Life in Modern Culture*, trans. Talcott Parsons, foreword by R. H. Tawney (New York: Charles Scribner's Sons, 1958); Gustavo Gutiérrez, *The Power of the Poor in History*, trans. Robert R. Barr (Maryknoll, NY: Orbis Books, 1983, 1984). Then we use sources that render perspectives on and a critique of historical materialism and the modern state: Anthony Giddens, *A Contemporary Critique of Historical Materialism* (Houndmills, Basingstoke, Hampshire, and London: Macmillan Press Ltd., 1981); Anthony Giddens, *The Nation-State and Violence: Volume 2 of A Contemporary Critique of Historical Materialism* (Cambridge: Polity Press, 1985); Anthony Giddens, *Capitalism and Modern Social Theory: An Analysis of the Writings of Marx, Durkheim, and Max Weber* (Cambridge, London, New York, Melbourne, and Sydney: Cambridge University Press, 1971); Benjamin Ginsberg, *The Fatal Embrace: Jews and the State* (Chicago and London: University of Chicago Press, 1993); Immanuel Wallerstein, *The Modern World-System: Capitalist Agriculture and the Origins of the European World-Economy in the Sixteenth Century* (New York, San Francisco, and London: Academic Press, 1974).

Although the above sources provide the context for reflection on the religious reality, we refer—in the final section of this chapter—to the studies of Guy E. Swanson, *Religion and Regime: A Sociological Account of the Reformation* (Ann Arbor: University of Michigan Press, 1967) and particularly Georgia Harkness, *John Calvin: The Man and His Ethics* (New York, Nashville: Abingdon Press, 1931) for a more detailed analysis of the role of religion (or lack thereof) in the rise of the modern nation-state.

Although it is older, the Georgia Harkness study is a classic. She does a clever study on the interrelationship among the forces of modernity, capitalism, and religion at the rise of the modern state. She critically analyzes the contributions of John Calvin, Max Weber, and R. H. Tawney as a basis to understand the clash that has taken place in modern society.

spawned by the rise of the modern nation-state and its legacy in the Atlantic world. This will be the first stage in a methodology whose intention is to shape the whole of this study into a theological critique of the modern state. The chapter also includes an effort to situate various ideologies of oppression that continue to threaten the security of the victims of the modern state.

This chapter is divided into three main sections to establish the background for and to give perspective to this theological undertaking. The first is a study of the politics of modernity that tells the story of the rise of the modern nation-state as a radical disruption with the traditional states. The modern state is the consequence of the combination of scientific and philosophical methods that has its origins in an Enlightenment rationality.

This section is an effort to situate the modern state and its politics and to provide the historical context for a creative analysis. The modern state has its ideological roots in Greece and Rome. This declaration might suggest a progressivist or evolutionist interpretation of history. However, theoretically, such a progressivist or evolutionist interpretation of the modern state is usually limited to the observation of successive changes in the forces of production. Yet a nonevolutionist interpretation of history is intent on explicating that the rise of the modern state is distinct from the teleological change or development of productive forces. Moreover, the secular theories of some of the principal thinkers have reinforced the modern state and its system.

In the second section, we shall examine the role of capitalism as a radical political expression of exploitive economic interests. If, as stated above, the rise of the modern state is distinct from the teleological change or development of productive forces, it might seem that a study of the role of capitalism in the modern state is contradictory. On the contrary, this study–in covering the rise of capitalism–will not only confirm that it was a radical break with its economic predecessors but will also expose its exploitive dimensions both in industrial Europe and in New World slavery.

Expanding markets and creative ingenuity resulted in the disintegration of the feudal and manorial systems as two significant means to the well-being of the peoples of medieval society. The breakdown of these systems gave way to a money economy, the rise of the industrial dimension of the modern state in general, and specifically the rise of modern slavery in the New World. Modern slavery was a radically new reality, distinct from its ancient and medieval counterparts, and principally a New World phenomenon. We shall see that some economists argued, however, that modern slavery also benefited the sovereign states of Europe, even if only briefly. Even so, the significance of modern slavery was in its role in building up the New World colonial interests of the merchants who were losing their influence in various monarchies.

By this time, several of the rising monarchies—even to their detriment—had expelled various merchant interests.

Slavery has always been the labor force for an agrarian and not a capitalist economy. The intention, at this point, is merely to situate slavery in the rise of modernity. It will be seen that the fullest meaning of slavery in the context of modern capitalism is not merely as an economic system. Slavery is also the vehicle for the expansion of modernity and the modern state into the New World. Slavery discloses the extent in which exploitation is associated with the progression of modernity.

In the final section, we examine religion in the modern state. Because of the nature of modernity and its relationship to reason, religion is not included in any of its projects, including the state. Here, one discloses that modernity establishes itself as a reasoned reality under the dictates of scientific rationality. This constitutes a redefined, adjusted religious understanding and practice.

Beginning with an outline presentation of religion in medieval society as a background, this study will examine the Protestant Reformation with specific emphasis on the rise of Puritanism in England. The importance of English Puritanism is in how it has become the shape of religious expression in the New World. Puritanism has left a deep mark on the New World, particularly in how it has adjusted itself to the interests of the modern state.

The religious discussion finally turns toward the thought of the sixteenth-century social religious thinkers caught up in the cross fire of declining traditional religious reality. It concentrates on the New World and considers itself to be "religiously" motivated, even though secular theories of the state neutralized religious ideas and values.

In the conclusion of this chapter, it is determined that the European social context yields its potential for grounding the critical theological reflection of this study. Viewing the New World or Atlantic world from its European background is a necessary ingredient in the critical analysis of religion in the rise of the modern state. European expansion, which has begun during the late fifteenth century, has forged the New World and has been the starting point of modernity, eventually to be grounded in the modern state.

Let us move now into the first part of this chapter. It is of significance to state at the outset that the modern nation-state has emerged within the context of modernity. Thus, as James Anderson says in his discussion of its meaning, *modern* is not synonymous with *contemporary*. Likewise, Anderson argues that though the sixteenth century—with the appearance of the absolutist state, the precursor of the modern state—is probably the early beginnings of the modern era, *modern* does not simply refer to the last five hundred years as a single historical period because of the time and discontinuous level of variations that has existed (*uneven and combined development* or, as we shall cite later, *space-time edges*).[11] Moreover, Anderson disagrees with the idea that *modern*, when applied to "states," merely refers to certain "standard features" such as monopoly power with standing armies to be used to create monopoly rights and protection mainly for the elite as suggested by certain thinkers.[12] Although Anderson does not refer to it in his study, these various determinations suggest an evolutionist or continuist approach to history that, of itself, does not adequately account for the radical transformation that we call modernity.

1.1. THE POLITICS OF MODERNITY: THE NEW REGIME

The rise of modernity and consequently of the modern nation-state gave rise to a new world, accompanied by explosions in learning, science, literature, art, economic expansion, and discovery. These "interacting processes" resulted in a new politics, economics, and (civil) religion. The new modern nation-state was the political expression of modernity. It was invented in such a way that both the security of economic well-being and the practice of religion were no longer contained within or reliant on unified political structures as they had been.

In this discourse on the modern nation-state as the political expression of modernity, it will be necessary to discuss the accepted definition of *modern nation-state*. Most thinkers will give a descriptive definition of *modern state*. Accordingly, a modern nation-state is an apparatus of authority or coercive power that organizes and rules a specific people (nation) who live in its territory and has a standing police or military that uses violence to preserve the rule. This idea of a modern nation-state also refers to the "social system that is subject to that government (apparatus of authority) or power."[13] Therefore, this definition of *modern nation-state* is characterized by a "centralized bureaucracy and taxation system, a regular standing army, and unified sovereignty over a clearly demarcated territory."[14]

---

[11] James Anderson, "The Modernity of Modern States," in *The Rise of the Modern State,* ed. James Anderson (Atlantic Highlands, New Jersey: Humanities Press International, Inc., 1986), 2–4.

[12] Frederic C. Lane, "The Economic Meaning of War and Protection," *Venice and History* (Baltimore: Johns Hopkins Press, 1966), 389. This work by Lane is cited in Wallerstein, *The Modern World-System,* 16.

[13] Giddens further distinguishes between the state and the civil society when he says, "I shall speak of 'the state apparatus' when I mean the administrative organs of government and 'society' or 'culture' when I mean the encompassing social system" (*The Nation-State and Violence,* 17).

[14] Anderson, "The Modernity of Modern States," 2; Giddens, in *The Nation-State and Violence,* 17–22. There, he uses the social scientist Émile Durkheim as a starting point for his definition of *state.*

Understanding the distinguishing characteristics of the modern nation-state, however, first warrants a brief analysis of the nonmodern or traditional state. It is commonly understood that the concept of state comes from the Greek notion of *polis* and that it means "city-state." It is vital to acknowledge that the term *modern* is not always synonymous with *state*, for there are both modern and nonmodern traditional states as well as a combination of both.[15] When used in conjunction with the concept of state, however, reference to the concept of modern delineates characteristics that are radically different from the social structure called the traditional state.

The traditional or nonmodern state consists in different types of intersocietal systems.[16] They are localized systems of tribal cultures, city-state systems, systems of feudal states, patrimonial empires, nomad or conquest empires, and centralized historical bureaucratic empires.[17] The paradigm for understanding the traditional state is the city-state and the large agrarian empire. The principal influence of this kind of traditional state is the administrative resources it generates. But these administrative resources are usually minimal because of the small population of the traditional city.

There were certain similarities in all traditional state-type societies; namely, "universal" architectural form and social characteristics. The city-state or the large agrarian empire type of city usually had a wall around it as a part of a defense system. In the center of the city were governmental and religious buildings with a marketplace in an open square. The center also contained the homes of the elite, with the poor living farther away from the center.[18]

Commerce was not the main factor that gave rise to the traditional states. They were, however, centers of technological innovation in the area of agrarian production.

---

[15] What this suggests is that the broader notion of state (e.g., those states centered on the Mediterranean world, which included northern Africa; Byzantine Italy city-states; the world of the Indian Ocean–Red Sea; the Chinese region; the area of central Asia; and the Baltic region) has existed before the actual delineation of the modern nation-state. Cf. Immanuel Wallerstein, *The Modern World-System*, 17; Anderson, *The Rise of the Modern State*, 2.

[16] Various studies can help derive a picture of the type of society called the traditional state. Giddens, *The Nation-State and Violence*, 35–41. In defining the nonmodern or traditional state, Giddens cites as his sources S. N. Eisenstadt, *The Political Systems of Empires* (Glencoe: The Free Press, 1963); H. J. M. Claessen and P. Skalnik, *The Early State* (The Hague: Mouton, 1978); John A. Wilson, "Egypt through the New Kingdom," in *City Invincible*, Carl H. Kraeling and Robert M. Adams (Chicago: University of Chicago Press, 1960); and Gideon Sjoberg, *The Preindustrial City* (Glencoe: The Free Press, 1960).

[17] Giddens, *The Nation-State and Violence*, 35, 77–78.

[18] Giddens, *Nation-State and Violence*, 36–37; Sjoberg, *The Preindustrial City*, 5.

These types of societies usually existed in relation to other nearby cities or villages. The political authority was centralized and loose in structure with a restricted use of military power. There were no standing armies in the traditional states, but rather, the armies were conscripted when there was a need for defense. There was usually no effort to consolidate several cities under a broader bureaucratic structure for governance. So each traditional entity had its own language, as well as political and economic identity.[19]

If we are to derive a more representative characterization of the modern nation-state beyond an analysis of its standard features ("centralized bureaucracy and taxation system, a regular standing army, and unified sovereignty over a clearly demarcated territory"), we must see it within the framework of modernity as abstract rationality. The characterization of the modern nation-state within the context of modernity results in a more intricate analysis of the questions of power and power relationships. As we shall see, it moves the discourse beyond seeing merely productive forces as a summarization of history, the most common understanding suggested by an evolutionist interpretation. In fact, an analysis of the modern nation-state from the perspective of its being the political expression of modernity reveals the roots of dominance within both authoritative and allocative resources of the modern nation-state. It gives us greater potential for addressing the problem of dominance from the underside of history.

Modernity is usually associated with abstract rationality; namely, a reasoned, planned, or ordered way of viewing or understanding the world. According to Georges De Schrijver, modernity is buttressed by scientific (Galileo, Kepler, and Newton) and philosophical (Descartes, Locke, Leibniz) methodologies. De Schrijver writes that modernity rests on five pillars: "confidence in science-based technology, the sovereignty of the nation-states, bureaucratic rationality, profit maximization, and the belief in steady progress."[20] He continues his characterization of modernity by stating that "the celestial explanation of order in nature and in human society was groundless, and had to be substituted with a new scientific approach, based on mathematically-constructed laws in physics and technology, and on the rational ordering subject (Descartes, Kant) in the domain of human society."[21]

At this point in his discourse, De Schrijver cites Stephen Toulmin, who makes the distinction between a "humanistic" modernity characterized by

---

19   Giddens, *The Nation-State and Violence,* 37–41.
20   Georges De Schrijver, "The Paradigm Shift in Third World Theologies of Liberation: From Socio-Economic Analysis to Cultural Analysis. Assessment and Status of the Question" (paper for Liberation Theology Symposium, KU Leuven, November 1996), 7.
21   De Schrijver, "The Paradigm Shift," 7.

the Renaissance and a "scientific" modernity usually associated with the Enlightenment of the seventeenth and eighteenth centuries. This is of interest and importance especially in that Stephen Toulmin dates the beginning of scientific modernity as the 1630s. This distinction between humanistic modernity and scientific modernity is significant because it is the exact distinction to be made in chapter 3, when we characterize the government of colonial Maryland (1634) as an enlightened feudalism.

The nation-state as a modern entity is both a bureaucratic rationality and sovereign. Georges De Schrijver distinguishes the nation-state from the state as he writes, "The nation-state began to be born, with its centralized and uniform organizational patterns in matters of jurisprudence, taxation, police, army, education, means of transportation and communication, language, culture policies, and after a while, geometrical city planning." De Schrijver continues, "The nation-state became the embodiment of rational order." Thus, the modern state is reason or rationality, basing society and the laws that shape it on "precepts of reason."[22] "Rational government meant the newly perceived malleability of social life, its needs to be shaped, its amenability to being remade according to designs embodied in the actions of external agencies—power being tantamount to the effectiveness of such action."[23]

Sovereignty, as a characteristic of the modern state, suggests the centralization of power within itself and the resistance to control from outside. For example, religion has not been seen as beyond the grounds of that sovereignty. Leadership in the nonmodern state has been ordained by God. The leader has acted within the state on behalf of God but not usually exacted a specific religion of the citizens. The modern state, on the contrary, is characterized by the separation of church and state. This means something radically different. Not only has the leader not exacted a specific religion of the citizens but the state has almost been totally free from the constraints of any kind of religion. Likewise, the sovereignty has been manifested in that only those who have been considered citizens have taken part in the day-to-day process of running the affairs of the state. Consequently, in accordance with the meaning of *modernity* as expressed earlier, one can say that the modern nation-state and its sovereignty are the practical expression of "science-based technology and bureaucratic rationality."[24]

Understanding the radical shifts that have taken place with the rise of modernity and the modern nation-state constitutes a problem of historical interpretation. The renowned historian Geoffrey Barraclough divides

---

[22] De Schrijver, "The Paradigm Shift," 8.

[23] Z. Bauman, *Intimations of Postmodernity* (London and New York: Routledge, 1992), 10.

[24] De Schrijver, 7–8; Stephen Toulmin, *Cosmopolis: The Hidden Agenda of Modernity* (Chicago: University of Chicago Press, 1990), 8–9.

European history into three periods based on what he calls the "three great problems" that have prevailed in Europe from the earliest records. These three great problems are (1) antiquity, (2) the investiture contest that has promoted what has been called the "great revolution," and (3) the Enlightenment. He parallels the age of discontinuity in Europe to a radical turning point in the life of the human person. Barraclough states that the changes in Europe have been like the growth and development of the human person from birth into adulthood and then on into life as an elderly person. The one strength of this approach is that, like those changes in the life of the human person, no single change in Europe takes precedence over another; neither are they derivative of the other. Accordingly, modernity is a radical turning point in Europe and not a derivative of an earlier period.[25]

The significance of focusing on European history the way Barraclough has done challenges us to acknowledge that it is no longer accurate to view the rise of modernity as merely a stage along an evolutionary, progressivist type of path.[26] Although Barraclough may not go far enough in his critique, he respects the radical disruption that takes place with the rise of modernity. His interpretation has the potential of explicating the powerful role of reason-enforced confidence in science-based technology, bureaucratic rationality, sovereign nation-states, maximization of profits, and belief in steady progress as constituting a radical break with the past.

Anthony Giddens has sought to outline and situate the rise of modernity and the modern capitalist nation-state in history more accurately. Such a task, according to Giddens, requires an adequate interpretation of history, a critical theory that includes an institutional analysis of modernity, and rejection of any idea that history creates and solves the problems of humanity. For example, Giddens sees that class struggle vis-à-vis Karl Marx is "both an expression of the social exploitation and at the same time the source of its transcendence."[27] Before presenting his nonevolutionary, discontinuist perspective of history, Giddens defines the evolutionary, continuist interpretation and engages in a critique of Marx's notion of historical materialism.

"An evolutionary interpretation of history in general, and modern history particularly, provides the customary approach to understanding the rise of capitalism. What this means is that as a result of some discernible mechanisms

---

25   Geoffrey Barraclough, *History in a Changing World* (Norman, OK: University of Oklahoma, 1955), 154–67.

26   Giddens, *The Nation-State and Violence,* 83–84. Giddens explains that the modern nation-state is not adequately explained by using a progressivist, evolutionary, or continuist interpretation of history. As we shall see momentarily, he develops what he calls a discontinuous interpretation.

27   Giddens, *A Contemporary Critique of Historical Materialism,* ix–x.

of change, there are trends of development in history which culminate in the emergence of modern, i.e. Western societies–these standing at the top of a hierarchy of types of society."[28] The evolutionary interpretation argues that even though there are some differences, there are "dominant continuities" that subsist throughout history. This approach, particularly with its evolutionary theories of social change, contends that the changes that are taking place are not so radically different from what has gone on before. Giddens, in explaining the evolutionary interpretation of history, says that "there are no fundamental discontinuities in social change. All phases of development that look like revolutions of one kind or another turn out to involve less turbulent, underlying processes of change that Giddens refers to as merely "social differentiation."[29] The social differentiation that takes place in the continuist interpretation of history is teleological, regulated by what is its ultimate or final cause. This means that there is an evolution whose stages progressively lead to

a high point of social development, "from the simple to the more complex."[30] In the continuist methodology, history (temporality) and social change are understood as "essentially" the same. As we shall see, a distinction between history and social change is necessary.[31]

During the earlier prehistoric era, changes were slight to almost imperceptible. The social structures underwent no recognizable change until the coming of agrarian-type societies. The pace of change increased with some of the nonmodern type of societies because of some economic and technological changes. In both the hunter-gatherer and the nonmodern-type societies, there was a distinct continuity in their social structures. Any changes were more likely adjustments of existing social structures for the sake of accommodation.[32]

In most forms of evolution, the continuities were portrayed as part of a generalized process of social differentiation.[33] But it was not until the rise of modernity and modern industrial-capitalist-type societies that there was a radical break with the earlier type of societies; thus evolved the modern nation-state.

---

[28] Giddens, *The Nation-State and Violence*, 31. Here, Giddens refers to chapter 5 of his work entitled *The Constitution of Society* (Cambridge: Polity Press, 1984), where he is laying the groundwork for his "discontinuist interpretation of history."

[29] Giddens, *The Nation-State and Violence*, 32.

[30] Giddens, The *Nation-State and Violence*, 31; Giddens, *A Contemporary Critique of Historical Materialism*, 69–70.

[31] Giddens, *The Nation-State and Violence*, 32.

[32] Giddens, *The Nation-State and Violence*, 32.

[33] Giddens, *The Modern Nation-State and Violence*, 31; Giddens, *A Contemporary Critique of Historical Materialism*, 69–89 passim.

Modernity and the modern nation-state, according to Giddens, constitutes a radical disruption or discontinuity that enforces a separation from the past. Therefore, modernity and the modern nation-state cannot be merely a stage in an evolutionary process. In this effort to provide an alternative interpretation of history, Giddens derives as his starting point "a critical appraisal of some of the main themes of Marx's historical materialism."[34] In this critical appraisal, Giddens takes exception to an evolutionary, continuist interpretation of history and opts for a discontinuist interpretation.

Giddens points to Karl Marx and his notion of historical materialism as continuist or evolutionary in that it focuses on social change as involving the progressive scheme of growth of the forces of production.[35] Historical materialism, according to Giddens, is "the conception that the history of human societies can be understood in terms of the progressive augmentation of the forces of production . . . the history of all hitherto existing society is the history of class struggles."[36] Using the Hegelian dialectical scheme, Marx establishes that capitalism is the summation of world history that will ultimately come to "revolutionary rupture" with the rise of socialism. In other words, Marx is stressing the significance of capitalism in bringing an end to human alienation. Giddens interprets Marx as saying that "capitalism is the class society which is to put an end to class societies; it is a society which maximizes human self-alienation, but in such a way as to open up the road to a new social order in which such self-alienation will be transcended."[37]

Besides its being evolutionary, the problem with Marx's theory–according to Giddens–is that it is reductionist when it focuses on the forces of production as the "summation of world history." Marx's materialist conception of history ultimately limits the understanding of history to a preoccupation with the allocative resources, leaving out the *institutional dimensions* that consist in the controlling "impact of the global nation state system and associated means of industrial, administrative and military power."[38]

---

[34] Marx's well-known theory of historical materialism is referred to here only as background. Giddens critiques historical materialism as teleological. Accordingly, Marx's theory is that "the driving force of the expansion of modernity across the world . . . is simply and primarily capitalistic competition" (Giddens, *A Contemporary Critique of Historical Materialism*, ix, 1; also, cf. Giddens, *The Nation-State and Violence*, 31). It is in chapter 3 of his work entitled *A Contemporary Critique of Historical Materialism* (69–89) that Anthony Giddens renders his critique of historical materialism.

[35] Giddens, *The Nation-State and Violence*, 31.

[36] Giddens, *A Contemporary Critique of Historical Materialism*, 1.

[37] Giddens, *A Contemporary Critique of Historical Materialism*, 75.

[38] Giddens, *A Contemporary Critique of Historical Materialism*, x.

Giddens's argument is that Marx's theory does not provide a "confrontation with various *institutional dimensions* of the modern order." There needs to be a strong critique of the institutional dimensions of modernity with its serious problems. Giddens lists four such problems. "One such problem is the polarisation of rich and poor, found not only within the developed countries but in much more acute form in the disparity between the wealthy and impoverished nations of the world. A second is the destructive impact of industry and technology upon the ecosystems of the environment. A third, linked to the intensifying of surveillance, is the repression of human rights within authoritarian political

regimes. Finally, there is the ever-present threat of large-scale war, whether or not such a war involves the use of nuclear weaponry."[39]

The discontinuist interpretation goes beyond any possibility of an evolutionary theory of history, such as the reading of history undertaken by historical materialism. History has to do with temporalities, and it is distinct from teleological change. The modern capitalist nation-state is a disruptive, discontinuist creation with no parallels in prior types of societies, nor is it teleological.[40] What has taken place with the rise of modernity and the modern capitalist nation-state has been radically different from the prehistoric period when humans have lived in hunter-gatherer societies.

The modern state has been radically different from what has been distinctive about the social world that capitalism has created as contrasted to other forms of social organization.[41] De Schrijver explains that the radical nature of the rupture that has created the modern state is rooted in modernity's powers of "abstraction and mathematization" of reality. In discussing modernity's role in undermining and superseding traditional ways of conduct, De Schrijver says that "modernity possesses and promotes a dynamic thrust towards change, precisely because of the propagation and universalization of abstract thinking."[42]

---

[39]   Giddens, *A Contemporary Critique of Historical Materialism*, xix.

[40]   Giddens, *A Contemporary Critique of Historical Materialism*, 69–73.

[41]   Giddens, *A Contemporary Critique of Historical Materialism*, 1–2.

[42]   Georges De Schrijver, "The Paradigm Shift," 12–13.

Also, cf. Giddens, *The Nation-State and Violence*; Giddens, *A Contemporary Critique of Historical Materialism*. In both of these works, Giddens argues that modernity constitutes a radical discontinuity with the past (Anderson, *The Rise of the Modern State*).

Immanuel Wallerstein places the creation of the modern world in the context of one of the two great "watersheds in the history of man"; the other was the Neolithic or agricultural revolution. Wallerstein says, "There seems to be widespread consensus that some great structural changes did occur in the world in the last several hundred years, changes that make the world of today

Giddens asserts that there are two common themes that exist in accordance with the Marxist-type evolutionist, continuist interpretation of history; namely, the "measure of the level of development achieved by any given society can be derived from how 'advanced' it is in terms of its capability of controlling the material environment–in terms of the level of the development of the productive forces. . . . [and] the heavy concentration, in many evolutionary theories, upon social development as an 'adaptive' process, where 'adaptation' is conceived of in an almost mechanical fashion."[43] Of course, in the case of the latter theme, knowledgeability is a central factor that has to do with practical consciousness, whereby "knowing that" and "knowing how" are determined by the hegemonic groups, those in more advanced societies. Giddens rejects these themes because, instead of their being transformative, they comprise an evolutionary approach to history that results in the reproduction of structures of domination.[44]

Thus, one also has to analyze the time-space constitution of social systems and their connection with structures of domination. Without becoming too detailed, it is sufficient for us to provide a brief explanation of the time-space constitution of social systems and how the problem of time and space is

---

qualitatively different from the world of yesterday" (*The Modern World-System*, 3). Wallerstein goes on to describe four major epochs of the modern world: "origins and early conditions of the world-system, still only a European world-system (1450–1640). . . . the consolidation of this [world-system] (1640–1815). . . . the conversion of the world-economy into a global enterprise, made possible by the technological transformation of modern industrialism. . . . This expansion was so sudden and so great that the system had to be recreated (1815–1917) . . . . The consolidation of this capitalist world-economy (1917–present)" (11–12).

   Peter Drucker, also an economist and historicist, would speak of these same realities in an even different approach. He would say that beginning at the time of World War II, we experienced the disintegration of the capitalist economy and the breakdown of the nation-state. He said that we entered into a new age of discontinuity. What he saw evolving since 1993 was a managerial estate. The impact of the managerial estate on its victims would be the topic of our future research. Peter F. Drucker, *Post-Capitalist Society* (New York: Harper Business, 1993). Cf. also with Peter Drucker, *The Age of Discontinuity: Guidelines to Our Changing Society* (New York and Evanston: Harper & Row, 1968, 1969) and James Burnham, *The Managerial Revolution: What is Happening in the World* (New York: The John Day Company, Inc., 1941).

[43]   Giddens, *A Contemporary Critique of Historical Materialism*, 82.
[44]   Giddens, *A Contemporary Critique of Historical Materialism*, 67–68, 82. In *The Power of the Poor in History* (87), Gustavo Gutiérrez critiques the replication of dominance as another form of domination. Gutiérrez writes that such replication is "a hollow cry . . . that actually only enhances the flexibility with which the prevailing system exercises its domination over the popular masses."

somehow, but not always, linked to social control. For just as distanciation in time-space relation "generates" abstraction and domination, it is simultaneously disruptive; it has the potential to generate revolution. De Schrijver claims that it is a mistake to think that modern abstraction and mathematization must necessarily lead to the creation of static life-forms. On the contrary, the capacity for abstract thinking makes it precisely possible for powerful changes to be ushered in. Mathematical time and space constitute, so to speak, the coordinates within which traditional, local, and time-bound social relations and practices can be broken down and rebuilt in a revolutionary way."[45]

Social systems operate in the environments of time (history) and space (geography). Here, one comes back to the problem of equating time with social change. Time is not identical with change in social systems. In the structuration of time, there is the distanciation between time and space, allowing for abstraction. "The equation of history (time) with social change must be resisted, as both logically mistaken and empirically wanting. If history is temporality–the temporal constitution of social events–it is clearly false to identify it with change."[46]

The time-space constitution of social systems and change consists in *episodic* characterizations and takes place according to *time-space edges*. The time-space constitution or structuration of time, as Giddens speaks of it, does not exist as a component or stage that is to be "supplanted by another." This means, for example, that nonmodern capitalist states "did not eliminate tribal type societies from around the world. Industrial capitalism has existed, and still exists, in conjunction with various other types of society (including socialism, recently) however strong its tendency to corrode or to absorb them."[47] Charles Long concurs with what Giddens is asserting. Long contends that viewing tribal-type societies as "embryonic stages or growths" that eventually will become modern nation-states is an evolutionary reading of history. In fact, Long contends that the contrary exists; tribal-type societies are not embryonic stages of growth. One of these various types of society not only might have contact with completely different types but they also might be interdependent.[48] This contact and communication is what is meant by *time-space edges*.

"*Episodes*' refer to processes of social change which have a definite direction and form, analysed through comparative research, in which major transition takes place whereby one type of society is transformed into another.

[45]   De Schrijver, "The Paradigm Shift," 10–13.
[46]   Giddens, *The Nation-State and Violence*, 32.
[47]   Giddens, *A Contemporary Critique of Historical Materialism*, 23.
[48]   Long, "Towards a Post-Colonial Method in the Study of Religion," *Religious Studies News* 10, no. 2 (May 1995): 4–5.

Episodes involve processes of structural transformation; but these do not have a mechanical inevitability to them."[49] Accordingly, societal development in this process is not evolutionary or the unfolding of one stage in a society into another based on some model of change (e.g., forces of production). However, the transitions referred to as episodes involve social change in which some structural transformation takes place.

Thus, "simultaneous, interconnected" types of society that exist in episodic transitions, like noncapitalist and industrial capitalist, are said to exist as time-space edges. "*Time-space edges* refer to forms of contact or encounter between types of society organized according to variant structural principles; they are the edges of potential or actual social transformation in the intersections between different planes of societal organization."[50]

The rise of the modern nation-state, according to Giddens, was not the result of evolutionary transformation from a traditional state. We shall now examine how, from its beginning as early as the sixteenth century, society took a radically new direction and form that resulted in the new world order. The radical transformation into the modern nation-state was the result of episodic relations that made even more manifest the existence of time-space edges.

1.1.1. THE RISE OF THE MODERN STATE

The rise of the modern state had its intellectual roots in the ideas concerning government from the Greek and Roman worlds.[51] The state and its role as a social

structure in the Greek society was the topic of Plato's *Republic* and Aristotle's *Politics*. Their ideas of state germinated as early as the fourth century BC. They included the notion of the *polis* as the community place where virtue

---

[49]   Giddens, *A Contemporary Critique of Historical Materialism*, 82–83.

[50]   Giddens, *A Contemporary Critique of Historical Materialism*, 82–83.

[51]   Starting with the notion that the modern state has its roots in the Greek city-states is not an evolutionary interpretation of history. We do not point to the Greek city-states as an early stage in the development of modern government. We are in accordance with Anthony Giddens when he asserts that "the 'Classical inheritance' was undeniably highly important in the subsequent emergence of modernity, as filtered through the influence of Rome and as appropriated in post-Renaissance thought. However, no other cases exist among the many documented histories of traditional states in which such ideas are developed in a comparable fashion. Greece is specifically untypical of traditional states, not a 'stage' in the progressive creation of modernity. Classical republicanism, Greek or Roman, was not an early anticipation of the 'impersonal sovereign power' found in the theory and practice of the modern state established in sixteenth and seventeenth century Europe" (*The Nation-State and Violence*, 57).

and goodness can be attained and of politics as the art of ruling and being ruled. These and various other social activities were centered within the context of the household. Aristotle, for example, theorized about authority in the state and its relationship to the household as well as ideas about democracy and the pyramidal structure (from the rich middle class to the poor) that existed in the state, including the place and role within the state of the labor system, including slaves. For Aristotle, the law was to be central to the maintaining of order in the state.

The Roman state relied more heavily on the rule of law whose role was the centralization of power. It was in the context of the Roman idea of state that distinctions were made between natural law and civil law.[52] Even more than the Greeks, it was the Roman practices of the execution of bureaucracy and sovereignty as well as the use of military power to enforce the security of its interests that became the paradigm of the modern state. The Greek and Roman state systems, however, were still traditional or nonmodern states.

It would be important to note that from the time Constantine came to power, *Europe* meant "Christendom." It became known as the "Catholic civilization" with a universal type of authority. It was the period when Roman Catholicism had the capacity for influence as a public authority. In this capacity, the church–mostly in connection with monasteries–was known for its role in being the point of reference.

Although the church over a period exercised universal authority, it would be important to recognize that it was never even as widespread as the Roman Empire itself. Though universal internally, the church was not so universal in its appeal. It had influence only in certain smaller parts of the continent. Giddens substantiated this position

when he said that "neither the Papacy nor the Holy Roman Empire were ever genuinely universal in their appeal."[53]

The fall of the Roman Empire was also the end of the imperial state method of government that had been centered on the Mediterranean. Thus, consolidated power ended except in the Byzantine Empire. The universal type of rule that was exercised by the Roman Empire was no longer. Out of this situation, there arose various kinds of more localized feudal type of states. European feudalism was the outcome of the "violent dissolution of older societies."[54] The status of rule in these traditional or nonmodern states became more tribal or patriarchal, based on spontaneous consensus or, what

---

[52] See definitions of *divine law, natural law,* and the *law of nations, infra,* footnote 80, page 28.

[53] Giddens, *The Nation-State and Violence,* 84.

[54] Marc Bloch, *Feudal Society* (Chicago: University of Chicago Press, 1961), 443.

was most common, a rule of violence. Because of its unique features, feudalism is important in the long-term development of the modern state.[55]

The European state became identified with the feudal state system with its monarchies, baronies, earldoms, free cities, and ecclesiastical principalities under the authority of both the emperor and the pope. These types of states became the most commonly used type of governance throughout Europe. Feudalism was a symbiotic grouping of people that existed to combat the scarcity resulting from generalized decline throughout Europe. It was considered by some to have been the most commonly used economic organization throughout Europe from the ninth century to the establishment of the absolutist states in the sixteenth century. Others, however, would see it–including both political and social dimensions–as important in its organizational system as well. Landlords, nobles, and knights were the authority of these state systems.[56] They acquired control of large tracts of land as they politically ruled and protected the inhabitants who dwelled there.

Feudalism was a crudely organized pyramidal agrarian-type social system in which "political power was treated as a private possession and divided among a large number of lords."[57] It carried with it specific rights and duties based on land tenure and personal relationships. It consisted of protectors and subordinates who exercised a modicum of security for those in danger from the hostility of the powerful abroad or beyond their borders. There was a clearly worked out hierarchy within the system, from the king, who was ranked the highest, to the lords or overlords to vassals and down to the serfs, who were the lowest in the pyramid. The relationship of the *king* to the *lord* to the *vassals* and the *serfs* was the foundation of the feudal system. This system

---

[55]   Giddens, *The Nation-State and Violence*, 83.

[56]   Wallerstein, 18; Giddens, *The Nation-State and Violence*, 79–80, 84–92; Anderson, *The Rise of the Modern State*, 25–29. This brief study of feudalism and its organizational structure also relies heavily on the following encyclopedic-type dictionaries: James Hastings, ed., *Encyclopedia of Religion and Ethics* (Edinburgh and New York: T & T Clark and Charles Scribner's Sons, 1920); David Patrick and Francis Hindes Groome, eds., *Chambers's Biographical Dictionary* (Philadelphia, London, and Edinburgh: J.B. Lippincott Company and W & R Chambers Ltd., 1902); *The Software Toolworks Illustrated Encyclopedia (TM)* (Grolier Electronic Publishing, Inc., 1991); Daniel G. Reid, coord. ed., *Dictionary of Christianity in America* (Downers Grove, IL: InterVarsity Press, 1990); Philip P. Wiener, ed., *Dictionary of the History of Ideas: Studies of Selected Pivotal Ideas* (New York: Charles Scribner's Sons, 1974); *The New Encyclopedia Britannica* (Chicago, London, Toronto, Geneva, Sydney, Tokyo, Manila, Seoul, and Johannesburg: Benton, 1943).

[57]   John P. McKay, Bennett D. Hill, and John Buckler, *A History of Western Society: From Antiquity to the Enlightenment*, vol. 1, 2nd ed. (Boston, Dallas, Geneva, and London: Houghton Mifflin Company, 1983), 280–81.

was completely interdependent and operated on a communal basis, with the king having authority over the lords and the lords being the authority over the vassals and the serfs.

In the feudalization of Europe, agriculture was the economic base of the feudal system, which consisted of landowners and landless serfs. The lords were those who had power and authority over others, an owner of land or other real property held in feudal tenure. The lord was also one whose right or title came directly from the king.

The vassals were those under the protection of the feudal lord who pledged to fight for and to serve the lord. In return for loyalty and service, the vassal was given a *fief* (beneficium, feudum, feud), which was something of value, mainly status. For as things went, that status meant that the lords maintained the vassal in their own households. This suggested that the fief was not synonymous with land. It was not until probably the tenth century that the fief became associated with land. The fief assured continuing mutual obligations between the lord and vassal. The vassals also provided the military protection for the feudal system. The fief received by the vassals by the tenth century was landed estates. At this later period, a vassal was sometimes a lord of his own estate but served as a vassal to a more powerful larger lord.[58] The vassal existed in a political relationship of dependency to the lord.

The serfs were bound to the land in a type of servitude whereby they not only provided food for themselves and their family but they also provided for the lord and vassal. In return for their service, they received the protection of the lord or vassal. The serf had an economic relationship to the lord in that he provided labor or rent to the lord or to a vassal. The serf remunerated the lord for the use of the land by giving his services and by sharing his crops with the lord. Production in the feudal system was for subsistence only.

The disintegration of feudalism was depicted as the beginning of the modern state but not in an evolutionary sense.[59] The feudal system lasted up

---

[58]   Wallerstein, *The Modern World-System*, 18–21.

[59]   Stringfellow Barr, *The Pilgrimage of Western Man* (New York: I. B. Lippincott Company, 1949, 1962), 17; Wallerstein, *The Modern World-System*, 15 passim, 36; Kenneth Scott Latourette, *A History of Christianity: Vol. II AD 1500–AD 1975* (New York: Harper & Row, Publishers, 1953, rev. ed. 1975), 330, 365; Georgia Harkness, *Man and His Ideas*, 192–94. Giddens, *The Nation-State and Violence*, 79–80, 83–85, 88–89 passim. Anderson and Hall, "Absolutism and Other Ancestors," 25–29. A comparison between the continuist interpretations with the notion of the discontinuist interpretation of history is above. The discontinuist interpretation is the basis of Anthony Giddens's critique of historical materialism.

Anthony Giddens, in his effort to show the discontinuity he sees existing between the traditional and modern state as well as to emphasize the influence of modernity on the evolution of the modern state, does not focus on feudalism

to the end of the fifteenth century. It was forced to submit to those who sought to centralize Europe into a sovereign state from as early as the late eleventh or early twelfth century. The centralized governing entities and their growing economic power were agents of the disruptive forces that unseated the lords and the security they had established for the peasants. Likewise, financial difficulties forced the feudal system to yield to the centralizing ambitions of monarchies. The monarchs allied themselves with the rising middle class of the cities, who were often the merchants and international traders. Then the centralized state with its salaried officials formed their own standing armies, which appeared for the first time in Europe. The militia or mercenary armies imposed sovereign order by warring against feudal lords. These forces resulted in the replacement of the feudal system.[60]

The agrarian structure of the feudal system was its weakness, and it could not withstand the onslaught of the merchants as it fell prey to their political and economic ingenuity. Wallerstein says, "The merchant class came from two sources: On the one hand, agents of the landlords who sometimes became independent, as well as intermediate size peasants who retained enough surplus after payments to the lord to sell it on the market; on the other hand, resident agents of long-distance merchants (based often in northern Italian city-states and later in the Hanseatic cities) who capitalized on poor communications and hence high disparities of prices from one area to another, especially when certain areas suffered natural calamities. As towns grew, of course, they offered a possible refuge and place of employment for peasants which began to change some of the terms of relationship on the manor."[61]

What one might conclude from what Wallerstein was saying was that the "agents of the landlords who became independent" were probably peasants who went to the cities to take refuge by the selling of goods. Wallerstein stated that the *kaufen* or merchant was not, at least at this point, a professional

---

as the crucible of modern state. He says, "In indicating just how different modern states are from all forms of the traditional state, I endeavor to highlight some key elements of the discontinuities of modernity." Here, we observe that Giddens is giving a new critique of historical materialism, one that renders forces other than economics or class as the basis for the emergence of modernity. His insight does include the merchants and their slave economics but in the wider context of modernity. Thus, feudalism is not a stage in the natural evolution of the absolutist state as much as a crucible from which the merchants have gained power and influence. With this approach, feudalism provides a "typological and comparative" entity within the context of the modern state.

[60] *The New Encyclopedia Britannica*, 1975 ed., s.v. "Armed Forces" by Jacques van Doorn; Anderson, *The Modernity of Modern States*, 26–27; Wallerstein, *The Modern World-Society*, 18.

[61] Wallerstein, *The Modern World-System*, 19.

tradesman.[62] The merchant (*kaufen*) was a salesperson who stood on the street with merchandise regardless of whether he produced them or bought them. Included in this group, according to Karl Bucher cited by Wallerstein, were a "confused medley of small tradesmen of the town, artisans and peasants."[63] Thus, in this sense, the peasant—when becoming independent of the feudal system—became a merchant. So a distinction can be made between this type of merchant engaged in local trade and one engaged in long-distance trade.[64] This type of local trade was supported by the feudal system; however, the feudal system could not withstand long distance trade. The disarray and discontinuity that resulted from the widening influence of the merchants contributed to commercial activity stemming from the feudal household and helped launch the age of modernity.

Manorialism coexisted with the feudal system and reached its pinnacle during the eleventh and twelfth centuries. Manorialism,[65] however, was quite distinct from feudalism in that the feudal system was a "political and legal structure regulating the relations among the various levels of nobility, and its structure stopped above the level of the peasant. Furthermore, early feudalism revolves around freely-chosen, non-heritable relations, whereas manorialism comprised inherited relations between peasants and their lords."[66]

The manorial system came into existence for somewhat the same reason as the feudal system. With the fall of Rome, great economic and political decline set in, forcing many to become bound to the land and engaged in subsistence farming. As stated, when referring to feudalism, the weaker became the victims of the stronger. They sought refuge from stronger neighbors who had the

---

[62] *Kaufen* is the word used to describe "buying." It derives from the word *Kaufmann*, which describes any person who sold wares in the market (the *mercatores* or *negotiatores*). According to Wallerstein, as he cites Karl Bucher, nowhere in the literature of the period does the term *kaufen* refer to professional traders. The merchant in the modern sense is "a specialized class of professional tradesmen who are as a rule still represented as wholesale merchants" (Wallerstein, 19).

[63] The text cited—Karl Bucher, *Industrial Evolution* (New York: Holt, 1901), 117–18, fn. 23—is found in Wallerstein, *The Modern World-System*, 19.

[64] Anderson, 27; Wallerstein, 17–21; Barr, 17; Giddens, 84–92.

[65] The word *manor* means "dwelling, residence, or homestead . . . the estate of a lord and his dependent tenants." For this section on manorialism, there is significant reliance on the work by John P. McKay, Bennett D. Hill, and John Buckler, *A History of Western Society: From Antiquity to the Enlightenment*, vol. 1, 2nd ed. (Boston, Dallas, Geneva, and London: Houghton Mifflin Company, 1983), 257, 319–326; *Software Toolworks Illustrated Encyclopedia (TM)* 1991 ed., s.v. "Manorialism" by James W. Alexander (Grolier Electronic Publishing, Inc.).

[66] McKay, Hill, and Buckler, *A History of Western Society*, 257; *Software Toolworks Illustrated Encyclopedia (IM)*, s.v. "Manorialism."

power to protect them against the onslaught of others. The result was a people even more tied to the land.

Like the feudal system, the manorial system, nonetheless, was agricultural; the peasants of the manor were farmers depending on the land for their survival. Another possible distinguishing characteristic between feudalism and the manorial system was that the feudal class, at the service of the nobility, was more of a leisure class, whereas peasants were hard laborers.

The land associated with the manorial system was divided into three categories: demesne, arable, and meadow lands. A demesne was land retained by the lord for his own use, arable land was distributed to peasants, and meadow lands were grazing lands for livestock and were shared by all the tenants. The meadow lands were also known as common lands.[67] In the manor system, land was owned by a lord who distributed portions of it to individual peasants or tenants. The right of the tenant to the arable lands of the manor system was derived from what was known as a tenure. The tenure gave rise to the heritable relationship between the lord and the peasant. In payment for use or possession of the land, the peasant would render money, crops, and services to the lord. Public service consisted in building roads, bridges, and dams as well as military service.[68] The manorial system also provided economic security and military protection for the peasants. The lord was usually in charge of the justice system, and his role was one of judge in the manorial courts. The laws were also passed from generation to generation.[69]

Peasants were either free or engaged in some form of bondage but not the same as slaves. Unlike free peasants, however, for economic reasons, bonded peasants were not usually free to break the ties that bound them to the lords. Whether the peasant was free or bonded, the closed system of the manor benefited both the lord and the peasant. "As manorialism grew and prospered, the tendency was for the size of manors to increase; the result was that more and more of a country's landed wealth lay in fewer and fewer hands. Monarchs began to amass vast manors, as did the church."[70]

Along with generalized social unrest, the deteriorating conditions of the peasants and the rise of cities during the late medieval period sowed the seeds for an end to the manorial system. "Monarchs were becoming stronger, and more and more economic and political power was being concentrated in the crown instead of in the hands of local lords. The rise of commerce and industry brought new power and prosperity to the cities, and peasants increasingly left

---

[67]   McKay, Hill, and Buckler, *A History of Western Society,* 320; also, cf. *Software Toolworks Illustrated Encyclopedia (TM),* s.v. "Manorialism."

[68]   *Software Toolworks Illustrated Encyclopedia (TM),* s.v. "Manorialism."

[69]   *Software Toolworks Illustrated Encyclopedia (TM),* s.v. "Manorialism."

[70]   *Software Toolworks Illustrated Encyclopedia (TM),* s.v. "Manorialism."

the land for these new urban areas."[71] Peasants who were left on the manors increased their agricultural output beyond production for subsistence. Many of the services and commitments were "converted into financial ones." Peasants were freed from bondage, while others purchased their freedom or escaped. And still others became independently wealthy.[72]

Because of the wars of religion and the plague of the fourteenth and fifteenth centuries, the numbers of peasants declined. This gave rise to a labor shortage that strengthened the position of the peasant. As a matter of fact, any effort at this point to impose serfdom of any sort was opposed by the peasants. For example, the Peasants' War (1524–1526)–which was both religious and social in nature–strongly called for the abolition of serfdom. Peasants also demanded "the reduction of rents and taxes, the resumption of the rights of village communities over common land, and the free election of ministries."[73] However, these efforts to revolutionize the manorial system failed. This failure was accompanied by the dispossession of the land of the peasants, land that had been the basis of the manorial system.

> The manorial community began to disintegrate. Common land was divided up, because it could be worked more intensively that way. The Lord moved to town and became absentee owner. The old relationship between the lord as protector and the serf as faithful follower began to crumble.[74]

Increased demands for production prompted the conversion of the common lands to gain land needed for greater production. Another factor that served to disrupt the lives of the peasants was the enclosure of land by the lords for the sake of sheep raising and hunting by the lords. Ultimately, the failure of the rebellion and the enclosures along with the growing power of the Crowns spelled the breakdown of the manorial system.[75]

Another important chapter in the rise of the modern nation-state was the absolute state.[76] The emphasis in the absolute state was the securing of larger territorial boundaries and the annihilation of the quasi-independence of the vassals.

---

[71]   *Software Toolworks Illustrated Encyclopedia (TM)*, s.v. "Manorialism."

[72]   *Software Toolworks Illustrated Encyclopedia (TM)*, s.v. "Manorialism."

[73]   *Software Toolworks Illustrated Encyclopedia (TM)*, s.v. "Peasants' War" by H. G. Koenigsberger.

[74]   Barr, *The Pilgrimage of Western Man*, 29.

[75]   *Software Toolworks Illustrated Encyclopedia (TM)*, s.v. "Manorialism."

[76]   Giddens, *The Nation-State and Violence*, 83–121, is the basis for this discussion of the absolutist state system.

Under absolutism, the state began to have more of a "pyramidal" character, even if the large majority of its subjects continued to live lives much as before [as separate entities]. The internal consolidation of the state served more clearly to accentuate its territorial form and it is during the period of absolutism that Europe became altered in respect of states' boundaries.[77]

The new reality for the absolute centralized state was the establishment of well-defined boundaries of influence with internal control of power while recognizing the autonomous nature and sovereignty not of its vassals but of the other centralized state. The "legitimacy of other states" prevented the universalization of the national laws to the detriment of another state.[78] The difficulty in all this was that, often, the territories were not contiguous, requiring even more by way of the "balance of power."

The period of the formation of the absolutist states–Spain, France, Great Britain–was also the period of the great "discoveries" that resulted from the mastery of the seas. Long-distance sea travel was made possible by the development of nautical technology and the emergence of world geography. Greater voyages led to the discovery and expansion of universal knowledge and new worlds that were maintained, supported, and strengthened by militarism and commerce.[79] "The period of triumph of capitalism as a 'world capitalist economy,' initiated in the sixteenth century, and continued through to the present day, is also a period eventuating in the world-wide triumph of the nation-state as a focus of political and military organization."[80]

The triumph of the nation-state constituted a basic change in the nature of sovereignty from that of the protection of private rights to the establishment of public laws and extreme political power. Again, we would come back to not only the role of the allocative resources but also the significance of the authoritative resources (power and domination based on scientific rationality). This reasoned, planned type of society crushed the privileges of prelates, pope, guilds, corporations, barons, and knights. It promised that it would take care of every person but in principle only. Bureaucratic rationality resulted in a kind of sovereignty that was secular (nonreligious) while using reformed notions of God.[81]

---

[77]   Giddens, *The Nation-State and Violence*, 85.

[78]   Giddens, *The Nation-State and Violence*, 86–87.

[79]   Giddens, *The Nation-State and Violence*, 91–92.

[80]   Giddens, *A Contemporary Critique of Historical Materialism*, 182.

[81]   See chapter 2 of this study, "The Struggle for Humanity in a Context of Religious Conflict," for a case study of this process of the triumph of the nation-state and

The consequences were that reasoned political and economic principles became the basis for social unity. Ultimately, the modern nation-state determined that either all would choose to serve the ends of the state or the violence of the state would eliminate anyone who rejected these ends. This period (seventeenth century) was full of religious wars, culminating in the Peace of Westphalia (1648). Also, the war between Spain and Great Britain was the period of the rise of the modern state.

There were several thinkers whose postulates were influential in the establishment of secular theories of the state. These political ideas became the foundation for the ideologies that had dominated modernity.[82] We shall study only briefly several of these thinkers from Niccolò Machiavelli to Thomas Jefferson.

1.1.2. SECULAR THEORIES OF THE MODERN STATE

The role of modernity as the adoption of scientific and bureaucratic rationality was most evident in the philosophical theories of the modern state. At this point in our study, we shall delineate some of these ideas. This would be, by no means, a complete study of any of the thinkers but only a noting of their most significant contribution in the establishment of the modern state.[83] We shall come back to some of these theories later, when we would discuss how these secular theories were responsible for the neutralization of religious ideas. Independence from church control (secularism) and from the emperor's universal claim on authority (antiuniversalism) were the principal attributes of the modern state.

---

its unique approach to sovereignty.

[82] Giddens, 94.

[83] The intention in this section is to trace the secular theories of the state associated with modernity. In doing so, we are relying on the following reputable histories of philosophy as general background sources, as well as on the specific works of certain of the thinkers: Frank Thilly, *A History of Philosophy*, rev. Ledger Wood (New York: Holt, Rinehart, and Winston, 1941; 3rd ed., 1966); Frederick Copleston, SJ, *A History of Philosophy*, book 2, vols. IV–VI (Garden City, NY: Image Books, 1963–1964; image edition, 1985); James Hastings, ed., *Encyclopedia of Religion and Ethics* (Edinburgh and New York: T & T Clark and Charles Scribner's Sons, 1920); Daniel G. Reid, coord. ed., *Dictionary of Christianity in America* (Downers Grove, IL: InterVarsity Press, 1990); Philip P. Wiener, ed., *Dictionary of the History of Ideas: Studies of Selected Pivotal Ideas* (New York: Charles Scribner's Sons, 1974); and the classic David Patrick and Francis Hindes Groome, eds., *Chambers's Biographical Dictionary: The Great of All Times and Nations* (Philadelphia: I. B. Lippincott Company; London and Edinburgh: W & R Chambers Ltd., 1902), s.v. "Machiavelli, Niccolò di Bernardo Dei."

Niccolò Machiavelli (1469–1527), who is considered to be the first modern political thinker and political scientist, has contributed to these ideas. His most renowned work, *Il principe* (1512–1513), is initially dedicated to Giuliano de' Medici, the third son of Lorenzo the Magnificent, and then rededicated to Lorenzo, Duke of Urbino, an original grandson of Lorenzo the Magnificent. In this work of Machiavelli, we understand why the adage "The end justifies the means"–which suggests unscrupulous political behavior–is applied to him. In his thought, Machiavelli is associated with what might be called the subversion of values. He describes the utilization of subterfuge for the purpose of conquest by a ruler.

His argument was that politics had laws of its own. In doing so, he advocated that to establish and maintain one's authority, the ruler was permitted to resort to any means necessary and that the worst and most treacherous acts of the ruler were justified by the even more wicked and treacherous state of the governed.[84] Machiavelli identified personal charism as the principal quality of the ruler. This implied that laws, bureaucracy, and centralization were subservient to the personal gifts of an individual ruler. In his eyes, universal authorities (like the papacy or the Ottoman Empire) were contemptible and weak. He wanted the state to be "free from domination by the Church in politics, science, and religion."[85]

In his thoughts on the state, Machiavelli uses two examples to focus on the important techniques for the seizure and retention of power in ways that seem to exalt reason as its basis rather than morality.[86] Thus, it seems that it is not so much a question of immorality that constitutes the survival of Machiavelli's state as much as it is placing "reason," one of the primary characteristics of modernity, above morality.

For Jean Bodin (1530–1596), the nation-state became the sole organ of political power, which meant that the social contract irrevocably transferred state sovereignty from the people to the ruler. Thus, he was the creator of the idea of an absolute ruler and the absolute state. The state must possess a single, unified, and absolute power.[87] Bodin went on to develop the doctrine of national sovereignty in all its administrative consequences and in its role as the source of all legal legitimacy. Corporate entities like the church or other

---

[84] Niccolò Machiavelli, *The Prince, A New Translation, Backgrounds, Interpretations, Peripherica (The Norton Critical Edition)*, trans. and ed. Robert M. Adams (New York and London: W.W. Norton & Company, 1977), 1–75, 26–28; 47–51; Patrick and Groome, eds. *Chambers's Biographical Dictionary*, s.v. "Machiavelli, Niccolò di Bernardo Dei."

[85] Thilly, *A History of Philosophy*, 274.

[86] Machiavelli, "On Those Who Have Become Princes by Crime," in *The Prince*, 25–28; Thilly, *A History of Philosophy*, 274.

[87] Thilly, *A History of Philosophy*, 275.

entities of the same type could remain as long as they become subservient to the sovereign will. Privileges that existed in the nonmodern state and passed for public law were, for Bodin, no longer possible. It was in this context that the nation-state had been the carrier of civil religion.[88]

The state is the supreme lawgiver and holds both administrative and allocative powers over its subjects. The lawgiver as arbiter of positive and civil law is not subject to the laws created by himself, though he remains subject to divine and natural law.[89] The lawgiver must also respect fundamental constitutional laws of the state as well as the property rights of the subjects of the state.

The modern state maintained sovereignty both internally and externally. For Bodin, the internal was maintained by the absolute ruler. But he held that the state was as absolute externally as it was internally. Thus, he became the founder of international relations and dealings by treaties between sovereign states.

Following on the heels of Jean Bodin was Thomas Hobbes (1588–1679), who extended the concept of political absolutism to a more basic level. His starting point was that the place of the human person, at the origins of human existence, was close to nature, like animals. In this natural state, there was no criteria for right or wrong, and no one distinguished between one another's possessions. People in this natural state, according to Hobbes, were nothing but brutes with hands raised against one another. This meant that people often

---

[88] Civil religion is a key element in understanding the religious way of thinking. For more insight into the concept of civil religion, see page 32.

[89] By the sixteenth century, the principal types of law are divine law, natural law, positive law, and the law of nations. With Hugo Grotius (1583–1645) also comes the development toward the supremacy of the natural law based on reason; cf. *infra*. The divine law is the law of God and pertains to the commandments as found in the Hebrew scriptures. The natural law pertains to specific principles held to be derived from nature and is considered to be universal and immutable and pertains to things that are self-evidently just. Thomas Aquinas, *Summa theologica*, trans. Fathers of the English Dominican Province (Westminster: Christian Classics, repr. 1981 under lic. granted by Benziger Brothers, Inc.), I–II QQ, 93–95.

The law of nations (jus gentium) or international law, unlike divine law and the natural law, is not about matters that are self-evidently just in themselves. The law of nations consists in human agreements made for the sake of peace and harmony and is classified by positive law, which is law deliberated on and approved at the level of government for and by human persons not including animals. The law of nations does not pertain to all living creatures, whereas laws that pertain to animals and all creatures are within the scope of natural law. Bernice Hamilton, *Political Thought in Sixteenth-Century Spain: A Study of the Political Ideas of Vitoria, de Soto, Suarez, and Molina* (Oxford: At the Clarendon Press, 1963), 98–100.

had to war against one another to survive. This situation could only be abated by people deciding to relinquish personal liberty into the hands of an absolute sovereign ruler (social contract).[90]

With a social contract, people agreed to give up their liberty to be obedient to the ruler. They gave up control of all aspects of life, including natural rights, except the right of self-defense. The sovereign, who was absolute, had to will all laws before they could be laws. Such a ruler created both positive law and standards of right and wrong for a civil religious doctrine. The ruler, for Hobbes, even determined public opinion. Thus, all justice was contained within the state, which for Hobbes was a closed system. "Hobbes turned justice into a by-product of power and denied any right of rebellion except when the sovereign became too weak to protect the commonwealth and hold it united."[91] Such a modern state system of its very nature gave states external sovereignty. The modern state, thus, was independent of every other state. Here, Hobbes was involved in a more complete expression of Bodin's notion of international relations.

As referred to before, sovereignty was not the principal quality of the state. The theories that explored the limitation of the state became the ideas that most contributed to the present-day notion of the modern state as exercised in the United States. It was the thinking of John Locke (1632–1704), whose two most important works were entitled *An Essay Concerning Human Understanding* (London, 1689) and *Two Treatises of Government* (London, 1690), that laid the foundation for the idea of the limited state. Locke's earliest political works were entitled *Essays on the Law of Nature* (1660) and *Essays Concerning Toleration* (London, 1666).[92]

Locke advanced the idea of the limited state to protect the natural law and individual rights. Thus, Locke differed from Hobbes in that he held the notion that the original situation of the human person was one of freedoms in which private property was recognized, but there was no personal security. He was reputed to not ever using the term *sovereignty* when referring to the state. Locke's liberal theory of the modern state was that it was the rule of an impartial judge established by voluntary agreement of the people. The ruler, according to Locke, was only enforcing God-given natural law and defending

---

[90] Thilly, *A History of Philosophy*, 298.

[91] Thilly, *A History of Philosophy*, 299.

[92] John Locke, *Essays on the Law of Nature*, trans. and ed. W. von Leyden (Oxford: At the Clarendon Press, 1954; orig. 1660); John Locke, *Essays Concerning Toleration*, trans. and ed. William Popple (London, 1689); John Locke, *An Essay Concerning Human Understanding*, 5th ed., Peter H. Nidditch (Oxford: At the Clarendon Press, 1975; orig. London, 1690); John Locke, *Two Treatises of Government, A Critical and Collated Edition*, ed. Peter Laslett (Cambridge: Cambridge University Press, 1960; orig. London, 1690).

natural property rights earned by one's work. His insistence on representative government placed further limits on the state. The representative legislative function of the government was amenable to popular control. For Locke, the people could even bring down a government if they deemed it to have failed to preserve the natural law and individual rights. Thus with Locke, the modern state took on liberal characteristics as he promoted a balance between the state and civil society.

It was Charles-Louis de Secondat, baron de La Brède et de Montesquieu (1689–1755), who emphasized, even more than Locke, the idea of balance in government of the state to control despotism. Thus evolved the process of checks to be implemented by intermediate bodies. For Montesquieu, the independently constituted executive, legislative, and judicial powers could provide the balance and promote a civic virtue that was once prominent in the ancient city-states.

Jean-Jacques Rousseau (1712–1778) disagreed that the original situation of the human person was warlike. To achieve protection, the rather timid person agreed to surrender individual freedom. From this, he drew the conclusion that the government must rest on the will of the governed. For Rousseau, the social contract preexisted any elaborate structure of law; the government cannot be based on force. Basing the idea of the social contract within original humanity, he laid the groundwork for revolt against the medieval and theocratic theories of state.

Two thinkers whose theories contributed to the development of the modern state were Immanuel Kant (1724–1804) and Georg Wilhelm Friedrich Hegel (1770–1831). Kant's thoughts regarding the state were centered on sovereignty. His focus was that the only natural political relation was that which existed between single individuals and the state. This view encapsulated the general post–French Revolution context. Before the revolution, there existed various entities that intervened on behalf of the individual. Kant's ideas gave the rational basis for the use of positive law as a means of dealing with the subject in the modernity state.

Hegel expanded the notions of Machiavelli regarding the qualities of the ruler. For Hegel, because the state was governed by law and bureaucracy, there was no need for the ruler to have any extraordinary personal qualities. The modern state was not only sovereignty and bureaucracy but also "mind" or "reason," the realization of rational freedom. Individuals in the modern state were civil servants who were moderated by rational, free institutions that secured the pursuit of absolute values inherent in philosophy, art, and religion.

Jeremy Bentham (1748–1832) saw the state's need to ameliorate the harshness of its governance. He knew that the state was not able to maximize the pleasure of each citizen. In light of this, his idea of the role of the limited state was the necessity of the control of serious crimes—murder and robbery—which were more harmful than the activity of the state itself. Similar to the philosophy of Bentham was the thought of Adam Smith (1723–1790), who held that the operation of economic laws was based only on supply and demand. This tactic permitted the state to no longer have any influence, thus allowing the interests of the dominant to thrive and the interests of the victims to be ignored.

Thomas Jefferson (1743–1826) studied John Locke and several of the French and British thinkers already mentioned. He sought to ground their ideas in the framing documents of the United States. For example, Jefferson set down his ideas regarding the modern state in his writing of the first draft of the Declaration of Independence of the United States in 1776. In this text, he heralded the establishment of a new society based on "life, liberty, and the pursuit of happiness" for all. In so doing, Jefferson promoted and accepted the basic framework of American civil religion.

Civil religion is a way of thinking that characterizes faith as the faith of a state or nation, focusing on the widely held belief in the history and destiny of a nation. According to Linder, civil religion is "a religious way of thinking about politics which provides a society with ultimate meaning (thus making it a genuine religion) which, in turn allows a person to look at their political community in a special sense and thus achieve purposeful social integration."[93]

Thomas Jefferson was a baptized Anglican, but as a government official, he attended no church and never referred to himself as a Christian, and he espoused no religion. Even though he insisted on his belief in God, Jefferson was considered by many to be a conservative but practical Deist. Jefferson's religious ideas related to the position he held regarding what had come to be known as "separation of church and state." He wrote a letter to the Danbury Baptist Association of Connecticut in 1802 in response to a letter from them expressing concern that an established church in their state still limited genuine religious liberty there. In this letter, Jefferson affirmed the intent of the founders to establish "a wall of separation between Church and State."[94] Separation of church and state is "the exclusion of civil authority from

---

[93] Reid, coord. ed., *Dictionary of Christianity in America*, s.v. "Civil Religion" by Robert D. Linder. Strong advocates of civil religion as an interpretation of religion in America are Robert Bellah, Richard Madsen, William M. Sullivan, Ann Swidler, and Steven M. Tipton, *Habits of the Heart: Individualism and Commitment in American Life* (New York and Cambridge: Perennial Library and Harper & Row, 1985); Robert Bellah, Richard Madsen, William M. Sullivan, Ann Swidler, and Steven M. Tipton, *The Good Society* (New York: Vintage Books, 1991).

[94] *Dictionary of Christianity in America*, s.v. "Civil Religion."

religious affairs and the institutional independence of organized religion from government sanctions or support."[95]

The effort in this section had been to characterize the role of modernity in the establishment of the modern state. It was inevitable—with the rise of individual autonomy and the establishment of laws, bureaucracy, and centralization of government—that a new kind of dominance was created in which all were forced to be subservient to the personal gifts of an individual. The state, which had received its authority from the sovereignty of God, now received it from the consent of the governed (which often meant only the protection of the interests of the merchant class). Thus, the state system exercised

external sovereignty. This ultimately meant that the state was dictated to by business interests instead of by the interests of those who would be victims of such business. With the advent of the separation of church and state, traditional religious principles just about lost its influence in the public arena.

In the cataloging of various theories that had been influential in the establishment of the modern nation-state, we had considered certain thinkers, the foundational ideas, and the scientific rationality on which the rise of the modern nation-state was based. The context during this period was one of radical social dislocation against the petrification of traditional religious and political structures (constitutional arrangements or political regimes), as well as of economic movements (mercantilism, merchant traders, and the rise of capitalism). It was the drive to human progress and mastery over the radical changes occurring in the modern social context that heralded a new age.[96]

Just as the modern nation-state has been the political expression of modernity, capitalism was its economic expression. The following analysis is an attempt to situate the rise of capitalism in the modern social context and how it has revealed itself in the New World labor system of slavery. Our claim is that modernity and the modern nation-state have reached its pinnacle in its capitalist expansion into the New World.

---

[95] Reid, *Dictionary of Christianity in America*, s.v. "Church and State, Separation of," by James E. Wood.

[96] R. H. Tawney, *Religion and the Rise of Capitalism: A Historical Study (Holland Memorial Lectures, 1922)* (New York: Harcourt, Brace & World, Inc., 1926; New York: A Mentor Book, 1954). For a fuller account of the revolutions of Europe, cf. Palmer and Colton, *Modern World*, 43–172, and Wallerstein, *The Modern World-System*, 15–63; Giddens, 35, 79–80, 83, 202.

1.2. THE MODERN NATION-STATE AND CAPITALISM

In this study of religion and the modern nation-state, situating capitalism is of paramount importance, especially in its expression in the New World; namely, as slavery and the slave trade. The emphasis will not be to view capitalism as simply a stage in the evolutionary history of productive forces. Capitalism seen within the broader context of modernity deals with the acquisition and distribution of the material world and exists in relation to power and domination in the modern nation-state.[97]

The source of power and domination in the modern nation-state rests not just in its forces of production alone but also in its being a planned, scientific, bureaucratic rationality. This perspective, as we have seen above, is suggested by Anthony Giddens in his rejection of a teleological reading of history. Giddens rejects historical materialism, which he defines as "the conception that the history of human societies can be understood in terms of the progressive augmentation of the forces of production. . . . that the history of existing society is the history of class struggles. . . . that the evolution of societies from tribal to ancient, to feudal to capitalist, to socialist incorporating the stagnant Asiatic mode of production is the basis for analyzing world history."[98] He suggests the intriguing alternative interpretation of history, which he calls time-space relations.

For Giddens, the distanciation of time and space provides a creative dimension from which to discuss capitalism and eventually slavery. Time-space distanciation is involved with the generation of power. In this structuration of time, "power is generated in and through the reproduction of structures of domination, which includes the domination of human beings over the material world (allocative resources) and over the social world (authoritative resources)."[99] This approach discloses that capitalism is an exploitative tool in the hands of the dominant or the powerful. With these presuppositions, let us examine capitalism and its role in the modern-state.

1.2.1. THE RISE OF CAPITALISM

Capitalism was extremely influential in the rise of the modern nation-state, though it was not reducible or inevitably tied to capitalism once it came into existence.[100] Giddens wrote, "The spread of capitalism is of fundamental importance to the consolidation of a novel world system from the sixteenth

---

[97]   Giddens, *A Contemporary Critique of Historical Materialism*, 91–92.
[98]   Giddens, *A Contemporary Critique of Historical Materialism*, 1–2.
[99]   Giddens, *A Contemporary Critique of Historical Materialism*, 91–92.
[100] Giddens, *The Nation-State and Violence*, 287–88, 312.

century onwards. Both capitalism and industrialism have decisively influenced the rise of nation-states, but cannot be reductively explained in terms of their existence. The modern world has been shaped by the intersection of capitalism, industrialism and the nation-state system."[101]

The birth of capitalism in Europe was a complete break with what had existed in feudalism. Initially, capitalism siphoned its energy from and drained the feudal system and then ultimately had a role in its collapse. With the rise of money, there began the shift from the natural economy of the feudal agriculture to a money economy, introducing for the first time a credit system. Thus, from the thirteenth century onward, forces external to the feudal system radically disrupted the medieval manors that had provided protection for the peasants. For example, one of those forces was the Crusades, which opened up trade options to the Orient, thereby enhancing mercantile relations. Exorbitantly priced Oriental goods were in great demand. This demand resulted in immense profits for the merchants and disruption of the just price structures that were based on labor.[102]

Thus, commerce was on the rise; and the guilds, which had been the impetus for industry and commerce, faltered. The rise of banks evolved whereby the properties made use of them to become even more endowed. Through the stockpiling of money, the purchasing power of these bankers was increased and allowed them to create monopolies in the area of land.

With the rise of cities and towns, people were more absorbed in the newly developing urban life. This resulted in the inability to produce their own food and allowed the moneyed class to corner the market of food production. Stock companies were also established, which encouraged investments in the various commercial enterprises and trading was on the rise.[103]

During the fourteenth and early fifteenth centuries, there was a gradual shift from a barter system to a money economy. In rural areas, this meant a shift from production for consumption to a heightened production that resulted in a surplus of goods. This then resulted in a change from a system in which services were returned for work done to a money labor system where profit was the order of the day.[104]

With the use of money came the possibility of hoarding and profiteering, large-scale commercial transactions on credit, large-scale investments in distant areas, large-scale production, monopolies, and a concentration of power in the hands of the moneyed few.[105]

---

[101] Giddens, *The Nation-State and Violence*, 4–5.

[102] Barr, *The Pilgrimage of Western Man*, 17–18.

[103] Latourette, *History of Christianity*, 657, 694.

[104] Harkness, *Man and His Ideas*, 192–94.

[105] Harkness, *Man and His Ideas*, 193.

It was not only the capitalists who loaned money at a profit to the "princes" but the "popes" also helped shape the birth of capitalism.

The position the church adopted was not a satisfactory one. While continuing to object to the new merchant-princes and usurers of the towns, the church itself tended more and more to make use of the money economy for its own ends.[106]

The definition of *capitalism* is not simply the impulse for the acquisition or the pursuit of gain of the greatest possible amount of money. Capitalism, more precisely understood, is the "maximization of profits" and "belief in steady progress." In its very core, capitalism is "identical with the pursuit of profit, and forever renewed profit, by means of continuous, rational, capitalistic enterprise."[107] Therefore, the impetus for the acquisition of money alone is not the complete delineation of capitalism. Significant in capitalism in the modern state is the maximization of profit and the belief in progress as well as the issue of control.

The capitalist system is controlled by interests whose sole purpose is acquiring profit. The means of acquiring the profit are ancillary to the profit itself. The modern state functions hereby as a rational political expression of private economic interests.

> Endowed with a bureaucratic apparatus of its own, created at the same time a free space for the citizens to take economically remunerating initiatives. This free space is technically called the "civil society" (see Hegel).[108]

Along with the desire to safeguard individual freedoms, there was also the intention to establish "a separate realm of 'civil society' [the private domain] free from arbitrary interference by the state. . . . [With the modern state there

---

[106]   Barr, *The Pilgrimage of Western Man*, 19.

[107]   Max Weber, *The Protestant Ethic and the Spirit of Capitalism*, trans. Talcott Parsons with a foreword by R. H. Tawney (New York: Charles Scribner's Sons, 1958), 17. Anthony Giddens's interpretation of Weber draws out the polyvalence associated with trying to define *capitalism*. Giddens iterates, "Weber defines 'capitalistic' enterprise as any type of economic action undertaken in anticipation of achieving profit through exchange." Then he proceeds to delineate that "this 'exchange' has existed all over the world and (here is the reference to the polyvalent aspect of capitalism) and in many different 'guises'" (Giddens, 126). Then he makes a clear distinction between various forms of mercantile capitalism and modern capitalism. He refers to expressions of capitalism existing at different stages (notice he uses *stages* here) of the rise of modernity (123–37).

[108]   De Schrijver, "The Paradigm Shift," 9.

emerged] forms of democracy whereby (some of) governed, at least in a formal sense, choose a government which reflects or represents their interests."[109]

The role of the state as a governing structure thus also became that of protecting the realm of the civil society. The state guarded itself against any interference into the free exercise of business conducted by the private sector. Thus, the ideals of democracy, free enterprise, and separation of church and state protected the interests of "(some of) the governed" and their property. These ideals or ideologies underlay the fabric of the modern state and fashioned that state into a partner in the political economy.[110]

The earliest examples of this type of profiteering existed in the late thirteenth century and the early fourteenth century in Italy (particularly Florence), Germany, and the Netherlands. Wealthy families such as the Medicis, the Fuggers, and Welders, to name a few, accumulated fortunes and even loaned money to popes and leaders of governments. This set up the first attempts at complicity between the wealthy and the church and state.

---

[109] Anderson, "The Modernity of Modern States," 3–4. According to Anderson and Hall, the contribution of Roman law to the rise of the modern state is its use of the Greek philosophical distinction between the public and private dimensions of the governing body, as well as its ideas regarding private property. The distinction is that the role of the *state* is associated with public affairs, while the role of the *civil society* is associated with the private sphere, the domestic household (Anderson and Hall, "The Absolutism and Other Ancestors," in *The Rise of the Modern State,* ed. James Anderson, 24.)

[110] For our purposes, we have defined *political economy* elsewhere as referring to all "aspects of a society or civilization: its political processes, how these relate to money and business, and how they are managed by technology. The political economy also determines behavioral patterns in the society, thereby forcing consent from its people and making its institutions, even religious institutions, subservient to it." Cf. Phillip J. Linden Jr., "Part Three: Review Symposium. Stephen Ochs's *Desegregating the Altar: The Josephites and the Struggle for Black Priests, 1871–1960," U.S. Catholic Historian* 11, no. 1 (1993): 138–40.

Immanuel Wallerstein, in the first of his four-volume work *The Modern World-System,* calls that broad type of definition of *economics* a "world-economy, not because it encompasses the whole world, but because it is larger than any juridically-defined political unit. . . . And because the basic linkage between the parts of the system is economic . . . reinforced to some extent by cultural links and eventually . . . by political arrangements and even confederate structures" (15).

Merriam-Webster defines *political economy* as a nineteenth-century modern social science dealing with the interrelationship of political and economic processes (*Webster's Ninth New Collegiate Dictionary,* 1989 ed., s.v. "Political Economy"). *The New Encyclopedia Britannica* says that the term *political economy* has been replaced by the modern science of *economics* in the twentieth century, and with this has come the expansion of the discipline into areas of specialty (*The New Encyclopedia Britannica, Micropedia,* 1975 ed., s.v. "Political Economy").

With the coming of merchant-bankers, operating for the sake of profit, came the dismantling of the old order and the capitalist form of domination. The "landed Church collided with the landed rulers . . . the medieval system was slipping."[111] Steady progress and the maximization of profits were the goals of the capitalists; the termination of peasant holdings was the result. Peasants had now fallen victim to the demands of the wealthy who now rejected subsistence as an incentive for economic well-being and who now thrived with profit as the incentive.[112] Thus, the developing capitalist order based on commerce was responsible for the shift from a land economy to a money economy. The landlords who lost money in the shift closeted their moral principles and, in turn, bled the peasants even more to recoup some of these losses. These landlords were called Junkers.[113] Such victimization of the peasants would later result in the aforementioned Peasants' War (1524–1526) in Germany.[114]

At its genesis, an essential ingredient in the rise of capitalism was the opening up of the Atlantic world, which increased and diversified commercial markets and their availability. Forced by the closing down of the land routes to the East due to the domination of that region by the Ottoman Empire, merchants invested heavily in sea ventures and discovery expeditions, which resulted in the founding of new sea routes, thereby gaining easier access to the markets of the East.[115] Palmer and Colton, in their history of the rise of the modern world, charted the course of the rising commercial revolution that took place in Europe, noting that the "opening up of ocean trade routes" was an intricate part of "the rise of a capitalist economic system and the transition from a town-centered to a nation-centered economic system." Palmer and Colton observed that "the new sea route to the East and the discovery of America brought a vast increase in trade not only of luxury items, but of bulk commodities like rice, sugar, tea, and other

consumer goods. Older commercial activities were transformed by the widening of markets."[116]

The Spanish "discovery" of America (1492) by Christopher Columbus geographically symbolized European expansion into the New World. This venture, however, was not the first of its sort. Columbus's contribution on behalf of Spanish merchant-traders was only a part of a long process that was

---

111   Barr, *The Pilgrimage of Western Man*, 29.
112   Palmer and Colton, *Modern World*, 100–2.
113   Palmer and Colton, *Modern History*, 101.
114   Wallerstein, *The Modern World-System*, 24.
115   Latourette, *History of Christianity*, 694–95. The development of sea routes down the coast of Africa is significant regarding the genesis of slavery and the slave trade.
116   Palmer and Colton, *Modern World*, 94–97.

begun by the Portuguese (1425). Under the direction of Prince Henry the Navigator, merchant-traders traveled down the African coast to the Cape of Good Hope en route to the Far East. The Portuguese had gained a certain leadership in nautical technology and naval construction and in the methods of exploration and colonization. They sailed down the western coast of Africa below the equator as far as Sierra Leone.

Slavery became the economic articulation of the expansion of entrepreneurial interests of the merchant-traders into the New World, for it cannot be denied that slavery played a key role in the conquest and colonization of the New World. For example, in 1440, Portuguese merchant-traders became the first to enslave Africans. These merchants, who eventually settled the Azores and Madeira, were the first to justify the enslavement of Africans.[117] Just as the merchant class cannot be considered apart from the rise of capitalism, neither can slavery. Slavery was of paramount importance as a labor force in securing trader interests in the New World. Thus, a specific look at slavery as a labor system and its relationship to capitalism was warranted. This was so because of the role of slavery not as an evolutionary stage but as a labor system used in the establishment of the modern nation-state.

1.2.2. CAPITALISM AND SLAVERY

Probably with the exception of the prehistoric era, there have always been those who have been enslaved. Not only does it seem that slavery has always existed but it also seems to have gone unchallenged.[118] *Slavery* can be defined as "the simple wish to use the bodily powers of another person as a means of administering to one's own ease or pleasure."[119]

---

[117] Winthrop D. Jordon, *White over Black: Attitudes toward the Negro, 1550–1812* (Chapel Hill, North Carolina: University of North Carolina Press, 1968), 56–57; David Brion Davis, *Slavery and Human Progress* (New York and Oxford: Oxford University Press, 1984), xvii.

[118] According to David Brion Davis in his work *The Problem of Slavery in Western Culture* (62–63), slavery was never seriously protested. For more on slavery in ancient times, see the following literature: Isaac Mendelsohn, *Slavery in the Ancient Near East: A Comparative Study of Slavery in Babylonia, Assyria, Syria, and Palestine from the Middle of the Third Millennium to the End of the First Millennium* (Westport, Connecticut: Greenwood Press Publishers, 1978), 123; Moses I. Finley, *Ancient Slavery and Modern Ideology* (London: Penguin Books, 1980); Moses I. Finley, "Was Greek Civilization Based on Slave Labor?" in Finley, *Slavery in Classical Antiquity: Views and Controversies* (Cambridge: Cambridge University Press, 1960), 61, 63–64; William L. Westermann, "Between Slavery and Freedom," *American Historical Review* 2 (January 1945): 213–16.

[119] Jewell C. Mazique, "Aristotle: A Study of His Slave Theory with Both Definite

The principal commodity of the capitalist economy in the New World, specifically in British America, was slavery, slave labor, and the slave trade.[120]

---

and Presumptive Evidence of Its Impact upon Western Civilization," *Dialogue: Journal of Phi Sigma Tau* 1, no.1 (April 1956): 24. There are other definitions of *slavery*, but all of them have the same basic characteristics as the definition of Sir George MacMann used by Jewell Mazique. Cf. *The New Encyclopedia Britannica*, 1943–1973 ed., s.v. "Slavery, Serfdom, and Forced Labor." *The New Encyclopedia Britannica* defines *slave* as "one who is owned by another and deprived of most or all rights and freedoms, hence the term chattel slave, denoting personal property at law. The slave is dependent on the whims of the owner, who may generally force him to any service and, at least in principle, may usually even dispose of his life." The slave owner is responsible for giving the slave minimal food, clothes, and a meager place to live. Often family members are separated at the whim of the owner, and marriages takes place only with permission. A slave is considered to be chattel, which means an article of property to be bought, sold, or just given away. Except in the ancient and classical worlds, slaves are not protected by the laws of the society and are victims of the police power of the state, especially since they are not considered to be citizens (Davis, *The Problem of Slavery in Western Culture*, 30–35, 224).

[120]   The following bibliography is by no means an exhaustive list of texts on slavery and the slave trade. However, it provides selected works to be used in the recounting of the complex problem of slavery. Other works more specific to slavery in British America can be found later in this chapter.

David Brion Davis, *The Problem of Slavery in Western Culture* (Ithaca, New York; London: Cornell University Press, 1966); David Brion Davis, *Slavery and Human Progress* (New York and Oxford: Oxford University Press, 1984).

Eugene D. Genovese, *The Political Economy of Slavery: Studies in the Economy and Society of the Slave South,* (New York: Vantage Books, 1967); Eugene D. Genovese, *The World the Slaveholders Made: Two Essays in Interpretation* (New York: Vintage Books, 1971); Eugene D. Genovese, *Roll, Jordan, Roll: The World the Slaves Made* (New York: Vintage Books, 1976); James C. Morgan, *Slavery in the United States: Four Views* (Jefferson, North Carolina; London: McFarland & Company, Inc., 1985).

An important study by E. Williams takes the position that "a racial twist has been given to what is basically an economic phenomenon. Slavery was not born of racism: rather, racism was the consequence of slavery." Eric Williams, *Capitalism & Slavery* (London: Andre Deutsch Limited, 1944); Frank Tannenbaum, *Slave and Citizen: The Negro in the Americas* (New York: Vintage Books, 1946); Ulrich B. Phillips, *American Negro Slavery: A Survey of the Supply, Employment and Control of Negro Labor as Determined by the Plantation Regime* (Baton Rouge: Louisiana State University, 1989); Kenneth M. Stampp, *The Peculiar Institution: Slavery in the Ante-Bellum South* (New York: Vintage Books, Alfred A. Knopf, Inc., 1956).

Mechal Sobel, *The World They Made Together: Black and White Values in Eighteenth-Century Virginia* (Princeton: Princeton University Press, 1987); Sterling Stuckey, *Slave Culture: Nationalist Theory and the Foundations of Black America* (New

Wide-scale slavery prompted the opening up of slave labor for the initial growing and mining of resources for the rising European industry during the late fifteenth and early sixteenth centuries as they traveled down the African coast to the East and finally across the Atlantic for the conquest of the Western Hemisphere.

The categories and the role of slavery in ancient and classical times as well as in the French and especially in the Spanish and Portuguese were radically different from modern slavery in British America and, later, the United States. Slaves in antiquity and classical times, for example, were often educated, could acquire property, and had the means of buying their freedom. They were considered to be fully human with personalities. Whereas in British colonial America, particularly after the 1660s, the slaves became slaves in perpetuity. It was illegal for slaves to get an education or to acquire property, and rarely could they buy their freedom. The slaves were usually tortured or mutilated or their children sold or they exploited by their labor, and therefore, they did not live long.[121]

Another difference between ancient and modern slavery is that slavery in the modern nation-state, where the enslaved were considered less than human, they were used for the sake of profit making. Slaves were considered to be but animals (cattle or oxen) and therefore were nothing more than a commodity. Slavery and the slave trade developed into the most inhumane, destructive institution to ever exist.[122] Let us first examine the various aspects of the profitability of slave labor and its relationship to modernity and the modern nation-state and then do a review of the overall survey of the history of slavery.

York and Oxford: Oxford University Press, 1987). The next work is a cliometric study of slavery. Cliometrics is a study that applies the methods developed in economics and statistics to the study of history. Robert William Fogel and Stanley L. Engerman, *Time on the Cross: The Economics of American Negro Slavery* (London: Wildwood House, 1974).

[121] Davis, *The Problem of Slavery in Western Culture*, 224–25.

[122] Mendelsohn, *Slavery in the Ancient Near East*, 121–22; Wallerstein, *The Modern World-System*, 88 (Wallerstein cites more recent texts on slavery as a resource for profits, supporting his argument that slavery in the modern system has become "preeminently a capitalist institution."); Sergio Bagli, "La economía de la sociedad colonial," *Pensamiento crítico*, no. 27 (abr. 1969): 53–61; also, cf. Eric Williams, *Capitalism and Slavery* (London: Andre Deutsch, 1964), 113. Anthony Giddens argues the theory that there is serious economic disadvantages to using slave labor in capitalist production. Giddens cites Max Weber to support his position against the use of slave labor where it will not be profitable. Giddens asserts that "the widespread employment of slave labour is only possible where slaves can be maintained very cheaply, where there are opportunities for regular slave recruitment and the production in question is agricultural" (127).

Slavery as a labor system in the modern state and its relationship to capitalism is taken up by the renowned historian David Brion Davis in his work entitled *Slavery and Human Progress*. Davis argues that it has been *progress* that has led to the modern nation-state's enslavement of Africans, and for him, progress has both quantitative and qualitative dimensions. The quantitative dimension refers to the organization of productive forces for profit through exchange (capitalist economics), technological development, material improvements, and a rising standard of living. The qualitative dimension refers to what Davis describes as "the highest aspirations of the human soul."[123]

David Brion Davis argues that there are two broad theoretical categories regarding slavery and economic progress. The classic liberal and fundamentalist Marxian is the first broad theoretical category. It sees slavery as necessary in its early stages (e.g., an alternative to killing prisoners of war). But ultimately, slavery has "impeded technological innovation as well as social and economic growth."[124] The second broad theoretical category is the view of various modern economists that slavery is compatible with the rise of modern technology and economic growth but has been abandoned just when it has begun to make an important contribution to Western capitalism.[125]

Davis says that literature on slavery separates these two broad categories into four theories. The first theory says that the earliest forms of slavery have been a stage in human evolution. On the one hand, it has been a necessary humane alternative to the killing of prisoners of war. On the other hand, it has served as a means to discipline and control native peoples.[126]

The second theory, rendered by Eric Williams and his followers, is that the enslavement of Africans has been necessary for the conquest of the New World. According to Davis, the thesis of Eric Williams is that "white Americans and Europeans progressed only at the expense of black slaves whose labor built the foundations of modern capitalism."[127]

The "Caribbean School" of economic history is well known for its thought on capitalism and slavery. It corresponds to the fundamentalist Marxian dimension of Davis's first broad category. The persons associated with this thinking are C. L. R. James, Eric Williams, and Walter Rodney.[128] William

---

[123] Davis, *Slavery and Human Progress*, xvii. The description of *capitalism* as the organization of productive forces for profit through economic exchange is used by Giddens in his work *The Nation-State and Violence* (p. 126).

[124] Davis, xiii.

[125] Davis, *Slavery and Human Progress*, xiii–xvi.

[126] Davis, *Slavery and Human Progress*, xiv.

[127] Davis, xiv.

[128] C. L. R. James, *The Black Jacobins: Toussaint L'Ouverture and the San Domingo Revolution* (New York: Random House, 1963); Williams, *Capitalism and Slavery*; Walter Rodney, *How Europe Underdeveloped Africa* (London: Bogle L'Ouverture, 1972).

Darity Jr. of the University of North Carolina, School of Economics, Chapel Hill, argues in conjunction with these thinkers that slavery and the slave trade are the foundation of modern capitalist political economy. Darity uses this Marxist perspective to "reveal why the origin of the Industrial Revolution is not a mystery for Marxist scholars and how the Marxist method of inquiry facilitates a clean break with the circularities that beset other 'theories' of early European industrialization."[129] Although a controversial position, Darity's analysis is not a new one. His reference to the Caribbean School suggests his exploration into the reason that "the interaction of the African and European modes of productions led to the triangle trade" and thus to European industrialization.[130]

According to C. L. R. James, Eric Williams, and Walter Rodney, the slavery of the New World (United States, Caribbean, and Brazil) was not an institution isolated from industrial Europe. The triangular New World trade was a three-dimensional commercial exchange. Slaves were captured and taken out of Africa to the New World, raw materials mined by the slaves were transported from the New World to Europe for use in the manufacturing industry, and the manufactured goods, rum, and weapons were carried back to Africa. The triangle was completed as the merchant-traders returned to the New

World with more slaves. Slavery probably benefited European industrial capitalism in that it provided the labor force to grow sugar, tobacco, and cotton crops and to mine raw products for the rising industrial complex of Europe. In that sense, despite its mainly industrial capitalist type of economics, slavery was a source and basis for great profits in Europe.

Continuing to emphasize the "role of productive forces" in establishing the Atlantic world, Darity reveals that Rodney and, before him, James and Williams unmask the role of slavery in the "uneven development" of the modern world. He says that "to tell the story of the split in world economic development from the 1500's to the present requires identification of the winners and losers in the Atlantic slave trade."[131] For example, Darity is strong in his analysis in stating that "the trade in Africans and the enslavement of Africans in the New World thoroughly aided the rise of the newer class in Europe, the capitalist class, both in its merchant and later in its industrial form." Darity continues, "[C]

---

[129] William A. Darity Jr., "Mercantilism, Slavery and the Industrial Revolution," *Research in Political Economy* 5 (1982): 1–21; also, cf. William Darity Jr., "The Political Economy of Uneven Development: From the Slave(ry) Trade to the Managerial Age" (unpublished manuscript, University of North Carolina, May 1991).

[130] Darity, "Mercantilism, Slavery and the Industrial Revolution," 3.

[131] Darity, "The Political Economy of Uneven Development: From the Slave(ry) Trade to the Managerial Age," 3.

apitalist development needed the enslavement of Africans to proceed–to break through the barriers to its development. The manifestations of this intimate relationship–merchant capital producing African slavery in the Americas and African slavery in the Americas facilitating the rise of industrial capital–are especially evident . . . in Williams' classic."[132]

The third theory would be the position taken by abolitionists and classical economists. From this perspective, slave labor was always seen as retarding long-term economic growth and curtailing social and moral progress because the oppressors were violating the laws of nature by the enslavement of humans. Accordingly, slavery would eventually be transformed by the laws of progress.[133]

The work by Ulrich B. Phillips on slavery entitled *American Negro Slavery* (1918) epitomized this third theory on slavery. Slavery stood as that which undermined both economic and social progress while bringing decline. Despite these negatives, slavery–through its paternalistic approach–did "civilize" the African savage.

Divergent still from the other theories, the fourth theory heralded slavery as progressive. Though there may have been some deprivations for the slaves, slavery was a special source of profits for the growth of the South. The work of Robert William Fogel and Stanley L. Engerman entitled *Time on the Cross* (1974) focused on this fourth theory. Although slaves were in permanent bondage, Fogel and Engerman denied that they were treated brutally and that they were poor as workers. Their position was that the slave received more than adequate benefits for services. This position considered it racist to describe the slaves as lazy, inefficient workers. The slaves themselves, even under the adverse conditions, developed family life and a rich cultural heritage. As an economic entity, slavery was on the verge of being the source of unparalleled growth when it was ended by the Civil War.[134]

In keeping with the theme of his book, Davis discusses slavery in terms of a shift from progressive enslavement to progressive emancipation. *Progressive enslavement*, in part 1 of his text, refers to "the expansion of European trade, technology, and religion . . . [by] Italian merchants; Iberian explorers; Jewish inventors, traders, and cartographers; Dutch, German, and British investors and bankers."[135] *Progressive emancipation*, in parts 2 and 3, refers to a movement that has recognized slavery as an obstacle to progress.[136] Those same societies that have profited from expansionist slavery have become the strongest advocates

---

[132] Darity, "Mercantilism, Slavery and the Industrial Revolution," 25. This is a direct reference to Eric Williams's *Capitalism and Slavery* (51–84).

[133] Davis, xiv–xv.

[134] Davis, xv–xvi.

[135] Davis, *Slavery and Human Progress,* xvii, 5–101.

[136] Davis, xvii, 107–315.

of emancipation as slavery has no longer been profitable. By the nineteenth century, the British who have profited by slavery have seen slaveholding as "retrogressive." In both progressive enslavement and progressive emancipation, slavery is examined as coinciding with progress.

Progressive emancipation demonstrates how slavery has become futile in the rising capitalist society. Giddens cites the thought of Max Weber to discuss "the disadvantages of organizing capitalistic production through slave labor." Giddens writes, "According to [Weber, the disadvantages] are quite formidable, and hence, the widespread employment of slave labour is only possible where slaves can be maintained very cheaply, where there are opportunities for regular slave recruitment and the production in question is agricultural. The employment of workers for wages or salaries involves much less capital risk and investment."[137]

Moses I. Finley, in comparing ancient slavery and modernity, also makes the connection between capitalism and slavery. He iterates that modern slavery considered within the framework of capitalism provides a "peculiar anomaly." Of its very structure, slavery is mainly suited for an agrarian-type society. However, Finley examines Karl Marx's brief scattered comments on slavery, which he has found in a published notebook of Marx entitled *Grundrisse*. Written during the winter of 1857–1858 but published originally in Moscow in 1939, *Grundrisse* makes the point that "'we now not only call the plantation owners in America capitalists, but that they *are* [italics in original] capitalists, is based on their existence as anomalies within a world market based on free labour.'"[138] This statement suggests that even Marx has thought that slavery as an economic system in the New World economy has been capitalist.

Therefore, slavery and the slave trade were an intricate part of the New World; and as a product of modernity, they were necessary to its economic expression of profit and profit making. The following historical overview was meant to point out the trends and development of slavery as an institution, emphasizing the distinction between ancient/classical and medieval slavery and slavery of the modern nation-state.

1.2.3. SLAVERY: ANCIENT AND CLASSICAL

Slavery in ancient times existed in the Near Eastern lands of Babylonia, Assyria, Syria, and Palestine from about the fourth millennium BC to the beginning of the Christian era. Its existence was revealed in the Babylonian Sumerian family laws of the fourth millennium BC and substantiated in the

---

[137] Giddens, *The Nation-State and Violence*, 127.
[138] Moses I. Finley, *Ancient Slavery and Modern Ideology*, 41; cf. Karl Marx, *Grundrisse*, trans. M. Nicolaus (London: Harmondsworth, 1973), 513.

Code of Hammurabi in the eighteenth century BC.[139] That it did not exist during the earlier prehistoric period of civilization was because those peoples depended on hunting and gathering for their survival. Hunting and gathering did not require such a complicated type of labor system as slavery. Slavery only came into existence with the rise of agriculture and the handicraft industry, both of which required cheap labor forces.[140]

Even as the livelihood of peoples changed and required a division of labor, there was still an insignificant number of slaves compared with free laborers. This was because those in the agricultural and handicraft industries were mainly engaged in production for consumption and not for profit. Thus, there was no need for a tremendous number of slaves.[141]

Although slaves of the ancient Near East were sometimes bought from foreign neighbors by merchants, generally, those who had been captured in warfare were the main source for slaves. In the earliest periods, captives in war were often killed. But changing times and expediency dictated that first women and then the men who were captured in war were saved and used as the servants of their captors. War victims especially were used in the households of royalty and as temple slaves. In fact, the largest number of war victims served in these two categories.[142] Slaves were either born in a household or purchased. Those born in a household were considered to be members of the family and were often treated better than those who were purchased.[143] Slaves also were natives who had defaulted on debts, those who sold themselves voluntarily because of unemployment, children who were exposed and kidnapped, or minors (mainly young girls) sold in payment of debts who became handmaids or concubines.[144]

---

[139] Mendelsohn, *Slavery in the Ancient Near East*, v, 19–21.

[140] *The New Encyclopedia Britannica*, 1975 ed., s.v. "Slavery, Serfdom, and Forced Labour."

[141] Michael I. Rostovtzeff, *The Social and Economic History of the Hellenistic World*, 3 vols. (Oxford: At the Clarendon Press, 1941), 74–125. Later works of Rostovtzeff that deal with the role of trade and even slave trade in the early Greek and Roman world are *Rome* and *Out of the Past of Greece and Rome*. Rostovtzeff gives a region-by-region accounting of slavery in fourth century BC. Although Finley agrees that slavery and free labor influence each other, Finley argues against Rostovtzeff's position that Hellenistic slavery "'differed from the modern economy only quantitatively, not qualitatively'" (Finley, *Ancient Slavery and Modern Ideology*, 54). *The New Encyclopedia Britannica*, s.v. "Slavery, Serfdom, and Forced Labour."

[142] Rostovtzeff, *The Social and Economic History of the Hellenistic World*, 192–94, 197, 203 passim, 1110–12; *The New Encyclopedia Britannica*, s.v. "Slavery, Serfdom, and Forced Labour."

[143] Mendelsohn, *Slavery in the Ancient Near East*, 66.

[144] Mendelsohn, *Slavery in the Ancient Near East*, 1–33.

Regardless of the source or circumstances of the enslavement, they were considered human; and their legal status in the ancient world permitted them to maintain families to marry, to enter into business, and to own property. And after the fulfillment of the terms of the enslavement, they were able to be freed.[145] Despite the more humane nature of ancient slavery and though the slave was considered to be a human being, the slave still existed on a lower plane than did the citizens of the society. According to Mendelsohn, the status of the slave in ancient society was as follows:

> The recognition that the slave, though legally a chattel, was a human being and that as such he possessed certain inalienable rights found its expression also in the law codes. The Hammurabi Code recognized as legally binding a marriage contracted between a slave and a freeborn woman, and although legally the slave with all his possessions was the property of his master, the children born of such a marriage were free, and the children born of a union between a master and his female slaves were freed after the father's death. The conception that the slave was a person half free and half slave is reflected in the fact that a master could not kill his slave with impunity. . . . When an unfree person denies his slave status he shall have his ear cut off by his master.[146]

Ancient slaves were not divided along racial or cultural lines because "the slave was generally [of] the same race, color, speech, and religion as his master. The great majority of the slaves was not even of foreign birth, but came from the ranks of the defaulting debtors, originally free members of the same community."[147] Although legally chattel, the status of the slave in relation to freedom was cast along a spectrum of degrees of freedom, depending on the personality of the slave master. They often worked alongside their master and were less numerous in skilled trades.[148]

Although slaves were designated for use in agriculture and industry, most farms and craft shops did not use slave labor. The farms were operated with tenant farmers or sharecroppers, and the shop owners often preferred a labor force of free craftsmen, even if they were unskilled. Therefore, positions were filled by free labor in ancient society that later would be filled by slaves.[149]

---

[145] Mendelsohn, *Slavery in the Ancient Near East*, 34–91.
[146] Mendelsohn, *Slavery in the Ancient Near East*, 122–23.
[147] Mendelsohn, *Slavery in the Ancient Near East*, 34–91, 122.
[148] Mendelsohn, *Slavery in the Ancient Near East*, 92–120, 122.
[149] Mendelsohn, *Slavery in the Ancient Near East*, 92–120, 122.

Slavery in Old Testament literature was coterminous with slavery in the ancient period. In biblical literature, slavery was presented as rigorous in submission, punishment, and the rightful designation for those captured in war. Except for what happened in Egypt in the book of Exodus, the period of servitude lasted for seven years, but it was not always honored. Moreover, biblical slavery had a dual character. It was seen, first, as subjugation from which God's people must be set free and, second, as bondage, which meant subordination, religious humility, and self-surrender. In this latter sense, God's chosen people were his slaves.[150]

Slavery was rampant in ancient Egypt and the societies of the eastern Mediterranean (Persia and the Aegean Islands). The most common source of slavery in Egypt and the regions of the Mediterranean was war captives just as it had been in ancient societies. The captives either became the private possession of kings or were kept for service in the temple or in the state. Owners of slaves had absolute rights over the slaves, whose heads were usually shaved to mark them out as slaves. In these cultures, slave breeding became another resource for slaves. Similar to Babylonia, the slaves of ancient Egypt were found in every field of work and therefore were of considerable economic significance.[151]

The existence of slavery in the classical world between the early period of the first millennium BC and the first millennium AD was best documented in the philosophical works on its social, political, and economic status by the Greek and Roman thinkers.[152] Aristotle was the first to define the legal status of the slave. He described the slave as in possession of a soul, and he asserted that slavery was rooted in nature and was seen as good and just.[153]

---

[150] Mendelsohn, *Slavery in the Ancient Near East*, 85–90; Davis, *Problem of Slavery in Western Culture*, 47–48, 63–65.

[151] Mendelsohn, *Slavery in the Ancient Near East*, 34, 40–42; *The New Encyclopedia Britannica*, s.v. "Slavery, Serfdom, and Forced Labour."

[152] Davis, *The Problem of Slavery in Western Culture*, 66–72. Davis studies the ideas of Plato and Aristotle and compares their theories on slavery. The purpose of referring to Plato and Aristotle is not to sustain an in-depth study of their theories. We seek only to substantiate the magnitude and the rudimentary ideas that have sustained slavery during the classical period.

[153] Benjamin Jowett, trans., *Politica*, I.4, 1254^{a15}; I.5, 1254; and I.5, 1255^{a1} in *The Works of Aristotle*, ed. Sir David Ross, vol. X, rev. ed. (Oxford: At the Clarendon Press, 1961); William L. Westermann, *The Slave Systems of Greek and Roman Antiquity* (Philadelphia: 1955), 1, 26. Moreover, in her work "Aristotle: A Study of His Slave Theory with Both Definite and Presumptive Evidence of Its Impact upon Western Civilization," Jewell R. Crawford Mazique argues that the thinking of Aristotle has had a strong influence on slavery, slave institutions, and the attitudes regarding slaves and the slave trade down through the centuries, particularly in the formation of modern slavery. Mazique suggests that one of the questions

In another place, Aristotle said that, "from the hour of their birth, some are marked out for subjection, others for rule."[154] Accordingly, Mazique paraphrased Aristotle's thought when she asserts that

"[n]ature itself had determined that some [humans] were physically and spiritually adapted for slave status and low class laborers as against those who were both spiritually and somatically unfit for such tasks, but fit for civilian life and its freedom.[155]

We can say ultimately that Aristotle developed a philosophy in support of slavery that met the social and political needs of his day. However, he ended up with the dichotomous task of explaining that all people were human. Nevertheless, contrary to modern society, the slave had a place in the classical society, in the *polis*. Because of the notion of the citizen as synonymous with the leisure class, the slave, of necessity, had to engage in work. Thus, the relationship between the slave and the free person was similar to and to be dealt with like other household relationships (e.g., husband and wife, parents and children).

The sources of slavery in classical Greece and Rome were similar to that of the ancient world: "war, insolvent debtors, piracy, brigandage, kidnapping, breeding, and import from barbarian lands." Both Greece and Rome were societies where even citizens were involved in work as peasants, craftsmen, or laborers. They even worked in the mines. It seemed that manual or managerial labor was done by citizens and slaves alike in society. Being subjected to the orders of another was what made work servile and degrading and was the distinguishing characteristic between the citizens and the slave in the work world.[156]

Insolvent debtors were source of slavery who were only enslaved during primitive periods but was forbidden and illegal by the sixth century BC in Athens and the fourth century BC in Rome. As the Roman Empire evolved throughout the Mediterranean region, so did the legal restraint on debt slavery. Another source of slavery in Greece was exposed and abandoned children and

---

of the arbiters of the modern state in the New World has been, what to do about slavery? She says that it has been Aristotle's ideas on the state in *Politics*, including his discourse on the place of the slave in that state, that have given the answer. Aristotle's justification of slavery is tied up with his notion of the pyramidal framework of the state with the aristocracy at the top. The master/ slave relationship will become the norm. However, the idea of "slave" used by the philosophers is not to be taken literally; "slave" is a metaphor for a subordinate position (e.g., of the industrial proletariat).

[154] Jowett, *Politica*, I.5, 1254^{a22}; Westermann, *The Slave Systems of Greek and Roman Antiquity* (Philadelphia: 1955), 1, 26.

[155] Jowett, *Politica*, I.5, 1254^{b25}; Mazique, 23.

[156] *The New Encyclopedia Britannica*, s.v. "Slavery, Serfdom, and Forced Labour."

children sold by poor parents and newborn infants, but by the sixth century, the Roman law declared all such children free. Sometimes those who were free could allow themselves to be sold into slavery, or certain crimes were punishable by sale into slavery.[157]

There were agricultural slaves and state-owned slaves, who did mining and worked on road gangs, had few rights, and were often treated brutally, while artisan slaves, public slaves who served in minor official positions (temples, secretaries, accountants, bank managers, secretaries of state, finance ministers, nurses, and sea captains), and domestic slaves often became eligible for manumission. Sometimes slaves of that period were often better off than many of the free citizens because they even occupied important positions in government.[158]

The conquests of the Roman Empire became the earliest source of slaves. However, by the second and first centuries BC with the expansion of the Roman Empire, peace and the suppression of piracy and brigandage eventually led to a scarcity of slaves. This scarcity was what ultimately prompted the importation of slaves from barbarian lands "beyond the Rhine, the Danube, and the Euphrates," and the breeding of slaves became necessary. The barbarian slaves created a new atmosphere in the Roman world.[159] One of the interpretations about what contributed to the downfall of the Roman Empire was not just economic changes and the weakening of the centralized power of the Greco-Roman world. That interpretation argued that the "numerical preponderance" of barbarian slaves who were a significant part of society was also an important factor.

Nevertheless, the classical world moved to new heights where slavery was concerned when the upper wealthy class began building large estates. Agricultural slavery was introduced on a large scale. Often because of the immense size of these estates, slave groups were used to cultivate the land, or the estates were divided up among the slave groups, making smaller herd farms. Just the sheer numbers of barbarian slaves prompted revolts against the sometimes brutal forces of the owners, especially as hereditary groups received tracts of land. Such acquisitions gave slaves rights from the masters, which put them on a par with free members of the society. Slaves developed into hereditary groups consisting of freed slaves who held important positions in various households and in public office. As slavery and especially hereditary groups became more accepted, relationships between slaves and slave masters became more indulgent. Davis wrote, "[D]uring the slow and profound

[157] *The New Encyclopedia Britannica,* s.v. "Slavery, Serfdom, and Forced Labour."

[158] *The New Encyclopedia Britannica,* s.v. "Slavery, Serfdom, and Forced Labour."

[159] Davis, *The Problem of Slavery in Western Culture,* 36; *The New Encyclopedia Britannica,* s.v. "Slavery, Serfdom, and Forced Labour."

transformation of the European economy, there was an overlapping and interpretation of the systems of slavery and serfdom, so that servitude and dependencies of various kinds were modeled on the prototype of hereditary slavery, and such words as *servus, Knecht,* and *vassus,* which had originally implied unlimited bondage, acquired new connotations of status, rights, and willing service."[160] We shall trace the point of termination of slavery and the rise of the feudal and manorial system.

1.2.4. FEUDAL OR MANORIAL BONDAGE: THE MEDIEVAL STRUCTURE

The origins of bondage in the medieval society came about as slavery of the Roman Empire evolved into hereditary slavery with its large tracts of land into what was called the *calani,* the tenant farmers who were independent owners of extremely large estates. In fact, the origins of serfdom in medieval Europe were in this mitigated form of "slavery" or bondage that was a system of feudal and manorial monarchies, duchies, and counties later called feudalism and manorialism.[161] The *calani* ultimately became the serfs in a feudal or manorial system. It was the banning together of various *calani* who surrendered their landholding to a proprietor in return for protection from invaders and oppressive neighbors that led to the feudal/manorial structures.[162] It would not be necessary to redescribe these systems at this point; however, it would be important for us to refer to them merely to situate them within this discourse on slavery.[163]

The labor system during the medieval period was centered on the feudal and manorial systems. Europe, for the most part, was an agrarian-type society

---

[160] Davis, *The Problem of Slavery in Western Culture,* 36–37; *The New Encyclopedia Britannica,* s.v. "Slavery, Serfdom, and Forced Labour."

[161] Rostovtzeff, *Social and Economic History of the Roman Empire,* vol. I, 192–254; Westermann, *Slave Systems of Greek and Roman Antiquity,* 109–13, 120, 140. Much has already been said about the feudal and manorial systems; see p. 18ff *supra.* By the ninth and tenth centuries, *calani*–also known as serfs–or *calani services* were the descendants of the former slave population of the Greco-Roman world. Although they were almost totally dependent on the lord, they achieved enfranchisement or manumission by their masters.

[162] Davis, *The Problem of Slavery in Western Culture,* 36–37; Rostovtzeff, *The Social and Economic History of the Roman Empire,* vol. 1, 192–254; Westermann, *The Slave Systems of Greek and Roman Antiquity,* 109–13, 120, 140.

[163] This study has covered more thoroughly the structure of feudalism and manorialism and how they functioned as a system of bondage. See *supra* p. 18ff. We refer to it here as we document its origins in the transfer of large estates to groups of hereditary slaves and freemen to form the *colony.*

whose workers were engaged in production for consumption, a rural type of subsistence economy. Most people grew their own food and provided what was necessary to maintain their status and relationship to the landlord. However, there were those who were made use of a more market type of economy. Daniel Thorner wrote, "We are sure to deceive ourselves if we think of peasant economics as oriented exclusively towards their own subsistence and term 'capitalist' any orientation towards the 'market.' It is more reasonable to start by assuming that, for many centuries, peasant economies have had both orientations [translation by author]."[164]

From the second to the twelfth centuries, discordant traditions resulted in the Catholic Church appearing to be ambivalent on the issue of slavery.[165] In fact, the formulation of Catholic teaching concerning slavery from the thirteenth to the mid-fifteenth centuries was influenced by the church's adherence to Greek philosophical thinkers and the Roman civil law (Thomas Aquinas). There were laws concerning slavery that regarded it as beneficial to both the slave and the master. Catholic church teaching took the more humane approach by accepting slavery for those enslaved usually as a captive of "just" warfare, especially those who were not Christian, criminals or debtors, or born to a slave mother, or as an ecclesiastical penalty.[166]

One of the concerns during the medieval period was the place of the human person in society. The question was, how could one be a slave while considered human, which was necessary for baptism? Christians would answer the dilemma of the humanity of the slaves by dividing the individual into two parts—a physical part and a spiritual part or Aristotle's matter and soul.[167] According to Thomas Aquinas, who Christianized Aristotle, the slave—even when baptized—still remained a slave. Baptism, according to church leaders, placed some limitations on the liberties of slaveholders in their relation with the slaves they owned. In the Catholic context, even the slave was managed with compassion—allowed to marry and have a family, given schooling, and had a recognized role in the existing society.

Studies on slavery and the Catholic Church stated changes even in church teaching from about the mid-fifteenth century because it was clear that modern slavery was distinctly different. John F. Maxwell, in his catalog of Roman Catholic church teachings on slavery, reveals that there was even a

---

[164]   Daniel Thorner, "L'économique paysan: concept pour l'histoire économique," *Annales ESC* XIX, 3 (May-June 1964): 422.

[165]   John Francis Maxwell, *Slavery and the Catholic Church: The History of Catholic Teaching Concerning the Moral Legitimacy of the Institution of Slavery* (Chichester and London: Barry Rose Publishers, 1975), 10–43.

[166]   Maxwell, *Slavery and the Catholic Church*, 44–49.

[167]   Mazique, 29.

new approach to its teachings.[168] Mediterranean slavery had been influenced by the ancient and medieval notions of slavery. What this meant, according to Maxwell, was that even though slavery was problematic, the slave and the master shared the same human nature–subject to the same laws of life and death–and were equally children of the same God and brothers and sisters in Christ.

The Catholic Church officially maintained its traditional attitude on slavery, which might be summarized as follows: "(1) [a]lleviating the hardships connected with it, (2) protecting the integrity of family life and safeguarding the natural rights of the slave, (3) insisting upon religious equality and sufficient instruction to insure an understanding of religion, (4) encouraging manumission. There was all too often a lag between the ideal and its practical application and the record of missionary labors abounds in expressions of regret and discouragement over the failure of slave owners to apply the teachings of the Church to the management of their slaves. Indeed a frequent source of conflict between clergy and planters throughout the colonial period lay in the insistence by the former that the slaves receive adequate religious instruction and participate freely in the religious life of the community."[169]

At the start-up of the modern world came the evolving merchant class, who were agents who functioned outside the feudal structure to sell acquired surplus goods.[170] And it was not until slave raiding in West Africa for profit, the discovery of America in 1492, and the conquest of the natives of Latin America during the fifteenth and sixteenth centuries that there was a change in church teachings "from pro to con" regarding slavery. The first of such denunciations of slavery by Roman Catholic Church, even though it was limited to opposing the enslavement of Christians, were rendered by Pope Eugene IV in 1433 and 1435, by Pope Nicholas V in 1452, by Pope Calixtus III in 1456, by Pope Pius II in 1462, and by Pope Sixtus IV in 1476, with all of them having excommunication as the punishment for anyone who were engaged in the enslavement of Christians.[171]

---

[168] Maxwell, *Slavery and the Catholic Church.*

[169] Madeline Hooke Rice, *American Catholic Opinion in the Slavery Controversy* (New York: Columbia University Press, 1944), 21. This summary of the traditional attitude of the Catholic Church of M. H. Rice is based on her study of Jean Baptiste Labat's *Voyages aux isles de l'Amerique (Antilles) 1693–1705.*

[170] Wallerstein, *The Modern World-System,* 19.

[171] Maxwell, *Slavery and the Catholic Church,* 50–51 ; Davis, *The Problem of Slavery in Western Culture,* 98–100; Rice, *American Catholic Opinion in the Slavery Controversy,* 11–24.

1.2.5. SLAVERY IN THE NEW WORLD

Excluding the conquest and enslavement of natives upon the arrival of Europeans into the Americas during the sixteenth century and the kidnapping of Irish Catholics in the mid-seventeenth century, the source of slavery in the New World was West Africa. The African slave trade began as early as 1425, when Spanish and Portuguese merchant-traders first went down the west coast of Africa, captured Africans, and returned them to the Iberian Peninsula. By 1492, the merchant class of Spain and Portugal was expelled and forced into the deep water ports of Holland (Dutch East India and Dutch West India Companies) and later to England (London Slave Company). With these events, the New World involvement in slavery and the slave trade had begun.[172]

Although there was no slavery in Europe, there is some question about its relationship to the European economy.[173] Slavery was probably not a *direct benefit* to the growing urbanized world of Europe as such. It was the merchant class of the rising European states (British, French, Dutch, Spanish, and Portuguese), however, that supported the slave merchants. The Crowns exchanged the opportunity for the merchant class to sail under the flags in return for taxes. Also, the various Crowns needed the raw materials of the merchant-traders if the newly forming industrialized societies were to grow. Europeans conquerors and settlers, however, heavily engaged in slavery in the Americas to derive raw materials for their industrial ventures.

Slavery became the principal business of those migrating to the Atlantic world. These ventures from their inception were entrepreneurial, establishing an extraordinary demand for human labor. The merchant class sought to create that new workforce first by the brutal conquest, detribalization, and enslavement of natives; then by the kidnapping and enslaving Irish Catholics; and finally by capturing, dehumanizing, and enslaving Africans.

1.2.5.1. SLAVERY IN SPANISH AND PORTUGUESE AMERICA

The natives were the first target when the conquistadores first landed at Rio de la Plata (1511) and then Asunción (1537). To exploit this newfound territory, the Crown in the 1520s–under the leadership of a rising bourgeois

---

[172] *New Catholic Encyclopedia,* s.v. "Slavery (History of)" by Charles Verlinden (New York: McGraw-Hill Book Company, 1979); Louis B. Wright, *Gold, Glory, and the Gospel: The Adventurous Lives and Times of the Renaissance Explorers* (New York: Atheneum, 1970).

[173] Again, confer with the works of the thinkers who view slavery as the basis of the modern political economy and as the economic expression of modernity. See *supra* p. 43ff.

elite–established an intricate cooperative system called the *encomienda-doctrina*. The encomienda system was a forced labor system instituted by the conquistadores, who were the merchant class of Spain and Portugal.[174] In the encomienda system, the colonists–in conjunction with the merchants–exploited, enslaved, and persecuted the natives. What the encomienda system did was tantamount to holding them as slaves. Any settler who was reluctant to take part in the encomienda system came into serious conflict with colonial authorities.

The encomendero, usually soldiers and conquerors called conquistadores, violently took the natives from their natural habitat into towns under their control. They were to exploit the land and its resources, to control the natives, to indoctrinate them in the Catholic faith, and to build and maintain churches, roads, and profitable shipping ports.

In theory, the encomienda was based on the interrelationship between the encomendero–the conquistador, whose responsibility was to oversee the forced labor of the native and defend the newly acquired territories–and the *doctrinero*, the church leader, whose responsibility it was to instruct the native in the Catholic faith. The native had to work and give tribute to the encomendero. Attacking the fiber of the existing native societies, the system actually neglected the care and education of the natives, forcing them to live in abominable conditions. There were even reports of torture. Through the encomienda process, the conquerors were ruthless in their pillaging and confiscating of natural resources.

The natives of the encomienda system consisted of two classes. The first class were the yanaconas (*originarios*), who were descendants of the captives of war who became slaves in perpetuity. The second class were the *mayans*, those who surrendered without fighting. The miatas were called *mityas tindarunas*, which meant that they were in forced labor. They grouped in towns and were used in mines for two months before they were freed. But mine work was usually fatal.

One of the efforts to deal with these attacks on the natives was inspired by the struggle of Bartolomé de Las Casas, the Paraguayan reductions of the Jesuits.[175] The reductions were described as follows:

---

[174] *New Catholic Encyclopedia*, s.v. "Encomienda-Doctrina System in Spanish America" by A. S. Tiebesar. The struggle against the *encomienda-doctrina* system as a struggle for justice is described in Lewis Hanke's *The Spanish Struggle for Justice in the Conquest of America* (83–105). The following texts were used to describe the encomienda system: Hanke, 5–13, 19–20; Tiebesar, 5:331–332; Latourette, *History of Christianity*, 3:92; Campbell, 300; Neill, 145; J. Aveling, *The Jesuits* (New York: Stein and Day Publishers, 1981, 1982), 149–50. Graham, 53–54; Caraman, 33.

[175] For further background on the Jesuit missions in Paraguay, confer with the following works: *Bulletin Signaletique* 527: *Histoire et Sciences des Religions* (Centre National

The most impressive achievement of the Society of Jesus on the South American continent was the series of missions, organized into Indian townships under Jesuit leadership, which we know from their Spanish title, as the Paraguay reductions. The venture has its origin in the intelligent planning of a Jesuit Provincial, Diego de Torres, who saw that the survival and the happiness of the natives in his new Province of Paraguay depended on insulating them against white penetration. The same idea has dictated Jesuit mission policy in many areas since that time, for sad experience had taught missionaries that their gift of the Christian message is too often followed by the trader or speculator's bestowal of gin, syphilis, and black-market firearms.[176]

Despite efforts by Bartolomé de Las Casas and later the Jesuits in the Paraguayan reductions to mitigate the cruelty of that system, the natives were decimated. They were unable to withstand the diseases of the Europeans, and if they did not die from the diseases, they were killed by the excessive hard work in the mines. The conflict with the Roman Catholic missionaries and the limited physical stamina of the natives led the merchant-traders to introduce African slaves as an alternative labor force.

With the introduction of black slaves during the sixteenth century, the emphasis of the labor force changed, but it did not put an end to the exploitation of the natives (e.g., peonage). As the production of sugar, coffee,

---

de la Recherche Scientifique-Centre de Documentation Sciences Humaines); L. Polgar, "Bibliographie de Historia Societas Jesu," *Archivum Historicum Societatis Jesu* (Roma) 48, no. 96 (1979): 345–420; notices and biographies of 114 Italian Jesuit missionaries to Paraguay by H. Storni, "Jesuitas italianos en el Río de la Plata (antioquia Provincia del Paraguay 1585–1768)," *Archivum Historicum Societatis Jesu* (Roma) 48, no. 95 (1979): 3–64. Kenneth S. Latourette furnishes the following in a list of authorities: W. H. Koebel, *In Jesuit Land: The Jesuit Missions of Paraguay* (London: Stanley Paul & Co., 1912), 381; Pierre François de Charlevoix, *Histoire du Paraguay,* 6 vols. (Paris: Desaint, 1757). Martin P. Harney, SJ, *The Jesuits in History: The Society of Jesus through Four Centuries* (Chicago: Loyola University Press, 1962), 244–49; *New Catholic Encyclopedia,* 15 vols. with supplements (New York: McGraw-Hill Book Company, 1979); Pablo Pastells, *Historia de la Compañía de Jesús en la Provincia del Paraguay,* 5 vols., (Madrid: Librería General de Victoriano Suárez, 1912–1933). Cunninghame Graham mentions the work of the Jesuit father Dobrizhoffer, *Historia de Abiponibus* (1784; English translation published in 1822). More recent works include the following: Nicholas P. Cushner, *Lords of the Land* (n.p., 1980) and C. J. McNaspy, *Lost Cities of Paraguay: Art and Architecture of the Jesuit Reductions, 1607–1767* (Chicago: Loyola University Press, 1982).

[176] Meadows, 34; Graham, 52–55; Caraman, 34.

and tea increased, the merchants and colonists established an intricate system of black slave plantations. This plantation system saw increased demands for labor for which the importation of massive numbers of black slaves was to fit the bill. It was with the failure of the natives to function well as slaves that the African slave trade became a reality.

1.2.5.2. THE SLAVE INDUSTRY IN BRITISH AMERICA

From its beginning in North America, slavery was a drive for profit and identified with the growth of commercial capitalism.[177] Therefore, one of the questions of grave significance is the British attitude toward slavery and the slave trade.[178] According to David Brion Davis, one of the renowned analysts

---

[177] Davis, 10.

[178] Initially, the basis of the economy in British America has been slavery and slave trading. The following selected bibliography certainly does not exhaust the studies on slavery in the States, but it provides an important insight into the role of the slave industry.

One of the foremost works on the slavery of British America is W. E. B. DuBois's *The Suppression of the African Slave-Trade to the United States of America, 1638–1870*. DuBois's work is significant because it is so thorough in its use of national and state governmental, legal, and historical sources (e.g., colonial statutes, congressional and state documents and archival materials, reports of antislavery societies, personal narratives, and monographs on slavery). Unlike most of the studies on slavery in British America, DuBois's work is the only one to make a strong link between the geography of the Atlantic seaboard and its impact on the specific investment of each of the colonies. His approach, unlike many studies on slavery, does not ignore the vital role of the Northern and New England colonies in slavery and slave trading. Most often, by stressing the use of slaves in the cotton, sugar, tobacco, and indigo industries, studies focus on the Southern colonies and states (Georgia, North and South Carolina, Virginia, West Virginia, and Kentucky) as the slave-bearing colonies so that, by the middle of the eighteenth century, it appears that the only colonies actively involved in slavery has been the Southern ones. In fact, that the impetus of the abolitionist's movement has come from Northern states does not mean they are blameless. The insight and research of DuBois translates instead into an effort to change the labor system from a slave to a free labor system. Such a move to free the slaves has promised greater profits in a rapidly changing economy. Prompted by the changes brought on by industrialization beginning in the mid-nineteenth century, slavery has no longer been the most profitable source of labor for the expanding commercial interests.

An early classic and challenging study on the slave industry in British America is Thomas R. R. Cobb's work *An Historical Sketch of Slavery from the Earliest Periods* (1858).

The following works also substantiate that the British America has been a society whose economy has been based on slavery: Davis, *The Problem of Slavery in the Age of Revolution 1770–1823*; David Brion Davis, "The Continuing Contradiction of Slavery: A Comparison of British America and Latin America," in *The Debate over Slavery: Stanley Elkins and His Critics*, ed. Ann J. Lane (Urbana, Chicago, and London: University of Illinois Press, 1971; Davis, *Slavery in the Colonial Chesapeake (The Foundations of America)* (Williamsburg, VA: Colonial Williamsburg Foundation, 1986).

Allan Kulikoff, *Tobacco and Slaves: The Development of Southern Cultures in the Chesapeake, 1680–1800* (Chapel Hill and London: University of North Carolina Press, 1986); Philip D. Curtin, *The Rise and Fall of the Plantation Complex: Essays in Atlantic History (Studies in Comparative World History)* (Cambridge and New York: Cambridge University Press, 1990); Robin Blackburn, *The Overthrow of Colonial Slavery, 1776–1848* (London and New York: Verso, 1988); Willie Lee Rose, ed. with commentary, *A Documentary History of Slavery in North America* (New York and London: Oxford University Press, 1976).

Edmund S. Morgan, "Slavery and Freedom: The American Paradox," *Journal of American History* 59, no.1 (June 1972): 5–29; Edmund S. Morgan, *American Slavery, American Freedom: The Ordeal of Colonial Virginia* (New York: W. W. Norton & Company, Inc., 1975); Helen Tunnicliff Catterall, ed., *Judicial Cases Concerning American Slavery and the Negro: Cases from the Courts of New England, the Middle States, and the District of Columbia*, with additions by James J. Hayden, vol. IV (New York: Octagon Books, Inc., 1968); William Hand Browne, *Archives of Maryland: Proceedings and Acts of the General Assembly of Maryland, January 1637/8–September 1664 and April 1666–June 1676* (Baltimore: Maryland Historical Society, 1883 and 1884).

Louis P. Hennighausen, *The Redemptioners and the German Society of Maryland: A Historical Sketch* (Society for the History of the Germans in Maryland, January 1888); Whittington B. Johnson, "The Origin and Nature of African Slavery in Seventeenth Century Maryland," *Maryland Historical Magazine* 73, no.3 (September 1978): 236–45.

The works of the Jesuits must be examined from two perspectives. The Jesuits existed as cofounders, collaborators, and investors in the founding of the Maryland colony. The literature on slavery, during this period, reflected a rejection of slavery and of slave-trading spirit. From the Puritan invasions of the Maryland colony between 1644 and 1646 to the period since the suppression and reestablishment of the Jesuits in 1773 and 1803, respectively, the Jesuits had been actively involved in slavery. The type of literature on slavery produced by Jesuits reflected a different spirit. This literature showed Jesuit support and participation in slavery.

The following are some of the Jesuit literature: Andrew White, *A Relation of Maryland* (orig., September 8, 1635; repr. Ann Arbor: University Microfilms, Inc., 1966); Joseph Zwinge, SJ, "Our Fathers in the Colonization of Maryland," *Woodstock Letters [WL]* 36: 78–92; Joseph Zwinge, SJ, "The Jesuit Farms in Maryland," *WL*, 39: 374–82; 40:65–77; 40: 180–99; 41: 53–77; 41: 195–222; 41: 275–91; 42: 1–13; 42: 137–50; 42: 194–200; 43: 83–89; 43: 336–52; "Papers Relating to the Early History of the Maryland Mission: Annual Letters, 1634–1642," *WL*, 10: 209–24; 11: 3–24; 11: 117–40; Peter C. Finn, "The Slaves of the Jesuits in Maryland" (thesis no. 4418, Washington DC: Georgetown University, May 1974); Emmett Curran, SJ, "'Splendid Poverty': Jesuit Slaveholding in Maryland, 1805–1838," *Catholics in the Old South*;

of the slave era in the United States, "[S]lavery a product of innumerable decisions of self-interest made by traders and princes in Europe and Africa, was an intrinsic part of American development from the first discoveries. The evolution of the institution was also coeval with the creation of the idea of America as a new beginning, a land of promise where men's hopes and aspirations would find fulfillment."[179]

Therefore, the intimate interrelationship between the rise of colonial America and the desire of the English and the Dutch to conquer the newfound land for profit was no longer questioned. The settlers, to respond to the rising demand for sugar and to a lesser degree to satisfy the escalating demands for coffee and cotton cloth, found it necessary to use more slave labor. Those involved in the slave industry even computed the possible rate of return and profit margins for those investing in the market.[180]

Considered to be an outgrowth of the late medieval concept of joint-stock companies, by the time of European expansion, slavery was widely accepted, and "only if there were

already tensions over slavery in [their] system of values" did the founders of colonial America have any problem or conflict with slavery.[181]

The founders of the Maryland colony, advocates of a type of "enlightened feudalism," however, initially resisted any involvement in slavery and the slave trade. Davis's insight, therefore, would certainly apply to Catholics. With what Davis said, it must have been the vision of George Calvert–the first Lord Baltimore himself–in conjunction with the influence of the Jesuits,

---

Gilbert J. Garraghan, SJ, *The Jesuits of the Middle United States*, vol. 1 (Chicago: Loyola University Press, 1983); Darold D. Wax, "Black Immigrants: The Slave Trade in Colonial Maryland," *Maryland Historical Magazine* 73, no.1 (March 1978): 30–45.

[179] Davis, *The Problem of Slavery in Western Culture*, 24.

[180] Fogel and Engerman, *Time on the Cross*, 3, 13–20, 67–78.

[181] Davis, *The Problem of Slavery in Western Culture*, 24–25. "Joint-stock companies were groups of capitalists who pooled their personal wealth in cash, acquired shares in a collective enterprise, divided the proceeds in proportion to their investment and were free to transfer their share to their heirs or sell it. From the end of the twelfth century this practice was common in the shipping business.... It was extended in the thirteenth century to the component parts of equipment under commission, and subsequently, at Genoa, to loans made to the militia ('column') and to syndicates formed in the first instance to recover debts in overseas countries and which in the end severely exploited the colonial provinces of the Republic. . . . In the fourteenth century, associations of capitalists were formed specializing in marine insurance, which was a source of considerable profits since at this time the fantastic risks from privateering and piracy were at their height" (Robert-Henri Bautier, *The Economic Development of Medieval Europe: History of European Civilization Library*, gen. ed., Geoffrey Barraclough [London: Harcourt Brace Jovanovich, Inc.; Thames and Hudson Ltd., 1971], 160).

especially Fr. Andrew White, that made the Maryland colony exclude slavery. In contrast, their closest neighbors–the Virginia colony, as well as the New England colonies–were organized as trader colonies and did not eliminate slavery and the slave trade in their plans.

George Calvert, because he was a member of the court of King James, was in the position to know the religious and economic atmosphere of British America. When George Calvert prepared the Maryland charter, like other colonial planners, he shaped the colony according to the needs of his potential settlers. Because most of the settlers in Maryland were Catholics who had known persecution in England, he wanted to make his proprietary colony inclusive of all peoples and their beliefs. As we shall see, this resistance to the slave industry would eventually lead to the undoing of Catholics as shown by the issues that surrounded the overrun of the colony in 1646. We shall come back to this later.

Now for a more specific review of the rise of the slave industry in British America, we have just seen some of the theoretical underpinnings of British slavery. The intention, at this point, is to provide specific documentation about the extent of slavery and to disclose further the context of the ensuing religious conflict within which the Maryland colony, specifically the Jesuit mission, has been founded.

The first known enslavement in the Americas was of the native peoples of Hispaniola. Shortly after his ascendancy to the Spanish throne in 1516, Charles V granted the first license to transport Africans as slaves. This license, granted to De Bresa, allowed the transportation of "none but grown males" to the island of Hispaniola.[182]

The actions of the Crown regarding slavery were almost always out of the hands of the religious, and *this* was especially true for Catholics. Slavery was almost totally in the hands of the adventuring conquistadores who wrenched authority from the Crown to initiate the primacy of enterprise in the Atlantic world. A Catholic who rendered strong opposition to slavery at this early period was Cardinal Jiménez. He opposed the slave charters granted by Charles V for the supplying of slaves to the West Indies, even though his motivation was to prevent slave revolts based on the sheer multiplication of numbers.[183]

The first record of any transaction regarding slaves as far as England was concerned was a report from the British economist Hakluyt. He stated that, by 1553, twenty-four African slaves had been brought into England.[184] In 1562, before the notion of chartered companies, Sir John Hawkins brought the first

---

[182] Thomas R. R. Cobb, *An Historical Sketch of Slavery from the Earliest Periods* (Philadelphia and Savannah: T & J. W. Johnson & Co.; W. Thorne Williams, 1858), 139.

[183] Cobb, 141.

[184] Cobb, 142.

British cargo to Hispaniola.[185] Other companies were developed by Queen Elizabeth in 1585 and 1588.

By the end of the sixteenth century, all eyes turned to the sugar industry in the West Indies. Several charters were granted to merchants to engage in the slave trade to enhance the production of sugar. Exclusive charters were granted to four companies that engaged in the slave trade between 1618 and 1672. James I gave a charter to Sir Robert Rich (1618), who carried slaves to Guinea. By 1631, the production of sugar had reached such a level in the West Indies that the bearers of early charters built forts for the "defense of commerce."[186]

In 1662, the Duke of York–brother of Charles II and owner of the Company of Royal Adventurers Trading to Africa–was granted a charter by the king "to furnish the West Indian colonies with 3,000 slaves annually."[187] However, this charter was surrendered by 1672 to a new company chartered by Charles II called Royal African Company. Even the king was named in this charter.[188] The Royal African Company functioned until 1688 at the dawning of the Glorious Revolution in England. At this point, after taking over ships of private traders, Parliament "abolished all exclusive charters."

From then on, the slave trade was opened by act of Parliament to anyone who sought to engage in it. The Royal African Company, from 1739 to 1746, was given money by Parliament to maintain itself. Private traders who paid duty of 10 percent on the English goods they exported to Africa were permitted to take part in the slave trade.[189]

By 1700, the slave trade had become the life of the colonies. According to the colonists, slavery had become the "the strength and sinews of [the] western world."[190] To begin with, all the colonies had slaves. The large number of ships and the statistics on the number of slaves were staggering. To discuss the impact of slavery on the colonies, the colonies might be divided into three types based on how they made use of slaves. They were planting colonies (Georgia, South Carolina, North Carolina, Virginia, and Maryland); farming colonies (New York, Pennsylvania, Delaware, and New Jersey); and trading colonies (Rhode Island, Massachusetts, New Hampshire, and Connecticut).[191]

The planting colonies were the "chief theatre of North American slavery," and their function became key to the future of slavery and the slave trade

---

[185] Cobb, 142; W. E. B. DuBois, *The Suppression of the African Slave-Trade to the United States of America, 1638–1870* (New York: Dover Publications, Inc., 1970), 2.
[186] Cobb, 143.
[187] Cobb, 143; DuBois, 2.
[188] Cobb, 143; DuBois, 2.
[189] DuBois, 2.
[190] DuBois, 4.
[191] DuBois, 7–38.

in North America.[192] These colonies were called planting colonies because of the climate with its long growing seasons and the quality of the soil. Even though slavery was to become the hallmark of the Virginia planting colony, the first Africans to set foot on colonial soil (1619) were thought to be indentures rather than slaves. Virginia was both an experimenter in the system of domestic slavery and the main producer of tobacco. These activities caused an enormous need for the use of slaves.[193]

Though North Carolina was ripe for the farming industry, because of the Quaker influence, there were no slaves at the founding of this planting colony (1660). However, slave labor was inevitable.

Slavery came with the settlement of the South Carolina colony in 1670. This planting colony was reputed to have had "one of the largest and most developed slave-trade of any of the continental colonies."[194] This success in the slave trade can be attributed to the colony's rate of development and its proximity to the West Indies. The numbers rose so rapidly and consistently that fear of the inevitable occurred, slave revolts.

The last of the planting colonies to be founded was Georgia in 1733. Its founders initiated a moral code in the colony ruling out rum and slaves. The settlers were bent on opposing such stringency and won out in the long run. By 1749, the restrictions were removed, and slavery abounded.[195] In his detailing of slavery in colonial America, Cobb did not mention Maryland, which supported what we had been saying: Maryland resisted slavery in its foundation. In fact, though it made use of servants, it was not until the mid-1660 that any mention was made of Maryland having slaves. Of course, this was after the major dethroning of Calvert's mission of toleration and inclusion in conjunction with the Jesuit missionaries. DuBois stated that Maryland, like Virginia, had a profitable business in slaves. However, he also inferred that because of the nature of the colony, slavery was delayed in becoming a reality. David Brion Davis, on the other hand, made it clear that Maryland and Virginia, to an extent, relied heavily on the use of indentured servants up to about 1660s.[196]

The farming colonies existed along the mid-Atlantic coast of colonial America in climatic circumstances that were not conducive to planting. The slaves that came to these colonies supplied the need for house servants. The settlers of these colonies did not make the use of slaves a priority, even though they were masterful in supplying slaves not only to the Southern colonies but

---

192 DuBois, 7.
193 DuBois, 12.
194 DuBois, 9.
195 Cobb, 151.
196 Davis, *Slavery in the Colonial Chesapeake*, 7–8. Cf. Cobb, 142–50.

also to the West Indies and to South America.[197] Another factor that made some of these colonies different was that, like the Maryland colony, the values they held placed them in opposition to slavery from its inception. However, they lost the battle to the powerful merchant-traders.[198]

The Dutch, who initiated the slave trade to the American continent, settled New Amsterdam in 1614. They were known for having conducted some of the fiercest slave trading, contributing immensely to the industry. For example, it was a Dutch trading company that brought the initial twenty slaves (or indentured) to the Virginia colony in 1619.

The founding of New Amsterdam, as New York was called initially, was done by one of the private Dutch joint-stock companies. The Dutch companies were the first to run what became known as the "triangle trade." They left Holland en route to Africa with the goods they would trade for slaves. Upon receiving slaves, they traveled to the West Indies or to Brazil, where they left the slaves. They then embarked on a trip back to Holland with sugar and other goods of the New World.[199]

By 1621, the Dutch had consolidated this operation into the Dutch West India Company. In 1626, the Dutch West India Company became the first to bring slaves to New Amsterdam and sold them at public auction.[200]

Because of the influence of the Quakers, Pennsylvania—which was founded in 1682—was one of those colonies that initially were less engaged in slavery. Several attempts at rejecting slavery were met with a lukewarm response. By 1750, Philadelphia had the most slaves in the colony. During that time, it was estimated that about one-fourth of the population of Philadelphia was slaves of African descent.[201] In an effort to resist the rise of slavery, Pennsylvania placed heavy duties and taxes on the transport of slaves. Likewise, rumors of slave uprisings were spawned in the colony, all in an effort to make slavery have a rough time succeeding in that colony.

The farming colony of Delaware was founded in 1638, with slavery being introduced in around 1688. The colony was originally designed for free labor, but slavery ultimately gained a foothold.

New Jersey, the last of the farming colonies, was settled in 1664. By 1665, the proprietaries of the colony—to placate the Duke of York, who was president of the Royal African Company—offered a bounty of seventy-five acres of land for each slave who was imported.[202]

---

[197] DuBois, 16–17.
[198] Ibid.
[199] DuBois, 17.
[200] Cobb, 148.
[201] Cobb, 149.
[202] Cobb, 149.

The remainder of the thirteen colonies (Rhode Island, Massachusetts, New Hampshire, and Connecticut) were known as the trading colonies. Since the climate of these northernmost ventures did not provide a very long growing season and the settlers did not personally make use of slaves, they were involved–like the Dutch colonies–in furnishing slaves to the other colonies. The trading colonies were engaged in the transport of slaves throughout all the other colonies.

Rhode Island was settled in 1636. With the exception of Providence–the home of Roger Williams, who saw blacks and whites on the same footing–Rhode Island was considered one of the colonies most conspicuously involved in the slave trade. For example, one of the most prominent slave traders was Aaron Lopez (1731–1782), a man of Sephardic background who came to Newport, Rhode Island, in 1752, where he renounced his Marrano past, remarried his wife in a Jewish ceremony, underwent circumcision, and became the leader of the Yeshuat Israel Congregation. Lopez built an extensive transatlantic slave dealing and mercantile empire. His fleet of twenty-six ships was engaged in shipping slaves all along the Atlantic coast colonies to the West Indies and to Latin America.[203]

Another slave trader of Newport, Rhode Island, was Captain Lindsay, who sailed a brigantine called *Sanderson*. He was reputed to have had many successful voyages in the "triangle trade route." "The trade formed a perfect circle. Owners of slavers carried slaves to South Carolina, and brought home naval stores for their ship-building; or to the West Indies, and brought home molasses; or to other colonies, and brought home hogsheads. The molasses was made into the highly prized New England rum, and shipped in these hogsheads to Africa for more slaves."[204] Therefore, though the New England trading colonies did not themselves use slaves in their society except as house servants, it can be stated that these colonists were the backbone of the slave trade even before their foundation. New England had their first slaves by 1644–1645 and, by 1754, reported a census of 2,448 Negro slaves.[205]

As early as 1641, the Massachusetts colony–settled in 1620–acknowledged as fundamental the "lawfulness of Indian and negro slavery" and granted an approval to the African slave trade. Puritans initially bought slaves and engaged in the traffic of war victims or those who were already "slaves in

---

[203] *Encyclopaedia Judaica*, 1971 ed., s.v. "Lopez, Aaron" by Stanley F. Chyet. Also, cf. *Encyclopaedia Judaica*, s.v. "New Christians," "Marrano," and "Marrano Diaspora" by Martin A. Cohen, as well as The Nation of Islam, *The Secret Relationship Between Blacks and Jews* (Chicago: Latimer Associates, 1991), 262–67.

[204] DuBois, 28.

[205] Cobb, 147.

Africa."[206] "The Biblical codes of Massachusetts confirmed slavery to lawful Captives taken in just warres, & such strangers as willingly selle themselves or are sold to us."[207]

New Hampshire, settled in 1623, was another one of those colonies whose initial opposition to slavery was eventually overrun by the influence of merchant-traders. Though the slave trade was not strong in this colony and they did make use of house servants, slaves were brought to the colony beginning only in 1730.[208]

By 1650, Connecticut–settled in 1634–either forced Indians to make retribution for injuries they inflicted on the settlers or captured and exchanged them for Negro slaves. Other debtors received the same fate. Connecticut, in slave-to-free ratio, had more slaves than Massachusetts.[209]

Finally, like Portuguese and French slave traders, English traders acquired asientos from Spain, seeking to engage in the slave trade with the various Spanish colonies. Spain had become a broke and broken nation after the fall of the armada in 1588. Spain had lost its sea potential, and they made use of British colonial traders to help supply their colonies. And they still had massive territories that needed slaves.

Thus, slavery was a dominant force in the colonies. Nevertheless, as we shall see, it was significant that the Maryland colony–because of its structure, namely, the feudal-type manorial colonial system, a nonmodern, traditional type of state–did not engage in slavery until the mid-1660s. After this, the original Maryland charter was abrogated both in the colony and by the Long Parliament of Cromwell in England. The manorial system was based on servants who would eventually purchase their freedom after a period of working out their indebtedness. It was only when slavery made survival in the manorial system economically impossible that the Maryland gentry engaged in the use of slave labor.[210]

---

[206] Cobb, 147.

[207] Cobb, 147.

[208] DuBois, 30.

[209] Cobb, 142.

[210] One of the factors in the system of bond servitude was the availability of those who were willing to serve. At that period (1660s), it must be noted that forced or slave labor had begun to dominate the British colonies. Later in chapter 2, we shall detail how the Marylanders under the original charter were forced to become subservient to the Puritan traders and their drive for conquest within the British colonies. The wills of the Maryland gentry had been broken, and they were no longer willing to confront the rising Puritans' influences. They remembered how they had been overrun and were constantly under attack. Resistance had become too costly.

Vestiges of the ancient and classical system were operative during medieval feudal times. However, the role and status of slaves radically changed as the feudal system failed. Unlike the Greek, Roman, or feudal/manorial societies, modern slavery in the New World saw the slave solely as an instrument for profit. Like cattle or chattel, the slave was not a person but a piece of property to be bought, sold, and bred. In fact, the principal debate among religious thinkers focused on the humanity of the slave. Even moral theologians in the church in the United States, to accommodate the existence of slavery, were reputed to have developed a theory called the "plurality of species." This theory meant that not all people were fully human. Some people (e.g., slaves) were less human than those who were not slaves.[211] Sydney Ahlstrom wrote that "slavery was a labor system, but more fundamentally it was considered an essential means of social control over a race which at that time was regarded by almost everyone (including most abolitionists) as an inferior branch of the human species."[212]

The indentured servant entered into bondage for a specific period, usually a three- or four-year term. People were also permitted to sell themselves into servitude. Sometimes, however, they were able to work off their time sooner than the designated period. For example, they often were able to acquire enough money to purchase portions of their time.

---

[211] Charles Randolph Uncles to John R. Slattery, November 8, 1886, *Slattery Papers*, 10-N-2 (Josephite Archives, Baltimore, Maryland). The notion of "plurality of species in man" was mentioned by Charles Randolph Uncles, a seminarian for the Josephite priesthood, in a November 8, 1886, letter to his superior general, Fr. John Slattery. Uncles cited that John C. Calhoun was arguing for a plurality of species in man. Calhoun took this position when he served as secretary of state of the United States. He rendered the idea of a plurality of species in man when he was pressed by the English government to abolish or mitigate the evils of slavery. Uncles went on to the question whether the plurality of species in man was based in "the study and adoption of false philosophical theories," or was it "welcomed, cherished, and industriously disseminated by a prejudice already existing"? He went on to say that if it was the former, then "it is more pardonable than otherwise." Uncles referred to this theory as being taught in Southern colleges, universities, and schools and written about in public journals during the late 1800s.

Compare Francis Patrick Kenrick's *Theologia moralis* (1840–1843), delineating a moral theological position similar to the commonly held notion of plurality of species in man. According to S. Y. Mize, Kenrick used a "scholastic approach, placing rational stability above slavery's abolition and states' rights" (*Dictionary of Christianity in America*, 1990). Joseph D. Brokhage demonstrated in his dissertation entitled "Francis Patrick Kenrick's Opinion on Slavery" (1955) that Kenrick fostered the support of the slave system over the humanity of the enslaved.

[212] Sydney E. Ahlstrom, *A Religious History of the American People*, vol. 2 (Garden City: Image Books, 1975), 99.

In the history of slavery, the United States as a nation held that all people were human and entitled to certain inalienable rights of freedom and equality but also set up (from colonial times to 1865) one of the largest and cruelest slave systems with full constitutional protection (1791).[213]

It almost went without saying that the Constitution tolerated slavery while expressing the belief that "all men are created equal." Loren Miller revealed in his study of the Supreme Court and the Negro that the enslavement of black Americans in the modern state had left them permanently scarred. Miller provided an appraisal of the discovered original draft of the Declaration of Independence in which Thomas Jefferson criticized King George III of England for violating humanity by his involvement in slavery and the slave trade and then for inciting slave uprisings in the colonies. Miller asserted, "The argument was a neat and telling one. Jefferson was at once making the King a scapegoat for the slave trade, which he detested, and absolving the colonists of blame for the institution of slavery that troubled his conscience and the consciences of many of his colleagues, although he and many of them were slaveholders."[214]

The question of whether the slave was human was a burning issue at the Constitutional Convention. The debate centered on the apportionment of representation and how to account for the slave in the Congress of the United States. The argument was whether slaves should be passed over as property or counted as human. The answer was found in Article I, Section 2 of the Constitution of the United States, where it referred to "all other persons." The statement "all other persons" was a synonym for the slave.

The decision made by the Constitutional Convention was that the slave was warranted only *three-fifth* representation (Article I, Section 9 and Article IV, Section 2). The statement in Article IV, Section 2 seemed to be a direct response to the British decision by Lord Mansfield in 1771 in the *Somerset* case where, under the common law, a slave gained permanent freedom when he set foot on free soil.[215]

---

[213] Ahlstrom, 99.

[214] Loren Miller, *The Petitioners: The Story of the Supreme Court of the United States and the Negro* (New York: Pantheon Books, 1966), 16. Loren Miller was a Supreme Court justice for the state of California. He argued that the intention of the framers of the U.S. Constitution was to preserve the interest of the slave industry. They did not want to see blacks because of their original slave status as having the same dignity "in principle" and not necessarily "de facto" despite the Thirteenth, Fourteenth, and Fifteenth Amendments to the Constitution of the United States.

[215] Miller, 19–20. Lord Mansfield rendered a landmark decision on behalf of Somerset. Somerset was a slave who had been brought to England on board a ship. His master allowed him to leave the ship during its stay in England. When the master decided to embark, the slave refused to return to the ship. The dispute went

The decision made by the founding ancestors of American freedom did not consider the slave to be a person, even though they were referred to as persons. The Constitution was not clear about how slaves were seen "in the eyes of the law," whether they were human or property. On this matter, the Constitution based itself on the natural law–the theory that every person was to be treated with dignity. However, as Miller declared, "[R]ecognition of slavery and its protection by the Constitution inflicted a mortal wound on the principle as far as Negroes were concerned." For according to Miller, "[T]he appellation *Negro* was synonymous with *slave*," and the slave was not considered a person.[216]

What this meant, according to Miller, was that "the Constitution protected slavery in the states in which it existed and that the legislative, executive, and judicial branches of the federal government were compelled to further that protection and there was a rising conviction that all doubts as to the constitutional meaning were being resolved in favor of the slave power by congressmen, the chief executive, and especially the courts. . . . The law of slavery, perforce, developed in the slaveholding states, which meant that it was favorable to slavery as *an institution of private property*."[217] That the slave was not considered human only furthered the interests of the profiteering related to slavery. That the slave had no rights, human or otherwise, left the slave and slave labor as only a market commodity.

1.3. RELIGION IN THE MODERN STATE: ISSUES OF ULTIMATE CONCERN

For Anthony Giddens, modernity questions everything, including religion and the degree to which it seeks to establish itself as a reasoned reality in conjunction with the dictates of scientific rationality. Thus, religion could only be included in modernity as a kind of fundamentalism unless it is reflexive.

Another way of viewing what has occurred regarding religion during the rise of modernity is to apply the theories of Guy Swanson. The reference is to an evaluation of the ultimate concerns that exist in a society and their interrelationship with the values that evolve in it. Guy Swanson says that "the things of ultimate concern are the spirit of a reality and he maintains that these things are generally spiritual powers or beings." He continues, "There is evidence that belief in such powers and beings grows from experience with the

---

before the court in England. Somerset sued for his freedom and won the case. In his decision, Lord Mansfield declared that "anyone who breathes the free air of England is free."

[216] Miller, 22.
[217] Miller, 30–31.

constitutional arrangements, with the regimes, of societies and other groups." Swanson also holds that "the ultimate concern is incorporated in particular times, places, and things . . . such objects become 'immanent.'"[218] Thus, if the modern state is a structured, planned system and a product of scientific rationality, then according to Swanson, it must engage in adjusting itself if it is to fit into modern schemes. It is the intention of this next section to discuss medieval religion as a starting point for explicating the adjustments made by religion to survive in the modern state.

1.3.1. MEDIEVAL RELIGION

At the beginning of the medieval period, the task of religion was the unification of Europe. Medieval religion was a combination of the three forces from whence it was born: "Palestinian religion, Greek philosophy, and Roman law."[219]

The medieval period up to the Enlightenment was often described as the Catholic era. The scientific and intellectual world as well as the social and political arenas rested in the hands of the Catholic Church.

For three hundred years, there existed an ecclesiastical domination. The Catholic Church and its values were absolute in Western culture. The church stood as the symbolic agent of God, directing all earthly affairs. Never before had the church enjoyed and, as we now knew, would enjoy such preeminence. "The 13th century, although followed by disruption, witnessed the pinnacle of the Church in control of secular and spiritual affairs."[220] The development of scholasticism reached its height at the end of the thirteenth century and provided theological support for the sovereign claims of the church in both ecclesiastical and political affairs.[221]

The religious and political atmosphere of the medieval period was restricted. Governments were dominated by Christian religion to the point that it was treasonous not to belong to the religion of the official state, and apostasy was punishable by death. Dissenters in Episcopal England could not live unmolested. The Inquisitions of Italy and Spain were renowned examples

---

[218] Guy E. Swanson, *Religion and Regime: A Sociological Account of the Reformation* (Ann Arbor, Michigan: University of Michigan Press, 1967), vii–x.

[219] Clifton E. Olmstead, *History of Religion in the United States* (Englewood Cliffs, NJ: Prentice Hall, Inc., 1964), 2.

[220] Clyde L. Manschreck, *A History of Christianity in the World: From Persecution to Uncertainty* (New Jersey: Prentice Hall, Inc., 1974), 149.

[221] Manschreck, *History of Christianity in the World*, 165.

of the intolerance of this period. Acts of sacrilege was punishable by death in France, and apostates were burned as criminals in Austria.[222]

Despite the sovereign and authoritarian control of people by the Catholic Church and by governments, this era before the Enlightenment provided an understanding of God, the world, and the human person that was the foundation for a society with spiritual values. Salvation was open to all; even the slaves, according to Aquinas, were to be baptized, manifesting concern for quality of life for all people. God was an absolute and transcendent being involved in the world through the church, which was the visible dispenser of God's gifts to every human person. Through grace, the human person–regardless of status–cooperated with God and attained eternal life. God was the definition of the person.

Though affected by sin and thus imperfect, the world was a redeemed place because of the incarnation. The church in the world had a divinely given authority and power to involve itself with government, securing an atmosphere for the survival of all people in this world with a promise of eternal salvation. These principles influenced the development of the medieval feudal society, which first provided favorable conditions for a thoroughgoing Christianization of social life.[223]

The controlling grip of the church and its medieval synthesis became disrupted and dissolved during the fourteenth and fifteenth centuries. The

---

[222] Frank E. Manuel, ed., *The Enlightenment* (New Jersey: Prentice Hall, Inc., 1965), 1–3.

[223] Ernst Troeltsch, *Soziallehren der christlichen Kirchen und Gruppen* (Gesammelte Schriften, Erster Band, 1961): "It was, he writes, only when the city which arose out of the disintegration and surplus of feudal land ownership had united its varied population drawn from all sorts of different social origins, that a ground was prepared on which the higher qualities of medieval society could be purified from the crudity and violence of feudalism. The very condition of existence of the city as an essentially economic association is peace, freedom and the common interest of all the citizens, together with freedom to work and the basing of property on personal effort and industry.

"In all these respects the city corresponded to a great extent with the demands of Christian ethics. As a non-military peaceful community of work, using the military element only for its defense and still devoid of capitalistic urban features, the medieval city was a pattern of Christian society as we find it in Thomist theory. From the political and economic point of view the period of civic culture which begins in the eleventh century may be regarded as a preparation and foundation of the modern world. But for the historian of ethics and the religious life it also appears, with its cathedrals and its intensive church life, its religious confraternities and guilds, its care for the spiritual and material welfare of its inhabitants and its educational and charitable institutions, as the highest point of the development of the medieval spirit."

people in the church began to liberate themselves from the "sacerdotal controlled, infused grace of a now worldly oriented Church."[224]

> The Renaissance (1300–1517) was a complicated period of social change which had many foci. Individualism, secularism, and rationalism were important motifs in the period, but so were other developments such as emerging nationalism, urbanization, and industrialization. Most of what we term modern had its roots or significant growth in the Renaissance. Industry advanced especially in the Low Countries and northern Italy, where cloth, arms, leather materials, and hardware were produced; capitalist forms of ownership developed; trading companies and corporations grew. Latin was still the international language, but national tongues were becoming stronger. Professional soldiers who served where they could get the highest wages were displacing the military obligations of vassalage.[225]

The Renaissance immediately antedated and ushered in the Enlightenment. The Enlightenment was that period in Europe that extended from about the early seventeenth century to the beginning of the nineteenth century. This period, also referred to as Aufklärung, was experienced on both subjective and objective levels. The subjective involved the ascendancy of the autonomous human person coming of age from a kind of infancy that kept humans dependent and without confidence in their own minds.[226]

Enlightenment might also be called the "age of reason" or "modernity," which constituted its objective aspect. In this sense, it was a cultural evolution in which reason became the absolute ruler of human life. The emphasis on the human mind led to scientific advancement and to the development of philosophical systems to explain what, until this period, had been explained by a higher authority.[227]

With the development of the above stages of modernity, religion was more and more becoming a matter of private opinion. The public life of the state and the intellectual community of culture had become almost entirely

---

[224] Manschreck, *History of Christianity in the World*, 163.

[225] Manschreck, *History of Christianity in the World*, 177.

[226] Anthony Flew, ed., *A Dictionary of Philosophy*, rev. 2nd ed., (New York: St. Martin's Press, 1979), 106; Dagobert D. Runes, ed., *Dictionary of Philosophy* (Savage, MD: Littlefield, Adams Quality Paperbacks, 1983), 107.

[227] Flew, *Dictionary of Philosophy*, 106; Runes, *Dictionary of Philosophy*, 107.

secularized.[228] But the roots of the Enlightenment went back to the early Greco-Roman culture. Greco-Roman philosophers looked at nature and concluded that the governing principle was the reasoning mind. Socrates, Plato, and Aristotle all focused primarily on the human person and ascribed a high value to human intellectual powers.

With the rise of Christianity, which was alien to the Greco-Roman idea of the human person, there was an ensuing struggle. Most of the early Christian converts were Greeks and Romans who never rejected their literature. So Christianity made cultural accommodations–Thomas Aquinas being the clearest example. During the Renaissance and at the rise of the Enlightenment, thinkers sought to recapture the spirit of Greece and Rome, resulting in a movement of thought and belief concerned with the interrelated concepts of God, reason, nature, and the human person. The Enlightenment's basic conviction was that, through reason, the human person could find knowledge and happiness.[229]

> During the Enlightenment natural religion (particularly Deism) and skepticism rose to challenge the basic tenets of Christianity, and the new nationalism arose in philosophical, political, and economic thought. Many intellectuals of the Enlightenment rejected the ancient world's cyclical view of historical change and instead looked upon history as the record of the progress of the person toward reason and perfection.[230]

The age of reason, the Enlightenment, seemed to be a reaction to what was the artificially structured and authoritarian nature of both church and governments. It propagated and spread the light of reason among wider groups and called for action on the basis of rational thought. Science was emphasized instead of faith, and doubt instead of authority.

The next section would give some indication about how the background of the splintering of Christianity during the sixteenth century into various sects was the outcome of vast economic changes, liberalism, and the liberation from traditional religious values. This task inevitably called for a probe into some of the ethical principles of the two primary protagonists of the Reformation, Martin Luther (1483–1546) and John Calvin (1509–1564). The question would be, what was there about their thinking that gave rise to the religious adjustments to modernity?

---

[228] *New Encyclopedia Britannica*, s.v. "The Enlightenment."

[229] *New Encyclopedia Britannica*, s.v. "The Enlightenment."

[230] *New Encyclopedia Britannica*, s.v. "The Enlightenment."

1.3.2. THE PROTESTANT REFORMATION

The shifts in religious understanding began much earlier than the late fifteenth century. It would be too simplistic to say that the shifts to a capitalist economy were caused by the Protestant ethic. Those economic changes became deeply rooted within the late medieval period. The complexity of the forces preempted any argument for a causal relationship between the two. For like the rise of capitalism, the origins of religious conflict preexisted what finally came to be known as the Protestant Reformation.

Historians agreed that the upheaval in the Roman Catholic Church dated from as early as the late medieval period. The papacy had struggled against severe attacks by imperium during the early Middle Ages. This prompted structural reforms in the church from as early as the fourteenth century. The movements at reform were by, among others, the Lollards, followers of Wycliffe; the Hussites; and the Anabaptists. The papacy and the structure it created was the source of strong criticism. Most of these attempts were interested in diminishing church influence that was orchestrated by the pope. Despite the shifts in the social order, the church still sought to maintain the traditional values. This was interpreted as pacification and not as reform.[231] In the late Middle Ages, the church continued its efforts to institute reforms.[232]

Another element that contributed to the Protestant Reformation in the late fourteenth and early fifteenth centuries was the influence of Jewish culture. Because of its liberalism, Jewish culture encouraged dissent from the structures and often promoted ideas for the sake of their novelty. It promoted liberal heterodoxy, which presented a formidable challenge to Catholic reform movements.

> The existence of the Jewish community, perpetually heterodox and protestant, constituted a challenge to static Christian thought; it gave to searching minds among non-Jews cause to ponder; it led them upon a quest for new views, merely in order to break the bonds of orthodoxy which dissenters rightly believed, served to enslave free thought.[233]

---

[231] F. L. Cross and E. A. Livingstone, eds., *The Oxford Dictionary of the Christian Church*, 2nd ed. (London and New York: Oxford University Press, 1957, 1958[2], 1974[3], 1977[4], 1978, 1983[6], 1984[7], 1985[8]), 1165.

[232] E.g., Gregorian Reform (1073), church councils Basel (1449), Lateran V (1512–1517), and Trent (1545–1563).

[233] Louis Israel Newman, *Jewish Influence on Christian Reform Movements* (New York: AMS Press, Inc., 1966), 135.

This period witnessed a new kind of tolerance from the church for Jews who were bankers in Europe.[234] What was described as an abuse of Jews resulted in their liberation throughout Europe. Because of the dominance of the Catholic Church, which forbade under the pain of excommunication the participation of Catholics in usury, Jews expanded their economic services for profit.

> It is difficult to say whether the Jewish communities flourished by reason of the freedom granted them under the aegis of liberalism, or whether liberalism arose as a consequence of tolerance for the Jews. The least that can be affirmed is that Jewish prosperity went hand in hand with intellectual emancipation not merely for Jews alone, but for all members of the larger community.[235]

This favorable change in the status of Judaism was an "open door" for heterodox movements and a Judaizing tendency. Where Jews flourished commercially and intellectually, so did widespread heresy among Catholics.

The economic revolution of the late Middle Ages, which heralded the modern era, fostered radical shifts in the social ethics that were quite divergent from that of the feudal system. The values of the feudal system upheld the concept that production was for use, not profit. Within that context, production was not the basis for competition rooted in supply and demand. Both Luther and Calvin, with their religious systems, promoted the shifts in social ethics but Calvin more than Luther. The new ethics, centered on the rise of capitalism, were among the issues that prompted Luther and Calvin to pursue reforms. It can be argued that "the most characteristic and influential form of Protestantism in the two centuries following the Reformation is that which descends, by one path or another, from the teaching of Calvin."[236]

Calvinism took on international significance, and unlike Lutheranism, from which it sprang, accordingly, Calvinism was "an active and radical force. It was a creed which sought, not merely to purify the individual, but to

---

[234] About the changing view of the church regarding Jews, R. H. Tawney says that in Florence, which was the financial capital of the medieval period, the church and civil officials initially place great restrictions on banking, and then they "imported Jews to conduct a business forbidden to Christians" (*Religion and Capitalism,* 39–40).

[235] Newman, *Jewish Influence,* 136.

[236] Tawney, *Religion and the Rise of Capitalism,* 91.

reconstruct Church and State, and to renew society by penetrating every department of life, public as well as private, with the influence of religion."[237]

So when Martin Luther raised his voice against the abuses in the Roman Catholic Church and when Calvin wrote his *Institutes* (1536), they had not begun a new movement. for both Luther and Calvin had previously witnessed the contradictions of religion and economics on the questions of salvation and survival. What was once the domain of the church in conjunction with the Crown was now being brokered through rising expansionist economic interests. Their discomfort with the growing transition from the familiar medieval feudal ways and the new philosophical questions being raised regarding the relationship between the church and the Crown gave rise to their protest. They both pursued an answer to the question of human justification. Such a pursuit sowed the seeds that would ultimately sow division throughout Christendom. It was Calvin rather than Luther, however, who had the more long-range impact on religion in the rise of the New World.

The teachings of John Calvin on predestination (the elect and *unelect* [emphasis added]) and then later on usury had a challenging long-range impact. These two areas of his thought were what led to the thesis of Max Weber connecting the seemingly disparate entities of religion and economics. Calvin's thought was not the genesis of the capitalist order but was seen as moving from a condemnation of many of the dictates of the rising new order to accommodation and finally to his giving his blessing to the new order based on the principle of the saved and the unsaved and to the practice of usury. It was from this view that Weber argued that the spirit of capitalism was born out of the Protestant ethic.

John Calvin's idea of predestination, when played out in history, meant that there were those who were set aside as saved and those who were, from their birth, considered unsaved.

> Scripture clearly proves that God, by his eternal and unchanging will, determined once and for all those whom he would one day admit to salvation and those whom he would consign to destruction. His decision about the elect is based on his mercy with no reference to human deserving. Equally, those whom he dooms to destruction are shut off from eternal life by his perfect, but incomprehensible, judgement. With reference to the elect, God's call and justification are proof of election which will be completed in glory. The unbelievers are cut off from the knowledge of his name and the sanctification of his Spirit, a preview of their coming

---

[237] Tawney, *Religion and the Rise of Capitalism*, 91.

judgement. I shall not bother to refute some of the stupid ideas men have raised to overthrow predestination, but deal only with genuine queries.[238]

There had been diverse interpretations given to the idea of predestination. One such view was that the doctrine of predestination, rather than being a "central premise of Calvin's thought, is an ancillary doctrine, concerned with explaining a puzzling aspect of the consequence of the proclamation of the gospel of grace." Nevertheless, "as Calvin's followers [especially Theodore Beza] sought to develop and recast his thinking in the light of new intellectual developments it was perhaps inevitable that alterations to his structuring of Christian theology might occur."[239] Their principal interest was the grounding of the teachings of Calvin in the context of the mentioned major shifts in the structure of ideas as well as in social structures. Thus was born one of the principal tenets of Calvinism, predestination.

The other tenet of Calvinism that had had great impact in the New World was usury. Before when we defined *capitalism*, we used Weber's distinction between the natural human desire to acquire money and property, which he referred to as "an impulse," and the use of money to make money to the detriment of others (usury).[240] During the late Middles Ages, though it was considered the sin of avarice, the practice of usury—as it was called—became more and more prevalent. Medieval economic life—on the basis of the just price whereby the producer received only what was necessary to pay for his labor, allowing only for subsistence—was being supplanted by modern capitalism, the competitive supply-and-demand type of economics so that, by the fifteenth century, usury was so widespread that most words opposing this practice went unheeded. Thus, it can be argued that the rise of the new Protestant spirit was the underpinning of the rise of money, mercantilism, and then capitalism.

---

[238] John Calvin, *The Institutes of Christian Religion*, ed. Toby Lane and Hilary Osbourne (London: Hodder and Stoughton, 1986), book III, chapter 21, par. 7, p. 216. Weber noted that the idea of predestination was not fully developed by Calvin until the third edition of *The Institutes* and "only gained its position of central prominence after his death" (*The Protestant Ethic and the Spirit of Capitalism*, 102).

[239] Alister E. McGrath, *Christian Theology: An Introduction* (Oxford: Blackwell Publishers, 1994), 71, 396–97. Theodore Beza succeeded Calvin as director of the Genevan Academy, which engaged in the training of Calvinist pastors for all Europe.

[240] Accordingly, Weber defines *capitalism* by stating that it is "identical with the pursuit of profit, and forever *renewed* profit, by means of continuous, *rational*, capitalistic enterprise [emphasis by this author]" (*The Protestant Ethic and the Spirit of Capitalism*, 17). It is the emphasis on "rational" in this definition that we can see a connection between capitalism and the modern project.

Usury was forbidden by the medieval church. The way of making money with money by charging interest on loans was condemned by the civil authorities. The basis for the condemnation of usury was a long-standing scriptural prohibition and that money did not labor and so, by its very nature, lacked the ability to produce.

> To take usury is contrary to Scripture; it is contrary to Aristotle; it is contrary to nature, for it is to live without labor; it is to sell time, which belongs to God, for the advantage of wicked men; it is to rob those who use the money lent, and to whom, since they make it profitable, the profits should belong; it is unjust in itself, for the benefit of the loan to the borrower cannot exceed the value of the principal sum lent him; it is in defiance of sound juristic principles, for when a loan of money is made, the property in the thing lent passes to the borrower, and why should the creditor demand payment from a man who is merely using what is now his own?[241]

The condemnation of usury had deep roots in the medieval period, and some of its earliest violators were those merchants who loaned money to the princes, cities, and even to the pope, all with interest. By the late thirteenth century, many ways were developed so that interests could be taken without it being seen as usury. As already stated, the events that led to the final cleavage in the church was their sale of indulgences to pay back a loan to the Fuggers, which had a large amount of interest.

In 1545, there was an exchange of letters between John Calvin and a person by the name of Sachinus, who was a friend of Calvin. The letter of Calvin to Sachinus was the first document ever that justified usury.[242] It seemed

---

[241] Tawney, *Religion and Capitalism*, 44–45.

[242] John Calvin, *Opera*, xa, 245. In a footnote regarding the letters, Harkness stated that Sachinus's letter was dated November 7, 1545. Calvin's letter entitled "De usuris. Jehan Calvin a quelqu'un de ses amys," on the other hand, was undated and thought to be written in 1545 because its title had been considered a response to Sachinus. There was a translation that can be found in John Calvin's *Economic Tracts* (32–36).

While I have had no experience myself, I have learned from the example of others how dangerous it is to give an answer to the question of which you ask for advice. For if we wholly condemn usury, we impose tighter fetters on the conscience than God himself. Yet if we permit it in the least, many under this pretext will take an unbridled liberty which can then be held in bounds by no restriction. If I were writing to you alone, I should have no fear, for I know well

that one of Calvin's fears in this letter was that greater permission would be gathered from his answer to the question about usury than he desired. But then he went on to answer the question, sanctioning usury based ultimately on the now prevalent changes in the economic situation in the world that warranted the acceptance of usury and would thereby solve the consciences of good Christians. Calvin no longer saw scripture as the delimiter of economic behavior. He closed the letter to Sachinus by saying that usury must not be gauged by any particular scripture passages but only by the rules of equity.[243]

---

your prudence and restraint: but since you are asking for another, I fear that he may gather a little more permission from my words than I wish. However, since I have no doubt that you will act with discretion according to the nature of the man and the circumstances, I will tell you how the matter seems to me.

The reasoning of Saint Ambrose and Chrysostom that money does not beget money, is in my judgement too superficial. What does the sea beget? What does the land? I receive income from the rental of a house. Is it because the money grows there? The earth produces things from which money is made, and the use of a house can be bought for money. And is not money more fruitful in trade than in any other form of possession one can mention? Is it lawful to let a farm, requiring a payment in return, and unlawful to receive any profit from the use of money? . . .

How do merchants derive their profit? By their industry, you will say. Certainly if money is shut up in a strong-box, it will be barren—a child can see that. But whoever asks a loan of me does not intend to keep this money idle and gain nothing. The profit is not in the money itself, but in the return that comes from its use. It is necessary then to draw the conclusion that while such subtle distinctions appear on the surface to have some weight, they vanish on closer scrutiny, for they have no substance. *I therefore conclude that usury must be judged, not be any particular passage of Scripture, but simply by the rules of equity.*" (Georgia Harkness, *John Calvin*, 204–6; italics in original)

[243] John Calvin, *Economic Tracts,* series of 1880–1881 (New York: Society for Political Education, 1882), 32–36. Calvin continues in the letter to Sachinus:

In the first place, by no testimony of the Scriptures is usury wholly condemned. For the meaning of the saying of Christ, commonly thought to be very clear, i.e., "Lend, hoping for nothing again" (Luke 6, 35) has been perverted. As elsewhere in speaking of the sumptuous feasts and ambitious social rivalry of the rich he commands rather that they invite in the blind, the lame and the poor from the streets who cannot make a like return, so here, wishing to curb abuses in lending, he directs us to loan chiefly to those from whom there is no hope of receiving anything. . . . The words of Christ mean that he commends serving the poor rather than the rich. Thus we do not find all usury forbidden.

The law of Moses (Deut. 23, 19) was political, and should not influence us beyond what justice and philanthropy will bear. It could be wished that all usury, and even the name, were banished from the earth. But since this is impossible, it is necessary to concede to the common good.

This sanction now placed usury outside the context of traditional Christianity. He equated taking interest to collecting rent on property. Though he cautioned against abuse, Calvin's ethics now accepted usury based on its being economically inevitable and advocated that scripture needed to be reinterpreted allowing for the open acceptance of usury.

What must be reiterated was that Calvin's doctrine was significant not only in that it was original but also in that it placed "the stamp of religious approval on a practice already widely prevalent."[244] With Calvin's doctrine, the capitalists and Christians alike now could exploit the poor with impunity.

> Calvin no more created the commercial enterprise of his day than the Pope created the empire of Charlemagne; but like the Pope [in the Carolingian period] he greatly furthered what was already in the process of development by conferring upon it a divine sanction.[245]

What can be said was that Calvin set in motion by his teaching the belief that all people were the servants of the profit systems or schemes. All must work diligently; the worker and the poor must be content with low salaries as

---

We have passages in the Prophets and Psalms in which the Holy Spirit inveighs against usury. Thus a city is described as wicked because usury is found in its market-place and streets. (ps. 55,11) But as the Hebrew word here means *fraud* in general, the passage can be otherwise interpreted. Even if we grant that the prophet speaks explicitly of usury, it is not surprising that among the great evils of his time he should mention it, for with an improper use of usury, cruelty and many evil deceptions are often joined. . . .

It is said in praise of a holy and God-fearing man that "he putteth not out his money to usury." (ps. 15,5) Indeed, it is a very rare thing for a man to be honest and at the same time a usurer. The prophet Ezekiel (Ezek. 22, 12) goes even further, for in enumerating the crimes which inflamed the wrath of the Lord against the Jews, he uses two Hebrew words, Nesec and Tarbit: one of which means usury and is derived from a root meaning to *consume*, while the second signifies an *increase* or *addition*, doubtless because each man contriving to further his own gain takes or rather extorts it at his neighbor's loss. . . .

Now it is said that today, too, usury should be forbidden on the same grounds as among the Jews, since there is a bond of brotherhood among us. To this I reply, that in the civil state there is some difference; for the situation in which the Lord had placed the Jews; and many other circumstances, made it easy for them to engage in business among themselves without usury. Our relationship is not at all the same. Therefore I do not consider that usury is wholly forbidden among us, except it be repugnant to justice and charity.

[244] Harkness, *Man and His Ideas*, 209.
[245] Harkness, *Man and His Ideas*, 200–1.

the wealthy created new markets and increased their profits. The poor ought to humble themselves in the face of their poverty and be subordinate to the technocrats of the capitalist structure. According to Harkness, it was Calvin's fiat in the usury controversy that first made religion an opiate of the people.[246]

1.3.2.1. THE RISE OF PURITANISM IN ENGLAND

The Reformation affected every country in Europe. As we stated, the reform movement had deep roots in the radical social, political, and economic changes that erupted in Europe from as early as the twelfth century. The intention of this section would be to situate the rise of Puritanism and touch on its impact on religiosity of British America from the colonial period and beyond. In fact, Puritanism can be described as the religious legacy of the United States.

When Henry VIII came to the throne in 1509 (1509–1547), England was existing in a consolidated peace that had come to the country after the Wars of the Roses. The Reformation in England took a unique shape probably because of its starting point, the controversy over the marriage of Henry VIII to Catherine of Aragon. By 1527 Henry VIII the drive that would end up in turmoil between himself and Rome.[247] The Church of England separated from Rome, condemning any relationship with the pope. The Church of England fostered the supremacy of the state over the Roman Catholic Church. Thus began the Protestant Reformation in England, which consisted in the institutionalization of a combination of Catholicism, Lutheranism, and Calvinism.[248]

Puritanism was the more decisive stage in the development of the Reformation in England. According to R. H. Tawney, in his effort to demonstrate the impact of Puritanism on English Reformation, it was "Puritanism, not the Tudor secession from Rome, that was the true English Reformation, and it was from its struggle against the old order that an England which was unmistakably modern emerged."[249] In fact, it was only with the beginning of Puritanism that the Reformation was considered to have come to England. Henry VIII had managed to overthrow more than nine hundred years of "undisputed papal authority" and "the entire edifice of medieval monasticism." "Yet doctrine was for the most part unchanged, popular piety

---

[246] Harkness, *Man and His Ideas*, 213.

[247] Ahlstrom, *Religious History*, vol. 1, 124–26.

[248] George M. Stephenson, *The Puritan Heritage* (Westport, Connecticut: Greenwood Press, 1952), 16.

[249] R. H. Tawney, *Religion and the Rise of Capitalism*, 165.

was relatively undisturbed, and parish life went on much as before."[250] Making use of Reformed theology derived from John Calvin, the Puritans were elect spirits, segregated from the mass of mankind by an experience of conversion, fired by the sense that God was using them to revolutionize human history."[251]

The word *puritan* was an adjective that was first used in the 1560s. "It soon came to mean precise, over-strict, over severe, failing to make allowances. As such it was used to ridicule those who were guilty of absurd severity or rigidity."[252] However, the Puritans were those who sought to "purify" the Church of England. There was a drive to cleanse the church of all Romanism. Olmstead asserted that the Puritans and Anglicans differed because of their distinctive "interpretations of the Scriptures and their role in ecclesiastical government."[253]

In England, there were two basic forms of Puritanism. There were Nonconformist Puritans, who critiqued the Church of England but did not wish to leave it. One of their strongest desires was to establish what they called a Presbyterian structure that meant the rejection of bishops. There also were the Independents or Congregationalists, who though limited saw the church as only for those whom they called the godly. They eventually separated from the Church of England and established small congregations, whereby they administered to one another.[254]

Moreover, Puritanism was considered a Calvinist sect and linked to Calvinism in that it applied the doctrines of John Calvin. R. H. Tawney argued even more strongly in a causal sense that Calvinism "as a way of life and a theory of society, possessed from the beginning one characteristic which was both novel and important. It assumed an economic organization which was relatively advanced, and expounded its social ethics on the basis of it. In this respect the teaching of the Puritan moralists who derive most directly from Calvin is in marked contrast with that both of medieval theologians and of Luther."[255] The Puritans used Calvin's doctrines to substantiate their moral ideas within a scriptural context. Many of the Puritan beliefs were influenced by the theology of John Calvin, which meant that the American Puritans took a Calvinistic outlook on the world. For example, like the Calvinist idea, Puritans held strongly to the doctrine of predestination. Likewise, both Calvin

---

[250]   Ahlstrom, *Religious History*, 126.

[251]   Alan Simpson, *Puritanism in Old and New England* (Chicago: University of Chicago Press, 1955), 39.

[252]   Owen Chadwick, *The Reformation (The Pelican History of the Church)*, vol. 3 (Harmondsworth, England: Penguin Books Ltd., 1964, 1966, repro. with rev., 1968), 175.

[253]   Olmstead, *History of Religion*, 15.

[254]   Stephenson, *The Puritan Heritage*, 17.

[255]   Tawney, *Religion and the Rise of Capitalism*, 91.

and the Puritans held that one could have saving faith without the assurance of salvation.[256]

Thus, Puritanism and Calvinism were not completely indistinguishable. "The Puritan ideal is best understood when seen among the Calvinists."[257] The two were linked in this sense. Puritanism, like Calvinism, can be described as fostering a private study and private interpretation of the Bible, believing "each congregation was a spiritual covenant" with predestination that leveled all classes. The stress on the covenant relationship can be called "federal theology."[258] Because of a growing dissatisfaction with the situation of religion in England and a concentration on the study of scripture, Puritanism might be characterized as a "movement of the Book."[259]

When James I came to power in England, he threatened the Puritans because of their rejection of *The Book of Common Prayer*. They still refused to conform, which resulted in their being outside the Church of England. Stephenson claimed that a contingent of the Puritans even promoted what developed into civil war.

The Puritans embraced the militant nature of Calvinism, making it impossible for it to reconcile with other sects. It was especially impossible for Puritanism to be reconciled with Catholicism. Calvinism had just about completely spread throughout England, thus allowing it to place its permanent mark on all English-speaking people.[260] The Puritans were the parents and the proponents of the principle of religious toleration as it developed in England and then later blossomed as they colonized the United States.[261] Though Puritanism no longer existed as such, its heritage had become a legacy to the Christian world of the United States since colonial times. Puritanism had left a deep mark on the English-speaking world.

1.3.3. THE DOMINICANS, THE JESUITS, AND THE LAW

At this point, the significance of any assertions regarding the thought of sixteenth- and seventeenth-century Dominicans and Jesuits and of the Dutch jurist Hugo Grotius was to highlight the religious problematic associated with the rise of the modern state. As referred to earlier in this study, law and its order were the topic of serious debate by the secular theoreticians of the modern

---

[256] Paul Helm, *Calvin and the Calvinists* (Edinburgh: The Banner of Truth Trust, 1982), 71–81.

[257] Chadwick, *The Reformation*, 176.

[258] Olmstead, *History of Religion*, 15.

[259] Ahlstrom, *Religious History*, 131–40.

[260] Stephenson, *The Puritan Heritage*, 18.

[261] Stephenson, *The Puritan Heritage*, 18.

state: Niccolò Machiavelli, Jean Bodin, and Thomas Hobbes. These secular theorists were in search of a rational method for understanding the real world that was free of ecclesiastical or religious dogmatism. They were engaged in a discourse on the relationship between the will and the intellect regarding law and nature. They sought a balance between political and economic necessity and general responsibility.

Ultimately, political and economic necessity dictated the implementation of the rule of Thrasymachus and Callicles found in the first book of Plato's *Republic* and in *Gorgias*, respectively. It was where one might derive the term *might over right*. These two protagonists basically argued along similar lines. Callicles said, "It is unjust and ugly to seek to get the better of the majority. But my opinion is that nature herself reveals it to be only just and proper that the better man should lord it over his inferior; it will be the stronger over the weaker. Nature, further, makes it quite clear in a great many instances that this is the true state of affairs, not only in the other animals, but also in whole states and communities. This is, in fact, how justice is determined: the stronger shall rule and have the advantage over his inferior . . . To my mind men are acting in accordance with natural justice when they perform such acts, . . . it is in accordance with law, too, the law of nature." Callicles continued to speak of what happened if an inferior, after being versed in the "incantations" that "equality is morality," became strong enough to break through these conventions. He said that such a person "will trample under foot our ordinances and charms and spells, all this mass of unnatural legislation; our slave will stand forth revealed as our master and the light of natural justice will shine forth."[262]

However, the rule of Thrasymachus was best expressed in the *Republic* by Thrasymachus himself. Thrasymachus, in a discourse on "what is justice?" with Socrates and companions, asserted that "the principle of justice is the interest of the stronger. . . . [D]ifferent forms of government make laws, democratical, aristocratic, tyrannical, with a view to their several interests; and these laws, which are made by them for their own interests, are the justice which they deliver to their subjects, and him who transgresses them they punish as a breaker of the law, and unjust. And that is what I mean when I say that in all states there is the same principle of justice, which is the interest of the government; and as the government must be supposed to have power, the only reasonable conclusion is that everywhere there is one principle of justice, which is the interest of the stronger."[263] The rule of Thrasymachus would be

---

[262]   Plato, *Gorgias*, trans. W. C. Helmbold (Indianapolis and New York: The Bobbs-Merrill Company, Inc., 1952), 51–52.

[263]   Plato, *Republic*, book I, trans. B. Jowett, ed. Louise Ropes Loomis (New York: Walter J. Black, 1942), 217–495, 236–37 passim.

summarized as follows: "[N]o one should pursue anything but what is in one's own interest, and since justice embodied in the laws of a state imposes the interests of another—namely, the stronger, who is sovereign—it is silly to obey them unless forced to do so."[264]

This approach to law inevitably favored the political, social, cultural, and economic interests of the absolutist sovereign powers of the modern state and its understanding of itself. However, the ensuing arguments by secular theorists for limiting the powers of the state would finally supplant the absolute powers of the sovereign state (Locke and Jefferson). Limiting the powers of the sovereign state and transferring those powers to the individual gave unlimited authority to those who "functioned outside the law." The contention of this study was that it was precisely this unlimited authority beyond the state that was the concern of the Dominicans and Jesuits. There was a strong effort on the part of certain scholars of these two religious orders to confront the interests of modernity. They thought that it was necessary for them to render moral religious insight and influence.

Hamilton said, "They had become conscious of living in an expanding world. This is what made them more aware of the unity of mankind and more anxious to assert it."[265] How to apply the laws to everyday problems was not an uncommon debate. For example, Hamilton stated, "In Spain the universities were consulted on a wide range of questions—legal, moral, political, and economic: the professors reflected on the questions and often used them as material for lecture courses, practicing the scholastic method with varying degrees of flexibility. Sometime after the end of a session they gave a public lecture or summary of the course (called a reflection). They also lectured on current problems about which they had not been consulted."[266] These thinkers dealt with divine law, natural law, and positive law not just in themselves but also in how these laws applied to the issues of the state, the high seas, church and state relations, the rulers and their subjects, and Christianizing/enslaving natives.

There were several religious social thinkers and a jurist of the sixteenth and seventeenth centuries who argued crucial issues concerning natives and their survival. The first of these thinkers belonged to the Dominican order. He was Bartolomé de Las Casas (1474–1566),[267] and he was called the "Apostle to

---

264   Paul Edwards, ed., *The Encyclopedia of Philosophy*, 1967 ed., s.v. "Sophists" by G. B. Kerferd.

265   Bernice Hamilton, *Political Thought in Sixteenth-Century Spain: A Study of the Political Ideas of Vitoria, de Soto, Suarez, and Molina* (Oxford: At the Clarendon Press, 1963), 98. Later, we shall see that Fr. Andrew White—cofounder of the Maryland colony—studied as well as taught at the colleges in Spain during the time of these thinkers.

266   Hamilton, *Political Thought in Sixteenth-Century Spain*, 6.

267   Lewis Hanke, *The Spanish Struggle for Justice in the Conquest of America*, 6th ed.

the Indians." After his ordination to priesthood in 1502, he became involved in the encomienda system in Cuba. The cruelty of the system was the impetus for his giving up colonizing and emerging as one of its foremost critics. "From 1515 to 1522 both in Spain and in America, he tried to win approval for a series of projects that, without ignoring the just interests of the Crown and of good colonists, would lead to the elimination of the disastrous practices of the encomienda system and military conquest and would foster peaceful colonization and the Christianization of the Indians."[268] After these efforts at radical reform were frustrated, Las Casas was received into the Dominicans, where he continued his argument, although somewhat unsuccessfully, for the suppression of the encomienda system. "He wrote many doctrinal treatises, letters, memorials, and pamphlets, of which the most famous, *Brevisima relacion de la destrucción de las Indias* (1542), is also the most stern indictment of the cruelty of the conquistadors."[269] It exposed the violence, cruelties, and injustices of the conquistadores.

Las Casas returned to Spain in 1547 and embarked on another one of his major contributions in 1550. He became engaged in the famous controversy and debate involving Juan Ginés de Sepúlveda on the question of wars of conquest in the Indies and slavery. The Crown suspended all military expeditions during this debate. Las Casas heralded the position of the Spanish Crown, which saw that there "was no advantage in slavery." Desirous of establishing colonies where natives and colonists would live peacefully together, the Crown found itself in conflict with the conquistadores.[270] "The Dominican [Las Casas] vigorously and lengthily defended the natural freedom and equality of the Indians and their capacity for self-government and Christianization. The outcome of the disputation is not clear, but it does stand as a high point in the struggle to secure justice for the oppressed native population."[271]

Francisco de Vitoria (1486–1546)[272], also a Dominican, taught at the University at Paris from 1523 until he came back to Valladolid in Spain in 1526.

(Boston: American Historical Association, 1949); *New Catholic Encyclopedia*, 1967 ed., s.v. "Las Casas, Bartolome de," by Andre Saint-Lu; *New Catholic Encyclopedia*, 1967 ed., s.v. "Latin America, Church and the Indian in," by Stafford Poole.

[268] *New Catholic Encyclopedia*, 1967 ed., s.v. "Las Casas, Bartolome de," by Andre Saint-Lu.

[269] *New Catholic Encyclopedia*, 1967 ed., s.v. "Las Casas, Bartolome de," by Andre Saint-Lu.

[270] *New Catholic Encyclopedia*, 1967 ed., "Slavery (History of)" by Charles Verlinden.

[271] Juan Ginés de Sepúlveda was a theologian in Spain who "applied to the Indians Aristotle's concept of natural slavery of inferior men and had upheld the justice of Spanish conquest" (*New Catholic Encyclopedia*, "Latin America, Church and the Indian in," by Stafford Poole).

[272] Hamilton, *Political Thought in Sixteenth-Century Spain*, 171–76.

He soon was appointed to a significant chair at the University of Salamanca (1526). The school of theology at Salamanca were endowed with humanism literature that incorporated into the scholastic framework. Vitoria, in his own theology, sought to "turn speculative moral matters to a practical everyday use, and this led to his being frequently consulted on topics of the day." For example, he had writings on the limiting of warfare, marriage of Henry VIII, and the Franco/Spanish conflict. He even chided priests and their neglect of the poor.[273]

Vitoria discussed in his lectures the colonization of the New World, which was alarming to those who had vested interest in these ventures. He taught that the natives were not foreigners but "vassals of the Emperor." He delivered the opinion on the rights of the king over the Indies and presented methods to be used in converting the Indians. Because several of his students taught at other universities in Spain, Vitoria had great influence regarding these matters in Salamanca. One of his influences was in the condemnation of Sepulveda's book on the Indies.[274] Victoria's lectures were also influential on the text entitled "New Laws of the Indies" (1542).

There was no reason why anyone should be forced to convert into the Christian faith. Vitoria dealt with this question in reference to the Moors. The issue was whether the threat of expulsion should be tendered to force conversion. Using Aquinas's ideas about reprisals for failure to convert, the key issue was that not only the failure to convert but also even blasphemy that was private was not ground for forced expulsion.[275]

The baptism of children without their parents' consent was another issue of importance, especially with regard to whether the parents were practicing in the church. Over and above the infringement of parental rights, it would expose the children to apostasy, but Vitoria did not agree that the validity of the sacrament was contingent on parental consent. This gave the option to baptize the child should there be other circumstances, such as if the spiritual care of the child were endangered, then parental consent might be preempted.[276]

---

[273]   Hamilton, *Political Thought in Sixteenth-Century Spain*, 174.

[274]   Juan Ginés de Sepúlveda was a sixteenth-century scholar who conducted a debate regarding the enslavement of natives in what was called the Indies (Central and South America). For Sepúlveda, the natural law contended that it was within the human person to distinguish between good and evil. There were two aspects to the natural law. It was common to all human beings and animals and bound them except when it came to self-defense and procreation. Natural law was rational and civilized nation, of which Spain was the most excellent (Hamilton, *Political Thought in Sixteenth-Century Spain*, 24).

[275]   Vitoria, *Commentaries*, vol. i, quo. x, art. 8, par. 5, 13.

[276]   Vitoria, *Commentaries*, art. xii, par. 1.

On the colonization of the New World, Vitoria was the principal thinker along with his student and then colleague and interpreter Domingo de Soto. Molina also often commented on Vitoria, while Suarez, who came later, also made use of Vitoria.[277]

Domingo de Soto (1495–1560),[278] a Dominican who was born in Segovia, studied in Paris and was considered one of the first converts of Vitoria to Thomism. After his profession as a Dominican in 1524, he was sent to Salamanca, where from 1525 he taught at the Dominican College San Esteban until 1532, when he substituted at the University of Salamanca for Vitoria, who had become ill. Again, de Soto replaced Vitoria at the Council of Trent in 1545, where he promoted dealing simultaneously with reform and dogma against those Romans who sought to postpone work on reform.

De Soto was preoccupied with the New World issues and had himself offered to go to America to deal with certain matters of grave concern. Instead, when he was not able to go, he was involved in sending missionaries whom he himself selected. In 1534, he wrote his ideas on the American missionary venture in an unpublished work called "De dominio." In this work, he argued regarding the difficulty of justifying the conquest of the native in the Indies. He served in an official capacity at the juntas of Valladolid during August/September 1550 and April/May 1551. His task was to summarize the arguments of Sepúlveda and Las Casas on the Indians. Because of the influence of de Soto, the juntas ultimately declared that conquest of the natives was unjust.[279]

Luis de Molina (1535–1600),[280] a Jesuit, wrote about the protection of missionaries, saying that they must not force the natives to accept the gospel message but that envoys of the Crown must see to it that the natives did not create an obstacle against the missionaries. Likewise, natives' refusal to accept the faith was no cause for retaliation by war. No one can be forced into the faith. He also strongly disagreed that "the unconverted could be coerced to follow the beliefs of the majority of the community."[281]

Francisco Suárez (1548–1617),[282] also of the Jesuits, in commenting on Vitoria in his work entitled *On Faith, Hope, and Charity*, agreed that the church not only had the right but also the duty to preach to natives and to defend those who preach and to punish those who, by force and violence, try to

---

[277] Hamilton, *Political Thought in Sixteenth-Century Spain*, 110.

[278] Hamilton, *Political Thought in Sixteenth-Century Spain*, 176–80.

[279] Hamilton, *Political Thought in Sixteenth-Century Spain*, 179.

[280] Hamilton, *Political Thought in Sixteenth-Century Spain*, 180–4.

[281] Hamilton, *Political Thought in Sixteenth-Century Spain*, 112–13; Francisco de Vitoria, *Comentarios inéditos a la II-II de Santo Tomac*, vol. i, quo. x, art. 7, "on whether infidels can be compelled to accept the faith."

[282] Hamilton, *Political Thought in Sixteenth-Century Spain*, 184–88.

prevent the missionaries from preaching.[283] Neither were the leaders of the settlement to war on the natives to occupy their territory or to exact payment for expenses incurred in the missionary venture. To do so would be coercion of religion and a violation of the law of nations and the natural law. Accordingly, the seizure of property of others against their will and waging an unjust war would make it difficult for the natives to accept the faith.[284]

In summary, these thinkers confronted the interest of modernity that sought to limit the powers of the state while transferring those powers to the individual. Such power given to the individual also meant unlimited authority to those who functioned outside the law (especially the merchant class). They were forced to render moral religious insight and influence in a context of radical change. They dealt with the three main stages of law as they applied to issues of the state, the high seas, the church and state relations, the Christianization of natives, and ultimately the question of slavery. All the issues were focused on the obligation of the missionary to preach, teach, and baptize as well as the obligation of the authorities to protect that responsibility and even the missionaries against harm from either settlers or natives. These efforts also took up the question of the rights of Spaniards over the New World. Now let us look at Hugo Grotius, who was not a missionary, a Spaniard, or a Jesuit or Dominican.

Huigh de Groot (Hugo Grotius) (1583–1645) was a Dutch jurist of a distinguished Calvinist family, was born at Delft, lived in Holland, and was commissioned by the Dutch East India Company to defend their "trade rights and their free access to the seas."[285] To achieve his task, he began by pursuing a discourse on the "sources and validity" of the concept of natural law–"inherent in human reason and immutable even against the willfulness of sovereign states are imperative considerations of natural justice and moral responsibility, which must serve as a check against the arbitrary exercise of vast political power."[286]

He started a discussion about the intrinsic "ground of obligation" of the natural law that was derived from the principles of reason. In postulating the ground of obligation, Grotius separated the natural law from the divine order

283   Francisco Suárez, *On Faith, Hope, and Charity* (Leon and Coimbra, 1621), xviii, sec. 1; Hamilton, *Political Thought in Sixteenth-Century Spain*, 110.

284   Hamilton, *Political Thought in Sixteenth-Century Spain*, 111.

285   *New Encyclopedia Britannica*, 1975 ed., s.v. "Philosophy, History of Western," by Albert W, Levi. The principal works of Hugo Grotius were *Mare liberum* (*The Freedom of the Seas*) (1609) and *De jure belli ac pacis* (*On the Law of War and Peace*) (1625). These works were the first codification of international law. Hugo Grotius, *The Rights of War and Peace,* trans. A. C. Campbell (Washington and London: M. Walter Dunne, 1901).

286   *New Encyclopedia Britannica*, 1975 ed., s.v. "Philosophy, History of Western."

and grounded it in the pursuit of a peaceful societal existence in accordance with the norms of human understanding as found in the human intellect. Grotius went so far as to posit the thesis that the natural law was intrinsically binding, even if God did not exist (*etsiamsi daretur non esse Deum*).[287] The natural law was so immutable that even God cannot change the "autonomous logical coherence" that existed. Grotius said, "Though God's omnipotence is infinite, he cannot alter some states of affairs that present themselves in the world. Just as God cannot make that two and two would not be four, he cannot determine that which is intrinsically wrong would cease to be wrong (or that which is intrinsically good would cease to be good)."[288]

Thus, for Grotius, there is no need to have "specific recourse" to God; there is no need to submit to God as the ultimate lawgiver. Recourse to God is superfluous. The human person is autonomous–infringement of as well as abiding by the law is based on conscious insight into the binding obligation that simply inhabits the natural law. It manifests itself immediately and autonomously, in its own right. The basic difference between Grotius and his predecessors is that, in his discourse, his emphasis is on the unique importance of the natural rights of the individual instead of on the natural law itself.

The discourse on natural law and the rights of the individual versus the rights of the sovereign was to answer questions that arose out of the desire to spread the gospel after the opening up of the Atlantic world and the colonization ventures into the New World. As we had seen, the starting point for each of them was the natural law. Further consideration of these thinkers was warranted in light of the specifics of their thoughts on the role of the Crown in colonization, the activities of missionaries, natives, slavery, and most especially the rights and obligations of the Crown in the New World or rights of the merchants on the high seas.

1.3.3.1. RELIGIOUS IDEAS NEUTRALIZED BY SECULAR THEORIES OF THE STATE

Out of the new secular theories, there developed a new understanding of God, the human person, and a society divorced from traditional Christian principles. Deism became the popular way of religious expression during the Enlightenment. This belief structure appealed to the human person's conscience and humanitarian feelings, its overconfidence in progress, the neglect of the person's metaphysical urges, and their materialism. Because the Enlightenment thinkers rarely completely rejected God and religion, Deism was a kind of middle point. The Deist rejected traditional revelation and, with

---

287   Grotius, *The Rights of War and Peace*, I, c. 1, X, 21–22.
288   Grotius, *The Rights of War and Peace*, I, c. 1, X, 21–22.

it, the dogma of the existing Christian churches. While accepting a God as a first cause and as a source of the good, the Deist built a view of the universe on the basis of rationalistic thought and mathematical laws.

With a deistic view of God and religion, the authority of scripture and traditional Christian values in the minds of people was permanently shaken, resulting in comfortable compromise. Religious ideas were neutralized by secular theories of the state. This made superfluous all that was contained in the traditional expression "Christian experience" because it tended to remove God from the needy human situation. With the deistic view, God was no longer active in the world of humans. With God removed from the situation, the secular rationalist's theories of Machiavelli, Jean Bodin, Thomas Hobbes, John Locke, Immanuel Kant, G. W. F. Hegel, Montesquieu, Adam Smith, and Thomas Jefferson (all covered above) substantiated the secular interpretation of the world.[289]

Just as a different view of God took hold, a new view of the human person evolved. The Enlightenment's emphasis on reason and the mind as well as the "this worldly," as opposed to the spiritual. The person's relationship to another and to property characterized this development of the person. In fact, the human person became redefined in terms of mind and was reducible to matter in motion.[290] Descartes also made his contribution by establishing a dualism of spirit and matter, which made all animals, including the human person, into purely mechanical structures.[291]

That which focused the person on self was the emphasis, and the human nature was good or at least capable of becoming good in and of itself. By nature, there was a natural benevolence and a natural sympathy for others. Natural reason was what ruled and led the person to the summit. This new anthropology concentrated the human person on self and ruled out a focus on the cosmos or God for meaning. The human person became the measure of and the ultimate definition of all reality. This focus even began to insist that human beings operated only out of self-interest and if free to do so would create an ideally good society based on the natural harmony of selfish interests.[292] Thus, the Enlightenment anthropology provided a redefinition of the human person, which was to profoundly influence the development of the new era.

---

[289] J. Edwin Orr, *The Light of the Nations* (Grand Rapids, MI: n.p., 1965), 14–15. A thinker not covered above was Thomas Paine, whose writings were immensely popular, and masses of restless people took hold of his ideas concerning the abandoning of Orthodox Christianity.

[290] La Mettrie, *L'homme-machine*, 1727.

[291] *New Encyclopedia Britannica*, 1975 ed., s.v. "The Enlightenment."

[292] Frank E. Manuel, ed., *The Enlightenment* (New Jersey: Prentice Hall, Inc., 1965), 5.

So the principal effect of the Enlightenment, although it was diverse in emphasis and interest, was its attack on established ways of life. The Enlightenment's conviction was that right reason could discover useful knowledge and aspire to the conquest of man's happiness through freedom. It may be said that the Enlightenment thinkers, by using these ideas, not only toppled the feudal, ecclesiastical establishment and the predominant Christian worldview but also, by freeing sciences and history from theology and metaphysics, fostered the basis for the materialistic secular modern culture.

This modern worldview, with its new understanding of God and its new anthropology, resulted in many developments, including the birth of the United States, triumph of capitalism, formulation of progress through education and judicial reforms, and rise of the ideas of national sovereignty and inviolable human rights and of liberal and democratic doctrines.[293] These new developments began a new type of society, the bourgeois social order:

> Appealing to values and principles which are universal in scope such as rule by law, the equality of all before the law, basic human rights, freedom of thought and express—in a word, life, liberty and the pursuit of happiness—they did so quite naturally in terms of the specific interests of the most progressive social class of the time and the one from which most of them sprang. In assigning to the middle class the task of realizing the "good life on earth," they tended to equate it with the good life of this class.[294]

Not only this but Thomas Paine and John Locke, as well as Thomas Jefferson, also became the preeminent philosophers who popularized this new modern society. They were the ones who, at least theoretically, parented the United States. They were described as translating the ideas of human rights based on the Enlightenment anthropology and the need to destroy outdated institutions into words that stirred hearts and minds. Therefore, the rise of the United States of America became the realization and fulfillment of the principles of the Enlightenment.

> The Old World imagined, invented, and formulated the Enlightenment, the New World—certainly the Anglo-American part of it realized it and fulfilled it. . . . It was Americans who not only embraced the body of Enlightenment

---

[293] Robert Anchor, *The Enlightenment Tradition* (Berkeley: University of California Press, 1967), 3–4.

[294] Anchor, *The Enlightenment Tradition*, 8.

principles, but wrote them into law, crystallized them into institutions, and put them to work.[295]

The Enlightenment philosophes, as they were called, and their thinking migrated to the newly created society–the colonies–and flourished. There were no Christian traditions, institutions, or structures that needed to be overthrown. There were no barriers to overcome. The Enlightenment philosophes were elected to the highest offices of the land. The Enlightenment not only survived in the United States but also triumphed, even though it preached liberty and practiced slavery.

In the United States, the Enlightenment principles of life, liberty, and the pursuit of happiness and the Enlightenment anthropology were not based on God. Rather, they were based on a scientific and reasoned approach to nature and progress. Progress established a society where the criterion for the human person's worth was ownership of property or the potential for such. That potential was often measured by ethnic origin, race, class, and sex. These were infallible criteria by which membership in the elect was determined.[296]

> [The elect] were a chosen company picked out of, perhaps, all the counties in England, and this by no human contrivance, but by a strange work of God upon the spirits of men that were, no ways, acquainted with one another– inspiring them as one person to secede into a wilderness they knew not where.[297]

---

[295] Henry Steele Commager, *The Empire of Reason: How Europe Imagined and America Realized the Enlightenment* (Garden City, NY: Anchor Press/Doubleday, 1977), ix. It seems that, from its earliest beginnings, modernity was more a matter for reflection among European thinkers rather than a reality. Henry Steele Commager cites Van der Kemp, a Dutch Enlightenment figure: "In America the sun has risen brightly, a promise to all of us if we will but see it. . . . America can lift us up. . . . It is the land of justice, we are a land of sin" (*The Empire of Reason*, 14).

Peter Gay goes even further and describes the Enlightenment as "a kind of paganism" that originally is "dependent upon the *paganism* of classical antiquity." Gay also says that the Enlightenment ultimately has even sought to be "emancipated from classical thought as much as from Christian dogma" (Peter Gay, *The Enlightenment: An Interpretation; the Rise of Modern Paganism* [New York and London: W. W. Norton & Company, 1977], xi).

[296] Thus, John Calvin's religious theory of the elect and unelect (saved and unsaved) resulted in the settlers' propagation of a social theory based on status rather than one based on one's graced relationship with God. The elect had come to the colonies in direct response to the command of God.

[297] Thomas Jefferson Wertenbaker, *The Puritan Oligarchy* (New York: Grosset & Dunlap, 1947), 74.

This perfected the social implications of the Calvinist principles setting up the Puritan aristocracy who embodied the principle of the elect. The values of this aristocracy were power, profit, privilege, prestige, and pleasure for the elect, buttressed by money, mercantilism, manufacturing, trading, and land speculation. These values fostered by the Enlightenment concepts of the human person shaped the rise of the profitable new economics, the slave industrial complex, in which colonialism and chattel slavery contributed to the success of the United States.

> The institution of slavery had fastened itself on American life, not only by reason of the activities of British slavers–at first directed toward the carrying of Africans to the Spanish possessions–but primarily because it offered to colonials an easy and profitable means of rolling back the North American wilderness and thereby laying out the exploiting plantations, and staffing the households of the wealthy with permanent servants. So between the years 1763 and 1775 fiery advocates of liberty–planters, merchants, lawyers, even ministers of the Gospel–saw apparently no moral inconsistency in openly offering rewards in newspapers for the return into captivity of some runaway black, while at the same time denouncing as "slavery" restrictions that the mother country had seen fit to place upon their freedom of action.[298]

The destiny of the "Enlightened" colonists freed from Europe became the burden of the slave on whose backs America was built.[299]

There are underlying questions that surface that involve a brief reflection on the basis for and the validity of the concept of the right to private property and the freedom that that implies and individualism. Both lead to "life, liberty, and the pursuit of happiness" for *all* people as ensured by the Constitution of the United States. In other words, how can a nation that has instituted and profited from slavery and the slave trade simultaneously profess freedom and justice *for all*? And how can anyone with a slave heritage in that nation conscientiously

---

[298]   Lawrence Henry Gipson, *The Coming of the Revolution: 1763–1775* (New York: Harper & Row, 1954), 5

[299]   As we shall see later, the resulting master/slave society saw Native Americans detribalized and their lands confiscated. Irish and other Catholics were kidnapped and brought to the colonies as servants, and later, they became enslaved. And Africans were captured and turned into slaves. Thus began what we shall call the dehumanization process that created the Negro with the permanent stigma or scar of slavery.

look to find "true" liberation through the use of the same Constitution, same economic principles, and same anthropological redefinitions that have been proffered to enslave them initially?

The right to private property is at the root of Locke's political theory, the basis for his ideas about equality. In his theory, it seems that one's personal worth and self-esteem—that which makes one a person—is related to ownership of private property or the potential for such protected by government.[300] Macpherson is convincing when he "tries to prove that Locke's civil society is totally subject to economic control. Therefore the issue of protecting individual rights belongs to the government.[301] Macpherson says that Locke's theory has culminated in justifying, even by law, the inviolability of modern property rights.[302] What this means is that if the right to private property is what constitutes freedom for all, then the contradiction lies in how the slave—who is property and perpetually so—could ever achieve full humanity.

The issue of individualism in the American culture states that each person is responsible for their own well-being. If one is willing to work, then one could make a living and prosper. You only have to save and show initiative, and by your own effort, you can get ahead. Dr. Louis Hartz, professor of government at Harvard University, while lecturing at a hearing in the Foreign Relations Committee of the United States Senate on the nature of revolution on February 26, 1968, admits that individualism is a theological concept. He adds that it comes out of the Protestant Revolution, the Reformation.

> I think individualism is a theological value in all Christian thought, and I think in the whole Judaic-Christian tradition individualism is important. Individualism is not important in other theological systems . . . there is no doubt that Western individualism and our whole faith in the individual in the

---

[300] C. B. Macpherson, *The Political Theory of Possessive Individualism* (Oxford: Oxford University Press, 1962), 97.

[301] To support *his* statement, Macpherson—in a note—cites Schlatter's *Private Property: The History of an Idea* (1951).

[302] Macpherson, 142. Also, according to Anthony Giddens, capital and private property are synonymous. Giddens says that even though Marx has "never analyzed [property] in detail," he (Giddens) has. Giddens says that "the chief form of private property in the means of production in class-divided societies is *land,* even if the formation of money capital through commerce and agriculture may be a far from negligible phenomenon. In capitalism the main forms of private property are factories, offices, machinery, etc., however much land (itself capitalised) might remain a necessary productive resource . . . 'Property', also implies normative rights of control of material resources" (*A Contemporary Critique of Historical Materialism*, 113–14).

West is grounded in our earlier religious experience. When you move into theological traditions outside that experience I think it becomes much harder to locate a historic sense for individuality.[303]

There is a conflict that arises in people when the paths to achieving certain goals set by the dominant values are closed. The enslaved, victims of racist oppression, for example, face a clash with these values. Is there not an inherent contradiction in the theology of individualism that reinforces and guarantees the economics and politics of "freedom and progress" in the States, a freedom and progress for the elect?

CONCLUSION

The creation of the modern nation-state with its profits and slavery and its development of new religious ideas stands as the legacy of the New World and its progeny down to the present. Likewise, the political, economic, and religious expressions of modernity resulted in a clash of cultures that has left permanent scars on the consciences of all its offspring. Beginning with its background in Europe, the genesis of the New World calls for a new interpretation, one that goes beyond the well-known approaches to understanding the past.

The purpose of this chapter has been to acquaint the reader with the new interpretation of what has transpired in the establishment of the Atlantic world during the last five hundred years. We have tried to uncover the *meaning* of the contradiction that has existed between traditional religion and the economics and politics of modernity. To achieve our objective, we have engaged in an analysis of the factors in the rise of the modern state, the capitalist political economy with slavery as its foundation in the Atlantic world, and the development of new religious ideas that have been adjustments to the traditional Christian view of the world.

Modernity has spawned a radical shift from an experience of the sovereignty of God that has characterized the medieval traditional state to the rise of the omnicompetence of reason, abstract rationality, individual autonomy, and the sovereignty of reason-based science and technology, bureaucratic rationality, belief in steady progress, and maximization of profits. The modern nation-state is the political expression of modernity.

Likewise, it is an apparatus of authority with coercive power (violence), which it uses to organize and rule its people. Such a state is characterized by

---

[303] Louis Hartz, "The Nature of Revolution" in *The Congressional Record* (Washington DC, February 26, 1968), 132.

a centralized bureaucracy and taxation system, a regular standing army, and a unified sovereignty over a specifically demarcated territory.

The rise of the modern nation-state constituted a radical break with the traditional state. It represented the complete breakdown of the feudal manorial societies, transferring the basis of survival from subsistence to the urban notions of production for profit, from the sovereignty of the lords to the sovereignty of the individual, ensconced in the absolute power of the state protecting the interests of the merchant class.

The theoreticians of the modern nation-state were philosophers who grounded the idea of this later type of sovereignty in terms of the law, ultimately completely changing the meaning of the law itself. The law, instead of protecting the good of the whole to the detriment of some of the parts, upheld the interests of the individual oftentimes to the detriment of the common good. This was demonstrated best in the second major section of this study, where we provided a new interpretation of the role of the capitalist political economy with slavery as its foundation in the Atlantic world.

As a reasoned, planned, or ordered way of viewing or understanding the world, the consolidation of the modern nation-state when viewed from the context of modernity becomes an analysis of power and dominance. The roots of dominance lie in authoritative as well as the allocative resources of the modern nation-state. A nonevolutionary approach looks beyond a purely economic interpretation of expansion into the New World, allowing us to account for the injustices that persist into the present. Such an approach takes us beyond an economic summarization of the last five hundred years into the massive dehumanization processes associated with the rise of modernity, including slavery, slave trading, segregation, denigration, and colonization, as well as the manipulation of reason-based science and technology, leading to the violation of the ecosystems of the environment up to what can be called the general undermining of the human spirit (technological eugenics).

Profits and slavery were vital in the rise of the modern nation-state, but the modern state as the product of modernity cannot be defined simply as the rise of money and profits and the use of slaves. The modern world, however, was shaped by the "intersection of capitalism, industrialism and the nation-state system." The radical shifts from an agrarian feudal economy to the capitalist political economy in the modern nation-state involved both profits and slavery. With the rise of the merchant bankers who sought profits came the dismantling of the old order. Belief in steady progress and the maximization of profits were the goals of those who helped shape the capitalist economy.

Slavery was not the same at every period of its history. Ancient and classical as well as medieval slavery made use of the slave but from the perspective of the household. The societies that permitted slavery had laws to govern the slave and slave owners. The slave was human in these societies; they could marry, have a family, and even eventually in some cases become freed.

Slavery of the modern state was distinctly different in that the slave was a tool of the capitalist merchant class and existed for the sole purpose of maximization of profits as the objective. Modern slave labor was used for the growing and the mining of resources for the rising industry from as early as the late fifteenth century and early sixteenth century. But slavery served a purpose that was broader than the role it played in the business of those who migrated to the New World. The slave ultimately meant total dominance of the enslaved by the enslaver. The slave was mere property and thus constitutive of the definition of freedom.

The third major section of this chapter considers the development of the new religious ideas that have been an adjustment to the traditional Christian view of the world. A consideration of religion in the context of modernity is complex. Modernity includes religion only as religion seeks to establish itself in conjunction with the dictates of scientific rationality. What this means is that religion is an evaluation of the ultimate concerns that exist in a society and their interrelationship with the values that evolve in it. Thus, religion must engage in an adjustment of itself if it is to fit into the structured, planned system called modernity. Thus, we spend time explicating the adjustments made by religion in the face of the omnicompetence of reason. Medieval religion has been land based, while modern religion is reason based. The impact of the reason-based reality of modern religion forced vast changes in its structures, particularly liberation from traditional religious values.

With the Protestant "revolution," as it might aptly be called, immediately obvious was the pursuit of heterodoxy by the merchant class and their hegemony. The most fundamental of traditional religious values had been that all human beings had souls and that salvation and survival was open to all. One of the earliest shifts away from traditional values was the redefinition of the human person (the slave as *only* an object for the maximization of profits) and the establishment of the Calvinist principle of the "saved and the unsaved."

Therefore, the adjustment of traditional values ultimately led to the establishment of new religious values that gave benediction to the individual autonomy and to long-standing ethics centered on the buying and selling of goods (slaves included) for profit as well as the relaxation of laws concerning usury.

There was no homogeneity regarding the adjusted religious reality. Several religious thinkers of the Dominican and Jesuit orders confronted the changing religious ethics, the interest of modernity, and its drive to limit the powers of the state while giving unlimited powers to the conquerors and merchant-traders who functioned outside the law. These thinkers took up the cause of the treatment of the natives and slaves and the rights of Spaniards over the New World. Their opposition was so strong that both orders experienced attacks, especially the Jesuits, who were suppressed.

In the meantime, the religious ideas became neutralized by secular theories as they took shape in the modern nation-state. These theories promoted a new understanding of God that was influenced by the Enlightenment's emphasis on the omnicompetence of reason. Thus arose a deistic view of God. Deism resulted in the shift from traditional religion, which espoused the sovereignty of God and the sacredness of humanity, to a comfortable compromise that allowed for the dehumanization process to gain footing with its emphasis on the buying and selling of human beings with impunity.

We shall now move on to the methodological part of this work, which shall not only give the theoretical ground for how we have presented this background chapter but will also substantiate the purpose of this entire study; namely, a view from the underside of the history of the United States.

CHAPTER TWO

Hermeneutics and Society:
The Political Theory of Paul Ricoeur

INTRODUCTION

THE PURPOSE OF pursuing a political theory is to provide a methodological basis and conceptual framework for a new interpretation of religion in the rise of the modern state and its legacy in the New World. As already suggested, our approach is from what we have described as the "underside of history." What we have done so far is to outline the history of the clash of cultures (religious) that has existed during the rise of the modern state in Europe (chapter 1). One of the pivotal aspects of this approach is contained in our disclosure of the "clash of cultures" that takes place with the rise of the merchant-traders and the "new theologians" who have neutralized traditional religious ideas with their secular theories of the state.

In this chapter, the focus is on the political theory of Paul Ricoeur, in itself, as a conceptual framework for understanding the cultural clash that has characterized the New World. We contend that this methodology is a foundation for any further insight into the impact of modernity in its political and economic expressions.

The notion of "political" or "politics" is essentially the process of acquiring and exercising power in human affairs as noted by Peter Berger and Richard J. Neuhaus. With this definition, "there can be no society, or no human group of even moderate size and continuity" that is not engaged in this power process.[304] Further nuancing of the meaning of *political* or *politics* is necessary to ward off the perception that one who takes a political stance is merely being *polemical*. The concepts of polemical and political can be defined as follows. *Polemical* is derived from the Greek words *polemikos*, which means to be warlike or hostile; *polemos*, which also means war; and *pallein*, which means to brandish, like a weapon. Whereas the concept "political" is the direct opposite of "polemical." *Political* is derived from the Greek *polis*, which refers to "city," "society," or even "civilization." "Society" and civilization" are broader in perspective than "city." These ideas traditionally refer to the idea of culture and point to religion within the context of culture.

A society in general is composed of institutions and structures around which its peoples gather. The people have the power to govern, organize, and control these institutions and structures. They are together for defending common beliefs and interests. Politics also refers to the network of relations among people in a society or civilization.[305]

Consequently, politics pertains not only to a geographical location and its inhabitants but also to reflections on the institutional and structural level and to the ideas that influence them. A study of these ideas and the history that undergird a society is philosophical in nature and culminates in a political theory.[306] By establishing the ideas of Paul Ricoeur into a political theory, we guard against this study being considered merely polemics.

The notion of a political theory might seem alien to the philosophical project of Paul Ricoeur.[307] However, from his completion of *La symbolique*

---

[304] Peter L. Berger and Richard J. Neuhaus, *Movement and Revolution: On American Radicalism* (Garden City, NY: Anchor Books, Doubleday & Company, Inc., 1970), 13.

[305] *Webster's Ninth New Collegiate Dictionary*, 1989 ed., s.v. "political," "politics," "polemical," "society," and "civilization"; Michael Curtis, ed., *The Great Political Theories, Vol. I: From Plato and Aristotle to Locke and Montesquieu* (New York: Avon Book Division, The Hearst Corporation, 1961), 13–21; *The Encyclopedia of Philosophy*, 1967 ed., s.v. "Political Philosophy, History of," by Peter Laslett and Philip W. Cummings, "Political Philosophy, Nature of," by Stanley L. Benn, 370–92; Mircea Eliade, ed., *The Encyclopedia of Religion*, 1987 ed., s.v. "Politics and Religion" by Max L. Stackhouse; Runes, *The Dictionary of Philosophy*, 241–42; Alan Robert Lacey, *A Dictionary of Philosophy* (London: Routledge & Kegan Paul, 1976), 163–64.

[306] Curtis, *Great Political Theories*, 13; Laslett and Cummings, "Political Philosophy, History of" in the *Encyclopedia of Philosophy*, 370.

[307] Paul Ricoeur, *Fallible Man*, trans. Charles Kelbley (Chicago: University of Chicago

du mal (1960), what Ricoeur refers to as the *poetics of will* has dominated his philosophical project. Apparently, Ricoeur has envisioned this idea of *poetics of will* theme to be a projected third part of his *Philosophie de la volonté*. Central to the process of deriving a poetics of will is Ricoeur's theory of imagination. In the poetics of will, the imagination is in the pursuit of meaning beyond discourse. Such a pursuit constitutes a shift from the theoretical sphere to the practical sphere. The pathway to such a poetics for Ricoeur has been through his various excursus on the human person in the sociopolitical context.

After the student revolts of 1968, however, Ricoeur has exhibited a keen interest in the conditions of the human person in the social arena.[308] It is in the context of his "excursus" on the human person that Ricoeur derives a hermeneutics of historical consciousness, which is the basis of his political theory.

The breadth of Paul Ricoeur's philosophical system rests in his willingness to expose his thinking to unprecedented challenges, particularly in the arena of the human sciences debate. In fact, it is the incorporation of these challenges into his philosophical project that suggests a Ricoeurian political theory. Ricoeur makes the following observation: "I am more and more coming to see that the emergence of a single, world-wide civilization, with the problems that this poses, constitutes one of the most important concerns for reasoned reflection. To recapture the full range of the meaning of our humanity and to open up the maximum number of possibilities for every person, is a challenge for thinkers in every human discipline."[309] Ricoeur adds that the "divergences

---

Press, 1965); Paul Ricoeur, *The Symbolism of Evil*, trans. Emerson Buchanan (New York: Harper & Row, 1967). Cf. Loretta Dornisch, "Paul Ricoeur and Biblical Interpretation: A Selected Bibliography," *Semeia* 4 (Fall 1975): 23.

[308] Paul Ricoeur, *Political and Social Essays*, ed. David Stewart and Joseph Bien (Athens: Ohio University Press, 1974), 3, 68–87. *Political and Social Essays* is one of the excursus of Ricoeur. It is a collection of articles that confront the political and social problems of modern society.

[309] Ricoeur, *Political and Social Essays*, ix. In *Political and Social Essays*, Ricoeur expressed similar concerns to the ones rendered by these other thinkers and disclosed the implications that these changes would have for the twenty-first century and the rise of the postcapitalist society.

One of the most significant of these types of discourses took place in 1968 when the United States Congress and Senate Committee on Foreign Relations conducted hearings entitled "The Nature of Revolution: The Significance of Revolutions Abroad for American Foreign Policy," 90th Cong., 2nd sess., February 19, 1968–March 7, 1968.

The following scholars were participants in the hearings: Dr. Crane Brinton of History Department, Harvard University; Dr. Richard Solomon of Political Science Department, University of Michigan; Dr. James C. Thomson Jr., History Department, Harvard University; Dr. Louis Hartz, Government Department,

of our economic and political systems should not be seen as a threat but as a locus for an expanding and continuing dialogue on basic human issues."[310] Of significance is that there are various other thinkers during that period of political upheaval in the late sixties and early seventies who have noted the changes that have taken place on the economic and political level.

In *Political and Social Essays*, Ricoeur discusses the meaning of man and culminates in a discourse on what it means for a person to be human. He says, "[One cannot] extract the essential points of a 'politics of culture'" without focusing on what it means to be a human person.[311] Accordingly, for Ricoeur, humanism is an acknowledgment that we are *only* mortals and not gods.[312] This definition signifies that there is a limitedness attached to being human that refers to the "philosophy of limits" whereby "meaning escapes us."[313] Ricoeur says that this is both Christian and Kantian.

In the Christian sense, the concept of limits means that we cannot claim absolute knowledge. The concept of limits suggests that history must look to what is beyond; namely, the eschatological, from whence final meaning is experienced. In the Kantian sense, the concept of limits refers to "limit-idea" in which the person is never able to know the "thing-in-itself." The *thing-in-itself* means thinking and demanding "everything" but never being able to "know" everything in itself. When this concept of limits is applied to history, we are faced with the limitations of being unable to know what the "total" meaning of humanity is.[314]

Within the grounds of Western culture, as we have seen, humanity constantly makes futile attempts to become god by filling up the limitedness of human life with materialism, exploitation, cultural dominance, and ultimate power experienced in the advancement of science and technology. David Stewart and Joseph Bien, editors of *Political and Social Essays*, call humanity's desire to become god a kind of resistance to being human. These authors even describe this desire as "the appearance of the demonic in the world," especially when humans conceal this drive to become god with a pledge to fulfill political ideologies.[315]

Therefore, there is a definite link between the understanding of humanism that Ricoeur defends and the problems of survival in the modern state.

Harvard University; Dr. John T. McAlister Jr., Woodrow Wilson School of Public and International Affairs, Princeton University.

[310] Ricoeur, *Political and Social Essays*, ix.
[311] Ricoeur, *Political and Social Essays*, 68.
[312] Ricoeur, *Political and Social Essays*, 86.
[313] Ricoeur, *Political and Social Essays*, 86.
[314] Ricoeur, *Political and Social Essays*, 86.
[315] David Stewart and Joseph Bien, introduction to *Political and Social Essays*, by Paul Ricoeur, 3.

The political implications of Ricoeur's philosophical project is our point of departure for an interpretation of religion in the rise of the modern state. Thus, we have the impetus for securing from the thought of Paul Ricoeur a politically constituted methodology whereby we are able to render an evaluative criticism of the religious conflict in the Americas.

Therefore, interest in the human sciences is significant in the thought of Paul Ricoeur.[316] Paul Ricoeur's works are a combination of his hermeneutics of history, historicality, and temporal existence, as well as his ideas about politics and society. His is not a closed system in that he is so diverse when he pursues what we have already described as his poetics of will; cf. *supra*. In fact, it is the inclusiveness of his system that has led to Ricoeur's exposure at the University of Chicago in 1973 to linguistic analysis, whereby he has then grafted it onto his phenomenological base. Specifically, this "grafting"–as he calls it–has radicalized Ricoeur's philosophical project and generated his hermeneutics. The hermeneutics has allowed for a mutuality between language and experience. It has allowed for a "lived experience to find its

---

[316] Paul Ricoeur, *History and Truth (Northwestern University Studies in Phenomenology and Existential Philosophy)*, trans. Charles A. Kelbley (Evanston, IL: Northwestern University Press, 1965). *History and Truth* considers the meaning, significance, and critique of history.

   Paul Ricoeur, *The Rule of Metaphor: Multidisciplinary Studies of the Creation of Meaning in Language*, trans. Robert Czerny with Kathleen McLaughlin and John Costello (Toronto: University of Toronto Press, 1977).

   Paul Ricoeur, *Time and Narrative*, trans. Kathleen McLaughlin, David Pellauer, and Kathleen Blamey (Chicago: The University of Chicago Press, 1984, 1985, 1988). The three volumes of *Time and Narrative* address the narrativity of all existence and are concerned with the temporal dimension of human activity and its implications.

   Paul Ricoeur, *Hermeneutics and the Human Sciences: Essays on Language, Action, and Interpretation*, ed. and trans. John B. Thompson (Cambridge: Cambridge University Press, 1981), 37–40, 197–221. Ricoeur comes the closest to discussing a political theory specifically in his article "A Response by Paul Ricoeur" in the book *Hermeneutics and the Human Sciences*.

   Paul Ricoeur, *Du texte a l'action: Essais d'hermeneutique II* (Paris: Editions du Seuil, 1986); Paul Ricoeur, *Lectures on Ideology and Utopia*, ed. George H. Taylor, delivered in English at the University of Chicago in 1975 (New York: Columbia University Press, 1986). In *Lectures on Ideology and Utopia*, Ricoeur deals with the hermeneutical structure of what takes place in the political dimension.

   Of course, of significant value is Ricoeur's work called *Political and Social Essays*, cited above, which is a collection of essays that have a retrospective value as they reflect on the fundamental questions facing peoples in the newly emerging economic and political systems of the late sixties.

clarification on the level of linguistic articulation" and for "language to find its origin and its referent in the deep-rooted expressibility of lived experience."[317]

Linguistically, when Ricoeur applies his hermeneutics, it means that he uses metaphor to disclose the nonsemantic dimension of symbol. Hermeneutics allows him the capacity to go beyond the literary that Ricoeur calls *semantic innovation*[318] (italics added). Moreover, when he applies his hermeneutics to lived experience, ordinary language about action becomes meaningful action beyond discourse. This meaningful action we call *praxis*. It is at this juncture that we are able to ferret out the Ricoeurian political theory. The political theory consists in the interaction between semantic innovation and human praxis, conjoined by a common element in the process, the imagination. This means that semantic innovation and human praxis, which stem from the imagination, are generative sources.[319]

A glimpse of a Ricoeurian political theory can be found in the Cerisy-la-Salle papers of Maria Villela-Petit and Serge Meitinger in which they apply the thought of Paul Ricoeur to particular questions of interest to themselves. Villela-Petit sees Ricoeur's "hermeneutics of historical consciousness" as a way of evaluating history, while Meitinger extends Ricoeur's use of metaphor into the field of lyric poetry in an effort to reveal the creative potential of imagination.[320] Maria Villela-Petit and Serge Meitinger give a survey of Ricoeur's approach to the methodology and epistemology of history.

In considering the historical problem, Villela-Petit stresses that the ultimate goal of Ricoeur's hermeneutical project is to understand the meaning of history and to establish a "historical" consciousness. Within the methodological and epistemological horizon of history, Petit argues that "the historical and the fictional narratives assembled are considered as essential contributions to the refiguration of the field of human action and suffering, in other words, to the refiguration of our historical condition. This refiguration has necessarily an ethico-political dimension, a dimension which has always been the *telos* of Ricoeur's thinking on history" (emphasis in original).[321]

---

[317] Ricoeur, "My Relation to the History of Philosophy," *The Iliff Review* 35, 3 (Fall 1978): 5–12, 11.

[318] The concept of semantic innovation will be discussed later.

[319] Ricoeur, "My Relation," 11–12.

[320] The Cerisy-la-Salle papers were published in T. Peter Kemp and David Rasmussen, eds., *The Narrative Path: The Later Works of Paul Ricoeur* (Cambridge: MIT Press, 1989). Maria Villela-Petit, "Thinking History: Methodology and Epistemology in Paul Ricoeur's Reflections on History from *History and Truth* to *Time and Narrative*," in *Narrative Path*, 33–46, and Serge Meitinger, "Between 'Plot' and 'Metaphor': Ricoeur's Poetics Applied on the Specificity of the Poem" in *Narrative Path*, 47–64, originally in *Philosophy and Social Criticism* 14, no. 2 (1988).

[321] Villela-Petit, "Thinking History," 42.

According to Villela-Petit, because Ricoeur's approach to history–as made explicit in *Time and Narrative*–is "more systematic than historical, [he] leaves aside one aspect of the 'reception' of history," its "mythic" use or misuse.[322] Then she explains that "[the misuse of history] corresponds to omissions or more or less subtle ideological prejudices which weighed down the writing of history itself. In that respect we have to talk not only of refiguration but also of defiguration of our human condition by historical narratives. Suffice it to remember that here too a 'critique of ideologies' is necessary."[323] Villela-Petit then sees Ricoeur's political diversion arising out of his understanding of the use of narrative as a refiguration of human activity as well as human history.

Serge Meitinger makes use of Ricoeurian theory by placing time and poetry in a nexus, in the same manner in which Ricoeur connects time to narrative. Meitinger makes the observation that "to establish this specific problematic, [he will] have to isolate at the very core of Paul Ricoeur's theoretical writings, a profound asymmetry between the field of lyric poetry and that of narrative."[324]

Where Villela-Petit gives insight into the methodology and hermeneutic for analyzing history, Meitinger looks at the field of poetry, recognizes Ricoeur's need to incorporate more explicitly the dynamics of poetry, and attempts to redress this by highlighting the asymmetry in the dynamic of both poetry and narrative.

The overall plan of this dissertation accepts the parallel between the Ricoeurian thought of Villela-Petit and Meitinger. Like Villela-Petit, we have sought to disclose the "misuse" of history as a critique of "ideological prejudices." Like Meitinger, we have sought to expose the nexus that exists between the temporal configuration and human experience and the role of imagination in each.

The chapter has three principal areas of study. First, we study the complex theory of imagination and discover that it is the metaphorical foundation of hermeneutical imagination. The hermeneutical imagination is engaged in the creation and transfer of meanings beyond the existing structures of meaning. It results in the creation of new meaning. Thus, the metaphor is at the foundation of imaginative production beyond the established discourse. The theory of imagination in its metaphorical sense thereby frees itself from the constraints of language and possibly even reason itself and extends itself into the whole field of action. The hermeneutic imagination, at this point, reaches through to the social dimensions by way of what Ricoeur calls the cultural

---

[322] Ricoeur, *Time and Narrative*. This work of Paul Ricoeur is a significant work in terms of what we are going to do in this dissertation.

[323] Villela-Petit, "Thinking History," 42.

[324] Meitinger, "Between 'Plot' and 'Metaphor,'" 47–48.

imaginative practices—ideology and utopia. In fact, reproductive imagination and productive imagination are accessible to us only through these imaginative practices. They function, on the one hand, as a principle of social integration, legitimation of power, and concealment and distortion. On the other hand, they function as a principle that stands against social integration or submission to the dominant culture and against excessive demands for legitimacy; and in their ability to dream, they enter into what might be seen as a kind of pathology that takes flight from the usual.

The second section considers the application of hermeneutical consciousness to the historical field, that is, the process of historical redescription prompted by the imaginative practices of ideology and utopia. At this point, we become engaged in the mimetic redescription that consists in the three moments of prefigured, configured, and refigured time. The prefiguration is the narrative description of events in terms of a plot that is rooted in a narrative preunderstanding that is structural, symbolic, and temporal in nature. It is a reference of the preliminary elements that can be used for setting up a plot as a part of the whole temporal structure. Configuration is the actual emplotment of the narrative. It is that which mediates between the structural aspects of action, overcoming the deficiency created between the interpreter of past events and the events themselves. The events are organized into a plot that brings together a series of events into a story, a meaningful whole. Refiguration is about the reception of the configured story. It is the application dimension of the reconstructed emplotment. When applied to the historical field, the mimetic spiral generates the potential for meaning of history beyond the classical notion of history as a science. This application of the mimetic spiral into the historical field assists in moving beyond the fictionalized data that is referred to as history.

We follow the dictates of the Ricoeurian theory of mimesis with its configuration act. We attempt to get beyond the classical notion of history by considering various notions of historical understanding. It becomes evident that the power of the mimetic spiral lies in its confrontation with the temporal order rendering a critique by its configurational power. Human action implies temporality that is denied in the rational constructs of the exact science philosophy of history. These historical constructs are reason-based "misuses" of history done to secure ideological prejudices. Thus, history is not just the accurate recording of facts but it must also be the interpretation of those facts. Therefore, in the third principal section of this chapter, we examine the relationship between mimesis and historiography. In so doing, we choose to follow the Fernand Braudel and the French Annales method of history.

Let us now begin this search for a new interpretation of the historical reality by demonstrating the foundation for a historical field that lies in a metaphorically based understanding of imagination.

2.1. THE THEORY OF IMAGINATION

2.1.1. BACKGROUND

Cognizant of his idea that there is no action without imagination, a succinct definition of Ricoeur's theory of imagination is necessary. The key to understanding Ricoeur's reading of history as political (cf. Villela-Petit *supra*) is to understand his theory of imagination, which functions as a bridge between discourse and action. The examination of the theory of imagination and the role of metaphor within that theory initiates the journey from discourse into social criticism and praxis, the principal components of any political theory. Ricoeur's way of reading history serves as the theoretical basis for what may be called a Ricoeurian political theory.

Imagination is generally understood to be "the power of forming mental images or other concepts not directly derived from sensation."[325] In other words, imagination is the power to see or to have mental images, ideas, or concepts of something or somebody. Imagination also refers to figures of speech that bring pictures to the mind.

Imagination offers a serious challenge for the philosophical project in general.[326] Besides its general definition, which is fundamentally based on perception/consciousness alone, there are various problems associated with the philosophical understanding of imagination. Ricoeur gives a survey of that ambiguity centered on the imagination theory. He discloses that there

---

[325] Paul Ricoeur, "L'imagination dans le discours et dans l'action," in *Savoir, faire, esperer: Les limites de la raison* (Bruxelles: Publications des Facultes Universitaires Saint Louis, 1976), 207–28, 216; Paul Ricouer, "Imagination in Discourse and in Action," in *The Human Being in Action: The Irreducible Element in Man Part II Investigation at the Intersection of Philosophy and Psychiatry* (*Analecta Husserliana*, vol. 7), ed. A.-T. Tymieniecka (Dordrecht, Boston, and London: D. Reidel Publishing Company, 1978), 5, 3–22, 3–4.

[326] Paul Ricoeur, "L'imagination," 216; "Discourse and Action," 3; and recently published in *Du texte a l'action*, Collection d'Esprit (Paris: Editions du Seuil, 1986); Richard Kearney, "Paul Ricoeur and the Hermeneutic Imagination," in *Narrative Path*, ed. T. Peter Kemp and David Rasmussen (Cambridge: MIT Press, 1989), 4; Joseph A. Komonchak, Mary Collins, and Dermot A. Lane, eds., *The New Dictionary of Theology* (Wilmington: Michael Glazier, 1987), s.v. "Imagination, Religious," by Stephen Happel.

is the common understanding that the imagination is a power of the mind.[327] Nevertheless, theories vary on the role and function of imagination in acquiring knowledge. For example, empiricist theories of knowledge have misused it; behaviorists and popular philosophers seek to negate its dominance. Two specific examples, given by Ricoeur, of the divergence in the understanding of imagination are the theories of Immanuel Kant (*Critique of Pure Reason*) and Gilbert Ryle (*The Concept of Mind*).[328]

According to Ricoeur, Immanuel Kant sees the imagination as a "single faculty" that functions in the knowledge process, fleshing out what is picked up by the senses only a piece at a time. The perception of reality is incomplete because the senses do not perceive the whole object directly. We see only certain parts of an object at a time, and the imagination "reproduces" what is not visible in its completeness (reproductive imagination).[329]

Ricoeur then says that, for Kant, the imagination combines experiential data into a single connected whole. Here, imagination exists before experience and functions as a synthesis of experiences, a procedure that provides images as well as produces coherence both from whence cognition originates (productive imagination).[330] According to Ricoeur, it is here that Kant finds difficulty seeing imagination as separate from understanding. "'The unity of apperception in relation to the synthesis of the imagination is the understanding;' and this same unity, with reference to the 'transcendental synthesis' of the imagination, the 'pure understanding'" (A119).[331] Thus, with his appropriation of Kant, Ricoeur sees imagination as either reproductive (of what is not visible in its completeness) or productive understanding that is the result of a synthesis of experiences.[332]

---

[327] Ricoeur, "Discourse and Action," 4.

[328] Ricoeur, "L'imagination," 214–15; Ricoeur, "Discourse and Action," 4.

[329] The theoretical basis of the political theory of Ricoeur is how he appropriates Kant's idea of imagination. He discusses his use of Kant when he is dealing with the role of the imagination in the configurational act and productive imagination. Ricoeur especially relies on Kant when he further develops the notion of productive imagination when he evolves the idea and role of *schematisms* in imagination. We will explicate this development later in this text (see p. 118 in this text) (Ricoeur, *Time and Narrative* 1:68; "Discourse and Action," 8). In his reflection on the productive role of imagination, Ricoeur is drawing on the following section of Kant's first *Critique*. Immanuel Kant, *Critique of Pure Reason*, trans. N. Kemp Smith (London: 1929), 141–150 (A115–A130).

[330] Ricoeur, "Discourse and Action," 8.

[331] To demonstrate Kant's emphasis on the unity that exists between the imagination and understanding, Ricoeur incorporates into his text a citation from Immanuel Kant's *Critique of Pure Reason* (143).

[332] Ricoeur, "Discourse and Action," 5.

According to Ricoeur, Gilbert Ryle stresses that imagination is not "a single faculty." For Ryle, imagination refers to various imaginative practices dealing with various distantly related experiences. These imaginative practices may even be "mock performances."[333] For example, when one is preparing a speech, one runs over in one's mind exactly how one will deliver the speech. Ricoeur corroborates that what Ryle seems to be doing in his thinking is even disassociating imagination from mental activity. Ryle says that a report in words is required to answer the instruction "Imagine what it would be like if . . ." Thus, the emphasis of Ryle is a clear reference to the linguistic or expressive dimension of imagination.[334]

Ricoeur summarizes the various theories of imagination by organizing them along two opposite axes in which he establishes a "wide range of basic significations"[335] (fig. 1). He continues, "The range of variation in these theories can be differentiated according to two opposite axes: with regard to the object, the axis of presence and absence; with regard to the subject, the axis of fascinated."

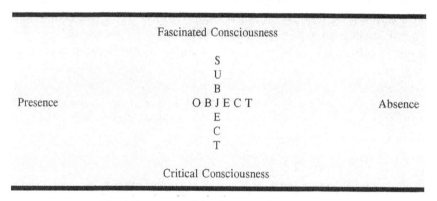

Fig. 1. Summary of the theories of imagination
consciousness and critical consciousness.[336]

Ricoeur describes the imagination theories at one end of the objective axis as a kind of presence. On this end of the objective axis, there is an image of

[333] Ricoeur, "Discourse in Action," 4. Here, Ricoeur has made use of Gilbert Ryle's work *Concept of Mind* (261); Gilbert Ryle, *Concept of Mind* (London: Hutchinson & Co., 1949), 260–61. Ryle spends a significant amount of time describing how his concept of imagination functions. In chapter VIII, entitled "Imagination," he discusses the variety of activities of the imagination (245–78).

[334] Ryle, *Concept of Mind*, 260ff; Ricoeur, "L'imagination," 214.

[335] Ricoeur, "Discourse and Action," 5.

[336] Ricoeur, "Discourse and Action," 5.

something that is perceived, but it is only a trace. Then Ricoeur says that "all theories of reproductive imagination tend toward this axis."[337]

Ricoeur views imagination theories at the other end of the objective axis as absence. This end refers to an image of something that is not really present but only seems to be present (e.g., a portrait, a dream, and fiction). It is, as Ricoeur says, other than present.[338] Interestingly, the two directions on the objective axis both fall along a spectrum of presence because absence is related, in a sense, to presence.

Ricoeur states that all theories of productive imagination tend toward the absence side of the objective axis.[339]

Imagination theories, however, also wind around a subjective axis. What characterizes this axis is attention to whether the subject of imagination is critically aware or is confused regarding the difference between the imaginary and the real. On the one end of the subjective axis, which Ricoeur calls fascinated consciousness, the subject lacks critical awareness and threatens to confuse the image with the real or takes the image for the real. The fascinated consciousness or "state of confusion" is a function of reproductive imagination. What dominates in the experience of the fascinated consciousness is the incapacity to discern between "lies and errors."[340]

On the other end of the subjective axis, which Ricoeur calls critical consciousness, the subject is critically aware. The critical consciousness or "act of distinction" consists in full awareness of the distance between the image and the real. The experience of the critical consciousness produces otherness. At this point, imagination functions as the "instrument of the critique of reality." The critical consciousness is a function of the productive imagination.[341]

The above summary by Paul Ricoeur exposes the ambiguity of imagination with various meanings that even tend to contradict one another. Finally, the question Ricoeur asks is whether "the philosophy of imagination is deficient or whether what is noted as a problem might be a structural trait of imagination itself."[342]

So far, except in a certain sense for Immanuel Kant, who is known for his a priori approach, imagination has been seen from a phenomenological perspective alone. The focus from that perspective is on a visual model of reality, namely, imagination is mainly a function of perception, and description

---

[337] Ricoeur, "Discourse and Action" (e.g., Ricoeur's use of Kant as described above in pages 112–13).

[338] Ricoeur, "Discourse and Action" (e.g., Ryle's linguistic formulation; see *supra*, p. 113).

[339] Ricoeur, "Discourse and Action."

[340] Ricoeur, "Discourse and Action."

[341] Ricoeur, "Discourse and Action," 216.

[342] Ricoeur, "L'imagination," 216; Ricoeur, "Discourse and Action," 6.

is its leading emphasis. However, Ricoeur is not satisfied with holding that imagination (the image) is derived solely from perception. He raises the question of how imagination can be derived from language. He says that the answer can be found when looked at from the hermeneutical perspective. More specifically, it is with metaphor and its potential for new meaning in the context of hermeneutics that Ricoeur suggests finding a better understanding of the theory of imagination.[343]

2.1.2. METAPHORICAL FOUNDATION OF HERMENEUTICAL IMAGINATION

At this point, imagination becomes a "method rather than a content."[344] Although Paul Ricoeur has introduced hermeneutics to his philosophical agenda as early as *La symbolique du mal* (1960), it is not until *La métaphore vive* (1975) that he has added the theory of metaphor and laid the groundwork for his own theory of imagination. Metaphor, generally speaking, is a hermeneutic principle that stresses a specific language use or figure of speech that extends the meaning of a word(s). Ricoeur will have us understand that metaphor pertains not only to the word but also to the sentence, the text, and finally to action itself.

It is now important to define *metaphor* and then present the background of its role in the theory of imagination. Metaphor has a long tradition that dates as far back as the Greek sophists and their use of metaphor in the context of rhetoric. In the introduction to *La métaphore vive* (1975), Ricoeur discusses how he derives the metaphoric principle. Ricoeur explains that

> [he] begins with classical rhetoric, passes through semiotics and semantics, and finally reaches hermeneutics. The progression from one discipline to the other corresponds to changes of the linguistic entity chosen for consideration: the word, the sentence, and then discourse.[345]

---

[343] Ibid.

[344] Ricoeur, "Discourse and Action," 8.

[345] Paul Ricoeur, introduction in *RM*, 3. Semiotics is a theory of signs and their applications in language, the study of all patterned communication systems. Semiotics is divided into three parts: syntactics, the study of grammar; semantics, the study of meaning; and pragmatics, the study of the actual purposes and effects of meaningful language. *Hermeneutics* is the term used to denote the discipline connected to the investigation and interpretation of human behavior, speech, institutions, and so on. (The meaning of all three of these terms were found in Flew, *Dictionary of Philosophy*, 323, 146, respectively.)

Thus, through a study of metaphor, it becomes possible to garner a clearer understanding of the role of imagination in Ricoeur's passage or shift into hermeneutics. It is precisely the connection between narrative and imagination, with their metaphorical base, that will give way to the hermeneutics of historical consciousness in Ricoeur.

The most precise definition of *metaphor* is found in Aristotle's *Poetics* as cited by Ricoeur (1457 b 6–9):

> [Metaphor] consists in giving the thing a name that belongs to something else; the transference being either from genus to species, or from species to genus, or from species to species, or on grounds of analogy.[346]

Metaphor is at the root of rhetoric and poetics, and its structure is that of the "transfer of meanings of words."[347] Metaphor uses words as carriers of the diverse intents of rhetoric and poetics. However, metaphor functions differently in each; in rhetoric, its function is rhetorical, while in poetics, it is poetical. According to Ricoeur, although both rhetoric and poetics deal with composition (emplotment), the manner in which metaphor functions in poetics is closest to narrativity as the following argument will demonstrate by the explication of metaphor in the context of rhetoric and then in that of poetics.

The significance of the difference is that rhetoric has to do with oratorical technique, and as a system, it is concerned with persuasion and defense. It engages in deliberation, seeking blame or praise; it has to do with the numeration or control dimension of reality. It deals with what Ricoeur calls "the art of inventing or proofs."[348]

Metaphor at the level of rhetoric and poetics is deviant and has the power of creating new meaning, but it is not limited to use of names or the redescription of names. Metaphor goes beyond the literal sense of a word, as well as a deviation of naming. At this point, metaphor crosses over into the area of what Ricoeur refers to as poetics or as the power certain fictions have to redescribe reality. Since the act of redescribing is *mimesis*, fictional redescription is the first definition Ricoeur has ever given of mimesis.[349]

---

[346]   Ricoeur, *RM*, 13 passim.
[347]   Ricoeur, *RM*, 12; Ricoeur, "Paul Ricoeur on Biblical Hermeneutics," in *Semeia* 4, ed. John Dominic Crossan (Chicago: Society of Biblical Literature, 1975), 75–76.
[348]   Ricoeur, *RM*, 12–13.
[349]   Ricoeur, "Biblical Hermeneutics," 76; Ricoeur, "Discourse and Action," 6–7. Mimesis will be dealt with later; cf. beginning p. 121.

Metaphor is the rhetorical process by which discourse unleashes the power that certain fictions have to redescribe reality. By linking fiction and redescription in this way, we restore the full depth of meaning to Aristotle's discovery in *Poetics,* which was that the *poiesis* of language arises out of the connection between *muthos* and *mimesis.*[350]

The definition of *poetics* can be found in Ricoeur's summary of his theory of interpretation as he derived it from Aristotle's *Poetics.* Ricoeur defines *poetics* as "that discipline which deals with the laws of composition that are added to discourse as such in order to form of it a text which can stand as a narrative, a poem or an essay."[351] The project of poetics is mimesis. *Mimesis* is that which composes a creative *imitation or representation/redescription* of lived temporal experiences by means of the plot. Mimesis or creative redescription is characterized by the active sense of organizing events into a narrative configuration. Mimetic activity is a dynamic "process of imitating and representing something."[352] "It [poetics] speaks the truth by means of fiction, fable, and tragic *muthos* (plot)."[353]

Ricoeur appropriates the Kantian notion of schematism to describe the method of giving an image to a concept. The method is "the very operation of grasping the similar," which is associated with the extension of the concept beyond its usual meaning to what it resembles. Schematism is the method whereby the phrase "seeing as" constitutes the restructure of the concept into new meaning (semantic innovation). It is in this transition into new meanings that the poetical dimension of imagination functions as an element of fiction, and metaphor thereby exposes itself as the foundation for the hermeneutical imagination.[354]

---

[350]   Ricoeur, *RM,* 7.

[351]   Paul Ricoeur, "On Interpretation," in *Philosophy in France Today,* ed. A. Montefiore (Cambridge: Cambridge University Press, 1983), 175–79, 177. The French translation was published later in *Du texte a l'action* and was presented in *L'Encyclopedie philosophique.*

[352]   Ricoeur, *Time and Narrative,* 1:33.

[353]   Ricoeur, *RM,* 13.

[354]   Ricoeur, "Discourse and Action," 8. This "as if" is extremely important in Ricoeur's definition of *emplotment.* For the term *fiction* designates "the configuration of a narrative for which emplotment is the paradigm, without regard for the differences that concern the truth claims of the two classes of narrative." Thus, *fiction* is both a "synonym for narrative configurations" and an "antonym to historical narrative's claim to constitute a 'true' narrative" (*Time and Narrative,* 1:64). See also *Time and Narrative,* 1:68, for reference to Ricoeur's use of Kant's concept of schematism.

In the hermeneutic sense, poetics becomes something more; it becomes the paradigm that expresses something that "reverberates" into imagination. Poetics seeks meaning in the face of one thing being said in terms of something else or several things at the same time, even resulting in the creation of new meaning. It is this process that narrative and metaphor come together with the temporal. Ricoeur writes,

> In both cases, [narrative and metaphor] the new thing–the as yet unsaid, the unwritten–springs up in language. Here a living metaphor, that is, a new pertinence in the prediction, there a feigned plot, that is, a new congruence in the organization of the events.[355]

Ricoeur considers that poetics and its ability to create new meaning play a significant role in the understanding of the theory of imagination. A poem, which is a work of language making use of a certain procedure that Ricoeur refers to as reverberation, is "a creation of language that comes to be at that moment without status in the language as something already established with respect to either designation or connotation."[356] Ricoeur writes, in the preface to the first volume of *Time and Narrative*, that the innovation produces a "new semantic pertinence" moving beyond the literal interpretation of the text. Ricoeur calls this poetical creation of new meaning "semantic innovation," and he sees that metaphor is absolutely necessary in that process.[357]

> Metaphor invites us to relate the imagination to a certain type of language use, more precisely, to see in it an aspect of semantic innovation characteristic of the metaphorical uses of language.[358]

Thus, the power in imagination that allows us to see something revealed or to understand consists in that aspect of imaginative production called semantic innovation. Semantic innovation is generated by metaphor.

It has a reference outside the established use of language. It is that aspect of metaphor that stretches imagination beyond its "ordinary" usage. In the context of emplotment, it is semantic innovation that functions to "confer a new intelligible significance on a course of events."[359] Metaphor and semantic

---

[355] Ricoeur, *Time and Narrative*, 1:ix.
[356] Ricoeur, *RM*, 98.
[357] Ricoeur, *Time and Narrative*, 1:ix; Ricoeur, "Biblical Hermeneutics," 79.
[358] Ricoeur, "Discourse and Action," 6.
[359] Villela-Petit, "Thinking History," 34; Ricoeur, *RM*, 98; Ricoeur, *Time and Narrative*,

innovation lead us to a more direct consideration on the referential dimension of imagination.

2.1.3. THE ROLE OF IMAGINATION IN THE CREATION OF ACTION

The role of metaphor in generating imaginative production has a referential dimension beyond the text itself, especially beyond established discourse. The notion of referring to something outside the text can be derived through an understanding that there is a distinction between *sense* and *reference* in the realm of discourse. The sense of the metaphorical statement receives its predicative structure from its reference.[360]

We have said that metaphor creates new meaning when it gives something a name that belongs to something else. The transfer of names is an extension whose predication speaks about resemblance or about the specific attributes of the subject. This process, according to Ricoeur, involves both sense and reference. *Sense* has to do with exactly *what* a statement says, and *reference* is *that about which* a statement is made.[361] Ricoeur explains that the meaning conveyed by the notion of sense has its own intrinsic composition. However, the concept of reference exists outside linguistic construction. Reference is real in that it refers to the world outside.[362]

In an effort to make clear the distinction between language and discourse, Ricoeur says that language functions "purely internally or immanently," referring basically to elements within the language of narrative configuration itself, whereas discourse is "open and turned toward the world it wishes to express and to convey in language." The indication is that the language, which is meant "to articulate our experience of the world, to give form to this experience," is discourse.[363] In hermeneutics, the concern then is about interpretation directed at what is "beyond" the text, viz., that about which language tells us something. For when you pay attention to the "world" arising "beyond" the text, you are doing hermeneutics. Language, therefore, is concerned about not just itself but also what is disclosed when referring to something outside itself, the "extra-linguistic *being* brought to language by the text."[364]

1:ix–x; Ricoeur, "Discourse and Action," 7.

[360] Ricoeur, "On Interpretation," 182–83.

[361] Ricoeur, "Biblical Hermeneutics," 81.

[362] Ricoeur, "Biblical Hermeneutics."

[363] Ricoeur, "Biblical Hermeneutics."

[364] Ricoeur, "A Response by Paul Ricoeur," in *Human Sciences*, ed. and trans. John B. Thompson (Cambridge, London, and New York: Cambridge University Press,

What has been discussed is hermeneutic imagination. Imagination is a "faculty" of human intelligence, the functioning of which can be analyzed. Hermeneutics deals with the understanding of texts and of that which is brought to language by the text. Indeed, it is through the semantic innovation of metaphor that hermeneutic imagination gives language a capacity that "constitute[s] a disclosure of unprecedented worlds, an opening on to other *possible* worlds which transcend the established limits of our *actual* world."[365] Ricoeur speaks of two orders of reference. The first has to do with the focus of ordinary language as it refers to empirical reality. The second order of reference is more significant for Ricoeur. According to Richard Kearney in his article "Hermeneutic Imagination," this second order refers to "a horizon of possible worlds." It ushers in the hermeneutic capacity of the imagination that focuses on the "world-disclosure yielded by texts."[366]

The theory of imagination frees itself from the constraints of language as a pure self-referential system and extends itself to the whole field of action. The issue here is that the fictive element has power to posit the existence of the reference. It is the redescribing power of fiction that is related to mimesis, which Ricoeur characterizes as a *heuristic force* that "has the capacity to open and unfold new dimensions of reality, suspending our belief in an earlier description."[367] Heuristic fiction surpasses a more perceptive approach to imagination that focuses on visual seeing and description–a visual model of imagination. The approach of heuristic fiction involves what Ricoeur calls the "iconic increase," which is the recreation of reality at a higher level. Ricoeur holds to his notion of imagination that, unlike the perceptive notion of imagination, it has a heuristic fictive element that strikes out traditional imagination based on the visual. Ultimately, the fictive element "remakes reality" in such a way that this remaking functions as a schematism of human action.[368] Meaningful action grafts itself on a schematism that mediates between the empirical awareness of diversity and the logic of narrative possibilities.

> This referential force consists in the fact that the narrative act, through the narrative structures, applied the framework of an ordered fiction to the diversity of human action. Between what could be a logic of narrative possibilities and

1981; Paris: Editions de la Maison des Sciences de l'Homme, 1981), 35.

365 Richard Kearney, "Myth as the Bearer of Possible Worlds," in *Dialogues with Contemporary Continental Thinkers* (St. Martin: Manchester University Press, 1988), 44; Richard Kearney, "Paul Ricoeur and the Hermeneutic Imagination," in *Narrative Path*, 5.

366 Kearney, "Myth as Bearer," 45; Kearney, "Ricoeur and Hermeneutic Imagination," 6.

367 Ricoeur, "Discourse and Action," 10.

368 Ricoeur, "Discourse and Action."

the empirical diversity of action, narrative fiction interposes
its schematism of human action.[369]

Ricoeur argues that the narrative process has a heuristic force that "open[s]
up and unfold[s] new dimensions of reality, suspending belief in an earlier
description." The process connects mimesis and redescription or, according to
Aristotle, mythos and mimesis. However, Ricoeur hereby advocates a poetics
of action that calls for something more than just a redescriptive function
with only a descriptive value. The mimetic function, if correctly understood,
requires more than an analytical description of the components of action
(mimesis); for the capacity to act–to be deciphered in the plot (mimesis$_2$)–
calls for a projective function of imagination, "which is part of the dynamics
of action itself" (mimesis$_3$).[370]

Ricoeur goes on to say that there can be no creative capacity for action
without imagination. He bases this idea on the role of imagination within
the context of individual action. There are three steps that specify the
schematization that yields an image of what it is to be done. The three stages
are as follows. First is a general projective scheme of the possibility of a project.
Second, one invents the scheme with what one figures to be the aspiration of
one's desires. The desires are concrete compared with the generality of the
projection scheme. Third, one comes to see that the "I can make this possible"
is within the reach of imaginative variants.

There is thus a progression from the simple
schematization of my projects, through the figurability of
my desires, to the imaginative variations of the "I can." This
progression points to the idea of the imagination as a general
function of what is possible in practice.[371]

Individual creative action, thus, reaches the point of extending itself and
grasping the ultimate consequence of redescription and imagination. However,
it still does not go beyond individual action itself into a relationship of people
with one another in the social context. If the hermeneutic imagination is
to serve as the underlying operating force of Ricoeur's theory of political
creativity, we must see how it can reach through to the level of the social.

The existential experience or the historical field calls for a social dimension
that is more encompassing than individual action. Ricoeur refers to the social
dimension as *intersubjectivity*. When two prospective temporal fields connect,

[369] Ricoeur, "Discourse and Action," II.
[370] Ricoeur, "Discourse and Action," 11–12.
[371] Ricoeur, "Discourse and Action," 13.

as it happens in the sociohistorical context, a relation of *pairing* takes place. On closer inspection, however, the pairing relation takes place not only between contemporaries but also between predecessors and successors. When the above-mentioned phenomenology of individual action is extended (extension of imagination in this sense), specific relations between the self understanding (and what we grasp from it of contemporaries, predecessors, and successors) begin to give birth to the awareness of the importance of the transmission of tradition. This looking back at history–in terms of a creative transmission of deep values–is what is called historical consciousness. The role of reproductive imagination at this juncture is critical. Ricoeur says that "the possibility of an historical experience in general lies in our ability to remain open to the effects of history." He asserts that it is the imagination in its social dimension that assists us in increasing our capacity to be affected (i.e., determined by the effects of history).[372]

Let us move on to discuss the social dimension of imagination, which is rooted in the wider principle of intersubjectivity. Ricoeur will now, in particular, flesh out the role of the social by the additional characteristic of the cultural.

2.1.4. THE SOCIAL DIMENSIONS OF IMAGINATION AND THE CULTURAL IMAGINARY

The social cultural imaginary is at the epistemological basis of the exploration of the historical field. *Social* refers to the roles of individuals within institutions as distinct from the political. *Cultural* refers to the "production of intellectual works through the medium of language and the creation of ideas."[373] Ricoeur uses the terms *social* and *cultural* interchangeably because "the form of the imagination [he] is concerned with is both social and cultural" (*Lectures*, 323). We will use the terms as almost equal qualifiers of creative imagination because, in the broader sense, they both refer to the same political reality. This aspect of the imagination establishes that the experience of the temporal field by another is analogous to one's own experience of the past, the present, and the future.

But the effects of history (the past, present, or future) can affect us only to the degree that we can be affected in that way. According to Ricoeur, it is the productive imagining of these analogies that gives us that capacity of receptivity, constituting the social dimension of the imagination. Thus, in the analogous exchange, the imagination is what transfers the meaning between

---

[372] Ricoeur, "Discourse and Action," 15.
[373] Ricoeur, *Lectures*, 323.

the interrelated experiences. Ricoeur labels this the social dimension of the imagination, which is also known as the cultural imaginary.[374]

To explain further, Ricoeur points out that the transfer of meaning that takes place in the cultural imaginary is at the root of what is called empathy (*Einfühlung*).[375] He states that, in this transfer, the power of the imagination generates new connections (diachronic). Imagination is productive, and its task is to work against the breakdown of human relations by manifesting the schemes of coherence that are precisely instrumental in establishing human relations (synchronic).[376]

It may seem here that in the transfer of the imaginary, resulting in new connections, Ricoeur is simultaneously speaking on synchronic and diachronic levels. Synchronic will be looking at history as from a "slice," and diachronic is an episodic manner. It is the latter that is important because of the focus on meaning as it is being transformed and changed in the course of the years. Both have to do with temporality, but the synchronic here will refer to the rules for doing history while the diachronic will have to do with its meaning. The simultaneity of the synchronic and diachronic levels is important in the search for meaning, particularly in the historical field. The imaginary on the synchronic level will be dealing with the science of history itself, while the diachronic focuses on interpretation and meaning. The synchronic must have the ability to take into account the changes in meaning suggested by the diachronic level. "A synchronic approach must precede any diachronic approach because systems are more intelligible than changes. At best, a change is a partial or a global change in a state of a system. Therefore, the history of changes must come after the theory that describes the synchronistic states of the system. This . . . postulate expresses the emergence of a new type of intelligibility directly opposed to the historicism of the nineteenth century."[377]

In this very process, Ricoeur states that it is the "competence" of the imagination "by way of identifying and keeping the analogy of the ego in its synchronic and diachronic relations preserving the difference between the course of a meaningful history and the flat course of things." Ricoeur says that "the possibility of a historical experience lies in our ability to remain open to the effects of past history," and it is the imagination that increases our capacity of so being "affected by the effects of history."[378]

---

[374]   Ricoeur, "Discourse and Action," 17.

[375]   Ricoeur, "Discourse and Action."

[376]   Ricoeur, *Lectures,* 261; Ricoeur, *Interpretation Theory,* 5.

[377]   Ricoeur, *RM,* 111.

[378]   Ricoeur, *RM.*

> The imagination has as its competence preserving and identifying the *analogy of the ego* in all relations with our contemporaries, our predecessors, and our successors. Its competence therefore lies in preserving and identifying the difference between the course of history and the course of things.[379]

If Ricoeur can be said to have a political theory rooted in historical consciousness, it is because that theory rests on the awareness of analogical utterances of the imagination in the course of history. The analogical power of imagination, whereby I see that the other person's temporal existence and experience is like (analogous to) my temporal existence and experience, is what constitutes the sociocultural aspect of imagination.

According to Paul Ricoeur, the analogical utterances of the imagination manifest themselves more, in particular, through the imaginative practices of ideology and utopia. Ricoeur appropriates the insight of Karl Mannheim, who correlates these two imaginative practices and looks at them as "deviant attitudes toward social reality."[380] In this particular instance, putting them in the same conceptual framework will make for a better understanding of the tension that exists *between* ideology and utopia–a tension that leads "from wholesome to pathological forms, from distorting to constitutive roles"–and *within* them, whereby one gains "a better grasp of their complementarity in a system of social action."[381]

Consequently, Ricoeur's hypothesis is that there are both positive and negative aspects to his correlating ideology and utopia into a single conceptual framework but also that this correlation manifests what critical imagination is about.

> The polarity between [the] two sides of each term may be enlightened by exploring a similar polarity between the two terms. My [Ricoeur's] claim is that this polarity both between ideology and utopia and within each of them may

---

[379] Ricoeur, *RM.*

[380] Ricoeur, *Lectures,* 1–2, 159–60; Paul Ricoeur, "Ideology and Utopia as Cultural Imagination," in *Being Human in a Technological Age,* ed. Donald Borchert and David Stewart (Athens: Ohio University Press, 1979), 107–8; Ricoeur, "Discourse and Action," 16.

Ricoeur became the first to attempt this process since Karl Mannheim did it in his work *Ideologie und utopie.* Many thinkers have dealt only with ideology while still others have centered their thoughts on utopia with no attention to ideology.

[381] Ricoeur, "Ideology and Utopia as Cultural Imagination," 107; cf. Ricoeur, "Discourse and Action," 16, and Ricoeur, *Lectures,* 1–2, 159–60.

be ascribed to some structural traits of what I call cultural imagination.[382]

This is also what poetic expression does for Ricoeur since the poetic dimension forces confrontation with culture.

According to Ricoeur, when our self-involvement in our own concept of ideology is extended, the result is universalization of ideology. When universalization occurs, the critique becomes constitutive of its own referent. In this sense, ideology gives ideas the form of universality.[383]

Ricoeur takes the concepts of ideology and utopia beyond even their literary and semantic expression to the level of how they function in society.[384] It is precisely at the level of the structural characteristics of ideology and utopia that Paul Ricoeur discusses them as *cultural or social imagination*.

Just as he has done with the metaphorical foundation of imagination (fig. 1 *supra*), Ricoeur also discusses *social imagination* as the variation along objective and subjective axes.[385] On the objective axis, whose scale goes from presence to absence, Ricoeur locates the shift from reproductive to productive imagination. The subjective axis harbors the two opposite dimensions of fascinated and critical consciousness.[386]

---

[382] Ricoeur, *Lectures*, 2.

[383] Ricoeur, "Ideology and Utopia as Cultural Imagination," 115.

[384] Ricoeur, "Discourse and Action," 16–17; Ricoeur, *Lectures*, 2; Ricoeur, "Ideology and Utopia as Cultural Imagination," 107.

[385] See the section on the two axes on pages 114, 115ff; especially see the diagram on pages 114–15.

[386] Ricoeur, *Lectures*, 3; Ricoeur, "Ideology and Utopia as Cultural Imagination," 122.

FASCINATED CONSCIOUSNESS
Reproductive Imagination
Ideology
(Preserves the existing order)

	replicates	*legitimates*	*falsifies*	
PRESENCE	Integrative	Legitimative	Distortive	**ABSENCE**
	subverts	*unmasks*	*explores*	

(Disruptive of the existing order)
Utopia
Productive Imagination
CRITICAL CONSCIOUSNESS

Fig. 2. Summary of the sociocultural imaginary.

The spectrum of ambiguities and complementarity in the social imagination moves from the integrative to the legitimative to the distortive assessment of reality (fig. 2). On the integrative level, the function of the social imagination is identification, which preserves or mirrors order and has the appearance of a clear picture. At this level, it replicates the features of dominance. The integrative dimension of the social imagination is constitutive of the cultural social and therefore preexists and will even outlive the existent dominance (i.e., because of the constitutive nature of integration). For example, an ideology constituted at the level of social action is necessary, similar to the way genetic systems determine biological life.[387]

On the legitimative level, the function of imagination is to give credence to authority. The legitimating quality of imagination prompts a mutuality between authority and those of whom it seeks belief. Such a system of legitimation is necessary because no system of leadership, not even government, can always rule by domination. In fact, even the dominant cannot sustain rule only by dominance. Thus, according to M. Weber, it is the role of legitimative imagination to secure the will of those in authority onto the governed. Legitimative imagination justifies the system of authority. Imagination on

---

[387] Clifford Geertz, "Ideology as a Cultural System," in *The Interpretation of Cultures: Selected Essays* (New York: Basic Books, Inc., 1973), 216; Ricoeur, "Discourse and Action," 17; cf. Ricoeur, *Lectures*, 12, 216, 256–57.

this level "mobilizes its forces to fill the gap between the demand from above and the belief from below."[388]

On the distortive level, the function of imagination is to disrupt. It might be described as "turning the real on its head." The "ideology in Karl Marx is determined not by its opposition to science," Ricoeur discerns, "but by its opposition to *reality*"[389] (emphasis in original). Ricoeur, however, is aware that Marx, in his later development, will focus on the opposition between ideology and science. At this level, it posits ideology as illusion or fantasy or even a false or inverted representation of reality. Ideology is only able to get away with this distorting activity because of the role of the integrative dimension of imagination and its preexistent state.[390]

To summarize briefly, in social life according to Ricoeur, imagination functions in two different ways. The three dimensions of the imagination–integrative, legitimative, and distortive–when related to the larger role of imagination, either function to preserve the existing order and are called then reproductive imagination or may function in a disruptive manner and are then called the productive imagination. Therefore, on the general level, we may deduce that imagination functions in two different ways: reproductive and productive.

Reproductive and productive imagination, in a sense, are synonymous with and accessible to us only through the *imaginative practices* of *ideology* and *utopia*.[391] It is ideology that seeks to mirror the existing order, prompted by the imagination. Its role is one of preserving and conserving what is. This reproductive kind of imagination has "the appearance of a picture" seeking to reproduce itself.[392] Utopia, on the contrary, functions in a disruptive manner in relation to the existing order. "Utopia has the fictional power of redescribing life."[393] In this fictional sense, it is always seeking to establish something else. This productive kind of imagination is "imagining something else, the elsewhere."[394]

---

[388] Max Weber, *Economy and Society*, 23–33 passim; Ricoeur, "Discourse and Action," 17; cf. also Ricoeur, *Lectures*, 13–14, 183–87 passim.

[389] Ricoeur, *Lectures*, 21.

[390] Ricoeur, *Lectures*. Cf. also Ricoeur, *Lectures*, 14, 22–25 passim.

[391] Ricoeur, "Discourse and Action," 15–16. *Ideology* is a reasoned/systematic reflection or the content of thinking characteristic of a particular individual, group, or culture, whereas *utopia* is a place of ideal perfection or an imaginary scheme for social improvement (*Webster's Ninth New Collegiate Dictionary*).

[392] Ricoeur, *Lectures*, 266.

[393] Ricoeur, *Lectures*, xxviii.

[394] Ricoeur, *Lectures*, 266.

The next section will point in more detail to how the three dimensions of imagination (constitutive/integrative, legitimative, and distortive) function in the imaginative practices of ideology and utopia.

2.1.4.1. THE FUNCTION OF IDEOLOGY

Ricoeur says that the function of ideology is social integration. In this sense, integration (identification) is the result of social messages communicated through certain cultural codes. This practical functioning of imagination operates at the basic level of human experience, which suggests that it is constitutive of human experience.

Integration is that aspect of the social imaginary that is related to the need every group has to give itself an image of itself or to represent itself. This is the most primitive level of ideology. Therefore, the relationship between domination and ideology exists at an even deeper level than the ruling class will have the power to institute. Ideology is why, according to Ricoeur, the ruling class has any power at all. In fact, the influence of ideology is more primitive than the analysis of the ruling classes and is capable of outliving class structure.[395]

Ricoeur seeks something more than the distorting notion of ideology– the reference to the integrative dimension of ideology. He searches into its presuppositions to demonstrate that, despite the negative dimension, ideology makes sense. Ideology is beyond the polemical. He concludes that "no social group can exist without this indirect relation to its own being through representation of itself." He continues, "The nascent pathology of the ideological phenomenon arises from its function of reinforcing and repeating the social tie in situations that occur after the fact."[396] Ideology takes on the function of interpretation as it produces social messages and cultural codes. This leads him to examine the further functions of ideology.

Ideology functions as a tool for legitimization of power. The role of authority in a system is a given. Every authority seeks to make itself legitimate. The ideological representations that make for integration into the society are monitored by a system of authority. The claim to legitimacy must be related to belief. However, there is a certain asymmetry between the authority and the believer. The claim coming from the authority always contains more than the belief that is accorded this authority.[397]

---

[395]   Ricoeur, "Discourse and Action," 17.
[396]   Ricoeur, "Discourse and Action."
[397]   This is a reference to force (police, military, or otherwise).

Ideology is also a "pejorative concept in which [it] is understood as concealment and distortion,"[398] and its function often produces an inverted image in which ideas become the real. In this pejorative sense, Marx writes,

> "[T]he ruling class establishes its power by concealing the ideas which express its interest." Thus the ideas of the ruling class are in every epoch the ruling ideas, i.e., the class which is the ruling *material* force of society, is at the same time its ruling *intellectual* force [emphasis in original]. . . . The ruling ideas are nothing more than the ideal expression of the dominant material relationships . . . grasped as ideas . . . the ideas of dominance.[399]

In the pejorative sense, ideas are separated from life and become autonomous reality. It is this dimension of ideology that is coopted and perverted by interest groups, which is why Ricoeur does not deny the legitimacy of the Marxist concept of ideology. On the other hand, Ricoeur seeks to relate Marx's concept to the broader symbolic structure of social life for the purposes of understanding how reality can become the victim of an idea for an illusion.[400]

2.1.4.2. THE FUNCTION OF UTOPIA

Now let us look at the other imaginative practice; namely, utopia. Utopia is not a literary genre in which one focuses on its realized content. *Utopia* literally means "nowhere" or "no place," a place that has no place, a ghost city, a river with no water, and a prince with no principality. Utopia implies the imaginative project of another kind of society, of another reality, another world. The utopian mode is to the existence of society what invention is to scientific knowledge.[401] The content of utopian themes are as follows: the status of family, consumption of goods, appropriation of things, organization of political life, and the role of religion.[402] In contrast to this function of ideology (viz., its function of social integration), utopia functions as a social subversion. Utopia makes possible what has been considered impossible. It proceeds from fantasy to reality.

---

398 Ricoeur, "Ideology and Utopia as Cultural Imagination," 108.

399 Karl Marx, *The Economic and Philosophic Manuscripts of 1844*, ed. C. J. Arthur (New York: International Publishers, 1964), 64.

400 Ricoeur, *Lectures*, 8.

401 Ricoeur, "Ideology and Utopia as Cultural Imagination," 118.

402 Ricoeur, "Ideology and Utopia as Cultural Imagination."

The function of utopia is that it stands against social integration and, ultimately, against the dominant culture and social submission to the dominant culture. In search for alternative ways of living, the field of the possible is opened beyond that of the actual. It provides imagination a constitutive role without the leap outside.

As already stated, power or the role of authority in a system is a given. This function of utopia, in contrast to ideology as an instrument for legitimizing a given system of authority, is its stand against the excessive demands for legitimacy in relation to the belief held by members of the community. Utopia seeks to unmask the pretension that is inherent in all systems of legitimation. This is why utopia must and does offer alternatives based on an effort to bridge the gap between authority and the victims of that authoritative system. Utopia espouses what results from the fantasy of an alternative society and its topographical figuration, "nowhere."[403] This is why all utopias, at one time or another, offer "other" ways of exercising power in religion, family, education, economic well-being, and politics.

The utopic consideration allows for a radical kind of structural analysis that is a search for the structural causes of poverty and injustice and the responsibility for institutional adherence to destructive value systems.

The problematic of power, however, is that utopia could be interpreted as the establishment of a power that replaces another power of the same caliber whether it be national, ethical, or void of power. The problematic of power in utopia occurs when one examines the actualization of utopia. The utopian spirit must be one that is more than a replacement of another negative power. The concept of utopia must become an experiment whose question is how to execute itself without resorting to the tyranny of power. The experiments testify to the seriousness of the utopian spirit because they demonstrate ways to address the "paradoxes of power."[404] The spectrum can be as diametrically opposed as a more rational or more ethical authority or the complete absence of power, if it is true that power, as such, is ultimately considered radically and inalterably evil.[405]

The next function of utopia corresponds to the distortive function in ideology. Its claim is that the *dream* of utopia is distortion; it is mad and a flight into the unreal. "Just as we are tempted to by the Marxist tradition to interpret ideology in terms of delusion, so we may be inclined to construe the concept of utopia on the basis of its quasipathological expressions."[406] However, the

---

[403] "The notions of conscientization and cultural revolution which are considered to be 'nowhere.'"

[404] Ricoeur, "Ideology and Utopia as Cultural Imagination," 121.

[405] Ricoeur, "Discourse and Action," 19.

[406] Ricoeur, "Discourse and Action," 119.

positive dimension of utopia is even contained in the pathology. The positive is that the "nowhere" develops an unsettling feature. Also, the flight can take the shape of a regressive nostalgia for a lost paradise hidden under the guise of futurism.[407]

As we shall see in the next section of this chapter, the issues that ideology and utopia raise are aspects of the sociocultural imagination that lead us directly into a hermeneutical methodology to express an alternative historical reality.

2.2. METHODOLOGY AND HERMENEUTICS IN THE HISTORICAL FIELD

The imaginative theory, with its metaphorical foundation explicated in the above sections of this chapter, is not only extremely important but also essential for the methodological component of our research. It is the linking of the imaginative theory to the historical field that results in the narrative reconstruction called a hermeneutics of historical consciousness that discloses "hidden," "forgotten," or "repressed" stories. Thus, the imaginative theory of Ricoeur functions in conjunction with hermeneutics to produce a political theory in the historical field, resulting in new understanding derived from hidden, forgotten, and repressed stories that has a power to redirect or transform society. Ultimately, the role of the hermeneutics of historical consciousness is to trace the interplay among the three components of the modern nation-state: politics, economics, and religion.

When preparing a methodology, it is necessary to clarify the presuppositions that underpin it. The hermeneutical presuppositions in this methodology have to do with the selection of data that will include God's oppressed, marginalized, and alienated in a new way.[408] The focus of this

---

[407] Ricoeur, "Discourse and Action," 20.

[408] Merle Miller, *Plain Speaking: An Oral Biography of Harry S. Truman* (New York: Berkley Publishing Corporation, 1973, 1974), 273. In her biography of former president Harry Truman, Merle Miller quotes Truman as saying, "The only thing new in the world is the history we do not know." This statement of Truman is almost a truism for the United States today as it is for the world. It is for this reason that this study attempts to trace the missing pages of history, to uncover the error of the omission of the victims of history.

A pursuit to discover the victims who have dropped between the lines of existing history requires a methodology that is both historical and hermeneutical. Such a pursuit necessitates combining new theories and new data to foster a new understanding of past events. The reference to new theories and new data is similar to the idea of Villela-Petit concerning the *misuse* of history characterized by *ideological prejudices*. Villela-Petit states that the "omissions . . . or *ideological*

methodology is to reinterpret history from the point of view of those who are proscribed. The hermeneutical presuppositions, especially in this kind of reflection on the past, warrant an adequate theoretical framework.

The problem is, how can such a critique of history be written without also falsifying the data? To preclude this falsification of historical data requires the systematic reexamination of sources that can be used in view of a scientific reconstruction of history. It also means selecting particulars from authentic materials, which culminates in a synthesis of those particulars into a "hermeneutics of historical consciousness."[409] Ricoeur's concept of the mimetic spiral becomes the theoretical framework of such a task to critique the past while preserving a sound grasp of the historical data.

Now this theoretical approach constitutes a time/narrative problematic. Time is not structured, which means that it is total fluidity except when characterized by vivid experiences. Narrative is the only way to structure time, the only way for it to lose its vagueness. Narratives are about particular things that are vast and all-encompassing. With narrative, things lose their vastness. Thus, it is through the mimetic redescription that Ricoeur resolves the narrative/time problematic.

Relying on Paul Ricoeur's insight called mimesis or imaginative redescription[410] allows us to survey the issue of temporality and how it affects human experience. The focus on praxis implies that this process is not static, which explains why the temporal dimension is constitutive of mimetic redescription. Therefore, mimetic redescription not only includes the act of imitating and representing the lived experience but it also is a productive, constructive dynamism that involves the temporal (synchronic and diachronic) process from which meaning and understanding is derived.

The question of mimetic redescription warrants balancing the historical knowledge of the past with a search for meaning. In the mimetic process, the narrator of events must weigh the data of the past against hermeneutic insight. The mimetic theory contends that, as the interpreter of events, you use a framework that has two constituent aspects–the historical facts and the exercise of temporality. The historical facts are brought within our reach in that they are brought into connection with a vivid experience of time. Ricoeur's problem now is that the time experience must be dramatized to

---

prejudices" demand the methodological and hermeneutical approach of not only "refiguration" but also "defiguration" (Villela-Petit, "Thinking History," 42).

[409]   David Pellauer uses the concept of "hermeneutics of historical consciousness" to describe the results of the function of the Ricoeurian mimesis or process of the redescription of reality, which will be explained later in this text. David Pellauer, *"Time and Narrative* and Theological Reflection," in *Philosophy Today* 31 (Fall 1987): 262–86, 276.

[410]   For a definition of *mimesis*, turn to page 117.

yield a message. This dramatization, as he states it, is brought about by using procedures of narration.[411]

The theoretical framework entails using the historical event and its trace found in historical documents. But also and most importantly, it involves explicating the emplotment, which is the mediating element between the temporal character of human experience and the narration of that experience. In other words,

> the poet is to provide that which comes [*apo*] from pity and fear through [*dia*] an imitation, clearly this effect must be embodied [*empoieteon*] in [*en*] the events of the plot.[412] (emphasis added)

In expounding the plot as the mediating element between time and narrative, Ricoeur develops a "hermeneutics of historical consciousness," which in the first part of this chapter has been generated by the imagination with metaphor as its foundation. The hermeneutics of historical consciousness is the potential for forming mental images derived from the productive imagination. Hermeneutics at this level means having the ability to create new meaning because of the ability to deviate even beyond the literal sense of a word or an event. For Ricoeur, mimetic redescription provides us with this potential.

Mimetic redescription consists in three moments: mimesis$_1$ or prefiguration, mimesis$_2$ or configuration, and mimesis$_3$ or refiguration.[413] Ricoeur describes the three moments of mimesis as a means through which past events impinge via their creative redescription on the present. These three moments are interrelated. As he states, "*We are following therefore the destiny of a prefigured time that becomes a refigured time through the mediation of a configured time*"[414] (emphasis in original), that is, through the structuring of time that is brought about by emplotment.

What follows is an explication and a description of the interaction among the three stages of mimesis and then a discussion of mimetic redescription and how it relates to the understanding of history.

---

[411] "[T]ime becomes human to the extent that it is articulated through a narrative mode, and narrative attains its full meaning when it becomes a condition of temporal existence" (Ricoeur, *Time and Narrative*, 1:52).

[412] In *Time and Narrative*, Ricoeur cites Aristotle's *Poetics* (53b12–13) to explain the mediation that takes place between time and narrative in the emplotment of an event(s) (Ricoeur, *Time and Narrative*, 1:45, 52–53).

[413] Ricoeur, *Time and Narrative*, 1:53.

[414] Ricoeur, *Time and Narrative*, 1:54.

2.2.1. THE PROCESS OF CREATIVE REDESCRIPTION: THE MIMETIC SPIRAL

2.2.1.1. MIMESIS₁ AND PREFIGURED TIME

In his analysis of language, Ricoeur is particularly interested in the use of metaphor as a means of bringing about *semantic innovation*.[415] Metaphoric language surpasses descriptive language in that it "produces a new semantic pertinence by means of an impertinent attribution."[416]

For example, when we say that nature is a temple, a new pertinence is established between nature and temple. With *semantic innovation*, there is an attribution that resists ordinary language and that points to a process of creative imagination. In a similar vein, Ricoeur wants to lay bare which procedure creates a new semantic pertinence in the narrated field of human action. And here, he sees the importance of the plot, which is comparable to the metaphysical utterance and which "redescribes a reality inaccessible to direct description."[417]

Plot, according to Aristotle, is the mimesis (or dramatic redescription) of an action. This redescription results from a synthetic "grasping together" into one whole and complete story, elements that are scattered in ordinary language; it is also a special structuration of our experience of time.

Now when mimesis is a semantic and unifying redescription of scattered events, it presupposes that these scattered elements lend themselves to such a creative reorganization or eventful configuration. The study of this potentiality for being redescribed is undertaken by Ricoeur on a preliminary level, that of mimesis₁.

Mimesis₁ asserts that the narrative redescription of events in terms of plot is rooted in a narrative preunderstanding that is structural, symbolic, and temporal in nature. These elements of preunderstanding are basically cultural presuppositions.

The structural elements refer to a conceptual network in which the separate material elements involved get their meaning from their purpose in conjunction with other terms of the whole network. For example, actions imply goals, motives, means, success, failure, help, and conflict. Actions entail someone's performance of the action in specific circumstances. The circumstances of action necessitate interaction with others as well as an outcome of the action. All this makes it clear that the dramatically evoked

---

[415] Ricoeur, *Time and Narrative*, 1:x.

[416] Ricoeur, *Time and Narrative*, 1:ix.

[417] Ricoeur, *Time and Narrative*, 1:ix.

action is a human action and is not a natural occurrence, for example, motion in physics.

The symbolic elements relate to the discursive character that is implicit in narrativity. The norms for describing actions are found within the symbolic framework of action. The symbol (i.e., the mediation of actions) makes it possible to narrate actions, for "before being a text, symbolic mediation has a texture."[418] This follows rules that are descriptive and enable understanding and also rules that are prescriptive and give an ethical dimension to actions. The prescriptive rules relate, for example, to manners and customs and are considered corresponding to the rightness or wrongness of the action, giving it its ethical characteristic that signifies that no action is neutral.

The final aspect that is presupposed at the level of preliminary elements that can be used for setting up a plot is the more complex whole of temporal structures. Action in the narrative context implies a temporal order. This is the most important and the most presumed aspect of this effort at narrative. The temporal features are the inductor of the narrative. When we cite Ricoeur's idea of temporal structures, we are at the key to what is basic to the whole issue of time and narrative.

Time has three dimensions: past, present, and future, which all show up in the now, in the mode of memory of the past, in attention to the present, and in expectation of the future. To a certain extent, Ricoeur adopts Augustine's solution that–at a basic level–says that time does not extend itself in space; it is only an extension in the mind (*distentio animi*). Here, Augustine is investigating the temporal structure of action that has a goal (its future) that uses means that are already known (its past) and is realized in the now (its present). The present mind simultaneously expects the future, attends the present, and remembers the past. "Time exists in the mental space stretched between memory of the past and expectation of the future."[419] Ricoeur attempts to translate Augustine's concepts in structural terms of action when he says,

> By saying that there is not a future time, a past time, and a present time, but a threefold present, a present of future things, a present of past things, and a present of present things, Augustine set us on the path of an investigation into the most primitive temporal structure of action. . . . The actual present of doing something bears witness to the

---

[418] Ricoeur, *Time and Narrative*, 1:58.

[419] Steven D. Kepnes, "Review of *Temps et récit* by Paul Ricoeur," in *Religious Studies Review* 12 (July/Oct. 1986): 251.

potential present of the capacity to do something and is constituted as the present of the present.[420]

Ricoeur wants also to go beyond St. Augustine's notion of *distentio animi* as a solution to the problem of time. He, with caution, seeks to incorporate Heidegger's concept of "within-time-ness" in *Being and Time* to focus on time.[421] Ricoeur agrees when Heidegger suggests that it is from the "present" place in the world that one raises the question of meaning. Within-time-ness is "centered on the relation to time as that 'within which' we ordinarily act."[422] "Within-time-ness is defined by a basic characteristic of Care, our being thrown among things, which tends to make our description of temporality dependent on the description of the things about which we care."[423] Ricoeur sees that maybe the solution is to integrate Heidegger's notion of care (*Sorge*) into the time experience and use this as a means to structure the present of present, present of past, and present of future. Linked to care (*Sorge*), linear time is done away with. As Ricoeur says, "The words 'future,' 'past,' and 'present' disappear and time itself figures as the exploded unity of the three temporal extases."[424]

There is a fundamental richness to this basic structure of temporality (to prefigured time respectively) because it is the starting point of narrative reflection on human events (action). The realm of action is a combination of the semantic network of phrases, the symbolic mediation of action, and the temporal structure. However, the point of Ricoeur's insight is that he sees that these structural features are only constituting the stage on which an action or a plot can take place. The recording of structural facts will have little meaning without mimesis$_2$, understood as dealing with the emplotment of events.

2.2.1.2. MIMESIS$_2$ AND CONFIGURED TIME

After the structural features of mimesis or the literary analysis of elements leading to action comes the configuration of a narrative for which emplotment is the paradigm.[425] Configuration mediates between the structural features of action (prefiguration[426]) and the way in which the emplotment of the

---

[420] Kepnes, "Review of *Temps et récit*," 1:60.
[421] Kepnes, "Review of *Temps et récit*." Cf. Martin Heidegger, *Being and Time*, trans. John Macquarrie and Edward Robinson (New York: Harper and Row, 1962), 456–88.
[422] Ricoeur, 1:61.
[423] Ricoeur, 1:62.
[424] Ricoeur, 1:61.
[425] Ricoeur, *Time and Narrative*, 1:64.
[426] Cf. above in the section on mimesis.

story is being received by the reader (refiguration[427]). The mediation by the configurational act must be understood in light of what might be described as an attempt at overcoming a fundamental deficiency; namely, the gap that exists between the creative perception of the interpreter of past events and the past events themselves.[428] After a description of the configurational act itself, we shall explicate how it is at the level of mimesis$_2$ that Ricoeur is able to overcome that fundamental deficiency.

Mimesis$_2$ rests on the "configurational act of 'grasping' together the detailed action or the story's incidents."[429] The author makes use of various artifacts creatively "[to] transform the succession of events into one meaningful whole, point, or theme."[430] On this level, Ricoeur asserts that these events are organized into patterns, making connections so that a traceable story evolves whereby a specific conclusion is induced. With these organized patterns, the assembling together of events differs from the event-by-event or episodic narration in that it confers a dynamic, experiential, and coherent dimension on the narrative.

The events are thus organized into a plot. The act of emplotment provides temporal characteristics of a synthetic nature to the narrative. It incorporates episodic time into the eventful. Emplotment mediates in three ways: (1) it brings together a series of events organized into a discernible whole into a meaningful story; (2) it unites heterogeneous elements such as "agents, goals, circumstances, means, interactions, circumstances, and unexpected results";[431] and (3) finally, it combines and unites both the chronological (episodic) dimension of the narrative, which deals with the various sequences of events, and its configurational dimension, which pulls together the specific actions into a meaningful whole.[432] Temporality is what Ricoeur adds to the concept of plot to provide the basis for understanding and followability of the plot.

Let us first distinguish between the episodic and configurational dimensions of time in the configurational act. On the one hand, the episodic dimension of a narrative is a rectilinear presentation of time in which events follow one another in such a way that they are related in an external way. There is usually no connecting link, neither of ideas nor patterns. The connection

---

[427]   The specifics of refiguration will be explicated below in mimesis$_3$.
[428]   Ricoeur considers Marrou and the French Annales school in "The Eclipse of the Event in French Historiography" (Ricoeur, *Time and Narrative*, 1:96–111). Further discussion of the historical event and the creative perception of the interpreter will be considered below in this chapter on page 154.
[429]   Ricoeur, *Time and Narrative*, 1:66.
[430]   Ricoeur, *Time and Narrative*, 1:67.
[431]   Ricoeur, *Time and Narrative*, 1:65. (Cf. also Ricoeur, *Time and Narrative*, in chapter 2, "Employment," 1:38–45.)
[432]   Ricoeur, *Time and Narrative*, 1:65–66.

is by way of like events, or for the most part, it is simply chronologically determined in an irreversible order of time. "The episodes follow upon one another in accord with the irreversible order of time common to physical and human events."[433]

On the other hand, the temporal features of the configurational dimension of the narrative are quite different from the episodic dimension. It first deals with what we have referred to as a configurational arrangement that transforms the events into a story. On this first level, the act of configuration brings together. This arrangement is carried out by a reflective act, which—comparable to Kant's act of judgment—"grasps things together" so as to extract a configuration from that which has previously been a mere succession of events. Concerning this approach, Ricoeur says,

> The configurational arrangement transforms the succession of events into one meaningful whole which is the correlate of the act of assembling the events together and which makes the story followable.[434]

The second aspect is precisely in the configurational retelling of past events that one imposes a "sense of ending." On the indefinite succession of incidents, the issue is not just to retell the story that is already known. This aspect commands us to see these often well-known events as leading to an end as suggested by the synthetic view through which they are configured.[435]

The third aspect adds another layer to the configurational dimension. It says that the first two aspects have established a new way of experiencing time—made possible by the emplotment as structuration of a narrative. Instead of time flowing from the past to the future, as in episodic time, the order is inverted. Time now flows from it—determined end to the beginning. Time is now reversible. What Ricoeur is dealing with here is his notion of meaning as derived from "sense" and "reference" but in reverse order. In reading the ending in the beginning and the beginning in the ending, we also learn to read time itself backward as the recapitulation of the initial conditions of a course of action in its terminal consequences.[436]

Now the next task in this section is the explication of the two features that assure the process that joins mimesis$_3$ to mimesis$_2$; namely, schematization and traditionality. These two are characteristic of the configurational act, and each is linked to time in a specific way. Each must be considered in terms of

---

[433] Ricoeur, *Time and Narrative*, 1:67.
[434] Ricoeur, *Time and Narrative*.
[435] Ricoeur, *Time and Narrative*.
[436] Ricoeur, *Time and Narrative*, 1:67–68.

their specific function in helping mediate the gap that could exist between the interpreter of the past and the past events themselves.

The schematization that is characteristic of the narrative function is the work of imagination, and more specifically, it is generated by the productive imagination. Here, as already seen, the productive imagination is not a psychological faculty; it is a transcendental (critical) faculty in the Kantian sense and is hence regulatory or rule governed. What this means is that the "categories of understanding are first schematized by the productive imagination."[437] The productive imagination does not produce from nothing; it is also synthetic, meaning—as we have already stated—that it grasps together or connects various already existing categories according to the rules of judgment. In similar fashion, like the productive imagination, emplotment synthesizes the theme of a story and the intuitive presentation of characters, circumstances, and so on from already existing categories called schematism.[438] Therefore, the configurational act of emplotment is based on a schematism created by the narrative function.

Ricoeur writes that schematism has this power because the productive imagination fundamentally has a synthetic function. Moreover, because of productive imagination, this synthesizing or "grasping together" of the configurational act makes the story followable. Thus, schematization in using productive imagination brings something to the plot, making it intelligible. This is where we shall see how tradition, the other feature that assures the continuity of the process of joining refiguration to configuration, becomes important. It is here that, together with tradition, schematization gives expression to refigured reality.

In the schematization process, schematism finds itself within a tradition in the sense of a "living transmission of an innovation always capable of being reactivated by a return to the most creative moments of poetic activity. So understood, traditionality enriches the relationship between plot and time with a new feature."[439] What this means is that schematization always relates to time by means of traditionality or a tradition.

In the schematization process, tradition has two poles: sedimentation and innovation. Sedimentation is almost literally a deposit or a part that is left or separated out. In the Ricoeurian context, sedimentation refers to *sedimented history* or a deposit or part that is separated out or the generally accepted arrangement of what has happened or how it is always explained. Thus, sedimented history is a paradigm.

---

[437] Ricoeur, *Time and Narrative*, 1:68.
[438] Ricoeur, *Time and Narrative*, 1:68.
[439] Ricoeur, *Time and Narrative*, 1:68.

Paradigm is necessary in the process of emplotment in that it keeps the plot in manageable levels. Sedimented history as a paradigm becomes well-known patterns whereby a reality becomes known. Paradigm, seen as a well-known pattern, is like a metaphor that is seen as the real, while what the metaphor really refers to is forgotten. What has happened is that the metaphor has become a paradigm. Therefore, according to Ricoeur, a paradigm or sedimented history is a history whose genesis has been deliberately repressed or forgotten. The paradigm comes out of sedimented history "whose genesis has been covered over."[440]

> As soon as a story is well-known—and this is the case for most traditional or popular narratives, as well as for those national chronicles reporting the founding events of a given community—to follow the story is not so much to enclose its surprises or discoveries within our recognition of the meaning attached to the story, as to apprehend the episodes which are themselves well known as leading to this end.[441]

Sedimented history or the creation of a paradigm happens on the levels of form, genre, and type. First, the paradigm at the formal level of a plot is a schematization of the narrative; and as such, it is of similar typology to sedimentation. According to Ricoeur, this level is called concordant discordance and may be paraphrased as innovative paradigms.

Second, at the level of genre, the paradigm is typified in Greek tragedy. It is both formal and restrictive. Paradigm gets beyond literary genre as suggested by the tragic poem. Finally, at the level of type or individual works, the paradigm—through an underlying causal ordering—establishes a universality or ordering that creates a certain "type" of work. Paradigm is more than just a successive ordering of events and more than the causal connection that orders itself into a type.

Thus, for Ricoeur, the production of these paradigms or sedimented history is born out of the formal principles of form, type, and genre and are a result of the productive imagination, which as we have noted is synthetic and regulatory. As a result, these paradigms are themselves regulatory. Ricoeur states,

> Paradigms furnish the rules for a subsequent experimentation within the narrative field. These rules change under the pressure of new inventions, but they

---

[440] Ricoeur, *Time and Narrative*, 1:68.
[441] Ricoeur, *Time and Narrative*, 1:67.

change slowly and even resist change, in virtue of the very process of sedimentation.[442]

But there is another pole of tradition called innovation. Insofar as every work or narrative is singular in character, then innovation is always present within the wider fabric of the paradigm that controls the form, genre, and type of the narrative. What this means is that paradigm controls the production of "good innovation," and innovation creates the "new" work that may bring about a deviation from the paradigm.

If this deviation is possible, it may occur on all levels of paradigm–form, genre, and type. Deviation of type is constitutive of every individual work. Each work stands apart from every other work. Change in genre is less likely because it is equivalent to a new genre. Deviation in form is more radical. Such a deviation could mean schism and perhaps constitutes the death of narrative itself, but if there is the possibility of deviation on this level that does not result in schism, then it must be written into narrative itself and is a "rule-governed deformation," which "constitutes the axis around which the various changes of paradigm through application are arranged."[443] So it is in innovation in traditionality that we see the possibility of deviation from the plot. This deviation then functions as a counterpoint to sedimentation and emplotment (both of which are of similar typology) and makes a narrative tradition possible. It does this because, as an aspect of tradition, innovation links the plot to time.

Innovation or the new invention, though creative and original, is already contained in the sediment or the paradigm. Innovation results from the labor of imagination, but it is still governed by rules, even when it seeks to distance itself from the tradition, and to deviate from the rule. With innovation, deviation becomes the rule on the three above-mentioned levels: the type, the genre, and the formal principle of concordant discordance. Thus, $mimesis_2$ exists in a process whereby the productive imagination uses sedimented paradigms as a basis for the configurational act–the creative redescription of the plot–and results in a story actualized in its being read. The reading of this newly created story is a new level of mediation between narrative and time that goes beyond $mimesis_2$ but is its complement. It is at this new level that narrative has its full meaning in that it is "restored to the time of action and of suffering."[444] Ricoeur labels this stage $mimesis_3$ or refigured time.

---

[442] Ricoeur, *Time and Narrative*, 1:69.

[443] Ricoeur, *Time and Narrative*.

[444] Ricoeur, *Time and Narrative*, 1:70.

2.2.1.3. MIMESIS$_3$ AND REFIGURED TIME

Mimesis$_3$ is centered on the reception of the configured story on the part of the reader and is called refiguration. It has to do with making present or reproducing for oneself what the emplotment–the creative redescription of the plot–is about. Mimesis$_3$ is the final stage in the resolution of the time/narrative problematic.[445] It is the "application" dimension of the reconstructed emplotment that links time to narrative and vice versa.

The explication of mimesis$_3$ reveals that "narrative has its full meaning when it is restored to the time of action and of suffering" and includes contemporary time.[446]

The explication of mimesis$_3$ and its transition from mimesis$_2$ are "brought about by the act of reading."[447] Ricoeur states, "The act of reading is thus the operator that joins mimêsis$_3$ to mimêsis$_2$. It is the final indicator of the refiguring of the world of action under the sign of the plot."[448] This seems to be more than just the reading of a text–it must also include something like "reading the signs of the time"–impressed by the creative redescription of a plot in the past. At this point, the world of the text and the world of the reader or hearer converge. This level in the narrative process is an interpretive exercise leading to an understanding of the meaning that is conveyed and its application to active history. This is an application of the meaning of the written work to the life of the current reader.

Here, Ricoeur draws on H.-G. Gadamer's idea of the "fusion of horizons" as he discusses the readers' reception of the text with their capacity of receiving it.[449] The *world* of the author or interpreter confronts the *world* of the reader (the addressee of the message). These horizons are to be brought into fusion in and through the process of interpretation. Gadamer suggests that there is a tension between the world of the reader (present) and the world of the author (tradition), which exists as a hermeneutical situation. Each has its own horizon. The reception of the text by the reader actualizes what has been configured. The action is produced by the fusion of the text and the reader into a joint work. In this sense, it is the reader who completes the work. It is the effect of the text on the reader that produces the present or actual meaning of the text.[450]

---

[445] Cf. *supra*, p. 135.
[446] Ricoeur, *Time and Narrative*, 1:70.
[447] Ricoeur, *Time and Narrative*, 1:76.
[448] Ricoeur, *Time and Narrative*, 1:77.
[449] Ricoeur, *Time and Narrative*, 1:77.
[450] Ricoeur, *Time and Narrative*, 1:77.

2.2.1.4. THE MIMETIC SPIRAL OR THE QUESTION OF REDUNDANCY

At this point, what about the objection that questions whether the spiral of mimesis—namely, the movement from prefiguration (mimesis$_1$) to creative redescription or emplotment (mimesis$_2$) to refigured time (mimesis$_3$) and then back again to prefiguration (mimesis$_1$)—does not constitute a vicious circle? The intersection of the three stages of mimesis does suggest a circularity. The reason is that mimesis$_2$—the creative redescription of the plot—has bridged the gap among time, experience, and narrative. Ricoeur continues, "[T]he end point seems to lead back to the starting point, or worse, the end point seems anticipated in the starting point."[451]

On the contrary, mimesis$_3$ is not simply the final link in a vicious circle, though it seems that it only leads back, in a circular fashion, to mimesis]. If the case were only a matter of the intersection between points, the "hermeneutical circle of mimesis and temporality would resolve into the vicious circle of *mimêsis alone*"[452] (emphasis added).

Although a type of circularity definitely does exist in mimesis, Ricoeur raises objection to the characterization of the mimetic spiral as being a vicious circularity.[453] He describes the linking together of the three stages as an "endless spiral that passes the same point a number of times, but at different altitudes."[454] Thus, mimesis in the Ricoeurian sense refuses to become a vicious circularity that is either a "violence of interpretation" or a "redundancy of interpretation."[455]

Ricoeur first raises an objection to the claim that his mimetic spiral ends up in a vicious circularity of violence of interpretation. He writes, "[N]arrative puts consonance where there was only dissonance. . . . [It] gives form to what is unformed."[456] Narrative often confronts the vastness of the unformed and gives it order or consonance. Ricoeur asserts that this formation of the unformed by the narrative is "suspected of treachery" because it offers consolation when, "at best, it furnishes the *as if* proper to any fiction we know to be just fiction, a literary artifice. This is how it consoles us in the face of death."[457] At this juncture, the options are either to be lured into accepting the consonance of the paradigms or to be caught up in the dissonance of the "absolutely

---

[451] Ricoeur, *Time and Narrative*, 1:71–72.

[452] Ricoeur, *Time and Narrative*, 1:72.

[453] For further study of Ricoeur's objections to the "violence of interpretation," see *Time and Narrative*, 1:72–73.

[454] Ricoeur, *Time and Narrative*, 1:72.

[455] Ricoeur, *Time and Narrative*.

[456] Ricoeur, *Time and Narrative*.

[457] Ricoeur, *Time and Narrative*.

unformed."[458] When one is no longer misled by the peace offered by the narrative or paradigm and there is a refusal to hold to the lie perpetrated by the narrative, one becomes aware of the violence. The violence is a result of an experience of the unformed (temporal dissonance) that prompts a short-lived drive for "radical intellectual honesty."

There is, however, an irresistible desire to return to some sort of order created by the narrative (consonance). At this point, the narrative consonance serves as a kind of opium of the masses forcing itself on the temporal dissonance. The insistence that the narrative consonance is a solution to the paradox is what Ricoeur calls the violence of interpretation.[459]

Ricoeur then raises an objection to a vicious circularity of redundancy of interpretation. If such a redundancy were to exist, it would be if $mimesis_1$ found its meaning only as an effect of $mimesis_3$ and if it would be created by $mimesis_3$. If redundancy exists between $mimesis_3$ and $mimesis_1$, then the function of $mimesis_2$ would be to restore in $mimesis_3$ what it receives from $mimesis_1$.[460] But $mimesis_2$ does not function in this manner; hence, redundancy does not occur. As one can see, redundancy is the type of circularity that feeds on itself; however, mimetic circularity does not feed on itself.

The strongest argument against redundancy, however, is rooted in an analysis of $mimesis_1$. The objection to redundancy in $mimesis_1$, specifically, manifests itself in the situation of the "(as yet) untold" stories. The "(as yet) untold" story suggests that action or experience itself is constitutive of the narrative and that $mimesis_1$ is not just an effect of $mimesis_3$. Let us examine the augmentative strength rendered by the "(as yet) untold" story.

Every experience has "an inchoate narrativity that does not precede from projecting literature on life but that constitutes a genuine demand for narrative" or a "prenarrative quality."[461] In other words, "action or experience is already in quest of narrative."[462] Again, this echoes the notion of cultural imaginative practices, especially the notion of the integrative dimension of imagination. The prenarrative quality of life states that experience is already mediated by the symbolic system called narrative almost imperceptibly.[463] The prenarrative quality of life is a quest for personal identity.

These statements about the prenarrative quality of experience, likewise, imply "that a life story proceeds from untold and repressed stories which

---

[458]   Ricoeur, *Time and Narrative*.

[459]   Ricoeur, *Time and Narrative*, 1:72.

[460]   Ricoeur, *Time and Narrative*, 1:74.

[461]   Ricoeur, *Time and Narrative*.

[462]   Ricoeur, *Time and Narrative*.

[463]   Ricoeur, *Time and Narrative*.

demand to be told."[464] In each story, there is potential for fulfilling the quest of each personal pursuit for completeness or personal identity. The discovery of personal identity is fulfilled through the creative narration of one's life story. Untold, repressed new stories evolve during this quest for personal identity. In this situation, the quest for personal identity finds completion only in the surfacing of the "(as yet) untold" stories within refigured time of the individual's life experiences and thus in the surfacing of new stories.[465]

The untold story "serve(s) as a critical example for every emphasis on the artificial character of the art of narrating."[466] Thus, the "(as yet) untold" story is evidence of an endless mimetic spiral of new narratives and not of redundancy. Ricoeur argues, "The manifest circularity of every analysis of narrative . . . is not a lifeless tautology" as long as there is the continuing effort to give a temporal dimension to one's narrative and a narrative dimension to one's time experience. "The hermeneutical circle of narrative and time never stops being reborn from the circle that the stages of mimesis form."[467] Interpretation of experience in time and that which allows that experience to have narrative structure is never lifeless because it is born out of the human historical quest for personal identity.

The untold stories or "missing pages" of history refer to those experiences of the oppressed that have been different from those of the dominant class and have not been a part of history. Since we have no way of having access to life experience except through stories that are told, the prenarrative–the "(as yet) untold story"–must be given expression in the spiral of mimesis.[468] Ricoeur states this in his discussion on the question of redundancy in the spiral of mimesis:

> We tell stories because in the last analysis human lives
> need and merit being narrated. This remark takes on its full
> force when we refer to the necessity to save the history of the
> defeated and the lost. The whole history of suffering cries out
> for vengeance and calls for narrative.[469]

We can see that the mimetic spiral is seminal to the political theory of Paul Ricoeur. However, the unique elements of the latter are not feasible in presuming that the mimetic spiral is sufficient as a method. Thus, it becomes

---

[464] Ricoeur, *Time and Narrative.*
[465] Ricoeur, *Time and Narrative.*
[466] Ricoeur, *Time and Narrative*, 1:75
[467] Ricoeur, *Time and Narrative*, 1:76
[468] Ricoeur, *Time and Narrative*, 1:75–76.
[469] Ricoeur, *Time and Narrative*, 1:75.

necessary to specify some of the elements used in applying the mimetic spiral to the historical field.

2.2.1.5. APPLICATION OF THE MIMETIC SPIRAL TO THE HISTORICAL FIELD

The mimetic spiral and its potential as a method for retrieving the past function as a historical principle. As such, it surpasses the classical notion of history used by historiographers. Indeed, the use of the mimetic spiral warrants exploring the evolution of historical understanding because it investigates some of the issues related to a general understanding of the meaning of history as a science and demonstrates that the mimetic spiral is part of the evolving notion of history, an aspect that makes it move "beyond classical history."

The events of human lives are the data of history. The question once more arises about the trustability or falsity of fictionalizing historical data. Marrou's qualified definition of *history* opposes *popularly accepted fabricated data*, which are data that are unfaithful to the historical trace and whose goal is often to legitimize the "interests" of the powerful. Here, Marrou says that "History is the very opposite of anything that is a false description of the past, or one that is distorted and untrue to the facts. It is unlike conceptions of utopia or imaginary history. It differs from myth, popular traditions and the pedagogical legends of a past that is depicted in 'patriotic' imagery, which in their pride great modern nations inculcate in the minds of their future citizens as early as the primary grades of the elementary school."[470] Fabricated data undermine as they seek to nullify the vital memory of the proscribed, the unelect.[471] This implies no real ethical concern for the future. Marrou feels this patriotic imagery is false, but he himself has no solutions for a mimetic spiral that includes a future–for an ethical reception of paradigms.

In doing history, only that which can be documented is considered authentic. Documents are the source of the trace, and through them, the narrator of the past must attempt to discover the "missing pages," the untold

---

[470] Henri-Irénée Marrou, *The Meaning of History*, trans. Robert J. Olsen, orig. *De la connaissance historique* (Montreal: Palm Publishers, 1966; Paris: Editions du Seuil, 1959), 33–34.

[471] This reference to memory and the proscribed is about the power acquired by the victims of the capitalist society as they remember the truth about how they have derived their oppressed status. They remember how their forebearers have suffered so that things could be better; thereby, they are inspired to commit themselves to the same struggle so that their ancestors have not died in vain and so that the hopes and values of the ancestors will be remembered and nurtured in their present situation. This memory is transformative and serves as a corrective for the generalized dehumanization of the poor.

stories. There are "missing pages," for example, from the standpoint of the victims of the rise of the Atlantic world during the sixteenth and seventeenth centuries. Dominant individualistic culture has not documented the history of the victims of the conquistadores over the natives.[472] Furthermore, the dominant culture has had a preeminent role in interpreting historical data.

> History has been written from the viewpoint of the dominating sectors… The perspective of history's vanquished is something else again. But history's winners have sought to wipe out their victims' memory of the struggles, so as to be able to snatch from them one of their sources of energy and will in history.[473]

Hence, one of the goals of the historian is to absent oneself methodologically from what can be called an "elitist" view of history.

We see that the latter way of narrating the past does configure facts; however, this configuration brackets vast amounts of data and threatens to leave out important aspects. It tends to take its lead from a reading that supports the interests of existing dominance that creates a situation whereby the victors obliterate the victims. This is a violation of true "indebtedness to the past."[474]

The fictionalization of history or the falsification of the historical past constitutes a problem, particularly for the victims of a particular era. Nevertheless, it is important to clarify Ricoeur's thoughts on mimesis or creative redescription as applying to both fictional genre and historical narrative. Thus, a distinction concerning mimesis must be made between both.

In *Time and Narrative*, narrative discourse is divided into two classes based on the two distinct senses of the term *fiction*.[475] *Fiction* is antonymous

---

[472] Though capitalism as such did not exist during the sixteenth and seventeenth centuries, the rise of industrialism with both the philosophy and the politics that was to be its foundation was already in full swing during this period.

[473] Gutiérrez, *The Power of the Poor in History*, 20–21, 206.

[474] Paul Ricoeur, *The Reality of the Historical Past (The Aquinas Lecture)* (Milwaukee: Marquette University Press, 1984), 2.

[475] From the very beginning when he was constructing his theory of narrative discourse (1977), Ricoeur made a distinction between the "true" narrative of historians and "fictional" narratives of storytellers. At this early stage of development, Ricoeur specified the distinction between these two different but interwoven narrative types at the level of sense and reference. At the level of sense, both fiction and history shared a *common narrative structure*. Whereas at the level of reference, they did not allude to the same reality. Paul Ricoeur, "The Narrative

to the historical narrative's claims of constituting a "true" narrative.[476] History stands opposed to fiction not because of its narrative structure but because of the "problems of reference or of truth," whereby it is characterized.[477] It is important to say that truth claims are decisive for discerning between creative historiography and fiction. The differences between history and fiction exist at the referential level. Ricoeur states that there is "undeniable asymmetry between the referential modes of historical and fictional narrative."[478] This asymmetry exists because, unlike fiction, history refers to empirical reality, events that have actually occurred. The referential mode of the historical narrative, through traces, is rooted in a real past. These past events, although determined through traces or historical documents of the past, have taken place.

> The past event, however absent it may be from the present perception, nonetheless governs the historical intentionality, conferring upon it a realistic note that literature will never equal, even if it makes a claim to be "realistic."[479]

The term *realistic* or *real* constitutes the difference between history and fiction. History relies on documents to reconstruct the past. It is through the use of documents and "by means of documentary proof, the historian is constrained by *what once was*" (emphasis in original).[480]

Fiction also is synonymous with narrative configuration that expresses the whole realm of the *as if.* Both fiction and history share this *common narrative structure.* Ricoeur continues,

> [T]he reference through traces borrows from the metaphorical reference common to every poetic work, inasmuch as the past can only be reconstructed by the imagination, and also what it adds to it, inasmuch as it is polarized by past reality. Conversely, . . . fictional narrative borrow[s] a part of its referential dynamics from this reference through traces.[481]

Function," *Semeia* 13 (1978): 177–202, 177; orig. given in slightly different form as the Leroy E. Loemker Lecture in Philosophy, Emory University, November 18, 1977.

[476] Ricoeur, *Time and Narrative*, 1:64.
[477] Ricoeur, *Time and Narrative*, 2:3.
[478] Ricoeur, *Time and Narrative*, 1:82.
[479] Ricoeur, *Time and Narrative*, 1:82.
[480] Ricoeur, *Historical Past*, 3.
[481] Ricoeur, *Time and Narrative*, 1:82, 2:3.

Though both history and fiction undergo distinguishing characteristics, they are the same at the level of emplotment because they borrow from each other. The word *fiction* is used, as Ricoeur writes,

> for designating the configuration of a narrative for which emplotment is the paradigm, without regard for the differences that concern the truth claims of the two classes of narrative.[482]

Ricoeur refers to the reciprocity in the borrowing of fictional and historical narratives, one from the other, as "the problem of interweaving." This interweaving of the two takes place through the "temporality of human action." It is "human time" that both history and literary fiction seek to refigure by the interweaving of their referential modes."[483]

Furthermore, the world—opened up by reference—does not so much entail "truthful" living as it does "expressive" living. Hence, "narrated time" becomes refigured time; and the plot, which creates a synthesis of "real" and "actual" experiences, becomes significant as a hermeneutical principle.

The issue of "untold stories" returns at this point as an application of what Ricoeur writes about as the referential mode of creative historiography. As seen in the argument against redundancy, Ricoeur uses the notion of "untold stories" as an objection to mimesis as vicious circularity. The application of "untold stories" at this juncture is disclosed at the level of preunderstanding. It becomes evident that the untold and repressed stories are the paradigm for the suffering from whose narrative expression of a life story proceeds toward personal identity. Ricoeur describes this process as an actual quest for identity.

The quest for identity exists at the prenarrative level and is a result of refigured or narrated time. With this notion of refigured time, Ricoeur makes an effort to bridge history and fiction using his theory of time and narrative in a dialectical sense. He says that the "poetics of narrativity responds and corresponds to the aporetics of temporality."[484]

Upon accepting the role of imagination as the hermeneutical foundation for a political methodology whereby one can give a new reading on history, the task in this last section has been to demonstrate how it functions in the historical field. We have called it the process of creative redescribing. What has been essential is to make clear why it is we can be selective of historical data in an effort to include God's oppressed, marginalized, and alienated in a new way. We have focused on a methodology which allows the reinterpretation

---

[482] Ricoeur, *Time and Narrative*, 1:64.

[483] Ricoeur, *Time and Narrative*, 1:82.

[484] Ricoeur, *Time and Narrative*, 1:84.

of history from the point of view of those who are proscribed warrant this kind of theoretical framework. As Ricoeur writes in the text "Imagination in Discourse and in Action," we have developed this methodology so that we might continue to "reanimate" the experiences not only of the rise of modernity but also of the Maryland colony in chapter 3, the possibility of "awakening dormant memories."[485]

Now let us look at the various notions of historical understanding. Getting beyond the classical notion of history, as dictated by the Ricoeurian theory of mimesis with its configurational act, is the topic of the next section of this chapter.

2.3. MIMESIS AND HISTORIOGRAPHY

Mimesis or creative redescription is the distinguishing characteristic between narrated history and what Ricoeur calls the "narrative character of history." The mimetic spiral, created by Ricoeur out of the metaphorical power of the imagination, is not just an exercise in theory.[486] The power of the mimetic spiral lies in its confrontation with the temporal order, refiguring it by the configurational act. Thus, mimesis by its very meaning is at the basis of history. Mimesis gives history its narrative character.

The world of human action, synonymous with intentionality of historical thought, always implies temporality. Ricoeur inserts history into life and into action with the help of a time concept that is dramatized through a plot. Historical reconstruction then becomes a "second-order reflection" because it takes place within a framework in which historical time and the time of action or narrative time are inseparable.[487]

Ricoeur states that history is of necessity connected to narrative understanding and synonymous with a basic competence for following a story.[488] With the mimetic process, Ricoeur stays clear of the methodologies of historical sciences as such while maintaining the fundamental character of the science of history.

In general, historical understanding as a science has evolved since the late eighteenth and nineteenth centuries. With its emergence as narrative interpretation along with Ricoeur's notion of creative redescription, it can be

---

[485] Ricoeur, "Imagination in Discourse and in Action," 8.
[486] Remember that mimesis is an excursus within the more comprehensive philosophical project of Ricoeur, viz., the *poetics of will*; cf. footnote no. 4, 48, pp. 104, 117.
[487] Ricoeur, *Time and Narrative*, 1:91–92.
[488] Ricoeur, *Time and Narrative*, 1:91.

said that history has evolved beyond a classical understanding.[489] Viewed in this way, history as a science must not only focus on the accurate recording of facts but there must also be an interpretation of those facts. Let us turn to a study of the historiography and the École des Annales as a way of clarifying our concern for events and facts in the problem of historical understanding.

2.3.1. HISTORIOGRAPHY AND THE ÉCOLE DES ANNALES

According to Paul Ricoeur, the principal problem in attempting to understand the events of the past is the "temporal distance." It is in his analysis of the contribution of French historiography to the theory of history, and particularly, it is his study of the École des Annales that Ricoeur finds new insight into the problem of "temporal distance." Their analyses support Ricoeur's theory that a narrative methodology combined with temporality is the most creative way to understand past events.

Contemporary critique of the narrative character of history has given rise to two schools of thought: the École des Annales and the neopositivists. They stand at opposite poles from each other but come together in their "denial of the philosophy of history" as well as in their "denial of the narrative character of history."[490] Neither sees how the narrative character can be a viable approach to history. The École des Annales mistrusts the philosophy of history, while the neopositivists insist that history be explained as an exact science.[491] The École des Annales's "eclipse of narrative proceeds from a displacement of the object of history which is no longer the active individual but the total social fact."[492] Neopositivists' "eclipse of narrative comes out of the epistemological break between historical explanation and our narrative understanding."[493]

---

[489] Karel Bloclex, "Introduction to Church History" (unpublished lecture notes, Katholieke Universiteit Leuven, May 1979), 1–18; Marrou, *The Meaning of History*, 9–28; J. Van Bavel, "Christology" (unpublished lecture notes, Katholieke Universiteit Leuven, 1979), 3–4; Patrick Gardiner, "Speculative Systems of History," in *The Encyclopedia of Philosophy*, vol. 7, complete and 7:518–23; H. P. Rickman, "Dilthey, Wilhelm," in *The Encyclopedia of Philosophy*, 2:403–7; W. H. Dray, "Philosophy of History," in *The Encyclopedia of Philosophy*, 6:247–54; Alan Donagan, "Collingwood, Robin George," in *The Encyclopedia of Philosophy*, 2:140–44.

[490] Ibid., 1:95.

[491] For more about the history of philosophy and how such philosophy eclipses understanding, see "The Eclipse of Understanding: The Covering Law Model in Analytical Philosophy," in Ricoeur, *Time and Narrative*, 1:111–20.

[492] Ricoeur, *Time and Narrative*, 1:96.

[493] Ricoeur, *Time and Narrative*.

The principal issue of both schools is temporal distance. They distrust the "temporal distance" that exists between *l'histoire événementielle* and the perception of its interpreter. In 1984, the Aquinas Lecture at Marquette University and, in 1985, Ricoeur have addressed this question of the temporal distance between the event and the interpreter directly by dealing with what he has called the "reality" of the historical past.[494]

In general, *l'histoire événementielle* means that which has actually happened in the past. Accordingly, it has two components, which Ricoeur calls the "pastness" of the event and the event done by a "human agent." The reconstruction of what has actually happened in the past confronts us with a communication problem due to the elapse of time that makes the "pastness" appear as "otherness." The event happens only once. It could have been done differently, but a gap exists between the event and its constructed model.[495]

Ricoeur appropriates the insight of several others to discuss his method for dealing with the problem of distance in the rewriting of history. Let us explore the applicability of these approaches by examining the significance these thinkers attach to the events in history and to the historical time span that separates us from them. This will permit us to see Ricoeur's reflection on the various aspects of the epistemology of history that are espoused by scholars like R. G. Collingwood, H.-I. Marrou, Marc Bloch, Lucien Febvre, and Fernand Braudel, authors of the École des Annales.[496]

A. R. G. COLLINGWOOD

As already stated, Ricoeur holds that "temporal distance" is the principal issue when dealing with the past. R. G. Collingwood's answer to the problem of historical distance was a method he called "reenactment."[497]

So for Collingwood, "reenactment" is a "de-distanciation or an identification with what once was."[498] Identification is a reconstruction of past events based on the reader being rendered contemporary with those past events. Identification is achieved in the three following ways: finding documentary evidence that is a trace of the past, rethinking what was once thought before, and possessing the events of past activity.[499]

---

[494]   Cf. Ricoeur, *Historical Past*; Ricoeur, *Time and Narrative*, 3:144–48.

[495]   Ricoeur, *Time and Narrative*, 1:96–97.

[496]   Villela-Petit, "Thinking History," 34–35; Ricoeur, *Time and Narrative*, 1:96–111; 1:208–17.

[497]   R. G. Collingwood, *The Idea of History* (New York: Oxford University Press, 1956), 205–324.

[498]   Ricoeur, *Time and Narrative*, 3:144.

[499]   Collingwood, *The Idea of History*, 10, 213–15, 246.

Ricoeur goes on to demonstrate that Collingwood's method does not heal the problems associated with temporal distance. He says that reenactment does not bridge the distance gap because reenactment is basically an extension of the historian's perception. Ricoeur says that the perceived world is other than the perceiver, an "otherness" that cannot be reduced to something atemporal; "reenactment," because of the changes and development that in the meantime has occurred, cannot bridge the temporal distance. Historians have to acknowledge that they do not really know the past but only their own thoughts about the past.[500] The past remains in the past, and research into the past that remains in the past is incomplete because the past must be dialectically related to the present tendency toward a not yet known future and its unexpected perspectives.[501] The dialectics suggest the paradigmatic character of the past emplotment for the present and its creative reading of history.

To further demonstrate the inadequacy of reenactment as an approach to understanding history, Ricoeur appropriates Marrou's criticism of Collingwood. Marrou states that "reactualizing," "reviving" the past as Collingwood desires to do, is impossible. Ricoeur continues,

> Marrou holds the reactualization of the past to be impossible for two reasons: first, the past can only be postulated; then, even if the past were accessible to us it would not be an object of knowledge because when it was present this past was, like our own present, confused, multifarious, unintelligible.[502]

In both instances, Ricoeur stands strongly against Collingwood's notion of the reenactment of the past.

B. H.-I. MARROU

Henri-Irénée Marrou, in deriving a definition of *history*, states that history is a *science* that deals with "*knowledge* of the human past"[503] (emphasis added). Of significance is the status of Marrou's idea of "knowledge."

---

[500] Ricoeur, *Time and Narrative*, 3:146–48; also, Ricoeur, *Historical Past*, 14–17.

[501] Ricoeur, *Historical Past*, 36. Here, Ricoeur places the past dialectically into the categories of "the same," "the other," and "the analogue" because, as he says, he wants to keep the narrator dependent on the memory of the past.

[502] Ricoeur, *The Contribution of French Historiography to the Theory of History*, The Zaharoff Lecture for 1978–9 (Oxford: Clarendon Press, 1980), 16–17.

[503] Marrou, *The Meaning of History*, 29; Ricoeur, *Contribution*, 9.

"Understanding" is implicit in Marrou's use of the word *knowledge*. The issue of understanding the past is, for Marrou, no different from "the understanding" of others in the present, except that it may be a document or a text. In doing history, one restructures the past events using documents. Hence, "historical understanding is '"not a science properly speaking, but only a knowledge by faith.'"[504]

> Historical knowledge, resting on the notion of testimony, is but a mediated experience of the real through a third party (the document) and is therefore not capable of demonstration, is not properly speaking a science but only knowledge by faith.[505]

So what the historian grasps (the document) is based on testimony that his reconstruction of the past boils down to an act of force. Marrou goes on to say, "We know of the past *what we believe to be true* on the basis of what we have understood, of what the documents have preserved"[506] (emphasis in original).

Research is the means of recovering such documents, and if "knowledge" implies the research whereby one derives data from these documents, then "knowledge" of the human past will imply not only the results but also the means for attaining the goal itself. Consequently, *knowledge* in Marrou's definition implies the authentication and explication of data that can be substantiated.

Consequently, one gets a clearer understanding of what Marrou means by *knowledge* in his definition of *history*. Reconstructing the past rightly depends on the text, that is, the available documents that are the trace on which a historian is indebted. But even then, history stands between a positivistic science and a fictional narrative because the trace of the past found in available documents is only the "effect and sign" from which you can read a meaning. Technically, the trace that has been left by the past is that which takes the place of–and represents–the past. Paul Ricoeur says that the historian owes a "debt of gratitude" to that trace of the past. Ricoeur explains that anyone who does historical research must become devoted to that trace because

> [i]t is left by the past, it stands for the past, it "represents" the past, not in the sense that the past would appear itself in the mind (Vorstellung) but in the sense that the trace takes

---

[504]   Ricoeur, *Time and Narrative*, 1:98. Ricoeur also cites Marrou's *The Meaning of History* (152).

[505]   Marrou, *The Meaning of History*, 137.

[506]   Marrou, *The Meaning of History*, 128.

[the] place of (Vertretung) the past, [which is] absent from historical discourse.[507]

The significance of the concept, "knowledge," in his definition of *history* is the rationale for choosing Marrou's definition of *history*. On the one hand, the definition is significant because it implies less than factual knowledge or its claims. It relates to documental traces and tries to reconstruct facts from them, facts almost in a positivistic sense. On the other hand, Marrou's idea of knowledge is based on understanding, which is the soul of his method. It fends against the positivistic idea because, for Marrou, understanding is inclusive. It includes the historian who is also caught up in an "existential" sense. Regarding this aspect of Marrou's method, Ricoeur adds that it includes "the interests the historian takes in the subject he has chosen and the questions [he] puts to his documents."[508] This is basically what protects the historian against being positivistic in the retelling of the past. Ricoeur is convinced that historical events come out of the past and that historians, as interpreters of these events, are influenced by their present concerns. More in particular, he maintains, "The initiative in history does not belong to the document, but to the question posed by the historian."[509]

Positivistic history is an event-by-event rendering of the past as past, which is simply a recalling of the past without any hermeneutic linking of the past to the present with a view to learning something about the future. Marrou, in his method of history, repulses the positivistic history. An epistemology of positivistic history has a one-sided approach to the heuristic and removes existential time from the human elements that give them meaning. This is not what we see in Marrou. Time considerations are present in the positivistic understanding–but only in the mode of succession of facts as if they were a succession of natural phenomena. It is the above-mentioned relationship between time and narrative that fulfills Ricoeur's quest for meaning. Therefore, Ricoeur's quest is in line with what Marrou refers to as "knowledge."

Marrou's insight on history, even if only to a lesser extent, incorporates the three dimensions of time–past, present and future–and it can be described as "inclusive." This definition dovetails into what Paul Ricoeur says about the interrelatedness of the past and the present, mediating the future. Marrou insists on a study of data not only as a past event but also as data that ought to be interpreted to confer a message to questions addressed to the past from the present. In other words, we can only look at that past event in terms of the present conjunctives. For history pertains to more than just an investigation of

---

[507] Ricoeur, *Historical Past*, 2.
[508] Ricoeur, *Contribution*, 15.
[509] Ricoeur, *Time and Narrative*, 1:99.

the past and is more than just narration of the past as past. This connection of the past through the lens of the present–which addresses questions of the past–is the basis for Marrou's methodology. The question of future-oriented time consciousness, however, is absent in Marrou.

Thus, Marrou is important for two reasons. First, he offers an encompassing definition of *history* as a form of knowledge through which there is a link between "the lived experience of people of other times and today's historian."[510] According to Marrou, history is the knowledge that binds the study of what has really happened to the present-day narrating of those events by the historian. The historian must interpret the trace that represents the past. Ricoeur has appreciated and been influenced by Marrou's insight on the "connection between understanding another person and knowing the human past." Second, this definition opens up the potential for a more dynamic view of history, one like Ricoeur's, which is philosophically based in a hermeneutics of meaning (mimesis). Ricoeur's focus on a hermeneutics of meaning goes beyond Marrou's definition of *history* by focusing on the ethical concern and responsibility for the future. Hence, Ricoeur's interest is in the past but only as a (flexible) paradigm.[511]

C. MARC BLOCH AND LUCIEN FEBVRE

Marc Bloch and Lucien Febvre founded *Annales d'histoire économique et sociale* in 1929, a venture that by 1945 became known as *Annales: économies, sociétés, civilisations*. The Bloch and Febvre definition of and approach to *history* served as what is to become an intermediary position between Henri-Irénée Marrou and Fernand Braudel.[512] Bloch focuses on the documented traces as testimonies that one has to decipher. One of the criteria in assessing the testimonies is to debunk the testimonies given by "privileged" witnesses with the help of testimonies that look rather accidental and that are to be found among other social classes and professions. His focus is thus the critique of testimonies from the background of psychosociology.[513]

Febvre opposes the notion of an impersonal submission of the historian to documents discussed by Marrou. Febvre states, "There is no history; there are

---

[510] Ricoeur, *Time and Narrative*.
[511] Ricoeur, *Time and Narrative*, 1:96.
[512] Marc Bloch, Lucien Febvre, and the contribution of the École des Annales to an understanding of history–especially the elements used in their facing up to the problem of the event, the longtime span, and the historian's relationship to both–serve as the point of transition between Henri-Irénée Marrou and Fernand Braudel.
[513] Ricoeur, *Time and Narrative*, 1:99–101.

only historians. . . . [The historian] finds the work already done for him in the documents."[514] This is very critical if one takes into account Bloch's critique of testimonies (traces). Ricoeur comments that, for Febvre, the work of the historian is mostly one of "analyzing and recombining."[515] In emphasizing this point further, Bloch cites Simiand's ideas about history. Simiand says that "if history is knowledge of the tracks left by all the activities of men of the past, then knowledge of the past is continuously transformed by the interpretation of these tracks."[516]

In their effort to bridge the gap created by the problem of the "otherness" of passed time, these two thinkers of the École des Annales make their greatest contribution; they reject the specific study of the chronological event and of the individual as the end point in historical analysis.[517] That form of history they characterize as "political [event] or diplomatic [battle] history."[518] Ricoeur describes the alternative to this form of history as "a history of the total human phenomenon, with, nevertheless, heavy stress on economic and social conditions." He continues, "[T]he majority of the works coming out of the French historical school are concerned with social history in which groups, categories, classes, town and country, bourgeois, artisans, peasants, and workers become the *collective heroes* of history."[519]

The successor of Lucien Febvre as the head of the Sixth Section at the École Pratique des Hautes Études was Fernand Braudel with his contribution called "geohistory." According to Ricoeur, Braudel's work will even more directly contribute to the breakdown of episodic history with its emphasis on individuals and battle histories.[520]

D. FERNAND BRAUDEL

Fernand Braudel has provided us with the manifesto of the École des Annales of historiography in his monumental work called *La Méditerranée et le monde méditerranéen au temps de Philippe II* (1949). In this work, Braudel solidifies the position of the École des Annales regarding events and individuals and the historians' perspective on what has happened. In so doing, Braudel wins Paul Ricoeur as a follower. Ricoeur appropriates Braudel's approach to history with specific corrections he makes to correspond with his own pursuit.

---

514 Lucien Febvre, *Introduction aux etudes historiques*, 253.
515 Ricoeur, *Contribution*, 9.
516 Ricoeur, *Contribution*.
517 Ricoeur, *Contribution*.
518 Ricoeur, *Contribution*.
519 Ricoeur, *Contribution*, 10.
520 Ricoeur, *Contribution*.

Like previous members of the École des Annales, Braudel is primarily engaged in a criticism of narrative history by way of a criticism of political history. Their complaint against an epic reconstruction of history is that it either consists in an interpretation that they categorize not as history but as philosophy of history or it presents things just as they are related in the sources (positivistic). According to Braudel, narrative history is not an objective method but itself a philosophy of history. His desire, according to Ricoeur, is for "a history of the total human phenomenon with strong emphasis on economic and social conditions."[521] Also, like the members of French historiography, Braudel rejects the positivistic tradition of historical studies.[522]

Braudel rejects the primacy of the individual and the event history. Unlike Ricoeur's more speculative approach that consists in a discourse on action or time, Braudel's rejection comes as a result of his efforts to go beyond the analysis of political history that links the events to the great achievements of an individual (a king, an emperor). He defines *event history* as merely the first stage of history that we must get beyond to see and tackle the various social realities.[523] Ricoeur cites an insight of Paul Lacombe, also shared by François Simiand and Henri Berr–three of Braudel's forebears–that states that the "'history of battles' and the 'history of events' go hand and hand."[524]

The contributions to historical methodology by the École des Annales are centered on their devotion to the study of social and economic history. In social and economic history groups, social categories and classes, and cities and country, the bourgeois, artisans, peasants, and workers become the collective heroes of history. Braudel himself comes up with what he calls the three levels of history "only as a means of exposition."[525] They are geohistory, social history, and individual or event history. As Braudel says in the preface of *La Méditerranée*,

> [Geohistory] exists almost out of time and tells the story of man's contact with the inanimate . . . [Social history] is the history of gentle rhythms, of groups and groupings . . . deep running currents . . . looking successively at economies and states, societies and civilizations . . . [Event history] is

---

[521] Ricoeur, *Time and Narrative*, 1:102–3.

[522] Ricoeur, *Time and Narrative*, 1:102.

[523] Fernand Braudel, *On History*, trans. Sarah Matthews (Chicago: University of Chicago Press, 1980), 8, 11.

[524] Ricoeur, *Time and Narrative*, 1:102. Cf. Paul Lacombe, *De l'histoire considérée comme une science* (Paris: Hachette, 1894); François Simiand, "Méthode historique et science sociale," *Revue de synthèse historique* 6 (1903): 1–22, 129–57; and Henri Berr, *L'histoire traditionelle et la synthèse historique* (Paris: Alcan, 1921).

[525] Braudel, 4.

traditional history . . . a surface disturbance, the waves stirred up by the powerful movement of tides. A history of short, sharp nervous vibrations . . . still simmers with the passion of contemporaries.[526]

Geohistory is the almost changeless history of humanity relative to our geographical surroundings. Social history attempts to demonstrate how the various forces that exist at the deepest level have an intricate part in the story that it seeks to unfold. Event history looks at the event in itself. *Event* here refers to what is called *l'histoire événementielle* by François Simiand. Event history "burns still, taken as the contemporaries lived it, described and felt at the rhythm of their life-span, just as brief as our own."[527] This event history is characterized by a short time span, despite that what happens in it may be experienced as extremely rich in humanity.[528] The event itself is the "most capricious and the most delusive of all."[529] To assess the events, they ought to be examined in light of a second-order reflection in which the event is seen in its broader context–that of the long time span of the slow development of civilizations.[530]

The longtime history (*la longue durée*) in Braudel's thinking becomes antithetical to the short time span and enters into a full critique of the history of heroes by reconstructing history from the background of slower developments that take place in human sociopolitical history. His insight is that, underneath the history of individuals and their frenzied time consciousness, a broader stream of rather anonymous events is deploying its slow, persisting rhythm of economic systems, of the sedimentation and slow changes in social and political institutions (e.g., the state), and in the world of ideas (*histoire des mentalités*). In this light, Braudel focuses on the geohistory of the Mediterranean (i.e., on the quasi-immobile history that links humans to their natural milieu and that creates a rather stable "geographical time" with *longue durée*). Grafted on this geographical time, he further distinguishes a "plurality of times," which means that each layer within the social history develops its own rhythm of stability and change. To lift history to the level of the long time span is to have new insights in the *evenemenrial* history. The real economic and social basis of history is not shaped by *evenemential* characters; on the contrary, these are shaped themselves by the (only slowly changing) socioeconomic basis.

---

[526] Braudel, 3–4.
[527] Ricoeur, *Time and Narrative*, 1:103–4; Ricoeur, *Contribution*, 10–11.
[528] Ricoeur, *Time and Narrative*, 1:104.
[529] Braudel, 28.
[530] Braudel, 25.

Ricoeur acknowledges that there is a certain wisdom in paying attention to "the extreme slowness of real changes." Additionally, he observes that Braudel has to introduce a new notion, that of *conjuncture*, to avoid a picture of history in which nothing new happens. In his review of Braudel's notion of conjuncture, Ricoeur's major difficulty is that Braudel analyzes the shifts in conjuncture with the help of quantitative measurements. This opens the avenue for a "serial history," "which rests upon the constitution of a homogeneous series of 'items,' hence of repeatable facts, eventually amenable to processing by a computer. All the major categories of historical time can be ever closely redefined in terms of a 'serial basis.'"[531] In practice, this means that mathematical procedures can tell us how a certain innovation (new conjuncture) in one domain is going to pass over to another domain.

Relying on Marx without appropriating his ideology, the École des Annales starts from the assumption that slow changes will happen first in the economic domain to spread themselves as new conjunctures in the other domains. But even then, the spreading happens automatically–traceable by mathematical procedures–without the special input of human agents or privileged actors in history: "So then the [new] conjuncture passes from economic history to social history, then to history in general, with the result that it can be conceived as a method for integrating at some given moment the greatest possible number of correlations between remote series."[532]

Ricoeur contends that even as the ideas centered on serial history tend to form into a structure, they must still retain their temporal character.[533] He also has difficulty with Braudel's long time span when it engages in a discussion of qualitative mathematics. It is in the construction of timeless models, as suggested by math sociologists, that the long time span becomes problematic for Ricoeur. His concern is that the long time span can become so long that time no longer exists.[534] Ricoeur will not allow the long time span to be "transformed into the negation of time, instead it must be understood as a plea for the plural character of social time."[535]

On the whole, it is clear that Braudel is critical of any narrative reconstruction of history that honors the creative input of historical actors. He rejects *l'histoire événementielle* in favor of the quasi-anonymous (slow) changes brought about in the series of new conjunctures of the long time span. But in spite of this project, which flatly contradicts his own, Ricoeur tries to give an

---

531 Ricoeur, *Time and Narrative*, 1:219.
532 Ricoeur, *Time and Narrative*, 1:221.
533 Ricoeur, *Time and Narrative*, 1:107.
534 Braudel, 38–47.
535 Ricoeur, *Contribution*, 12.

original rereading of Braudel by pointing out that what the latter understands by the long time span can also be understood as part of an emplotment.

Braudel's main achievement, Ricoeur says, was his idea of the "plurality of social times," that is, "history whose passage is imperceptible," along with history "of slow but perceptible rhythms." But this "decomposition of history into various plans" of the same time raises the question whether Braudel does not tacitly start from a principle of unity to draw the distinctions between "quasi-immobile history, a slowly rhythmically developing history on the scale of individuals, namely, that history of events which the history of the long time-span is to dethrone."[536] Another contribution of Braudel is that despite his disdain for the narrative, he has implicitly developed a new form of plot that extends itself throughout the whole work.

Ricoeur describes the concept of the long time span as the principle of unity that keeps together the different spans of time employed by Braudel in his work *La Méditerranée*. Even more, the long time span is a transitional structure that functions like Ricoeur's own concept of employment, which combines time and narrative through the configurational act. The function of the long time span is similar to the mediational potential of configuration (mimesis$_2$), the place where Ricoeur speaks of the past, which has gained an intelligible structure through the plot impinging on the present and projecting itself into the future. The new form of plot (the long time span for Braudel) in *La Méditerranée* functions as a transitional structure that links the first part of the work, which refers to the economic geography of the Mediterranean Sea, with the third part that refers to Philip II. The long time span provides for the "overall coherence of the work" resulting in what Ricoeur calls a "quasi-plot."[537] This concession to Braudel is constitutive of Ricoeur's own final insight, namely, emplotment for Ricoeur and the long time span for Braudel are structures that are attentive to "pointlike phenomena" but whose reference is the slow-moving, broad stroke of a more major event.[538]

In Braudel's *La Méditerranée*, the first level called geohistory is held together by the transitional structure of the long time span. When the work shifts into the second level, that of political history, its coherence is attained by conjuncture of economies, empires, societies, and civilizations.[539] Thus, Ricoeur rereads Braudel's work as a "mimesis of action." By using the long time span, Braudel has actually created "a new type of plot (virtual-or quasi-plot) . . .

[536] Ricoeur, *Time and Narrative*, 1:208. Ricoeur is citing Braudel's *On History* (20–21).
[537] Ricoeur, *Time and Narrative*, 1:208–9.
[538] Ricoeur, *Time and Narrative*, 1:217.
[539] Ricoeur, *Time and Narrative*, 1:210–14.

[that] teaches us to unite structures, cycles, and events by joining together heterogeneous temporalities and contradictory chronicles."[540]

Ricoeur corrects Braudel by insisting that emplotment is not limited to the third part of *La Méditerranée*; all three levels of that text contribute to the overall plot.[541] Ricoeur, at this point, cites Aristotle to define *plot*. Ricoeur believes it must "include not only an intelligible order but a magnitude that cannot be too vast, or it will be unable to be embraced by our eye" (51a1).[542]

Thus, Ricoeur states that Braudel is rendering a plot when he depicts "the decline of the Mediterranean as a collective hero on the stage of world history. The end of the plot, in this regard, is not the death of Philip II. It is the end of the conflict between the two political leviathans and the shift of history toward the Atlantic and northern Europe."[543]

Ricoeur states that because of Braudel's effort to be "analytical and disjunctive," he ends up with only a virtual or quasi-plot.[544] This is also Ricoeur's eventual position in which "the event is not brief and nervous, like some sort of explosion. It is a variable of the plot."[545] Braudel separates the parts into what Ricoeur says are "sub-plots," providing only an implicit image of the whole that may be seen as *the* plot (emphasis added). Thus, Ricoeur rereads Braudel's work as a "mimesis of action." By using the long time span, Braudel has actually created "a new type of plot by uniting structure, cycles and events by joining together heterogeneous temporalities and contradictory chronicles."[546]

CONCLUSION

Slavery, religion, and regime as a dissertation topic and its Ricoeurian conceptual framework raise several questions: What insight can the thinking of Paul Ricoeur bring to an understanding of the apparent deviation in history that has taken place with the rise of modernity–the problem of slavery and its interrelationship to religion and politics? What, if anything, can the ideas of a European philosopher whose project has been hermeneutic phenomenology bring to this theological discourse? Why attempt to answer the questions

---

[540] Ricoeur, *Time and Narrative*, 1:216. At this point, Ricoeur speaks about the structuralism of Braudel in which he sees the short term as a "conjuncture which is a grouping of events in the same area. (Braudel, *La Méditerranée*, 1244).

[541] Ricoeur, *Time and Narrative*, 1:214–15.

[542] Ricoeur, Ricoeur, *Time and Narrative*, 1:215.

[543] Ricoeur, *Time and Narrative*.

[544] Ricoeur, *Time and Narrative*, 1:216.

[545] Ricoeur, *Time and Narrative*, 1:208–17, specifically 1:217.

[546] Ricoeur, *Time and Narrative*, 1:216–17.

centered on slavery by rereading the history of the opening up of the Atlantic world and the rise of the modern state?

To give a methodological response to these questions, this chapter has been seeking an answer to two other questions: what is history, and what is historical method? The answer to these last two questions contain the substance of the political methodology and conceptual framework for this study.

After a study of Ricoeur, it is clear that an understanding of imagination is vital to the ultimate *hermeneutics of historical consciousness*, which constitutes the political theory of Paul Ricoeur. Imagination is not a reference to some illusion or fantasy, but it is the use of imagination as a creative force in connection with the role of metaphor, which serves as the foundation for the hermeneutics of historical consciousness.

The crux of the Ricoeurian methodology comes at the point when imagination in conjunction with metaphor breaks through to the field of action. At the level of action, the sociocultural imagination is either reproductive or productive. Reproductive imagination and productive imagination are synonymous with its dynamic practices of ideology and utopia. The social dimension of imagination manifests itself in the historical field. The connotation is that imagination (in the present) offers a point of identification or a criticism of history (the past), as well as a potential for exploring the possible (the future).

For Ricoeur, it is essential to link the imaginative theory to the historical field. It is this linkup that results in the creative redescription that Ricoeur calls a *hermeneutics of historical consciousness*, where hidden, repressed, or forgotten stories are unmasked. This hermeneutical dynamic begins with what Ricoeur calls the mimetic process. The mimetic process, he claims, gives intelligibility to traces of the past, its emplotment confronts what is happening in the present along with its implications, and it touches the future. Such a process rests on the examination of the relationship between time consciousness and narrated history.

There are various ways of defining the concept of time in history. There is the abstract, rectilinear, event-by-event, moment-by-moment view, in which the points of time follow one another like a dotted line. This view states that the past is behind us; it is over, while the future is yet to come. There is no real place for the interpretative dimension in this approach to history.

Antithetically, there is also the dynamic, configurational perception of time that is a more experiential concept of time. The configurational perception views the past, the present, and the future as one coherent, temporal structure. In this concept, the diverse periods form a unity.

In the former episodic perspective of time and history, the historical data are of great importance. The phases of history are described as functioning almost in isolation from one another. Historical data are determined through the criteria of scientifically established facts (the ideal of the positivistic sciences), eliminating symbols, myths, and fables from what it postulates as real. The only thing that is real in this process is that which can be verified in a positivistic sense.

In the mimetic conception of time and history, there is not an overemphasis on the historical fact or the event as scientifically or rationally constructed. The phases of history are seen as more interrelated with one another; however, it is history and not fiction because of the truth claim associated with history. Both historical and fictional narratives are the same at the level of emplotment because they borrow from each other, but the distinguishing characteristics is the truth claim of these two classes of narrative. This dynamic historical thinking includes the living development by and the active involvement of the interpreter in the doing of history. The more dynamic configurational approach to time and history leads us to a combination of the past with the present and the future through a hermeneutic or a hermeneutics of historical consciousness.

The integral ingredients of this methodology for an interpretive understanding of the past consist in a pursuit of the truth, an understanding of the past, and a hermeneutical dynamic for understanding the text. Pursuit of the truth is crucial in this process, though the answer is difficult to achieve. The effort to reconstruct the past is done by an interpreter who is conditioned by contemporaneity. Consequently, reconstruction of the past raises the questions how do we come to know the truth, and as a corollary how do we express that truth?[547] Understanding of the past entails defining whether to use an event-by-event or a configurational approach. The hermeneutic phenomenological approach to the text, which Ricoeur calls the mimetic spiral (prefiguration, configuration, and refiguration), provides a new and dynamic kind of interpretation of well-known past events, whose meaning ought to be deciphered.

The mimetic spiral creatively bridges the gap between the past and the present, with the present effectively entering in dialogue with the past. Ultimately, the spiral allows the rewriting of a historical plot that dramatizes the time experience. The link between time and narrative acknowledges that there is a temporal dimension involved in the experience of the particulars and makes it possible to synthesize those particulars into a narrative.

An objection to this mimetic process is that the dimension of these constituent elements together gives rise to a type of circularity in the

---

[547] Ricoeur, *Historical Past*, 2.

interpretation. Ricoeur objects to the possibility of circularity and redundancy of interpretation that can be found at the first level (mimesis$_1$) of the spiral. He says that prefiguration (mimesis$_1$) is not the product of refiguration (mimesis$_3$) because of the potential of prefiguration to open up "as yet untold stories." These untold, forgotten, repressed stories are constitutive of prefiguration, which means they do not derive nor are effected by refiguration.

The mimetic spiral operates in the realm of discourse. But the question is, how can a narrative be constructed to include ideas and experiences that have been continually left out of the discourse? And as long as this oblivion persists, one does not deal with the realm of practice where political theory functions. To move from the theoretical to the practical and to apply the mimetic spiral there, one must take seriously Ricoeur's notion of imagination. In the delineation of the mimetic spiral, there was already the presupposition of semantic innovation. Therefore, the interpretation of history as proposed in the mimetic spiral converges with the practical, giving way to the transformation of historical understanding. According to Ricoeur, the imagination is central to the new historical consciousness. Imagination is an important link between hermeneutics and the historical field. This is because, as Ricoeur iterates, imagination gives language the capacity of disclosing or opening onto various possible worlds that transcend the established limits of our actual world.

The mimetic theory of Ricoeur confronts the problem attached to a factual relating of history bereft of interpretation while avoiding the tendency of history to be exclusive and elitist. The structural features of mimesis ultimately have the strongest potential for the reconstruction of the "missing pages" of history, the "untold stories," through creative redescription.

Paul Ricoeur rounds out his methodology by explicating the contribution of French historiography to an understanding of the past. He examines the École des Annales; especially, he rereads and appropriates specific aspects of the methodology of Fernand Braudel. Braudel sees the limitations of "event by event" history; moreover, the solution for Braudel is the existence of three levels of time. He establishes a transitional structure that allows the consideration of history in both short and long expanses of time arranged in terms of "quasi-plot(s)." Braudel's other contribution to Ricoeur deals with the long time span (*longue durée*), which permits an observation of the "slow changes" taking place in the social and economic dimensions. These "slow changes" include new events (quasi-plots) that are like explosions, which he calls conjunctures. In using the long time span, a new kind of plot emerges whose objective is to get beyond individual event history (*l'histoire événementielle*).

Therefore, in this chapter, "Hermeneutics and Society," Paul Ricoeur provides an epistemological and methodological framework that is central to this study. Through an understanding of Ricoeur, his notion of imagination, his development of the mimetic spiral and its role in a hermeneutics of historical consciousness, and finally how he appropriates the École des Annales, especially his use of Braudel's long time span (*longue durée*), whereby we can use a new and innovative context for our search for the root cause of an apparent historical deviation experienced as a result of modernity and its creation of the modern nation-state.

In conclusion, this theoretical framework of Paul Ricoeur allows us to discover the "untold stories" of the founding of the Catholic Church and its survival that has taken place in a "protestant society" of slavery and the slave trade. This story of Catholics, though a conjuncture (quasi-plot), is central to the *longue durée* that constitutes the powerful clash of religious forces that has characterized the last five hundred years. The *longue durée* unmasks the oppressive ideologies in the creation of the Atlantic world with its laws and bureaucratic rationality; with slavery, which was the foundation of capitalism; and with the adjustment of religious understanding are all secondary to the process of structuring the modern state with its political economy.[548]

The task now is to use the Ricoeurian "political methodology" to do an interpretation of religion in the rise of the modern state, the speculative dimension of the overall project. Achieving this goal consists in engaging in a reading of the religious reality of the Americas as it has existed at the time of the founding of the Maryland colony.

---

[548] As I have defined in another place, "Political economy [today] refers to all aspects of a society or civilization: its political process, how these relate to money and business, and how they are managed by technology. The political economy also determines behavioral patterns in the society, thereby forcing consent from its people and making its institutions (even religious institutions) subservient to it" (Linden, "Review Symposium," 138–40).

CHAPTER THREE

The Struggle for Humanity in the
Context of Religious Conflict

INTRODUCTION

THE PURPOSE OF this chapter is to focus on the establishment of the Maryland colony (1634) in British America as the grounding of the dehumanization process (chapter 1) in a specific historical context. The colony presents a unique contradiction to the ideology of the rising modern nation-state and the violence of the merchant conquest in the Atlantic world, where the decimation of the native, slavery, and the slave trade have been dominant.

The context of the New World by 1634 was one of religious conflict between two competing forces, the new world religion represented by a reality built on the political and economic expressions of modernity and a "particular type" of religion represented by the enlightened feudalistic state sponsored by Maryland Catholics. At this point, British America had formed a society whose underlying principles actually meant *freedom from religious* constraints and profits at any cost.[549] This freedom ultimately meant religious toleration

---

[549]   Jewell R. Crawford Mazique, "The Role of the Christian Church in the Establishment of Slavery and Segregation in the United States" (unpublished

for all the other colonists of British America but intolerance and subjugation for the Catholics of the Maryland colony.

The enlightened feudalistic state of the Maryland colony was a development out of the more humanistic, traditional-type state characteristic of the medieval old-world religion and not compatible with the new world order politically and economically as highlighted by the modern state. Their existence was doomed not because of their religion as such or because of shortsightedness or error of the expedition. It was doomed because, in the new world order, the possibility of the existence of such a reality was limited and proscribed. Their establishment of the enlightened feudalistic state represented the old politics and economics being rejected by the new world order in the building up of the Atlantic world. Therefore, the struggle was that Catholics established a manorial construct in opposition to the expansionist spirit of the Atlantic world.[550] By 1689, the original vision of Maryland lost out and with

manuscript, Washington DC, May 1954).

The insight of Jewell R. Crawford Mazique was that, because of the primarily enterprising nature of European and British expansion into the Atlantic world, "disunity" was the foundation of the Christian Church in America. She also argued that "freedom from religion" rather than "religious freedom" was the impetus for expansion into the Atlantic world. The modern nation-state established itself by capturing Africans, kidnapping Irish Catholics, and detribalizing Native Americans.

Jewell R. Crawford Mazique has been engaged as an intellectual, scholar, theoretician, activist, and freelance writer in the struggle for justice for sixty years. Her work as a freelance writer has been syndicated and appeared between 1958 and 1962 in four major African American newspapers: *Courier Correspondence* of the *Pittsburgh Courier* (Pittsburgh, PA), *Herald-Dispatch* (Los Angeles, CA), *Afro-American Newspapers* (Baltimore, MD, and Washington DC), and the *Capital Spotlight* (Washington DC). Other works of Mazique are as follows: "Soviet Women. Seeing the Soviet Woman through Negro Eyes Is a Strike in the Direction of Peace," *New World Review* 28, no. 3 (March 1960): 12–18; "Change and Challenge in Desegregated America: The Negro and Social Psychiatry," *Journal of the American Association for Social Psychiatry* 1, no. 2 (February 1960): 82–89; "Aristotle: A Study of His Slave Theory with Both Definite and Presumptive Evidence of Its Impact upon Western Civilization," *Dialogue: Journal of Phi Sigma Tau* 1, 1 (April 1956): 23–35.

See also Phillip J. Linden Jr., "The Founding of the Catholic Church and Its Survival in a Protestant Society of Slavery and Slave-Trading: The Maryland Colony 1634–1646" (licentiate thesis, Faculteit Der Godgeleerdheid, Katholieke Universiteit Leuven, 1988); also, Linden, "Review Symposium," 138–40.

550   The Portuguese and Spanish conquistadores, with their "adjusted" form of Christian values, had already swept through the Western world about a century before the British and Dutch ventures. In their entrepreneurial efforts, the conquistadores had come up against the vision and ideas of the missionaries, which included the

it all hope of ever overcoming what had become British America's colonial heritage, the enterprise of "slavocracy" and the establishment of the modern nation-state.

Let us now make the link between the methodology of the second chapter and what is to follow in this chapter. That link, as we have said, is rooted in the metaphorical foundation of imagination and its potential for emplotment. These two are the bases for the hermeneutical dimension that manifests itself in what Ricoeur calls the mimetic spiral of prefiguration, configuration, and refiguration. The mimetic spiral results in a hermeneutics of historical consciousness that embodies the critical functioning of imagination at the social and cultural level. What is called for methodologically at this point is a Ricoeurian reading of the Maryland colony.

Mimesis₁ or prefiguration declares that, when narrating events, we confront a reality whose elements consist in cultural presuppositions surrounding the events before the words are written down. There is a preunderstanding whose components are structural, symbolic, and temporal.

Prefiguration, when applied to the idea that religion is a significant force in the creation of the Atlantic world, implies that there are underlying elements that preexist any textual emplotment of the story of the development of the enlightened feudalistic state and the issue of slavery in southern Maryland. Such presuppositions consist in the drastic changes existent in the Maryland colony as it has undergone attack from its colonial neighbors, even before its actual settlement. The pursuit of truth in this case is related to the understanding of the elements involved in the move from a feudal manorial colony with a Christian foundation (a society that has stood against slavery and the killing of native peoples) to facing a dilemma of choosing between being persecuted and being followers of trader principles.

The narrative requires symbols through which the descriptive and even the prescriptive rules can express what has taken place. Descriptive symbols use words and even grammar to communicate the event, whereas prescriptive symbols relate to customs and give action its ethical character. No action

preservation of the natives against slavery (e.g., the Jesuits in Paraguay). According to Arnold Toynbee, the British and Dutch conquerors knew that the interference of the missionaries in the affairs of the Portuguese and Spanish conquistadores had impeded their business interests. So the British and Dutch were determined not to have this occur with them. Toynbee said, "The Protestant Christian Western empire-builders of the second wave deliberately subordinated religious missionary work to commercial and political considerations. They discouraged and discountenanced their own missionaries when these created embarrassments of the Western trader and the Western administrator" (Arnold Toynbee, *An Historian's Approach to Religion,* Gifford Lectures, 1952–1953 (London, New York, and Toronto: Oxford University Press, 1956), 159–60.

is neutral though. Both ethical and religious actions of the founders of the Maryland colony have been influenced by their culture and customs.

The events surrounding the founding of the Maryland colony have a temporal character (past, present, and future). The *understanding* gained by remembering the past affects the present-day life of all the proscribed, the unelect, and the oppressed not only of the United States but also of the world. Thus, this *understanding* (of the past) influences the response to future challenges.

These events have a narrative character that consists in the means whereby the truth of the past is transmitted. Whether written or oral, the communication of the past and its truth–if it is to touch the present and deal with future challenges–must be transfigured in the present. The combination of a pursuit of the truth of southern Maryland with the interrelationship between the temporal character and the narrative is the basic aspect of this theoretical framework.

Concerning the interpretive dimension of this text, there are several methodological issues to be considered. These forthcoming considerations of the interpretive dimension will seek to establish the benefits of the Ricoeurian methodology as a conceptual framework. The task here is to concretize the role of religion as the space or context for a new understanding of society.

The collection, analysis, and synthesis of the material for this study is what confirms this project as a study of the history of religion. The result of these efforts is the imaginative redescription or configuration (mimesis$_2$) of what has happened in southern Maryland. We emplot the events of the early settlers who have been entrusted with a charter having as its goal the establishment of a type of colony that will obviate the elitist religious struggles and persecutions of the rising merchant class. With the process of creative redescription, we draw together the various parts of evolution of the Maryland colony into an intelligible narrative picture (emplotment). We reveal that, for twelve years (1634–1646), the Maryland colony–because of its structure–has not only struggled against trading for profit but has also been opposed to the rise of slavery and slave trading. The colonists have been committed to the mission of making life possible for all, regardless of their religious beliefs.

In 1646 and again in 1654, Puritan slave traders occupied the Maryland colony and ousted the Catholics. In the 1646 attack on the colony, the Jesuit priests were kidnapped and brought back to England, where they would be executed as priests who were in violation of the law. This perverse spirit undermined the Catholics, exposing them to persecution. The Catholics, Indians, and free Africans were forced to act out slavocracy, slave-trading practices, and so on, which comprised the ultimate accommodation of the Catholics to the ongoing direction of the other colonies toward investment in slavery and slave trading. It would be important to note that, by 1790, the slave traders had already determined that slavery would be at the core of the political economy and that the majority of the English colonial settlers supported it.

Mimesis$_3$ or refiguration refers to the core reception of the text. This stage of the mimetic spiral is already beyond the configuration or the restructuration of the plot. At this stage, the mimetic process is engaged in "doing history," which not just comprises the reception of events in the abstract but also is an interpretation of these events in the concrete.

The interpretation we render also contains a critique of events. At this point, imagination takes the creative role of rendering a political appraisal on the level of practice.

The view from the level of the reader gives an interpretive dimension to the narrative process. When refiguration is applied to our Maryland story, the question that is raised has to do with the victims' "repressed stories." Through the narrative function, victims are confronted by their absence from history; and thus, for the victims, refiguration necessitates confronting the text as produced by the elite. This confrontation leads to a reinterpretation of commonly accepted understanding with a view toward challenging and confronting the void. What this means is that the children of the victims of early Maryland, through this process, are compelled to redefine themselves in light of their own status in the culture and society they find themselves in. They become interpreters of the events of early seventeenth-century Maryland and, during this process, coax to the surface the "untold stories" of the proscribed.

The next step in the process is to return to newly developed cultural presuppositions that exist at the level of prefiguration. The newly derived underlying elements consist in a structural network, symbols, and a temporal dimension but moving in an upward spiral. The story told by many historians leaves out the victims and emphasizes the side of the victors. This incomplete picture will be disclosed to a more complete meaning.

Such a project means seeing the settlement of the Maryland colony and its survival in British America as emplotted subplots/quasi stories or "transitional structures" that contribute to the slow-moving progress of the long time span (*longue durée*). In these quasi-plots/stories of the Maryland colony, there is "overall coherence" arranged in such a way that the entire work might be viewed in terms of its quasi-plot.[551] Let us look at these subplots and quasi stories or *conjunctures* as something more—as the context of extremely slow changes.

---

[551]   Ricoeur, *Time and Narrative*, 1:209.

According to Ricoeur, these quasi stories foreshorten the memory. Ricoeur appreciates the contribution of Braudel and cites him as seeing that this process of the *longue durée* with *conjunctures* is similar in effect to that of a sped-up film. The conjunctures are an effort to expose, even though in some sort of slow motion, that there are realities in the history of Maryland that are beyond and behind it that, in some way, needs to be conveyed. In this process, Ricoeur "[joins] history together with disciplines for which time is not a major category"–such as sociology, economics, and politics–to get beyond a less complex chronological, event-by-event understanding. This is called the history of *mentalities*.[552] The quasi stories are "slow but perceptible rhythms" of what ultimately is the "imperceptible" forging of the Atlantic world into a regime that lives on into the present and looks toward the future.[553] Thus, we use the Ricoeurian methodology to look at the story of the Catholics and the Maryland colony as a quasi-plot in the overall story of the rise of the Atlantic world.

The chapter is divided into three principal sections. The first section focuses on the political, economic, and religious context in which the Maryland colony has been born in British America. It also touches on the early attempts at migration in which some of the earliest theories of colonization have been established.

The second section is on the Maryland colony specifically and focuses on the conflict of religion, which is at the foundation of the rise of the Atlantic world. It gives the background of the Calverts and their relationship to the Jesuits. It also discusses the Newfoundland experiment and how it has ended in being overcome by harsh climate and French Huguenot merchants who have conducted attacks on the fledgling colonial venture. It has been at this early date that there has been some of the first resistance to the expansionist spirit in the English-speaking world with its adjusted religious values and new world order. In the remainder of this section, we engage in a discourse on the establishment of the Maryland colony, the special palatine privilege in the Maryland charter that provides the platform for the enlightened feudalistic state, religious liberty and its limits particularly as the Catholics have lost out and been completely overrun by Puritan merchants in 1646, and the consequent introduction of slavery into the colony in the 1660s.

Finally, we take the issue of the specifics of the struggle for humanity. Implied in this section is that liberty is connected to ownership of property.

---

[552] Ricoeur, *Time and Narrative*, 1:109; Catherine L. Albanese, "Refusing the Wild Pomegranate Seed: America, Religious History, and the Life of the Academy," *Journal of the American Academy of Religion*, 1994 Presidential Address LXIIII2 (Summer 1995): 205–29, 218–19.

[553] Ricoeur, *Time and Narrative*, 1:208.

This presupposition regarding property has also determined who is human or not. It has been the disenfranchisement of Catholics in general and Jesuits specifically that has resulted in the dehumanization process, applying even to the church.

As shall be seen when we move into the body of this chapter, the disclosing of events centered on the establishment of the Maryland colony not only unmasks the past of Catholics in the United States but also reveals the conflict that is at the roots of the commodification of politics and religion.

3.1. RELIGION, POLITICS, AND THE BRITISH COLONIAL VENTURES

Even though the Catholics of seventeenth-century Maryland are often heralded for their role in the establishment of the traditional American freedoms recognized in the Constitution of the United States, it can be said that they have been the victims of the political and economic expressions of modernity. The renowned Catholic historian John Tracy Ellis states it as follows: "The experiment in Maryland put Catholics and Protestants side by side on terms of equality and toleration unknown in the mother country. 'In that respect,' says one historian, 'the settlement of Maryland holds a unique place in the history of English colonization.'"[554]

To corroborate the theory of the contribution of Catholics to American freedoms, Gerald P. Fogarty, SJ, contends that Catholics have contributed the principal ingredient for the establishment of traditional American freedoms. Fogarty divides the stages in achieving these freedoms into the three following periods:

1. From 1634 to 1689, Catholics—while under constant attack—are said to have worked out the relationship between church and state;
2. From 1690 to 1718, Catholics have been faced with severe anti-Catholicism; and
3. From 1718 to 1790, Catholics have moved from not being permitted to own property to being among the first to sign and ratify the Constitution of the United States.[555]

---

[554] Tracy Ellis, *American Catholicism* (Chicago: University of Chicago Press, 1956), 25. In this quotation, John Tracy Ellis cites Charles M. Andrews, *The Colonial Period of American History*, 4 vols. (New Haven and London: Yale University Press, 1936), 2:290.

[555] Gerald P. Fogarty, SJ, "Property and Religious Liberty in Colonial Maryland Catholic Thought," *Catholic Historical Review* 72, no. 4 (October 1986): 573–600.

Fogarty, like Thomas O'Brien Hanley, SJ, claimed that religious liberty was linked to and based on the right to own property. Unlike in England, where people were deprived of their property because of their religious beliefs, religion in the colonies functioned in the private realm and was not an obstacle to the ownership of property. In making religion a private matter, the state could deprive no one of property because of their religion.[556]

> The church and state were vied, not so much in terms of union or separation, but as two sovereignties. The essential functions of each were clearly recognized, and any usurpation by either was detected by this essential reference. In a distinctive manner, this tradition demanded reserve in the exercise of authority by each sovereignty in mixed temporal and spiritual matters.[557]

However, liberty and equality–as manifested in the concepts of "religious toleration" and "separation of church and state"–existed for everyone in British America except Irish Catholics, Africans, and Native Americans.

Notwithstanding the insights of Fogarty and Hanley, the Roman Catholic Church was established in the United States within the context of bitter religious conflict. Instead of being considered the founders of the American liberty, the early Catholics of Maryland were progressively undermined. The religious struggles against the Puritans of England followed them to the new land. They were imperceptibly caught in a struggle, pitting themselves against the establishment of the modern religious creation, the commercial cult. This new religious creation, with its commercial interests, resulted in individualism, slavery and the slave trade, and extermination of the natives. As we shall see, Catholics not only failed to halt the oppressive dominance but also themselves were its victims.

To the degree that they resisted the modern spirit were Catholics denied freedom. "Catholics and their religious understanding fell victim to the hegemony created by the newly developing political organization of the economy. The original Catholics and their descendants had religious and political ties to the Europe from which the new colonies sought a clean break. So, in this process religious toleration, which was to be enshrined in the Constitution of the United States, was anything but tolerant toward

---

[556] Fogarty, "Property and Religious Liberty"; cf. Thomas O'Brien Hanley, SJ, *Their Rights and Liberties: The Beginnings of Religious and Political Freedom in Maryland* (Westminster: Newman Press, 1959).

[557] Hanley, *Their Rights and Liberties*, 121.

Catholics."[558] Let us reiterate that there was opposition to Catholics because they represented strong opposition to the rising dehumanization process.

Intolerance and subjugation of Catholics and of the Maryland colony was a clear victory for those engaged in establishing the newly adjusted religious understanding that would never oppose or clash with the political and economic expressions of modernity. Thus, to tell the story of the Catholics of early Maryland from the perspective of their contribution to the great freedoms established by the Constitution of the United States would be to eliminate crucial pages of history. It would mean to conceal the "repressed" stories of the victims, whose voices were still crying out to be heard.

In general, the history of Western expansion from the perspective of the victims is actually concealed. It is a history of terror for the victims who are overrun by the merchants and their drive for the profits derived from land speculation, slavery, and violence. Hearing these voices renders a critique, a fracturing of the exploitative dominance of the modern state. The problematic involves seeing that the modern ideology that has fostered individual autonomy and limited the power of the state simultaneously has been an enslaving and undermining ideology.

The period was also one in which the adjusted new religious values sanctioned the violent detribalization and overthrow of long-standing native societies, along with their traditions and values; the kidnapping of the Irish and other proscribed peoples of Europe; and the capture of Africans. Therefore, what was thought to be development by the adventurers was an age of brutal invasion and destruction for these victims.

Thus, the opening up of the Atlantic world conducted by the wealthy bourgeoisie merchants of Spain and Portugal was followed during the next three centuries by the French, Dutch, and British. These breakaway forces engaged in the creation of a new type of society based on economic enterprise, free from traditional religious constraints. The spirit of those times found the adventurers influenced by the notion of freedom of religion, meaning that traditional religious ideas and values were no longer normative.

It is important to look specifically at the British colonial venture and its religious and political milieu, including a general survey of the rise of the British slave industry.

Then we shall examine the founding of the Maryland colony and what we will see as its complete demise due to its traditional roots. We shall see that with the overthrow of the initial ideas around which that colony has been organized has come the dethroning of traditional religion itself as a meaningful entity.

---

[558] Linden, "Review Symposium," 139.

Our focus on the economic and the religious expressions of modernity is not meaningful in themselves. Their significance is in the role they have in the dehumanization process, which in our interpretation is a by-product of the modern state. This kind of interpretation is possible because of the Ricoeurian methodology. Its stress on the role of productive imagination allows us to read the economic and religious dimensions involved in the rise of the Maryland colony as commodified and modernity's way of securing the dehumanization process.[559]

3.1.1. BRITISH AMERICA

Before a discussion of the actual settlement of the Maryland colony, it is imperative to situate it in its wider historical context by surveying the religious and economic context of British America. The author Daniel-Rops contends that the British colonies have "originated to some extent from Protestant intentions or Protestant enterprise."[560] The impact of these forces on each other is the subject of this chapter and the underlying rationale for combining the elements of Protestant society and slavery and slave trading. Though it is complicated to do so, an effort will be made to delineate briefly the role of each force and how it has affected the Maryland colony.

To begin with, let us survey the religious force. Daniel-Rops characterizes the religious situation as follows:

> [The British colonies are a] cross-section of the Churches and other groups deriving from the Protestant Reformation. British America would end up being the receiver of Anglicans, Presbyterians, Congregationalists, Quakers, Scottish Calvinists, Dutch Mennonites, Lutheran Germans, Baptists, and Moravian Brethren. All these Protestant groups were transferred into and were dominant in the British colonies for over a century and a half of the colonial period. All were united in that they possessed one quality–strong religious convictions.[561]

---

[559] Cf. chapter 2 of this dissertation, especially the sections "Process of Creative Redescription" and "Mimesis and Historiography." Also, regarding the critique of an evolutionary history, see chapter 1, where we discuss the problem of productive forces alone being the "summation of history."

[560] Henri Daniel-Rops, *The Church in the Eighteenth Century*, trans. John Warrington (Garden City, New York: Image Books, 1966), 233.

[561] Daniel-Rops, *The Church in the Eighteenth Century*, 234.

Daniel-Rops also adds that the members of these churches have been "descendants of men whose defense of their faith had created a world"–a world of religious conflict.[562]

By the time the Maryland settlers disembarked at Saint Clements Island in 1634, there already were three British settlements, namely, Virginia (1602), Massachusetts Bay (1607), and Plymouth (1620), each a separate sanctuary of elitist religious beliefs. The background for the conflictual religious atmosphere in the colonies had been transplanted from the British homeland. The struggle back in England of the English Catholics and the Puritans against each other and both of them against the Roman Catholics was the historical paradigm of the religious conflict that would eventually surround the settling of the Maryland colony.[563]

The British colonials brought with them all the beliefs, the hatred, and the prejudices they had inherited. Diverse groups of Puritans had tried to take the Crown, along with the Church of England, further in its reforms than it was willing to go.[564] Yet it was mostly Puritans who were the early settlers of the New England area of North America, while followers of the Church of England had settled in Virginia.

The earliest settlements formed two distinct governmental constructs; the New England group (Massachusetts Bay and Plymouth) formed a theocracy, while Virginia formed a civil state with an established religion. Accordingly, Williams said that it would be important to note that the two groups of colonies had two things in common: all three–the English Catholic colony and two New England Puritan colonies–exploited the natives and hated Roman Catholics.[565]

The religious systems, the theocracy of the Puritans, and the established church of the Virginians were protected by particular laws, which set them poles apart from each other. They even viewed each other as proscribed; nevertheless, they clearly stood together in the eventual exclusion of Roman Catholics from their midst and from any other place in the newfound British territories.

---

[562] Daniel-Rops, *The Church in the Eighteenth Century.*

[563] Michael Williams, *The Idea of Maryland* (galley manuscript, n.d., Special Collections, Georgetown University Library, Washington DC), 1. This text was an unpublished manuscript. When this galley was written, Williams was listed as an editor of the popular Catholic journal the *Commonweal.*

[564] Jack P. Greene, ed., *Settlements to Society: 1584–1763*, vol. 1, *A Documentary History of American Life*, gen. ed. David Donald (New York: McGraw-Hill Book Company, 1966), 2.

[565] Williams, *The Idea of Maryland*, 1.

> The very charters granted by the English monarchs to the settlers of Massachusetts Bay and Virginia, when not actually forbidding the entry of [Roman] Catholics into the colonies, contained provisions curtailing freedom of worship and the exercise of their political rights.[566]

Even though religion was one of the motives for the Puritan and English Catholic, it should be noted that it was not a desire for religious toleration at all. The stimulus was not the setting up of exclusive religious sects. Freedom of religion was not the deeper motive for the colonies as it had traditionally been held.

The founding of the Maryland colony disclosed another motive that sparked the colonial society in British America. The dominant motive force operating in British America was an entrepreneurial one, which ultimately left the colonists open to the newly developing slave market. This was substantiated in that the early founders of colonial America had sought to escape the social revolutions taking place all over Europe; they were not revolutionists. Europe was engaged in broad-based social change, still disallowing structures and systems for the full-scale profit desired by the bourgeoisie, and the old regimes were still holding on. "American liberal culture was established by the Puritan migration of the seventeenth century, rather than by a social revolution. [T]he process of migration [made] possible a remarkable degree of ease and success for the liberal movement in America, since the old feudal enemies [were] left behind in Europe."[567] It was not so much to escape religious intolerance as to be grounded in a kind of liberalism that would promote economic profit. The founders boasted of their purity of intention in establishing a new city on the hill, "a new Jerusalem," and living out a new covenant that, we would contend, was a capitalist economy supported by the newly evolving modern state.[568]

---

[566] Williams, *The Idea of Maryland*.

[567] In 1968, Dr. Louis Hartz—then a professor of Harvard University—testified at a hearing in the United States Congress, Senate Committee on Foreign Relations entitled "The Nature of Revolution" (110), where he discussed individualism as a theological value of the elite. Here, he sought to establish that the very foundation of the Atlantic world, of America, was to establish a liberal philosophy rather than to engage in a social revolution.

[568] "The Nature of Revolution"; also, cf. Anton Weiler, "The Experience of Communities of Religious Refugees," in *Concilium: Exodus–A Lasting Paradigm*, ed. Bas van Iersel and Anton Weiler, English ed. Marcus Lefebure, 189, (February) 63–71; Werner Sombart, *The Jews and Modern Capitalism*, trans. M. Epstein, Social Science Classics Series (New Brunswick; London: Transaction Books, 1982), 43–44 passim; Weber, *The Protestant Ethic and the Spirit of Capitalism*, 164 passim; George M. Marsden, ed., *Religion and American Culture* (San Diego, New York,

Also supporting this view was the theory that the British and its colonizing effort was not primarily due to religious discontent or to dissatisfaction as a result of being mistreated.[569] It was known that there were some who had legitimate complaints with regard to religious intolerance. (For example, it can be said that Catholics certainly were among those who had legitimate grievances.) However, the colonies were not founded as a result of dissent and discontent.

> [The British colonies] were founded by enterprise directed from above: by good and solid greed, and by the quite normal expansion of generally accepted attitudes and purposes prevalent in the governing order in the realm of England . . . There was no question of disruption, none of rebellion. Those colonists, leaders or followers, wanted one main thing from their enterprise: to better themselves by adding to the wealth they had and the wealth they could create for others.[570]

This argument was supported by demonstrating what life was like for the people in England during the seventeenth and eighteenth centuries. During the Elizabethan and Stuart England, compared with our age today with its advances in medicine, science, and technology, life was rugged. From time to time, they were at war, and the people had been overrun by the plague. This period also can be characterized as having serious "political disaffection," but the people generally lived more or less happily. "Discontent existed, but it did not drive people overseas. Contentment, more widespread and prominent," continued Elton, "positively operated against emigration."[571] Thus, there had to be stronger motives for emigration than dissatisfaction or adventure, according to Elton.

Chicago, London, and Toronto: Harcourt Brace Jovanovich, 1990), 142–47.

There is also an issue that is discussed by Martin E. Marty; namely, the relationship between the expulsion of the Jews from Spain and Christopher Columbus's voyage of 1492 and the founding of colonial America. Martin E. Marty, *A Short History of American Catholicism* (Allen, Texas: Thomas More, 1995); Solomon Grayzel, *A History of the Jews: From the Babylonian Exile to the Present, 1728–1968* (New York; Scarborough, Ontario; London: A Mentor Book, 1968; orig. Jewish Publication Society of America, 1947), 473–85.

[569] G. R. Elton, "Contentment and Discontent on the Eve of Colonization," in *Early Maryland in a Wider World*, ed. David B. Quinn, St. Mary's College of Maryland (Detroit: Wayne State University Press, 1962), 105–6.

[570] Elton, "Contentment and Discontent," 118.

[571] Elton, "Contentment and Discontent," 113.

Before its interest in colonial America, England's early involvement in expansion economics was its colonization of Ireland. The expansionist spirit of the British ventures into Ireland revealed "the common and acceptable human emotions of greed and the search for greater wealth."[572] For the English society, like the rest of Europe of this period, the ownership of land, not money, constituted wealth; it was central to achieving economic status. Elton referred to England as a land-oriented society before its expansion efforts. "[England] was a landed society, a society which regarded only land and landed wealth as ultimately acceptable in creating status."[573] Most land, up to that point, was inherited by the eldest son, who in turn passed it down to the following generations; and if you did not receive it by inheritance, you could find it somehow. Before 1560, there was available land because of the great confiscations of ecclesiastical properties (churches, monasteries, etc.) and their being disbursed for immediate financial resources. This made it possible for those who did not have an inheritance to acquire land and status as well as to furnish a lucrative source of compensation for the Crown.[574]

But during the 1560s, this method of deriving status and wealth in England was slowly being closed off. There were no longer free gifts of land; moreover, whatever land the Crown owned it leased instead of sold because it was a source of ongoing resource to the Crown. So many people of this era were becoming landless.

> You could not found status upon leaseholds, though you could add to your wealth by acquiring them; you needed freehold property before you could gain the position of a landed gentleman, or even of a man of weight in your county. Only freehold, for instance, qualified you for the parliamentary franchise.[575]

Two aspirations would be fulfilled with the founding of colonies: England would grow in the geopolitical arena, and those who pursued the land would have the opportunity at the vast regions that the colonies promised. Both the individuals and the Crown were to profit from these ventures, and thus, the settlements were set up and, for the most part, governed by the Crown through charter. The involvement of the Crown in the political benefits of

---

[572] Elton, "Contentment and Discontent," 114. It cannot be denied that the conflict between Ireland and Great Britain today stems from the period when Cromwell has sought to empty Ireland for the sake of profit.

[573] Elton, "Contentment and Discontent," 115.

[574] Elton, "Contentment and Discontent."

[575] Elton, "Contentment and Discontent," 116.

colonization motivated their executing controls, even in the planning process. The emigration movement in America was a "developmental" process.

> [The process would be led through] various stages of planning, to summer visits for mainly trading purposes, to small-scale experiments in colonization, and finally, through many interim stages, to the creation of new European social and economic groupings across the Atlantic by the exploitation of natural resources in different regions, mainly in eastern North America.[576]

In the name of their nation, in these early stages, the plans of the settlements by the British included the exploitation of the resources and the large groups of native peoples. The natives and their rights "played a surprisingly limited role in the planning of permanent settlements.... [The settlers] cut and carved North America on paper many times" without any regard for the natives.[577]

The colony had to be granted a charter sealed by the king, thereby making it part of the English kingdom. The New World settlements were an "organized, controlled, and licensed transfer of English existence to the American continent. When the organizing agents settled the North American continent, they were not cutting loose or turning their backs on Europe; they were simply finding new areas for the exercise of their entrepreneurial qualities of which they had given sufficient evidence in England and Ireland for years before that."[578]

Thus, the economic and religious expression of modernity are the principal grounds for the British settlements. The religious motives of the early founders of the colonies, when unmasked, point to the entrepreneurial nature on which the colonial society of British America has existed. In fact, Richard Hakluyt (1552?–1616)–a cleric, geographer, and advocate of English colonial expansion–holds that the priority for expansion has been economic first. Jack P. Greene, who has edited a collection of selections on the early settlements in the English colonies, restates a Hakluyt comment as follows: "the clearest and most comprehensive statement of the motives–economic, patriotic, religious, and social–that impelled Englishmen to risk their lives and their fortunes in overseas enterprise."[579] Hakluyt is considered to be an authority on the issues

---

[576] Quinn, "Why They Came," in *Wider World*, 119.

[577] Quinn, "Why They Came."

[578] Elton, "Contentment and Discontent," 116–17.

[579] Greene, *Settlements to Society*, 4. Citing Richard Hakluyt, "Selection 1, Arguments for Planting English Colonies in America: Richard Hakluyt, 'A Discourse Concerning Western Planting (1584).'" This selection of Richard Hakluyt is

surrounding the period of British colonization. The following is the initial point of his "A Discourse Concerning Western Planting":

> The soyle yeldeth, and may be made to yelde, all the several comodities of Europe, and of all kingdoms, domynions, and territories that England tradeth with, that by trade of marchandize cometh into this realme.[580]

Hakluyt, however, also saw British expansion as an extension of Protestantism in a competitive sense. For Hakluyt, British expansion must be an expansion of Protestantism over against Catholic expansion of the Spanish Empire to the south. In fact, William Warren Sweet reflected on Hakluyt's argument when he wrote that British expansion was a "crusade against Catholicism." Citing a passage of Sir Walter Raleigh, Sweet continued,

> The policy instituted by the crown in separating the English Church from the Papacy was eventually to mean that religion was to be a major motive in laying the foundations of empire. The call of the mission field and the conversion of the heathen were given lip service by all the early writers on colonization, but it produced little immediate fruit. The Elizabethan seamen were Protestants of the Protestants when it came to hating Roman Catholicism, but their personal religion was a strange compound of "fervid patriotism, a varied assortment of hates, a rough code of morals, and an unshaken trust in the providence of God. To the heathen they brought not peace but the sword.[581]

In summary, we can say that it was the English mercantile community that sponsored the colonial movement using a scheme of evangelization of the heathens. However, their "crusading zeal was aimed primarily at Roman

---

reprinted from Collections of the Maine Historical Society (thirty-five vols., 1831–1906, series 2, volume II, 152–61). The original document is entitled "Divers Voyages Touching the Discovery of America and the Islands Adjacent to the Same, Made First of All by Our Englishmen, and Afterwards by the Frenchmen and Britons," in *Documentary History of the State of Maine*, vol. II (Cambridge, 1877). See also, George Bruner Parks, *Richard Hakluyt and the English Voyages* (New York: American Geographical Society, 1928), special publication no. 10.

[580] Ibid.

[581] William Warren Sweet, *Religion in Colonial America* (New York: Charles Scribner's Sons, 1942), 8.

Catholicism."[582] It was the overseas trading network, as he called it, that desired amassing capital for investment in joint-stock companies. He said the early "conglomerates" let individuals combine their resources and direct them into the colonial enterprise. Greene concluded his commentary on Hakluyt: "Virginia, Plymouth, and Massachusetts Bay were each sponsored by English merchants organized into joint stock companies."[583]

Despite the above arguments to the contrary regarding the British colonial ventures, the Maryland venture seemed to have strong contrasting motives to what had been discovered regarding the general colonization process in the other colonies. The Maryland colony, unlike any of the others, spoke of escape from religious persecution as its principal motive.

Thus, the most important issue was the question of religious tolerance. It must be noted, however, that in advertisement documents for the Maryland colony, there was discussion about the possible economic gains for those who joined the colony. The best example of such a document is the work *A Declaration of the Lord Baltimore's Plantation in Mary-Land*:

---

[582] Sweet, 8.

[583] Sweet, 2. In a recent history of the colonial experience of Catholics, Jay P. Dolan would strongly apply the above motive of economic profit to the Maryland colony. He disagreed with Elton and argued that the founding of the Maryland colony was for entrepreneurial rather than religious reasons. "[T]he Maryland colony was not founded primarily as an asylum or refuge for Catholics. Maryland was established first and foremost as a commercial enterprise, with profit, not religion, the primary impulse" (Jay P. Dolan, *The American Catholic Experience: A History from Colonial Times to the Present* [Garden City, New York: Image Books, 1985], 72).

Dolan described the Maryland colony as a commercial enterprise allowing Catholics to engage in profits, uninhibited by British hatred of Catholics. He argued that prosperity was the principal objective and that they exploited religion and manipulated the already persecuted Catholics. He suggested that Calvert would not have set his colony up with such a variation on the feudal structure using enlightened concepts of leadership (Dolan, *The American Catholic Experience*, 72). To support his argument, Dolan used John D. Krugler's doctoral dissertation: John D. Krugler, "Puritan and Papist: Politics and Religion in Massachusetts and Maryland before the Restoration of Charles II" (unpublished doctoral dissertation, University of Illinois), 10.

Dolan used Krugler to support his argument in another way. He argued that Calvert's resignation as secretary of state was not for religious motives. He suggested that George Calvert had been Catholic from birth and ultimately would not have left the high position of secretary of state in the British government where he had already acquired such an influential status among his Catholic peers (John

D. Krugler, "Sir George Calvert's Resignation as Secretary of State and the Founding of Maryland," *Maryland Historical Magazine* 68, no.3 [Fall 1973]: 239–54).

[All who joined would] commit their men and money to my Lords Officer appointed for that purpose: or to any other who will take care of them and it, and receive and use the dividend of land for their benefit: [they] shall receive of my Lord a mannor of good land, to the full quantity of 2000 Akers, for them and their heyres for ever in that Country.[584]

This promise to potential settlers was called a proprietary grant, property secured by Lord Baltimore from the Crown that he could hold without qualification. He had dominion over every part of it and was responsible for an annual tax. Baltimore then, in turn as a proprietor, gave the properties as proprietary grants to the settlers.

All Marylanders were tenants in the household of Baltimore because the Maryland grant was a feudal type. Some historians of early America described the proprietary grants in this way: "Estates in Maryland could be awarded by the Calverts to whom they chose, and remained with the tenants of their choice so long as the holders paid their quit-rents to the Proprietor."[585] They were to hold these grants with only one qualification, that "sufficient 'provisions of victuall' should be planted yearly before labor could be diverted to other channels."[586]

Through this qualification, Calvert sought to avoid some of the mistakes of the Jamestown and Plymouth colonies that held property in common and tried to produce for profit without growing enough food for the people. Calvert managed this by assuring through the proprietary grant that each freeman become an owner with the direct command to provide provisions for all. "Even those who were bound out in service for a term of years could look forward to the future when they would be freemen and owners of property."[587] At this point, however, it would be important to look at the background of the early

---

[584] Fr. Andrew White, *A Declaration of the Lord Baltimore's Plantation in Mary-Land; Wherein Is Set Forth How Englishmen May Become Angels, the King's Dominions Be Extended and the Adventurers Attain Land and Gear; Together with Other Advantages of that Sweet Land*, ed. and intro. Lawrence C. Wroth, John Carter Brown Library (June 10, 1929), reprinted by Maryland Hall of Records Commission (June 20, 1983).

[585] R. B. Nye and J. E. Morpurgo, *A History of the United States: The Birth of the United States*, vol. I. (Harmondsworth, England: Penguin Books Ltd., 1955; reprinted in 1961), 61.

[586] Matthew Page Andrews, *The Founding of Maryland* (Baltimore: William & Wilkins Company; New York and London: D. Appleton-Century Company Inc., 1933), 68.

[587] Andrews, *The Founding of Maryland*. For more on slavery in British America, see the section in chapter 1 called "The Slave Industry in British America."

Catholic migration into British colonial territories and an understanding of why Catholic.

3.1.2. EARLY ATTEMPTS AT MIGRATION

The Maryland colony[588] was established as a "new type of colony," a development from what had been attempted in the Virginia and Massachusetts Bay colonies.[589] Maryland was to become the haven for Catholics and thus, as presented briefly above, distinct from all the British settlements that had preceded it. Maryland was the manifestation of a new direction that had begun over fifty years before. The Catholic exile movement to America began during the late sixteenth century after the Tudor rise to power with a centralized government extending throughout all English territories, including Ireland. Henry VIII had appropriated an independent authority that the church had executed for years and had subsumed the powers of the Catholic nobility of England, of Scotland, of Wales, and of Ireland. Only local aristocracy, usually Protestant, had authority. Catholics were relegated to the status of entry.

---

[588] The background for this historical study of the Maryland colony is based on evidence collected from original sources. These collections consist of original documents (e.g., letters, printed sources, judicial cases, Land Office patent records, logs, early Maryland General Assembly proceedings, pictures, artists' conceptions based on archaeological finds, and various other artifacts).

To gather the data for this part of the research, time was spent at the various original sites. Visits were made to the following archives and collections: the Archives of the English Jesuits at Farm Street in London, England; the Mrs. Jewell R. Crawford-Mazique Special Collections and Papers, Washington DC; the Georgetown University Archives and Special Collections, Washington DC; the Archives of the Jesuit Fathers of the Maryland Province, Baltimore, MD.

Visits were also made to the following original sites in the Maryland colony: Saint Clements Island, Maryland, the site where the *Ark* and the *Dove* disembarked in 1634; Saint Marys City, Maryland, the site where the colony originally settled; Saint Inigoes, Maryland, the site of the first land grant to the Jesuits in 1635; Kent Island, Maryland, the site where William Claiborne–the trader and agitator of the Catholic colony–had his trading post.

Finally, this investigation involved visiting the site of an archaeological dig at Saint Marys City in southern Maryland. The site of the dig was the "great brick church built by Father Andrew White," who was the cofounder of the Maryland colony and founder of the Catholic Church (the first Jesuit mission) in English-speaking North America. The quest for the untold story of the undermining of religion in general and Catholicism specifically had been the foundational structure on which the historical framework of this chapter was built.

[589] Quinn, preface to *Wider World*, 9.

Running concomitant with the expanded authority of the Crown was the resistance to it. However, no opposition to the Crown was tolerated until the Stuarts came to power with a greater degree of balance between centralism and local autonomy. A more open society was being envisioned by some, but their enthusiasm was submerged, until the Civil War in England (1642–1648) gave them body and strength, thus expanding their power as owners. Quinn said that there were

> [l]arger groups who looked backward to a truly hierarchical society to a utopia in which landowning might come again into its own as a symbol not only of wealth but of political and judicial power.[590]

In 1569, a struggle took place resulting in the Catholic aristocrats having some of their autonomy restored. Additionally, the distance of Ireland from the Crown made it an ideal breeding ground for the revival of the feudal-type utopias.[591]

> Between 1568 and 1576 feudal grants were discussed and, on some occasions, granted for parts of Ireland, foreshadowing the principal lines of planning that led toward American experiments and which were to culminate (in one form at least) in the Maryland of 1634.[592]

An example of these settlements was the attempt by Sir Thomas Gerard of Bryn, Lancashire, who sought to become lord of County Antrim. But it soon failed because of his persistent requests for assistance from the Crown.[593] These aristocrats, after much struggle, failed to establish these independent feudal-type principalities in Ireland. So when the ventures to Ireland failed, they set their goals toward greater autonomy, which they envisioned as possible for the new colonies to be established in North America.

There had been other attempts by aristocratic gentry, mostly land-hungry younger Protestant gentlemen whose interest was in becoming wealthy, to join in the venture to Ireland. It was a way for them to acquire land from which they had been excluded in England through the laws of primogeniture, whereby only the firstborn sons would inherit already existing lands that belonged

---

[590] Quinn, "Introduction: Prelude to Maryland," in *Wider World*, 12.
[591] Quinn, "Introduction: Prelude to Maryland," 12–13.
[592] Quinn, "Introduction: Prelude to Maryland," 13.
[593] Quinn, "Introduction: Prelude to Maryland."

to their families.[594] These primogeniture laws denied the younger sons from becoming wealthy landowners in England. The younger sons would own the land settled by the colonists and derive land revenues through quitrents.

The beginning of the English colonization in North America took place when two such Protestant aristocrats, Sir Humphrey Gilbert and his half brother Sir Walter Raleigh, of Anglican background and commercial intentions received from Queen Elizabeth, who also was of Anglican background, what were called the letters patent in June of 1578. The letters patent granted clearance for them to colonize land in North America that had not yet been settled.

> [The patent covered] any lands that were not occupied by Christian people. This he [Gilbert] took to apply to the whole of eastern North America and, by elimination of some northern areas, the coastline and hinterland between the Cape of Florida and Cape Breton.[595]

Queen Elizabeth stated in the letters that the purpose was "for the inhabiting and planting of [British] people in America."[596] Up to that point, charters had only been given to trade companies. Even so, the charters— except for the one to be granted to the Maryland colony—were for joint-stock companies.

Catholic recusants[597] were often persecuted throughout England for failing to submit to the Church of England in both civil and ecclesiastical courts,

---

[594]   Quinn, "Introduction: Prelude to Maryland," 14.

[595]   Quinn, "Introduction: Prelude to Maryland," 15. Cape of Florida was the southernmost tip of the peninsula of Florida, not including any of the early Spanish settlements; Cape of Breton was the easternmost point of the Breton Island in Nova Scotia, Canada, 59°48'W. This massive territory was the place of the settlement of the British colonies and of what became English-speaking North America. European expansion into continental United States, however, did not consist in only the British colonization on the easternmost coast of North America. From the sixteenth through the seventeenth centuries, other European nations (Spain, France, and Holland) were involved in colonizing even some of the original thirteen colonies. Spain (1539–1542) discovered, explored, and settled the southwesternmost part of North America along with Florida; after earlier discovery and exploration in 1524 and 1534, France (1608) began in Quebec to settle the territory, which ultimately extended from southern Canada down the Mississippi River to the Gulf of Mexico. Holland (1609) settled what was New Amsterdam, later to be called New York.

[596]   Sweet, *Religion in Colonial America*, 1.

[597]   *Recusant* is derived from the Latin *recusare*, "to refuse." In English law, recusants or refusers described especially papists who refused to attend divine worship

receiving penalties from each court. Sometimes recusants were prohibited from traveling beyond five miles from their dwelling place. They were also excommunicated, forced to relinquish their civil rights, and refused burial. There was also, after 1689, what was called "constructive recusancy." This referred to those who were found guilty but whose punishment was only exacted sporadically.[598]

During this period, Catholic churches were looted; and monasteries, abbeys, and other church lands and buildings were confiscated. The laity were also exploited by exorbitant fines and forced to forfeit their estates. Only those who were very wealthy could afford to pay the fines. Even tighter regulations were enacted and enforced against Catholics (e.g., An Act against Fugitives over the Sea [1578]). The fugitive statute was passed to prevent Catholic recusants from leaving England.[599] If they left and it was discovered, they were forced to return and repent. If they would refuse to repent, they were disenfranchised, and their prospective property in the colony would be confiscated.

To circumvent these statutes and the exorbitant fines, Gilbert included a saving petition in his charter that, in effect, exempted any Catholics who became a part of the expedition from the provisions of the fugitive statute.[600]

---

in the established church as dictated by the 1559 Uniformity Act. This law was reinforced by later statutes. Recusancy laws were in effect beginning with the reign of Elizabeth I (1558–1603) and lasted until the reign of George III (1760–1820). The intent of these laws was to force people to embrace the Church of England. If a recusant was caught, conviction carried with it stiff penalties and fines.

The recusant was first given a chance to reject the papacy and papal supremacy and to embrace the established church. The penalty for holding firm to the papacy meant being forced to leave the country, after which returning without permission was a capital felony, which could mean execution. They could not return to the country without permission. For the most part, conviction resulted in financial penalties that were so steep that everyone but the very wealthy would be relegated to poverty. The penalty was a payment of twelve pence originally, but it later increased to twenty pounds a month. Later statutes gave the monarch the power to seize the goods and two-thirds of the lands of a recusant in lieu of the fine.

[598] Paul Kevin Meagher, "Recusants," in *Encyclopedic Dictionary of Religion*, ed. Paul Kevin Meagher, Thomas C. O'Brien, and Sr. Consuelo Maria Aherne (Washington DC: Corpus Publications, 1979), 2986–87; J. A. Williams, "Recusants," in *NCE*, 12, 135.

[599] Quinn, "Introduction: Prelude to Maryland," 15–16; J. Moss Ives, *The Ark and the Dove: The Beginnings of Civil and Religious Liberties in America* (London: Longmans, Green, and Co., 1936), 22

[600] Ives, *The Ark and the Dove*, 23; William J. P. Powers, "The Beginnings of English

Gilbert persuaded the secretary of state, Sir Francis Walsingham, to sign the petition for the new colony by explicating its value as a present and possible future source of revenue (fines and penalties as well as continuing taxes to be levied against the colony) from the wealthy Catholics. The petition allowed Gilbert to take "[wealthy Catholics] whose finances would enable them to discharge the 'penalties due to her Majesty, I and such others who were not able to pay the fines and penalties of their religion but might be able to pay them later."[601]

The first venture took place during 1578–1579 with Sir Humphrey Gilbert aboard the ship called the *Falcon* along with 7 other ships and 350 voyagers, most of whom were Catholics. They were turned around by encounters with the Spaniards and unbearable weather, and so the venture failed.[602]

Sir Humphrey Gilbert's plan for colonization was becoming fully developed. Many of the problems of the earlier venture were solved. He now focused on Catholic recusants of England. Gilbert began to realize that Catholics were pivotal for his newly generated colonization theories. They had been the victims of religious strife and were eager for a society in which the state did not interfere in their relations. The wealthy Catholic recusants Sir George Peckham and Sir Thomas Gerard were the first to join Gilbert's attempt at a Catholic colony. Quinn postulated that, by deciding to migrate Catholics to the New World, "the Catholic gentry [would form] the core of his [Gilbert's] conceptual scheme [the "feudal pyramid "] for an American landed empire."[603]

Sir Humphrey Gilbert's motive for focusing on Catholics, namely, to become wealthy, was tempered by his desire to assist them in finding a place to be free to practice their faith. He set sail with a fleet of five ships and some two hundred men; most of them were Catholic recusants. Gilbert was able to establish Newfoundland (1583) as a settlement. In an effort to survey the land to the south, which was also part of the grant, Gilbert's ship was wrecked. Heavy storms and inclement weather forced the failure of this venture south,

---

Catholic Emigration to the New World," in *Records of the American Catholic Historical Society of Philadelphia* 9 (March 1929): 15. For further detail on the Reformation in England, the following works can be consulted: Kenneth Scott Latourette, *A History of Christianity*, 2 vols., *Reformation to the Present* (New York: Harper & Row, Publishers, 1953; rev. ed., 1975), 2:797–835; John M. Todd, *Reformation* (London: Darton, Longmans & Todd, 1971); and Chadwick, *The Reformation*, 97–136.

[601] Ives, *The Ark and the Dove*, 23; Powers, "The Beginnings of English Catholic Emigration," 15.

[602] Powers, "The Beginnings of English Catholic Emigration," 15; Ives, *The Ark and the Dove*, 23.

[603] Quinn, "Introduction: Prelude to Maryland," 15; Ives, *The Ark and the Dove*, 23.

and of the five ships that started out, only one accomplished the entire journey as planned; Gilbert was lost at sea.[604]

Thus, Sir Humphrey Gilbert–in his efforts to assist Catholics–became the father of the colonization theories for eastern North America.

> The importance of [his] voyages lies in the fact that by them was abrogated the law of 1571, by which Catholics were forbidden to leave the realm, thereby setting a precedent for all future exile movements. The words of the letters patent were to the effect that in Sir Humphrey was vested the authority to make all laws, political and religious, for his colony, provided, of course they were not against the true Christian faith, i.e., the Church of England. The phrase "the true Christian faith" was a stock phrase taken from the Magna Charta of 1215 and it was capable of being interpreted, as it was by Calvert in 1634, to mean the Catholic faith.[605]

According to David Quinn, Gilbert developed his colonization theories based on his knowledge of "the feudal law and institutions" as well as "the wide powers the Spanish crown conferred on its conquistadors" in southwestern North America and in Latin America from the early sixteenth century.[606]

---

[604] Edwin Scott Gaustad, *A Religious History of America* (New York: Harper & Row, 1966, 1974), 30.

[605] Powers, "The Beginnings of English Catholic Emigration," 17.

[606] Quinn, "Introduction: Prelude to Maryland," 14. It can be argued that Gilbert, in including in his theory "the wide powers the Spanish crown granted to the *conquistadors*," was able to establish a "feudal pyramid" that existed outside the control of the British Crown. The conquistadores were principally conquerors and not settlers of the Atlantic world. They initially conquered the natives before the coming of those who would settle the land. For example, the ancient Inca society was overthrown by a relatively small group of conquistadores who accompanied Hernán Cortés, one of the two principal conquerors (Francisco Pizarro was the other conquistador involved in the conquest of Mexico) of the Atlantic world. (Cf. *New Encyclopedia Britannica*, 1975 ed., s.v. "Colonial Latin America and the Caribbean" by Benjamin Keen.

As we have seen *supra*, the encomienda-*doctrina* system was an intricate cooperative system established by the rising bourgeois elite, the conquistadores. The goal of the encomienda-*doctrina* was to exploit land and its resources, to control natives, to indoctrinate them in the Catholic faith, and to build and maintain churches, roads, and profitable shipping ports. The encomienda-*doctrina* system was established with the use of soldiers. The encomienda system sponsored the "civilizing" mission of the conquistadores. The conquistadores violently took the natives from their natural habitat into towns under their control

Gilbert parented the concept of the actual colonization of the eastern part of North America for Great Britain, superseding both Spain and Portugal. He also fostered the idea that North America could be structured into a wholly feudal society that included commerce. The "rights" of the natives, however, were irrelevant to him.[607]

> Gilbert gradually built up . . . a remarkably consistent body of theory on the articulation of a renewed feudal society. He knew what elements of authority should adhere to the lord proprietor and how much autonomy he could, in turn, allow to his tenants, ranging from poor, landless emigres to lords of immense areas of soil and their subtenants, in the elaborate social pyramid which could be constructed.[608]

Though the Calverts[609] knew of the Gilbert theories, it would be important to note that the Maryland colony was not to be a direct descendant of Gilbert.

---

and used them as slave labor to extract the resources from the land for profit. They attacked the fiber of the existing native societies, forcing them to live in abominable conditions. Often there were reports that the natives were tortured. The conquistadores were ruthless in their pillaging and confiscating of both human and natural resources throughout the various Spanish possessions.

As seen above, for further background on the encomienda-*doctrina* system, see *New Catholic Encyclopedia*, 1967, 1979 ed., s.v. "Encomienda-*Doctrina* System in Spanish America" by A. S. Tiegesar; R. B. Cunninghame Graham, *A Vanquished Arcadia: Being Some Account of the Jesuits in Paraguay, 1607–1667* (London: Century, 1988), 12; Jay P. Dolan, "Conquest and Conversion in the New World," in *The American Catholic Experience: A History from Colonial Times to the Present* (Notre Dame and London: University of Notre Dame Press, 1992), 15–42; Stephen Neill, *A History of Christian Missions* (Baltimore: Penguin Books, 1964); Hanke, *The Spanish Struggle for Justice in the Conquest of America*. See also note 58, 149.

[607] Quinn, "Introduction: Prelude to Maryland," 15.

[608] Quinn, "Introduction: Prelude to Maryland," 14.

[609] Sir George Calvert, the first Lord Baltimore, was originator of the ideas of a colony for Catholic refugees. At his death, he was succeeded by his first son, Cecil Calvert, who became the second Lord Baltimore. Although Cecil Lord Baltimore as proprietor of the Maryland colony originally planned to reside in the colony, we shall see that he stayed in England to protect the interests of the colonists against those who would undermine it. Then there was Leonard Calvert, the second son of George Calvert and the first governor of the Maryland colony. The history of the Maryland colony centered on this second son of George Calvert. Then there was the third son, George Calvert, the namesake of his father, who also traveled in the original voyage to the colony with his brother Leonard. George was named the first lieutenant governor, but he died within six months after

Gilbert's principles contradicted those whereupon Maryland was eventually founded. Gilbert's theories included two elements that were absent from the Maryland foundation: the Maryland charter required the principle of the advice and consent of the governed, and it secured a place for the native peoples.[610] It would be important to state that Cecil Calvert's charter for the Maryland colony as well as the Virginia colony and other commercial interests only provided confirmation that the Maryland charter was radically different. Rather than just model itself on Gilbert's theories, the Maryland charter challenged the developing trends regarding settlements in the New World.

For the most part, it was the poverty of English Catholics and the growing opposition among Catholics toward England in general, along with threats of war between Spain and England, that combined to end any further attempts on the part of Catholics at colonization in the New World during the late sixteenth century.

Wealthy Catholics were few in numbers; therefore, they were limited in participation in any new venture. The two sides in the opposition among Catholics were between those who desired to be involved in colonization efforts. On the one hand, there were those who saw that these overseas ventures were not the best way to deal with their own poverty and persecution in England. Additionally, they thought that they could give "political allegiance to the crown without violating the tenets of their faith."[611]

On the other hand, being involved in Gilbert's expeditions was perceived now as a kind of cooperation with the English government, an early contradiction on the part of the prospective Catholic settlers. Commitment to Gilbert's plans also went against the designs of the Catholic party sponsored by the Spanish government. This party favored a strong resistance to the English Protestant government, and it sought the restoration of Catholicism in England.

The Spanish ambassador to England was also head of the Spanish-sponsored Catholic party in England. He used his power to prompt Catholics to oppose the involvement of Catholics in Gilbert's schemes. The reason for the opposition was not a lack of empathy with the persecuted Catholics. It was mainly because involvement with persecuted Catholics threatened the Spanish hegemony in the Atlantic world.[612]

---

the settlement at Saint Marys City (Harry Wright Newman, *The Flowering of the Maryland Palatinate: An Intimate and Objective History of the Province of Maryland to the Overthrow of Proprietary Rule in 1654, with Accounts of Lord Baltimore's Settlement at Avalon* [Baltimore: Genealogical Publishing Co., Inc., 1985; originally published in Washington DC, 1961]).

[610] Newman, *The Flowering of the Maryland Palatinate*, 15.

[611] Ives, *The* Ark *and the* Dove, 23.

[612] Ives, *The* Ark *and the* Dove, 24.

It can be seen that the ventures were mostly supported by wealthy Protestant gentlemen, land- and profit-hungry younger sons of mercantilists who had a vision of amassing wealth by the confiscation of the mineral resources of these newly founded markets.[613] They believed they could achieve this by exploiting the dissatisfied and disillusioned Catholic gentry of England. Yet along with this drive for wealth was a dominant, unconcealed anti-Catholic spirit. The context was one in which Spain had become identified with Catholicism around the world of that day.

So the waning of its hegemony of Spain was seen as a weakening of Catholicism, and John Tracy Ellis said, "[A] unifying theme in the English propaganda for colonies was that every advance made against the Spaniards was a blow against the papacy."[614] Ellis proceeded to say that the wealthy Englishmen, "freebooters" as they were called, reveled in anything that helped diminish the influence of the Catholic Church.

Tracy Ellis stated that, even though their ventures were peopled with Catholics, the efforts of Gilbert, Raleigh, and others—for example, John Hawkins, Francis Drake, and Martin Frobisher—"were credited with advancing the Protestant cause" because these expeditions were competing for English supremacy over Spain.[615] "There was joined to avarice for material wealth, anxiety to grasp unclaimed lands, and jealousy for the mastery of the seas, as leading motives for English efforts in the new world, a determination to crush Catholicism."[616] Gilbert's attempts might be summarized in the following way:

> [Gilbert's] ideas and master plan lived on in documents and in the minds of men throughout the fallow period of the Spanish war between 1585 and 1604, to be revived and experimented with during the following generation. The plans showed no realization of what colonization in America involved in physical and economic terms, let alone in connection with the resident inhabitants, but the ideas of territorial lordships in North America in one form or another was to last for well over a century.[617]

---

[613] Cf. Judith Mara Gutman, "The Merchant-Adventurer's World," in *The Colonial Venture: An Autobiography of the American Colonies from Their Beginnings to 1763* (New York: Basic Books Inc., n.d.), 1–48.

[614] John Tracy Ellis, *Catholics in Colonial America*, Benedictine Studies: Eight (Baltimore: Helicon Press, 1965), 316.

[615] Ellis, *Catholics in Colonial America*.

[616] Ellis, *Catholics in Colonial America*.

[617] Quinn, introduction to *Wider World*, 17.

Sir Walter Raleigh explored and collected data on the North Carolina and Virginia areas (1585–1603). He established settlements in the area of the city he named Raleigh in North Carolina. At this early period of British exploration, Raleigh even explored the possibility of establishing a military-type naval base that would serve as a kind of reconnaissance headquarters for testing the land and climate and for initiating and securing collaborations with the natives. But this idea never materialized because the Crown demanded that his ships be returned to England to defend against the Spanish armada.[618] Raleigh eventually lost his title to the American land in 1603. He tried to live peacefully with the Chesapeake Indians of that region, but he and his settlement ended up being wiped out by the Indians in around 1606/7.[619] But it must be remembered that in some sense, though the Gilbert and Raleigh schemes failed, the ideas lived on in the minds of the generations that followed, resulting first in the Virginia Settlement Company (1607–1624) and then in the development of the other colonies giving rise to the British colonial period. Unlike the earlier Catholic ventures, these latter colonies utilized the expertise of the merchant class, who introduced the profit motive.[620]

The period after these first attempts at colonization that were based on the escape of Catholics from England during the time of persecution saw the distinctive beginnings of the idea of the Maryland colony. After King James I came to power in 1603, he refused toleration of Catholics. The problem of toleration was not because James I was unfriendly to the Catholic aristocracy, for a number of them found themselves appointed to James's court (e.g., Sir George Calvert, later to be first Lord Baltimore, originator and founder of the Maryland colony). The problem was that James I made toleration of Catholics dependent on "the formal renunciation by Catholics of papal authority in temporal matters."[621]

It was at that time that the migration movement started up again after twenty years of no attempts on the part of Catholics. At this point, there was Lord Thomas Arundel, a nobleman and later to be the father-in-law of Cecil Calvert, son of George Calvert, who at the death of his father would

---

[618] Quinn, introduction to *Wider World*, 18.

[619] Quinn, "Prelude," 18.

[620] The plans of Gilbert and the experiments of Raleigh provided valuable information regarding the expense of these colonial ventures. This information resulted in the later adjustments used in the establishment of the Virginia Company. These later ventures brought to bear a combination of merchant expertise with its profit motive, and the theories of Gilbert combined with the ambitions of recusant Catholics wedded to the experiments of Raleigh allowed for the establishment of settlements over an extended period. Ibid., 18–19.

[621] Ibid., 19.

become second Lord Baltimore. Arundel became interested in establishing a settlement but was discouraged by both priests and friends.

In spite of their discouraging him, Arundel continued his plans; and in 1605, Easter Sunday, the *Archangel* with George Weymouth as its captain set sail for the Maine coast. However, no permanent colony would be established, and so they sailed back to England. Like earlier expeditions, this was just another attempt by Catholics to get away from persecution.[622]

From Gilbert's first attempt at colonial settlement during a period of eighty years up to the Arundel-Weymouth settlements in Maine, there were fifty-nine charters issued by the British Crown in a territory from the Gulf of Saint Lawrence down to the Amazon. All were granted for the propagation of Christian religion through the English church. According to Thomas Hughes in his monumental work on the history of the Jesuits, these charters were strongly saturated with antipopery and anti-Catholicism. As an example, the Virginia charter in 1609 declared,

> Because the principall effect which Wee cann desier or expect of this Action, is the conversion and reduction of the people in those partes unto the true Worshipp of God and Christian Religion, in which respect Wee would be lothe that anie person should be permitted to passe that Wee suspected to affect the superstitions of the Churche of Rome, Wee doe hereby declare that it is oure will and pleasure, that now be permitted to passe in arne voiage from time to time to be made into the saide countrie, but such as firste shall have taken the oath of suprematie; for which purpose Wee doe by theise present give full power and authoritie to the Tresorer for the time beinge, and anie three of the Counsell to tender and exhibite the said Oath to all such persons as shall at anie time be sent and imploied in said voige. Although expresse the mention, etc. In witness whereof, etc. J.r. [Jacobus Rex] apud -xxiii. die maij. Per ipsum Regem.[623]

---

[622] For example, Ives discovered a "relation" in the work *Purchas his pilgrimes* (Glasgow, 1906, xvm, p. 335 et seq.), which referred to a man named James Rosier, thought to be a Jesuit priest who accompanied an adventurer by the name of Bartholomew Gosnold on an expedition to New England in 1602. *Purchas his pilgrimes* made the reference in the following statement: "The religious tone of his letters indicated that he was a priest and there is no doubt but that he was sent on a second expedition by Lord Arundel." This expedition was not a permanent settlement, and the Rosier "relation" was the only record of the voyage (Ives, *The Ark and the Dove*, 26).

[623] Thomas Hughes, *History of the Society of Jesus in North America: Colonial and Federal.*

After England became prominent in the Atlantic world with its victory over the armada (1588), Spain was subservient to England. Catholics, by then, were forced out in the face of Protestant ascendancy in Western expansion. Protestant dominance, with its aforementioned concentration in a Calvinistic religious system of the "saved and the unsaved," was a ready construct for the furthering of the cause of modernity in the dehumanization process in English-speaking America up to the present day.

To securely ground these facts, it is necessary to present specific historical data. Though the data might be detailed, it in no way is meant to suggest that this is merely an event-by-event presentation. We are crawling back through the history of this period to not only chronicle the age when modernity has taken shape in the Atlantic world but also demonstrate how economics and religion have become the ready tools of the dehumanization process.

3.2. THE MARYLAND COLONY

3.2.1. THE CALVERTS IN ENGLAND

The focus on the Calverts; the Jesuits, especially Fr. Andrew White; his companions; and their role in the founding of the Maryland colony was a contingent element in an understanding of the religious ideas that clashed the rise of the Atlantic world. As the Maryland historian Matthew Page Andrews stated, "The founding of the Maryland colony represents the fruition of an idea; and the plan of settlement offered a solution for the most difficult political and social problem of the Christian era."[624]

The significance of the Calverts in the ascendancy of the Atlantic world with its newly developing political economy rested in the role George Calvert (1580–1632), the first Lord Baltimore, would play in the British government and in his vision for a settlement in British America for Catholic recusants. George Calvert's government service and his connections with some of the earliest British settlers, specifically his membership in the Virginia-London Company and the New England Council, provided him with the rich background and experience. Let us look more specifically at the role of George Calvert, the first Lord Baltimore, and at the colony he fashioned.

George Calvert was born the eldest son of Leonard Calvert and Alice Crossland at Kipling, Catterick Parish, North Riding and Yorkshire. Leonard Calvert of Kipling in the chapelry of Bolton, Yorkshire, descended from

---

Text, From the First Colonization till 1645 (London: Longmans, Green & Co., 1907, 1908), 1:150–51.

[624] Matthew Page Andrews, *History of Maryland: Province and State* (Garden State, NY: Doubleday, Doran & Company, Inc., 1929), 1.

"the ancient and noble house of Calvert in the earldom of Flanders."[625] Alice Crossland was the daughter of John Crossland, of Crossland, Gent., one of the ancient families of England.

George Calvert's parents were probably recusant Catholics in England, and he was born at the time of serious religious problems for Catholics.[626] Religious restraints sought to undermine the family's attachment to Catholicism until they were forced to relinquish their commitment to Roman Catholicism and to embrace the Church of England.[627] Thus, one became stigmatized by any religion that did not conform to the rising interests of modernity. Such a religion had the potential of confronting the status quo and would not be tolerated. Therefore, any attempts at a Catholic education for George Calvert, during the early years of his life, were thwarted. As a boy of thirteen, he studied under a Protestant tutor at York for two years. Then admitted as a "gentleman commoner" at age fifteen in 1593, he went for formal studies at Trinity College of Oxford, where he received his bachelor's degree in 1597.[628]

The "patronus" of George Calvert from as early as 1597 was Sir Robert Cecil, the Marquess of Salisbury. He met Sir Robert Cecil while on a tour of Europe.[629] By 1605, soon after receiving the master of arts degree at Oxford, George Calvert began his career of public service by becoming the personal secretary to Sir Robert Cecil, who had great political power in the Crown during the reign of James I. Sir Robert Cecil was created Earl of Salisbury, of Oxford, and of Northumberland.[630] Through Sir Robert Cecil's patronage, Calvert rose rapidly in the service.

---

[625] Henry Foley, SJ, *Records of the English Province of the Society of Jesus. Historic Facts Illustrative of the Labours and Sufferings of Its Members in the Sixteenth and Seventeenth Centuries*, 8 vols. (London: Burns and Oates, 1877–1883), 3:324.

Newman states that "it was perhaps in the fourteen-hundreds that the English progenitor crossed the channel and settled in County York and became a breeder of sheep—no doubt sending the wool back to his kinsmen in Flanders to be made into cloth—for Flanders in that day was the principal center of the textile weaving industry" (*The Flowering of the Maryland Palatinate*); Andrews, 1–2.

[626] As it shall be seen, George Calvert's religious background emerges as significant in terms of the establishment of the Maryland colony. The issue of the Catholicity of the Calverts will be looked at *infra*, page 207 passim.

[627] Krugler, "Sir George Calvert's Resignation," 239–54, 242.

[628] Foley, *Records*, 3:324; Celestine Joseph Nuesse, *The Social Thought of American Catholics, 1634–1829* (dissertation, Catholic University of America Studies in Sociology), vol. X (Washington DC: Catholic University of America Press, 1945), 11; Krugler, "Sir George Calvert's Resignation," 242.

[629] Krugler, "Sir George Calvert's Resignation," 243.

[630] Andrews, *The Founding of Maryland*, 19.

[He] served as Clerk of the Crown and Assizes in County Clare, Ireland, as one of the clerks of the Privy Council, and as the king's agent on special missions to the Continent; he also served in parliament in 1609.[631]

George Calvert's career in Parliament extended over two decades, first for Bossiney, Cornwall, in 1609; then for Yorkshire in 1621; and for Oxford in 1624.

After the death of Sir Robert Cecil in 1612, George Calvert succeeded him as Earl of Salisbury. He also became the correspondent for King James I in matters that related to Spain and Rome. George Calvert was sent to Ireland to mediate the conditions of Catholics in 1613. He became even more recognized for his public service when the king knighted him in 1617, and on February 1, 1619, he was appointed as one of the principal secretaries of state. He now became known for his familiarity with both Continental as well as domestic issues.

As an administrator, George Calvert was featured not in the role of policy maker but in the role of advising the king in important matters of state. His position demanded that he be the king's voice in Parliament on the following sensitive issues: the rise of the Puritans, the struggle over subsidies, the Catholic question, the Spanish dominance, and other foreign policy issues.

Seventeenth-century Europe was a time in which people generally were forced to conform to specific professions of faith or be seen as rebellious, for nations were identified with a specific form of worship.[632] So George Calvert became increasingly caught up in the political and religious crosscurrents that flourished among the king, the Parliament, and the dominant religious elements during this troublesome period.

By 1623, George Calvert had become involved in issues that would ultimately force his resignation. He found himself under pressure as he served as an emissary of King James I, who was now tempered with age. Becoming embroiled in the king's foreign policy politics, he conducted the negotiations for the proposed marriage between Prince Charles Stuart of England to Infanta Maria of Spain and a proposed treaty with Spain.[633] The match was against the will of the Puritan faction of England, who felt strongly that the Roman Catholic influence of Spain would undermine Puritan religious interests. When this marriage and alliance failed, Prince Charles pursued an

---

[631] Krugler, "Sir George Calvert's Resignation," 239–54, 243. According to Krugler, Calvert was "a painstaking, cautious and faithful servant," characteristics that he manifested especially in a controversy involving the Dutch theologian Vorstius in 1609, whereupon gaining the attention of the king.

[632] Andrews, *The Founding of Maryland*, 19.

[633] Hanley, *Their Rights and Liberties*, 60.

alliance with Princess Henrietta Maria of France, thus changing the support of England from Spain to France.

The Parliament had not favored Calvert's proposed alliance with Spain, which it interpreted as negative, and thus chose to enter into a hostile foreign policy with Spain. Calvert's credibility in foreign policy waned as the spheres of influence changed in these last years of the king's reign. Calvert was made Lord Baron of Baltimore, County Longford, Ireland. This honor came from James I on February 16, 1624, as a reward for his years of service.[634]

Then when Charles I succeeded his father to the throne in early 1625, he invited all the members of his father's council to continue to serve in their existing capacities. George Calvert ended up resigning as secretary of state, and it was believed to have been for religious reasons. Even though he was reputed to have been born of Catholic parents, it would be important to note that George Calvert lived as a Catholic probably for only a brief period in his early childhood.

At the time of his resignation, George Calvert was not forced but chose to reveal that he was a Catholic; and as already stated, he may have been such all his life.[635] There were various interpretations of this coincidence between his announcing he was a Roman Catholic and his resignation as secretary of state. Even though there was no existent infant baptismal record of George Calvert, it was the general practice in a Catholic family to baptize the newborn shortly after birth.[636] Therefore, George was probably already a Catholic; but after his father's forced disavowal of Catholicism when George was a child, he lived a life committed to the Church of England.

One interpretation was that, with the death of the king, George Calvert's "conversion" was little more than an open acknowledgment of a long-held secret; namely, that he was "secretly a Papist" and was a Spanish spy operating in the inner circle of James's government. This position was only an assertion and would have warranted little or no connection to the proclamation of 1625.[637]

Another interpretation was that George Calvert converted to Catholicism in late 1624 or early 1625, which in turn caused or forced him to withdraw from politics. This interpretation had a long-standing history, argued by prominent

---

[634] Carr, x.

[635] Cf. *supra*, p. 204. Krugler, "Sir George Calvert's Resignation," 243–52; Andrews, *The Founding of Maryland*, 21–25; James McSherry, *History of Maryland*, ed. and continued by Bartlett B. James (Baltimore: Baltimore Book Co., 1904), 20–21; Hanley, *Their Rights and Liberties*, 59–61.

[636] Krugler, "Sir George Calvert's Resignation," 239–54, 238–42.

[637] Krugler, "Sir George Calvert's Resignation," 240.

historians of Maryland, particularly Matthew Page Andrews and Thomas O'Brien Hanley.

M. P. Andrews said, "[The] change of spiritual allegiance *caused* him [Calvert] to resign his high office and greatly strengthened his desire to found a successful settlement in America, which, in Newfoundland, he had already begun" (emphasis added).[638] Thomas O'Brien Hanley, who concurred with the position of M. P. Andrews, held that Calvert had ventured into an unsure political situation due to his "conversion." The conversion of Calvert caused his resignation from the council of Charles I. To support the stance he took, Hanley cited Charles M. Andrews's use of a letter from the Florentine ambassador to the Grand Duke of Tuscany, April 11, 1635, in his work *The Colonial Period of American History*. According to Andrews, the ambassador said, "Everyone knew him [George Calvert] to be a Catholic, he could not serve him [Charles I] in the same high office . . . nor was he willing to take an oath so wounding to his religious feelings."[639]

Thus, M. P. Andrews and Hanley thought that Calvert's conversion was actually what "forced" or "caused" his resignation. For them, Calvert's resignation was connected to his commitment to the church. According to Krugler, however, their argumentation was based on a misunderstanding of how Stuart politics functioned at that period. He said that, because of the events leading up to a conversion, Stuart politics would have made it necessary for Calvert to leave office and then convert to Catholicism. Yet this was not how it occurred.[640]

According to John D. Krugler, the interpretation that was most likely was that George Calvert was probably baptized at birth and was reared as a Catholic; but later, his family was forced to submit to the Church of England. In 1625, George Calvert experienced personal crisis as he was witness to the unfair treatment of Catholics. This prompted him to revert to his childhood religion and vie for the establishment of a colony.

Krugler's argument was that religion, as such, was not the only motive for Calvert's resignation but his diminishing political influence in the court as well.[641] Calvert's statement to the king about his conversion was no more than an acknowledgment of his Catholic past. The decision to resign as secretary of state was only the occasion for Calvert to announce his Roman Catholicism.

---

638 Andrews, *The Founding of Maryland*, 24.

639 Charles M. Andrews, *The Colonial Period of American History*, 4 vols. (New Haven, Connecticut, 1937), 2:277–78; Hanley, *Their Rights and Liberties*, 59; "Historical Manuscripts Commission: Second Appendix to Fifth Report"; "Appendix to Sixth Report"; and "Fifth Appendix to Tenth Report."

640 Krugler, "Sir George Calvert's Resignation," 240.

641 Krugler, "Sir George Calvert's Resignation," 252–54.

Thus, the resignation of George Calvert as secretary of state was not entirely caused by his "conversion" to Catholicism. On the contrary, it seemed that his resignation was prompted by his escalated desire to shape a new type of society whose goal would be to try to escape the tense religious and economic conflicts that had become common on British soil.

For Calvert, colonization would be the solution to the conflicts that had already begun during the latter years of his involvement in the court of James I. It would be important to note that, even though other historians differed from Krugler about what prompted the resignation of George Calvert, M. P. Andrews and Hanley argued along with Krugler that the resignation was directly related to his interest in establishing a colony.[642] He wanted to establish a settlement in the New World, which would be a haven for English Catholics.[643]

Lois Carr, a more recent historian of Maryland, seemed to concur with John Krugler that George Calvert was born into a Catholic family and was probably baptized as an infant. Carr also stated that the family had been under pressure and was abused by England's laws demanding that Catholics conform to the Church of England instead of being faithful to Rome. George Calvert's father, but probably not his mother, consequently submitted to the Church of England and left the Roman church. However, Calvert finally sided with the struggle of Catholics and wanted to work toward the founding of a colony.[644]

Therefore, George Calvert's interest was in the founding of a unique colony with broader liberties than earlier charters possessed.[645] He wanted no clauses resisting the migration of Catholics. Thereby, Catholics could escape the oppression of the English church and state, and all sects would be allowed to exist in harmony.[646] He knew that the other colonies that had been established offered a similar solution had the idea of a sanctuary as their goal. But his vision was to be different still. Unlike those colonies that had preceded,

---

[642] Krugler, "Sir George Calvert's Resignation," 253–54; Andrews, *The Founding of Maryland*, 24; Hanley, *Their Rights and Liberties*, 60.

[643] When he was in Parliament, George Calvert had been an emissary of the king in the Virginia-London Company (1609), which was based on the theories of Gilbert and Raleigh, and he also had membership on the New England Council (1621). Andrews, *The Founding of Maryland*, 21, 47–48.

[644] Krugler, "Sir George Calvert's Resignation," 239–54, 239–40; Lois Green Carr, "The Charter of Maryland," in *A Declaration of the Lord Baltimore's Plantation in Mary-Land*, Maryland Hall of Records Commission (June 20, 1983), viii.

[645] It must be noted that, at this period, the Virginia (1607), the Plymouth (1620), and the Massachusetts Bay (1628) colonies already had been established.

[646] Hanley speculated that Calvert, during his stay in Parliament, "could not escape a debate with himself over the nature of a church and state which was at the bottom of the problems of religious conformity" (*Their Rights and Liberties*, 60).

Lord Baltimore did not want a colony just for his persecuted "coreligionists." He envisioned the founding of a colony whereby all people, including the native peoples (even if they did not convert to Catholicism), might be able to worship in peace.[647]

3.2.2. THE NEWFOUNDLAND "EXPERIMENT"

George Calvert was an official representative of the Crown on several settlement committees. Among them were the London and Virginia Company, possibly the East India Company, and the Newfoundland Committee.[648] It was the Newfoundland Committee, tended by the British nobleman Sir William Vaughan, that purchased Newfoundland between 1616 and 1620 at the time of the Arundel-Weymouth expeditions.[649] Newfoundland was a section of the New World north of Maine that comprised the whole southern part of the Avalon Peninsula. Calvert became involved in Newfoundland in 1620 and purchased part of this grant from Vaughan. Calvert's original purchase was only "a narrow strip of land running east to west from the Atlantic seaboard to Placentia Bay; it was bounded in the north by Caplin Bay (now Calvert) and in the south by the headland between Aquaforte and Fermeuse. This lot included the harbor of Ferryland."[650]

On August 4, 1621, George Calvert established a settlement of twelve fishermen at Ferryland of Newfoundland under the command of a Welsh soldier and sea captain named Capt. Edward Wynne. As early as 1623, before he left his position in the British court, Calvert began preparing a charter for a colony at Newfoundland that was to be submitted to the king for approval and seal. He had in mind developing a charter that would be different from the stock company of New England or the royal company of Virginia.

At this early stage in almost experimental fashion, George Calvert sought "to negotiate for a charter that was . . . a palatinate or proprietary colony."[651] Additionally, the palatine concept–implied in the Newfoundland experiment–and the proprietary concept were to be used interchangeably.

---

[647] Andrews, *The Founding of Maryland*, 24.

[648] Russell R. Menard and Lois Green Carr, "The Lords Baltimore and the Colonization of Maryland," in *Early Maryland in a Wider World*, ed. David B. Quinn (Detroit: Wayne State University Press, 1982), 167–215, 173.

[649] Hanley, *Their Rights and Liberties*, 63; R. J. Lahey, "The Role of Religion in Lord Baltimore's Colonial Enterprise," *Maryland Historical Magazine* 72, 4 (Winter 1977): 492–511. See Arundel-Weymouth expeditions *supra*, pp. 201–2 passim.

[650] Lahey, "The Role of Religion in Lord Baltimore's Colonial Enterprise," 494. Lahey is using a description from a map of Newfoundland found in Sir William Vaughan's *Golden Fleece*; also *Purchas his pilgrimes*, 4:1873.

[651] Hanley, *Their Rights and Liberties*, 63.

The palatine or proprietary type of colony was an enlightened feudalistic-type state (humanistic as opposed to rationalist state of modernity) whose emphasis was on settlement and in which all the authority would be held by the owners of the land. Those landowners would have the ultimate powers to make the necessary laws for the good of the colony but only in conjunction with settler participation of "advise and assent."[652] Later, we would explain the difference between the two types of colonies and discuss the notion of the palatinate.

Then on April 7, 1623, Charles I–to demonstrate the appreciation of his father, King James I, for George Calvert's loyalty, integrity, and years of exemplary service rendered to the court–endowed him with a colonial charter. The Calvert settlement was to have "the royalties of a Count Palatine" in Newfoundland, which he named *Avalon*.[653] Finally, George Calvert would be able to fulfill his vision of a colony in the New World for his persecuted coreligionists.

In the meantime, with the two ships *Ark of Avalon* and *George*, George Calvert set out to visit his colony on April 27, 1627, disembarking at Avalon in the summer of 1627. George Calvert returned to England and eventually to his peerage in Ireland.[654]

In the spring of 1628, he made a second voyage to Avalon, bringing his wife; his children, except for Cecil, his eldest son; his two sons-in-law, Sir Robert Talbot, Knt., and William Peasley, Esq.; and their household goods and over sixty settlers, most of them Irish Catholic.[655]

Demonstrating that the new colony was to be sensitive to the religious rights of all, Calvert brought priests as well as Protestant ministers to satisfy the spiritual needs of all colonists. By providing places of worship for all Christian religious groups, Calvert had advanced beyond his time. This settlement had achieved something that was beyond the thinking of most of

---

[652] Hanley, *Their Rights and Liberties*, 63–64. John Gilmary Shea, *History of the Catholic Church in the United States*, vol. 1, *The Catholic Church in Colonial Days: The Thirteen Colonies–The Ottawa and Illinois Country–Louisiana–Florida–Texas–New Mexico and Arizona, 1521–1763* (New York: John G. Shea, 1886), 1:30–31.

[653] Andrews, *The Founding of Maryland*, 25; Foley, *Records*, 3:325. According to M. P. Andrews and the Jesuit historian Henry Foley, Newfoundland–which was the first Christian settlement in the English-speaking New World–was given the name *Avalon*. The reason for this name was so that the colony might bear the same name as the place of the "first fruits of Christianity in ancient Britain," namely, Glastonbury, Somersetshire, which was also called *Avalon*. Though he admitted that the Newfoundland charter was not accessible to him, Fr. Henry Foley refers to Avalon as a "count palatine."

[654] Newman, *The Flowering of the Maryland Palatinate*, 7.

[655] Newman, *The Flowering of the Maryland Palatinate*, 7–8.

his contemporaries.[656] Lord Baltimore's desire to have all the settlers at Avalon worship freely was soon to be the source of the charges brought against him, especially because it allowed Catholics to be free of the English penal code.[657]

The settlement at Newfoundland, along with its palatine privilege, turned out to be an experiment that did not last long for George Calvert, his wife, his children, and the settlers. They were not prepared for the terribly cold winters. Not only was the climate a serious problem but the soil also did not lend itself to growing crops. The greatest enemy to the Calvert settlement in Avalon was that of the French Huguenots from Canada, whose ships of war tried to overrun the Avalon colony. The Huguenots were Protestant merchants who were against the establishment of the Catholic colony by George Calvert. Additionally, it can be established that the Huguenots desired new economic markets, and they saw Avalon, which was primarily a peaceful exclusive refuge for the persecuted of England, as a threat to their business enterprise.[658]

Studying a letter to the Duke of Buckingham regarding what occurred with the French, we would begin to have insight into the unique character of George Calvert and the characteristics of his colonial effort. What appeared at this early date were the religious conflicts that so dramatically characterized the opening up of the Atlantic world. The Catholics, in escaping the long arm of rising mercantilism, ran headlong into it at the very beginning of their sojourn in America. As Calvert himself said in a letter to the Duke of Buckingham, "*I came to build, and settle and sow; and I am fallen to fighting Frenchmen* [italics in original]."[659]

---

656   Lahey, 499 passim; Nuesse, *The Social Thought of American Catholics*, 12; Shea, *History of the Catholic Church*, 31.

657   Shea, *History of the Catholic Church*, 32. The Newfoundland experience prepared George Calvert, Lord Baltimore, well for when he would write the charter for the Maryland colony. He would not set up places of worship himself, but all religious beliefs were free to provide their own ministers and places for worship or not worship at all. Religious practice and a place for worship for all would not be mandated in the Maryland charter. Calvert, however, would still insist on the inclusion of all sects in the colony, even though it would eventually work against him as the Puritans would invade the Maryland colony in 1646. See the section on the Puritan invasion *infra*, p. 70.

658   Andrews, *The Founding of Maryland*, 26–27; Newman, *The Flowering of the Maryland Palatinate*, 8.

659   Andrews, *The Founding of Maryland*, 26–27. The letter of Calvert gives an account of just one of the attacks of the French traders on his settlement at Newfoundland:

I remember that his Majestie once told me that I writt as faire a hand to looke upon a farre off as any man in England, but that when anyone came neare itm they weare not able to read a word; whereuppon I gott a dispensation both from his Marie and yor Grace to use another man's pen when I write to eyther of you, and I humblye thanke you for it; for Writting is a greate payne to mee now.

This account of the Newfoundland experiment painted an imaginative landscape of the entrance of the Calverts into the Atlantic world. The Newfoundland experiment depicted the incipient stage of the clash of religious ideas that was taking place in the Atlantic world. To the tradesmen above, the Calverts represented the old regime–Catholic manorial Europe–while the merchant-trader forces they confronted in the Newfoundland experiment represented the newly developing ideology of the modern state, which was ultimately to characterize the political hegemony of that world up to the present.

Calvert's vision that he could establish a colony in the New World for his persecuted coreligionists had come to an end. The business interests and the attack on his settlement at Newfoundland by the French Huguenots, presumably in their interest of mercantilism, apparently gave the initial definition of the idea of *protestant* in the rise of the Atlantic world.[660]

By August 19, 1629, Lord Baltimore considered the Newfoundland colony a failure. In another letter, he petitioned Charles I for a change of location and

---

One de la Rade of Dieppe with three ships and 400 men, many of them gentlemen of quality, and La Fleur de la Jeunness de Normandy (as some Frenchmen here have told us) came first into a harvour of mine called Capebroile not above a league from the place where I am planted, and ther surprising divers of the fishermen in their shallops at the harbour's mouth, within a short time after possed themselves of two English ships within the harbour, with all their fish and provisions, and had done the like to the rest in that place had I not sent them assistance with two ships of mine, one of 360 tons and 34 pieces of ordance, and the other a bark of 60 tons with 3 or 4 small guns in her and about 100 men aboard us in all.

The ships being discovered to move by a scout whom the French kept at the harbourls mouth, they stayed not weighing anchor, but let slip their cables and away to sea as fast as they could, leaving their booty and 67 of their own men behind them on shore for haste. We gave them chase but could not overtake them, and that night I sent a company to fetch the 67 men out of the woods, fearing that being well armed, as we understood they were, and then in desperation, they might force some boat or weak ship, or do other mischief, and the next morning they were brought unto me hither, where I have been troubled and charged with them all this summer. . . . Your Grace's most faithful and humble servant, George Baltimore Ferryland, 25 August, 1628.

[660] It is important to note that Protestantism in this history of Maryland is not a discourse on religious difference as much as it is a reaction against any movement that has refused to be wholly motivated by "business" or any movement that has possessed the potential to reject "business" and its meaning. The distinguishing ingredient of protestantism manifested in the interchange between Calvert and the Crown at his entrance into the Atlantic world is that being protestant became synonymous with being more interested in trading than in establishing a settlement.

cited the harsh climate as the reason for the failure. However, the historian M. P. Andrews suggested the contrary. M. P. Andrews stated that Calvert's letter not only revealed the "attitude and outlook" of Calvert but it also asserted that Calvert was deceived by "certain men of prominence" who, in the interest of their own commercial and political advantage, misdirected Calvert's attention to Newfoundland."[661]

George Calvert requested of the king that he leave a contingent of settlers, mostly fishermen, at Newfoundland in the interest of maintaining the Crown's possession. The above statements in his letter to the king said the intentions of Calvert to support the public interests of the Crown to increase the boundaries of the British domain in the New World. Thus, Calvert requested permission from the Crown to take with him forty Avalon colonists and, while still under the Newfoundland charter, survey the possibility of settling in the region of Virginia. His wife and children had already gone ahead of him to the warmer climate of Virginia.

Lord Baltimore favored the Virginia region, but he soon found that there was great hostility to Catholics from the rising Puritan population in Virginia. The governor of Virginia, John Potts, along with the other leadership of that colony insisted that he and his company take the oath of supremacy and allegiance so they could remain.[662] Lord Baltimore refused to take such oaths as they were drafted. So he drew up his own form, which he and his followers would take, but this proposed oath was repudiated. The long-term open strife particularly directed at Catholics had now manifested itself in Virginia. What was significant in light of future developments was that Catholics could not live in harmony with the other colonists. These disappointments, however, did not deter George Calvert from his commitment to the formation of a permanent Catholic colony.

With the experience of hostility fresh in his mind, Lord Baltimore returned to England during the late summer of 1629, requesting a grant for the Virginia region. Calvert was met with resistance similar to his experience while visiting the Virginia colony. In England, Lord Baltimore found himself facing even

---

[661] Andrews, *The Founding of Maryland*, 27.

[662] Andrews, *The Founding of Maryland*, 30–31; Ellis, *Catholics in Colonial America*, 325. Also, cf. Shea, *History of the Catholic Church*, 1:32. Shea stated that William Claiborne, secretary of the Virginia colony, was present and also insisted on the Calvert's colonists taking the oaths of allegiance to the Crown and supremacy of the Church of England. Shea also quoted two sources regarding this incident (n. 1, 1:32). He cited Sainsbury: "In justifying their course, Potts and his associates boasted 'that no Papists have been suffered to settle their abode amongst us.'" Then he cited Neill: "Virginia broke up a French Catholic settlement in Maine, and at a later day had prevented Irish Catholics from landing" (Sainsbury, "Calendar of State Papers," i, 104; and Neill, "Founders of Maryland," 45).

more serious opposition from members of the British-based Virginia Company, of which he was formerly a member. But he found support from Sir Thomas Arundel, a Catholic, who along with Sir George Weymouth had already been engaged in pursuing a solution to the "problem of religious conflict."[663]

In 1631, Charles I, king of England, granted Lord Baltimore the territory south of Virginia. Again, the Puritan-influenced faction of the Virginia colony–Claiborne included–reared up against and resisted the Calvert venture being placed so near to Virginia. Finally, Charles I resolved the issue by granting a patent for the territory north of Virginia, the Chesapeake region, which would be called Maryland in honor of Queen Henrietta Maria.[664]

The notion of the palatine privilege was only implied in the Newfoundland charter. Maryland was the first clearly defined proprietary or manorial system based on the palatine privilege in the New World *under English rule*, a kind of landed estate in which the tenants who occupied it paid quit rents, as they were called, to the proprietor of the colony (italics added).[665] The Maryland palatinate was considered to be special because unlike the Plymouth, Massachusetts Bay, or Virginia colonies, Maryland was the only colony with such a degree of independent administration.

There was also another feature that made Maryland unique; namely, the palatinate. Despite the feudal-like structure and the fact that the palatinate was tightly controlled by the authority of Lord Baltimore and his successors, the palatinate was also much more democratic than other colonies because the charter also "provided the legal basis for representative government."[666]

> [The charter] specified that the laws of the province had to be "of and with the advise, assent, and approbation of the

---

[663] Hanley, *Their Rights and Liberties*, 63. Arundel was involved along with Sir Francis Walsingham in establishing refuge colonies for Catholics. Arundel had also distinguished himself in voluntary service of Austria, where he took part in a battle against the Turks. There, he gained recognition by the Crown.

[664] Ellis, *Catholics in Colonial America*, 325; Andrews, *The Founding of Maryland*, 28–32.

[665] The phrase *under English rule* was used because Spain and Portugal must have had comparable institutions transplanted into the New World (e.g., the encomienda-*doctrina* system in Mexico and Central and Latin America). The manorial system must have been something as a common denominator to which the "palatine privilege" added supplementary rights. More would be written on the palatine privilege (1632/3) and its relationship to an earlier notion, the Paraguayan reductions (1610), and how both combatted the interests of the conquerors or conquistadores, as they were called in Latin America. See pp. 224, 242.

[666] Edward C. Papenfuse, introduction to *The Charter of Maryland*, Maryland Hall of Records (June 20, 1982).

free-men of the said province, or the greater part of them, or
of their delegates or deputies."[667]

This democratic element made the notion that Maryland was an
"enlightened" feudalistic state.

Calvert, in 1631, made a formal appeal to Father Blount,[668] the English
Jesuit provincial, for priests to be missioned to his American project.[669]
Moreover, Father Blount had to petition the Jesuit general M. Vitelleschi
in Rome to authorize priests to work as missionaries in the English colony.
Several letters exchanged hands between Blount and the Jesuit general before
permission was granted to Father Blount.[670]

Here was how this seemed to have occurred. In 1631, Father Blount sent
his letter requesting permission to send Jesuits to establish a mission in the
Maryland colony. But the issue of sending a priest into an English colony
required serious deliberation. The reason was that this would be the first
New World mission of the Jesuits that was not a Roman Catholic (i.e., French,
Spanish, or Portuguese) government-sponsored venture.[671]

The Jesuit general M. Vitelleschi responded to Father Blount's letter by
requesting more specific information, deciding to delay a decision until he

---

[667] Papenfuse, introduction to *The Charter of Maryland.*

[668] The Jesuits, now intensely engaged in missionary activity in England, created
a vice provincialate to facilitate their work. One of the most prominent Jesuits
during this period (1619–1635) was Fr. Richard Blount, who became the first to
fill the post of vice provincial of England. As vice provincial, Father Blount had
jurisdiction in England and was answerable only to his superior, the general in
Rome, M. Vitelleschi. Father Blount functioned in this capacity until Fr. Henry
More took over in 1635. Ives, *The* Ark *and the* Dove, 69–70.

[669] Fr. Edward Knott, the English Jesuit provincial between 1641 and 1642, presented
to the cardinal secretary of state or to the secretary of the Holy Office at the
Vatican an account of the issues between himself and Lord Baltimore. He said
that, before the establishment of the Maryland colony, Lord Baltimore had
sent letters to Fr. Richard Blount, English provincial, requesting Jesuit priests
for the Maryland mission. Knott stated that Provincial Blount received letters
("Addiditque litteras ad P. Generalem") from the baron that contained the original
formal request by George Calvert to the superior general of the Jesuits to assign
priests to the Maryland mission. "Addiditque litteras ad P. Generalem enixe rogans
uti habere posset selectos aliquot patres tum ad catholicos confirmandos, tum ad
haereticos convertendos, qui ad earn regionem incolendam destinandi erant, tum
etiam ad fidem apud infideles et barbaros propagandam" (Hughes, *Text*, 1:248,
249; Ibid., *Documents*, 1,1, no. 18, 178–81.)

[670] Reference to the correspondence between Vitelleschi and Blount is found in
Hughes, *Text*, 1:201, 246–47, 266–67.

[671] Hughes, *Text*, 1:201.

had that information. On June 4, 1633, the Jesuit general–still not having received the information he desired–issued a letter praising the potential of such a venture but again requesting more information that would help him in his decision to authorize the Jesuit priests to participate in the mission to the English colonies in America.[672]

In the meantime, on May 13, 1633, Father Blount had sent a second urgent letter requesting that Jesuits commit themselves to a mission in the Maryland colony. This second letter took three months to reach Rome. Apparently, this last letter still did not fulfill the Jesuit general Vitelleschi's request. Finally, it was not until late in the year of 1633 that the Jesuit general received adequate information to make the decision regarding sending Jesuits into the Maryland colony. He received the information he needed in the document "Declaratio coloniae" (1633), in brochure form, written by Fr. Andrew White.[673]

"Declaratio coloniae" made the call for settlers to make the voyage to Maryland. This colonization tract described the venture for those who might join it and provided the *first conditions of plantation*. The document stressed the location, the reasons for the settlement, and its potential benefits for its respondents. The declaration even encouraged investment into the venture by those who, for some reason, had to delay their presence in the colony.

The first conditions of plantation also stated that each one who joined the expedition either by paying one hundred pounds for every five able men they transported or by committing their men and money to the Lord's colonial office or to the care of someone else in the colony would receive a manor consisting of two thousand acres.[674] The first conditions of plantation was

---

[672] Hughes, *Text*, 1:246–48. Cf. Hughes, *Documents*, 1, 1:19, where in his letter Vitelleschi states, "[Y]our Reverence has a strong desire . . . to obtain from me the requisite authorization for sending some of ours on a mission, in company with English gentlemen or merchants, who are thinking of looking for new abodes in the Indies of the West, beyond the limits of those countries occupied by the Catholic King (of Spain) [and also of France and Portugal]" (translation).

[673] The full English title of the document as copied by Hughes is *A Declaration of the Lord Baltimore's Plantation in Mary-Land, Nigh upon Virginia: Manifesting the Nature, Quality, Condition and Rich Utilities It Contayneth* (February 10, anno 1633). Cf. Hughes, *Text*, 1:249–51. The historian Lawrence C. Wroth, in a monograph, contends that the Latin version, whose English form has been published earlier, has been expressly prepared by Father White to provide the specifics for the Jesuit general (White, *A Declaration of the Lord Baltimore's Plantation in Mary-Land*). Lawrence C. Wroth has edited and introduced a facsimile of the document, which has been published by the John Carter Brown Library on June 10, 1929, and reprinted by the Maryland Hall of Records Commission on June 20, 1983 (7–10). See also Robert Emmett Curran, ed., *American Jesuit Spirituality: The Maryland Tradition, 1634-1900* (New York; Mahwah: Paulist Press, 1988), 47.

[674] White, *A Declaration of the Lord Baltimore's Plantation in Mary-Land*, 22.

significant, especially in light of the land controversy between the Jesuits and Lord Baltimore, to be dealt with later in this chapter.

The Jesuit general wrote in an earlier letter to Father White that he highly commended him for offering his services. In a new letter (dated June 4, 1633), after he had received the "Declaratio coloniae," the general not only gave permission for Jesuits to join the Maryland expedition but also focused on the qualifications required in a foreign missionary using White as an example.[675] Blount not only appointed Fr. Andrew White (1579–1656) but also, at this time, assigned another priest and a lay brother for the venture, Fr. John Gravener, alias Altham (1589–1640), and Bro. Thomas Gervase (1590–1637), respectively. Both, like Father White, had made known their desire to work in the missions of America.[676]

Special emphasis needed to be given to what probably was of serious concern for the Jesuit general regarding the shape of the colony. The Jesuit general knew of and had given approval to the Jesuit missions called reductions in the Spanish colonial context. It was probably only after he received word regarding the palatine privilege of the Maryland charter that he gave permission for Jesuits to work in the missions associated with the British Crown. It was the Calverts with the insight and vision of the Jesuit social policy in Latin America, as it would be seen, along with freedom of religion and a palatine construction, warranting an internal independency of policies, that alone seemed to alleviate the Jesuit general's concerns.

Only after the approval from the Jesuit general did Fr. Andrew White and the Jesuits become involved in the colony. They even sponsored the venture, seeking to influence as many British Catholics as possible to join the venture. Although most of the advertising was done via person-to-person communication, the Jesuits also did some direct promotion with their publishing of Andrew White's *Declaration*.

In the meantime, after petitioning for Jesuit priests and applying for another colonial grant to settle in the area to the north of Virginia on the

---

[675] Hughes, *Text*, 1:246–48. "If you consider Father Andrew White to be well suited for that mission, and if he himself desires it so ardently, I see no reason why I should object to his being sent thither. But one point I cannot do otherwise than commend with all earnestness to your Reverence: it is that, in the choice of those whom you think of sending forth on that new expedition, you not only make much account of their inclination and desire—since, if people are unwilling or are not so will disposed for a long voyage like that, no great good can be expected from them—but also that you scrutinize most diligently their virtue, prudence, and zeal, especially in the case of those who are to lay the foundation of the mission; that they be such as the others who came afterwards may look up to, walking in their footsteps and following their example as a rule and model of action."

[676] Hughes, *Text*, 1:198–200; Ellis, *Catholics in Colonial America*, 327.

Potomac River and while making all the necessary preparation for the new colonial venture, the first Lord Baltimore, George Calvert, died on April 15, 1632. He was buried in the chancel of old Saint Dunstan's, Fleet Street, London.[677] Cecil Calvert, George Calvert's eldest son, at twenty-six years old, became the second Lord Baltimore and inherited his father's vision and all his plans. He started the royal bureaucratic process for a new warrant and charter draft, ending with a charter by June 20, 1632.[678]

He maintained the same good relations with the Jesuits as his father had. In fact, Cecil–upon the death of his father, even though he decided to leave the matter of religion in the colony to the colonists themselves–"availed himself of his father's appeal to the Society of Jesus to interest itself in his colony."

George Calvert's idea in the Newfoundland experiment, however, of bringing with him to Newfoundland and trying to support "Protestant and Catholic ministers of religion" had not been so successful; it had incurred severe criticism from all sides. George Calvert was accused of acting against the Crown (criminally) in setting up Roman Catholics. In setting up the Protestants, he was accused of being insincere in his religious profession as a Catholic.

So Cecil, to avoid possible conflict, would make a change in the charter contrary to his father's original idea about how religion was to be executed in the Maryland colony. It was a development in the trend toward religious freedom. Even though Cecil took advantage of his father's appeal to the Jesuits for involvement in the colony, he ruled out the support of any specific religion by the colonial government. Religious practice was left up to the settlers; it became a matter of a private decision (the first indication of the separation of church and state). This change was the earliest sign of compromise leading eventually to what was to become toleration of all religious groups except for Catholics.[679]

Before examining the palatine privilege, it is essential that we consider the background of the most significant Jesuit priest who has been cofounder of the Maryland colony and established the Roman Catholic Church in British America.

---

[677] Foley, *Records*, 3:325.

[678] Carr, "The Charter of Maryland," xviii–xxii. For treatment of the Maryland charter, see *infra* p. 229.

[679] Carr, "The Charter of Maryland," xviii–xxii; Ives, *The* Ark *and the* Dove, 69; Ellis, *Catholics in Colonial America*, 326–27; Andrews, *The Founding of Maryland*, 149–50.

3.2.3. FR. ANDREW WHITE, "THE APOSTLE OF MARYLAND"

Fr. Andrew White, heralded as the Apostle of Maryland, has been immediately associated with the Calverts, appointed chronicler of the Maryland colony, and as stated earlier motivated the research from whence the idea of the palatine privilege was developed.[680] Father White, even today, is a "saint" to many for whom he is the gyroscope for traditional old-world religion. He is the person who stands as a contradiction to the ultimate compromise by the Jesuits in the Atlantic world.

Father White was born in London in 1579, and like George Calvert, he was of a proscribed recusant background.[681] Unlike Calvert, however, not much was known of his early childhood or of his family. His initial education was in the English College at Douai in Flanders in early 1593, a place for Roman Catholic refugees. From November 1, 1593, until 1595, he studied at Saint Alban's College in Valladolid, Spain. He also studied at Saint Hermenegild College and Saint George's College at Seville, Spain, but returned to Flanders and to Douai College in June of 1604. In 1605, he was ordained a secular priest at Douai College.[682]

Fr. Andrew White volunteered to work in the mission in England. But upon arriving there, he found himself living the lifestyle of the hunted. It was at the time of the Gunpowder Plot (1605), which was an attempt by Catholics to seize power in England by using gunpowder to blow up the king and the Houses of Lords and Commons. Some priests were executed during this time, but Father White was arrested under the antimissionary priests' laws, imprisoned, and then permanently banished from England to Douai in Flanders along with forty-six other priests on July 24, 1606.[683] It would be

---

[680]   Maryland Historical Society, *The Calvert Papers*, Fund Publication No. 28, 209; J. A. Leo Lemay, *Men of Letters in Colonial Maryland* (Knoxville, Tennessee: University of Tennessee Press, 1972), 8.

[681]   For details regarding recusant, see *supra* p. 194.

[682]   Lemay, *Men of Letters*, 8–9; Cooper, "White, Andrew," in *Dictionary of National Biography*, ed. Sidney Lee, vol. 21 (London Smith, Elder & Co., 1909), 32.

[683]   Cooper, 32; Edwin H. Burton and Thomas L. Williams, eds. *The Douay College Diaries 3rd, 4th, 5th, 1598–1654 with the Rheims Report, 1570–1580*, vol. I (London: printed for the Society by John Whitehead & Son Ltd. of Leeds; also Catholic Records Society Publication, 1911), 74. The diary list was also printed in the memoirs of Bishop Challoner (*Memoirs of Missionary Priests*, 11, 14). The following section from the *Diaries* confirmed that Father White was among the Jesuits who were expelled: "Die 24 [July 1606] ad nos pervenerunt sacerdotes ali qui nuper in exilium jussu Regis Angliae deportati, plures vero diebus succedentibus secuti sunt. Ejecti item erant ex regno per varias portus et vias quandraginta septem sunt nomina." (D. Andreas Whitus was listed.)

important, in light of future events, to note that White was warned that he would be executed if he ever returned to England.[684]

While he was in Belgium, Father White applied for membership in the Society of Jesus. In February 1607, he entered Saint John's, the newly constructed novitiate of the Jesuits in Leuven, Belgium.[685] Father White made simple vows on February 2, 1609, and upon leaving the novitiate, he was chosen by the Jesuits to teach.[686]

In 1619, while still in simple vows, Fr. Andrew White returned to Spain, where he taught the humanities in the halls of various Jesuit colleges, including Saint Hermenegild College and Saint George's College at Seville and Saint Alban's College at Valladolid. White also taught theology at the Jesuit College in Leuven, where the Faculty of Theology at the Katholieke Universiteit Leuven now stood.[687] Father White made his final profession as a Jesuit on June 15, 1619, in that college.[688]

From 1619 to about 1622, Father White was again engaged in missionary activity in England, and it was at this time that White first met George Calvert and became interested in his colonization plans. However, Father White returned to teaching in 1623 and worked as professor of theology at Leuven. He went to Liège in 1624, where he became prefect of studies in the college in 1625. In this position, Father White was only a qualified success.

Father White held a strict interpretation of the Jesuit seminary program as well as espoused a strict interpretation of Thomas Aquinas.[689] Because of this, he was met with opposition and was at odds with the rector at Liège, and he only remained there until 1629, when he went back to England. Upon his

---

[684] Lemay, *Men of Letters*, 9; Bernard Bassett, "Three Men from Maryland," *Jesuit* (Spring, 1974): 10–11.

[685] Hughes, *Text*, 1:159–60; Gerald Walsh, "Father Andrew White, SJ–'Apostle of Maryland,'" *Baltimore Catholic Review*, Tercentenary Edition, Supplement (June 15, 1934), 6; cf. also Lemay, *Men of Letters*, 9. Further background regarding Fr. Andrew White includes the following: Thomas Talbot was novice master at the novitiate at Saint John's House, Leuven, until it moved to Liège in 1614. John Gerard then became novice master and rector of the college. William Flack (alias Flock) was rector at Saint Omers, appointed in 1592–1594. John Foucart succeeded him (George Oliver, *Collections: Toward Illustrating the Biography of the Scotch, English, and Irish Members of SJ* [London: F. C. Featherstone, 1838], 204–5.

[686] Oliver, *Collections*, 204.

[687] Walsh, "Father Andrew White," 6.

[688] Oliver, *Collections*, 204.

[689] Henry Warner Bowden, *Dictionary of American Religious Biography*, advisory ed. Edwin S. Gaustad (Westport, CT; London: Greenwood Press, 1977), 502.

return to England, he was assigned for the next several years at the mission of Saint Thomas in Hampshire County.[690]

During the time that George Calvert was involved in the Newfoundland experiment, he corresponded with Fr. Andrew White in Liège. Because of his interest in the New World missions, White had maintained this relationship with George Calvert. Then in a letter written between 1627 and 1629, Calvert communicated with Father White again in Liège and offered him to share in planning the immigration to the New World. So when George Calvert returned to England from Virginia in 1629 to pursue a charter for the Maryland colony, Father White was his confidant and support.[691]

Father White received a letter from the Jesuit superior general in Rome that stated that, sometime either in late 1628 or in January of 1629, he requested to be assigned to the mission in America. The general responded in a letter dated March 3, 1629, approving of his interest in the American mission to Maryland and encouraging him to fulfill the wishes of the provincial, Richard Blount, regarding this matter.[692]

After volunteering for the planned mission to Maryland, Father White was a cofounder with George Calvert, first Lord Baltimore. Father White wrote the document in which the new venture was advertised. However, his most significant contribution was the establishment of the Jesuit mission in the colony after its arrival on the Maryland shores, March 25, 1634.

The securing of the palatine privilege embodies the special significance of the Calvert venture beginning with its only being an "experiment" in the Newfoundland venture. Let us now examine it as it has blossomed in the Maryland colony.

3.2.4. THE PALATINE PRIVILEGE

Until the Maryland colony, the original colonial ventures under the British Crown were stock and royal-type colonies. The founders of the Maryland colony sought to establish a radically different type of colonial structure, a palatinate. The resource for the palatine privilege was either the result of the creative historical research of George Calvert and his expertise as a diplomat while still a member of Parliament or the result of the direct influence of the Jesuit associates of George Calvert.[693]

---

[690]   Lemay, *Men of Letters*, II.

[691]   Maryland Historical Society, *The Calvert Papers* (Baltimore: 1889–1899), 1:205.

[692]   Hughes, *Text*, 174; Hughes, *Documents*, 1, 1, no. 5, A, 16–17.

[693]   According to Thomas Hughes, the persecutions of the Jesuits resulted in the destruction of most of the documents that might have substantiated the relationship between George Calvert and the Jesuits during the planning stages of

There was a distinct difference between the palatine privilege and the stock or royal type of colonies. The stock and royal-type colonies had as their primary focus the securing of a haven for the economic interests of the adventurers, derived through trading and conquest. These stock-type colonies were investment oriented for profits and patterned on the powers Spain had granted to the conquistadores.[694] The stock colonies did not focus on settlements as such; they merely established trading or outposts, which were places where merchants and traders would come together to buy and sell their commodities, a buying and selling that inevitably included slaves.

The palatine privilege meant "that the laws that governed it [the colony] might take exception to those that prevailed in the mother country." Thus, the palatine privilege was attractive to those with civil disabilities resulting from the particular design of their respective Crown. Also, "the proprietor operated the colony as a capital investment, selling and leasing, and looking to a return from certain fixed taxes."[695] Without belaboring the point, the palatinate was similar to the stock or royal-type colony except that the palatine privilege was an enlightened feudal-type colony employed for religious purposes and gave the proprietor almost absolute rule.[696]

---

the Maryland colony. Hughes said, "Much more could be said about our English Mission, but the violence of the last persecution . . . did away with almost all our documents; while whole libraries of ours [the Jesuits] were pillaged; all our desks with their papers and notes were robbed; so that it is not strange if much is wanting here which we hope is written in the Book of Life" (*Text*, 1:66–67). Hughes was using a quotation from a Jesuit cited in the Stonyhurst MMS (*Anglia Historia*, vol. vi, n. 204: *Annual Letters, 1685*.

[694] For an understanding of the significance of the conquistadores in the motivation of George Calvert, Lord Baltimore, see *supra* on page 224. Also, reference must be made at this point to the Jesuit settlements called Paraguayan reductions, which were not only different from but also set against the encomienda system (see *infra* p. 48). The natives came willingly into reductions, whose main purpose was to Christianize and to protect them from the rise of "civilization" and its cutting edge, manifested by the mamelucos and the Paulistas, who were slave traders.

[695] Hanley, *Their Rights and Liberties*, 64.

[696] We have used this term several times before. By enlightened feudalistic-type state was meant a more humanistic state as opposed to the rational state of modernity. The palatine privilege allowed for this kind of manorial/feudal type of government. This approach of government was what we would describe today as socialist. It did not have capitalist profit as its principal goal, and it refused to do violence on the natives. The manorial/feudal system was organized around the idea of shared responsibility of all those involved and not exploitation. For example, as we shall see, there were no slaves permitted in the colony until after the 1660s, after the overrun of the original settlers and the undermining of the original charter.

Jesuit interest in the palatinate itself can be traced back to the Jesuit social policy that became operative in countering the Atlantic world. For example, the Jesuits had acquired privileges and exceptions that, with respect to their establishment of reductions at Paraguay, had already existed since 1610.[697] There was a strong similarity between the privileges acquired by the Jesuits in the establishment of the Paraguayan reductions and those derived through the palatine privileges that the Jesuits acquired in collaboration with George Calvert. It was probably such that the Jesuit general would not have given permission for Jesuits to involve themselves in the Maryland venture without such assurances and protection as given by the palatine privilege.

It was certain that as early as 1622, before George Calvert "reconverted" and resigned from the Parliament and the Privy Council of King Charles I, he found the Jesuits to be his allies. So it was most probable that it was the connection between Calvert and the Jesuits that motivated the search for an English paradigm that would assure the same type of independence as Paraguay from the Crown. One such Jesuit priest in Calvert's life was Sir Tobie Matthew (1577–1655), who was considered to be significant because of his work converting those of high rank in the English court. There was evidence

---

[697] There were tracings that suggested that the suppression of the Jesuits, first in France (1763) and then worldwide (1773), might very well be due not only to "a host of European resentments and jealousies," as E. S. Gaustad stated in his work *A Religious History of America* (26). It was more likely the social theory of the Jesuits et al. (cf. *supra* Las Casas, Vitoria, de Soto, Suarez, and Molina) as expressed in the Paraguayan reductions. What might be called the social policy of the Jesuits against slavery and the slave trade (like other religious orders [e.g., Dominicans, Franciscans, and Mercedarians] who engaged in varying degrees of resistance) offered strong resistance to the efforts and interests of the merchant class in the Atlantic world from the Bourbon regime in France to the reductions in Paraguay to the Maryland colony.

For further background on Jesuit missions in Paraguayan reductions and the Jesuit social policy against slavery and slave trading, which led ultimately to their worldwide suppression in 1773 (except in White Russia), see the following texts: *Bulletin Signaletique, 527, Histoire et Sciences des Religions,* Centre National de la Recherche Scientifique-Centre de Documentation Sciences Humaines; L. Polgar, "Bibliographie de Historia Societas Jesu," *Archivum Historicum Societatis Jesu* (Roma) 48, no. 96 (1979): 345–420; Lewis Hanke, *The Spanish Struggle for Justice in the Conquest of America,* American Historical Associations, 6th ed. (Boston: American Historical Association, 1949; reprinted by Boston: Little, Brown and Company, 1965), 83–105; M. Mourre, "Paraguay," *Dictionaire Encyclopedique D'Histoire* (Paris: Editions Universitaires, 1978), 3384; *The New Catholic Encyclopedia,* 1967, 1979 eds., s.v. "Reductions of Paraguay" by H. Storni; and W. H. Koebel, *In Jesuit Land. The Jesuit Missions of Paraguay* (London: Stanley Paul & Co., [1912]), 381; also, see bibliographic listings in note 58, 149.

that George Calvert was "brought back" into the Catholic faith by Sir Tobie.[698] To substantiate this fact, Hughes used a document called "Massachusetts Historical Society Collections" (1792), which said that Sir Tobie Matthew was the person around whom "the whole history of incipient Catholicity in English America revolves" because of his role in the reconversion of George Calvert.[699]

During the latter years of his tenure in the court, another Jesuit who actively influenced George Calvert in the design of the colonial project based on religious liberty was the Jesuit priest Fr. Henry More, the great-grandson of Sir Thomas More; he would eventually become the Jesuit provincial in England.[700] Fr. Henry More became the spiritual counselor of George Calvert during the time of his reconversion. Calvert was aware that the ideas of Sir Thomas More, the chancellor of Henry VIII, were being argued by Catholics in defense of their existence in the Crown. Furthermore, Calvert had the responsibility of keeping abreast of all the important issues of his day. Thus, at the suggestion of Fr. Henry More, it was likely that George Calvert read Sir Thomas More's *Utopia* to gain a useful interpretation of the problem that existed in the struggle between religious conscience and the rights of the state.

The person who was most important in demonstrating the link between Calvert's idea of the palatinate and the influence of the Jesuits was the Jesuit priest Fr. Andrew White. There was evidence that George Calvert was a correspondent and close friend of Fr. Andrew White as early as 1622.[701] It was also probable that the relationship between George Calvert and White ultimately led to White's being considered cofounder of the Maryland colony along with George Calvert. The exchange between them extended between the year 1622 and the year the Maryland charter was approved (1632).

Fr. Andrew White was the principal connecting link between the palatinate and the Paraguayan reductions.[702] He received his education and even taught in Spain at the Jesuit universities of Valladolid and Seville, where

---

[698] It was probably at the time that Lord Baron of Baltimore "converted" or, according to Krugler, reconverted to Catholicism that he became friends with the Jesuits. Krugler, *MHM* 78 (Fall 1973): 239–254, 252.

[699] Hughes, *History of the Society of Jesus*, 2:5.

[700] Hanley, *Their Rights and Liberties*, 8–9; Andrews, *The Founding of Maryland*, 147.

[701] Lemay, *Men of Letters*, 10. In this work, Lemay stated that Fr. Andrew White most likely met George Calvert and became interested in the Calvert colonization plans shortly after he was professed as a Jesuit on June 15, 1619. Lemay cited Hughes and quoted Foley to corroborate White's being in England during that time, assigned to different missionary posts (Hughes, *Text*, 1:170 n. 6). According to Foley, George Calvert wrote Fr. Andrew White from Newfoundland in 1627/28. Father White was not in England after 1622; therefore, he concluded, the two of them must have met before 1623.

[702] For more details on the Paraguay reductions, see *infra* p. 242.

the Jesuit social policy against many issues of the Atlantic world was born. It can be demonstrated that these two universities were centers where the Jesuits developed and honed the enduring social policy for Central and Latin America. It was from these universities that ideas like the reductions received support from Jesuit superiors and ecclesiastical approval.[703] The reductions, as seen above, probably motivated Calvert to search into English ecclesiastical history and to settle on the idea of the privileges granted to the bishop of Durham as a model for his newly developing colonial charter. The palatine privilege was clearly defined in the Maryland charter:

> Together with all and singular the like, and as ample rights, Jurisdictions, Privileges, Prerogatives, Royalties, Liberties, Immunities, Royal rights, and franchises of what kind soever temporall, as well by Sea, as by land, within the Countrey, Iles, Iletts, and limits aforesaid; To have, exercise, use, and enjoy the same, as amply as any Bishop of Durham, within the Bishoprick, or County Palatine of Durham, in our Kingdome of England, hath at any time heretofore had, held, used, or enjoyed, or of right ought, or might have had, held, sued, or enjoyed.[704]

Durham in Northern England was a palatinate that existed in the north of England near the border of Scotland, stretching to the Tweed River. The idea of the palatinate was derived from the ecclesial juridical powers held by the bishops of Durham of the Roman Catholic Church in England as early as AD 634. With this type of authority, even though Henry VIII reduced their jurisdiction, the bishops of Durham executed powers that were even more extensive than that of feudal nobles.[705]

Two elements of the palatine privilege would characterize its significance for George Calvert. The privilege was based on an ecclesiastical model, a bishopric of the Roman Catholic Church. This provided the juridical context that made the Jesuit general more apt to sending Jesuits to the region. Moreover, the proprietor, who was to be the principal ruler of the colonial

---

[703] Other type of manors were entrusted to religious orders, for example, the encomiendas. The reductions were more independent (not dependent on the control by the Crown) than the encomiendas. The palatine privilege was anchored in a privilege granted to an ecclesiastical entity (the bishopric in this case).

[704] Maryland Hall of Records Commission, *The Charter of Maryland* (June 20, 1632; reprinted June 20, 1982).

[705] Hanley, *Their Rights and Liberties*, 66–72; Andrews, *The Founding of Maryland*, 42; Carr, "The Charter of Maryland," xiv; Quinn, "Introduction: Prelude to Maryland," 23.

venture, was also to be independent like a king in his own domain, separate from the Crown.[706]

Quinn commented,

> The "bishops of Durham" clause . . . gave the grantee exemption from the statute [cf. note below]. In his territory he could also prosecute war; institute martial law in the face of rebellion, tumult, or sedition; proclaim ordinances; pass laws under certain limitations, establish courts; issue pardons; and appoint officials necessary to maintain peace and administer justice. He could regulate trade, impose taxes and customs duties, and incorporate cities. Such power represented a formal delegation of sovereignty unparalleled for centuries, but necessary for the government of a dependency at such a distance from England.[707]

Additionally, it should be noted that the common saying during the feudal period of England was "What the King is without, the Bishop of Durham is within."[708]

That the first Lord Baltimore and then later his son Cecil, the second Lord Baltimore, were motivated to use the idea of the palatinate as a model of ruling the colony demonstrated that they were motivated by more than just the desire to profit from the venture. They had religious and political reasons for such an arrangement, namely, to offer a stable refuge for their coreligionists away from their persecutors in the homeland. Therefore, by so setting up the charter, settlers as well as the natives were untouchable even by the Parliament.[709]

The proprietary system was based on the European feudal or manorial concept. Lord Baltimore himself, to whom the charter was granted, was the proprietor. The charter of the Maryland colony was issued by the king to the

---

[706] Andrews, *The Founding of Maryland*, 42; Carr, "The Charter of Maryland," xiv; Hanley, *Their Rights and Liberties*, 66; Quinn, "Introduction: Prelude to Maryland," 23; Gerald W. Johnson, *The Maryland Act of Religious Toleration: An Interpretation* (Annapolis, MD: Hall of Records Commission, Department of General Services, 1973), 5–6.

[707] Quinn, "Introduction: Prelude to Maryland," 23. Quinn mentioned that the palatinate of Lord Baltimore would even be exempt from the Statute of Quia Emptores of Edward I, which had denied "subinfeudation," the right to create feudal manors and the titles, honors, and so on associated with their establishment. The dependency on the Crown was an autonomous dependency.

[708] Hanley, *Their Rights and Liberties*, 66.

[709] Hanley, *Their Rights and Liberties*.

proprietor; he was the principal owner of the venture. All those involved in the venture were responsible to the proprietor.

The proprietary or manorial system consisted of manors, which were estates ruled by the lord, who had charge of the land and the tenants. All the settlers were tenants in the house of Baltimore because the grant was a feudal-type land grant. "Estates in Maryland could be awarded by the Calverts to whom they chose, and remained with the tenants of their choice so long as the holders paid their quit-rents to the proprietor."[710]

The manor was a unit of English rural territorial organization, and lords were the only ones with a right to erect a manor. The manor was the source of social control as well as a provider for the community. The "rights and duties of the inhabitants" (rules) of the manor were established by the lords and sealed by a charter (king).[711]

"Mary-land may (without sin, I think) be called Singular." Sydney Ahlstrom, the historian of American religion, used this quotation of an early chronicler of Maryland to discuss the uniqueness of Maryland.[712] The Maryland charter, therefore, was unique. Contrary to earlier British ventures, in an effort to be inclusive of all peoples, for the first time, the charter introduced the ideas of toleration and of separation of church and state. Consideration of religious liberty as the principal element of the charter of the Maryland colony was significant for this study.

3.2.5. THE MARYLAND CHARTER AND RELIGIOUS LIBERTY

George Calvert died (April 15, 1632) only a few months before the Maryland charter was sealed by Charles I (June 2, 1632). He had originally wanted Catholics to see themselves as members of one sect among many others. Cecil Calvert focused on the principles of freedom of conscience and separation of church and state. He insisted that church and state were separate and that religion was a private activity. From this emphasis, Cecil Calvert deduced that no one would be allowed to say anything negative against the

---

[710] Nye and Morpurgo, *Birth of the USA*, 61.

[711] Menard and Carr, "The Lords Baltimore," 176–78. Carr, "The Charter of Maryland," xvii.

[712] Hanley, *Their Rights and Liberties*, 47; Ahlstrom, *Religious History*, 405. Ahlstrom noted that neither James I nor Charles I really supported the Protestants during the Thirty Years' War and that Charles's grant to Calvert demonstrated that Catholics had the sympathy of the Crown. Therefore, it was the Puritans who dominated Anglo-America and probably not the Crown who were the persecutors of Catholics in the New World.

beliefs of another and that, without further qualifications, a person could "vote, hold public office and participate fully in the society regardless of religion."[713]

Although he did not change his father's policies regarding religion, Cecil applied for certain changes to secure a more formally established haven for Catholics in his new colony. He sought to make explicit what had only been implied in the Avalon charter regarding the bishop-of-Durham clause, the palatine privilege. Such specification abrogated the restriction of the palatine privilege to the region of Durham itself, allowing it to be applied in the Maryland colony. He wanted full power as proprietor, with the degree of independence in which there would be little restraint on his proprietary authority. He wanted his sovereignty to suffer no interference from the Crown. He also sought changes that would free the proprietor from any military commitments.

He saw that the colony could avoid the rigors of the penal code by inviting England's "liberties rather than its penalties." So he kept the language of the charter ambiguous and chose to deal with unanswered questions about the freedoms that would be allowed Catholics by personal communication between himself and his brother Leonard Calvert, who was to be the governor of the Maryland colony.[714]

Another issue he emphasized in the charter was the proprietor's right to create titles of honor and subgrant land with the rights to erect manors. This was done so that he could more easily recruit the wealthy younger sons prohibited from inheriting any wealth from their families due to primogeniture laws.[715] These potential adventurers would fund the settlement and could be appointed leadership positions in the colony as lords of the manors. These manors, each with a lord appointed by the proprietor, would produce the legal basis for the much needed governmental structure for the colony.

Other emphases of Cecil in adjusting the charter for Maryland were certain aspects of the religion clauses. In the Newfoundland experiment, for example, George Calvert actually supported Protestant and Catholic churches. As already mentioned, this drew adverse criticism and therefore was not successful.[716]

To secure the new religious emphasis, the Maryland charter advocated statutes of "patronages and advowsons" as well as the removal of the "mortmain" statute, which was part of the Newfoundland charter.[717] These

---

[713]   Wroth, *Declaration*, xx.

[714]   Ellis, *Catholics in Colonial America*, 326; Andrews, *The Founding of Maryland*, 150.

[715]   For more details on the laws of primogeniture, see *supra* on page 193.

[716]   See *supra*, p. 219.

[717]   *Webster's Dictionary* defines *advowson* and *mortmain* as follows: *Advowson* is the right in English law of designating an ecclesiastical benefit. *Mortmain* is the condition of

statutes of patronages and advowsons ultimately allowed the proprietor to protect the practice of religion as he so willed; the proprietor was considered by the charter to be the patron of religion. This was a vague statement saying that the proprietor and his progeny were only expressing a general religious spirit and not a prescription.

Unlike the Newfoundland charter, as stated, the Maryland charter no longer supplied ministers or churches for the various religious entities.[718] The section of the Maryland charter that referred to this type of church-state relationship read as follows:

> And furthermore the Patronages and Aduowsons of all Churches, which (as Christian Religion shall encrease within the Countrey, Iles, Iletts, and limits aforesaid) shall happen hereafter to bee erected: together with licence and power, to build and found Churches, Chappells, and Oratories, in convenient and fit places within the premises, and to cause them to be dedicated, and consecrated according to the Ecclesiasticall Lawes of our Kingdome of England.[719]

Ellis described the tenets of this section of the charter in the following three points: "1) the proprietor was given express and absolute liberty to erect and found all churches and chapels; 2) the right of control was vested in him as patron for all churches of whatever kind; 3) he was expressly exempted from all laws of mortmain which otherwise would have made it impossible for him to convey properties to religious bodies."[720]

Cecil built on these ideas by inviting people of all denominations to participate in the new venture, and in his private instructions to the departing colonists, he insisted on the inclusion of all beliefs. Also, before embarking from London, Cecil delivered to Leonard Calvert a document entitled "Instructions to Colonists," dated November 15, 1633. "Instructions" manifested Cecil's

---

property or other gifts left to a corporation in perpetuity for religious purposes; the influence of said property and gifts of the past regarded as controlling the present.

[718] Carr, "The Charter of Maryland," xv–xvii; Papenfuse, introduction to *The Charter of Maryland*; Hanley, *Their Rights and Liberties*, 66–69; Andrews, *The Founding of Maryland*, 36–46.

[719] Maryland Hall of Records Commission, *The Charter of Maryland*.

[720] Ellis, *Catholics in Colonial America*, 326. This idea of religious liberty is very Jesuitical (i.e., dialectical). By affording religious freedom to Protestant proprietors, the religious freedom of Catholics proprietors is at the same time being safeguarded–a model the Catholics will wish to expand over the other colonies.

anxiety over the freedoms of the Maryland charter.[721] It dealt with several points; two of them would be significant for this study: how the citizens of the colony were to conduct themselves during the trip and how the leadership was to deal with the Virginians, particularly William Claiborne, the Puritan trader who occupied a trading post on Kent Island, which was a part of the Maryland grant.[722]

First, Cecil's main concern was that the openness regarding religious freedom would endanger the peace, so he ordered that they should not violate each other's religion. Thus, Cecil Calvert–for the colonists to effectively carry out his directive–prohibited all religious discussions on the trip over and charged in the introductory paragraph,

> His Lordship requires his said Governor and Commissioners that in their voyage to Mary Land they be very careful to preserve unity and peace among all the passengers on shipboard, and that they suffer no scandal nor offence to be given to any of the Protestants, whereby any just complaint may hereafter be made by them in Virginia or in England, and that for the end, they cause all acts of Roman Catholic religion to be done as privately as may be, and that they instruct all the Roman Catholics to be silent upon all occasions of discourse concerning matters of religion; and that the said Governor and Commissioners treat the Protestants with as much mildness as favor as justice will permit. And this [is] to be observed at land as well as at sea.[723]

And in the "Instructions to Colonists" (art. 6), he prescribed formalities to be observed upon arriving in Maryland and on the inauguration of the plantation. Jay P. Dolan put it this way:

> These instructions clearly indicated the mind of Cecil Calvert regarding the place of religion in colonial Maryland. Since civil harmony was the primary consideration, religion

---

[721] Cecil Calvert, Lord Baltimore, "Instructions to Colonists," *Calvert Papers*, 131–40; Hughes, *Text*, 1:251–52.

[722] William Claiborne is a significant figure in the religious conflict that has undermined Catholics in colonial Maryland. There will be more on Claiborne passim.

[723] "Instructions to the Colonists by Lord Baltimore," November 13, 1633, in *Narratives of Early Maryland, 1634–1684*, ed. Clayton Colman Hall, 16. Cited in Johnson, *The Maryland Act of Religious Toleration*, 6–7. See also *Calvert Papers*, 131–40; Newman, *The Flowering of the Maryland Palatinate*, 18; Hughes, *Text*, 1:251.

was to remain a private affair, neither shaping the destiny of the colony nor impeding its progress.[724]

Second, disputes about the establishment of their kind of colony continued to rage right up to the time they were to depart; it even caused some delays. Moreover, Cecil chose not to sail with the colony because he thought he needed to stay and continue to defend the Maryland charter.[725] Thus, the colonists were to monitor all arguments against the colony. They were not only cautioned that the Virginia colony might continue its opposition to their settlement as they had to the palatine privilege and the separation of church and state of the Maryland charter but they were also warned about William Claiborne, who had appropriated a part of the territory they had been granted. Thus, all colonists were cautioned regarding how they should deal with both their neighbors in the adjacent colony to the south, Virginia and William Claiborne. Regarding William Claiborne, the "Instructions to Colonists" (art. 5) stated that a letter be written to Claiborne soon after their arrival. They were told by Cecil Calvert to give William Claiborne notice of their arrival and of the authority (the palatine privilege and separation of church and state) granted them by the charter. They were told to treat him courteously and to seek a response from him.[726]

The intervening year after the charter was approved was used to make the project known and to attract Catholic settlers. Attention must now be given to the actual planting of the colony in the Atlantic world.

3.2.6. THE SETTLEMENT

The expedition to Maryland embarked in September 1633, more than a year after the king's approval of the charter (June 20, 1632). Cecil appointed his brother Leonard as the lieutenant general or the first governor of the palatinate. He also appointed George Calvert—a younger brother named after his own father, Sir George Calvert, first Lord Baltimore—to the post of deputy governor and Jerome Hawley and Thomas Cornwallis as commissioners.[727]

The settlers for the Maryland colony had been chosen by Cecil Calvert. They had to be committed to the plans as well as have the necessary economic means to assist the colony in its early stages.[728] The process of choosing the

---

[724] Dolan, 74.

[725] Menard and Carr, "The Lords Baltimore," 168.

[726] Hughes, *Text*, 1:262.

[727] Andrews, *The Founding of Maryland*, 55.

[728] John A. Doyle, "The First Century of English Colonization, 1607–1700," in *The Cambridge Modern History*, vol. 7, *The United States*, ed. A. W. Ward, G. W. Prothero,

members who were to contribute to the colony took place over a year before departure.[729] This first Maryland colonial expedition, however, consisted of sixteen to twenty "gentlemen adventurers," all Catholic except for one; their families; and those they were transporting; namely, "a host of servants, mechanics, artisans and laborers, the majority of whom were Protestant."[730] Many of the Protestants who were a part of this venture converted to Catholicism after they were in the colony. Vital to the expedition were the Jesuits who were to establish the mission in the colony, Fr. Andrew White, Fr. John Altham (Timothy Hayes), and Bro. Thomas Gervase.[731]

The *Ark* and the *Dove*, 360-ton and 60-ton vessels respectively, left London in September of 1633 but were ordered to return to Gravesend, where the emigrants had to take the oath of supremacy.[732] Since most Catholics refused to take the oath and did not wish to cause humiliation for Lord Baltimore, they retired to Cowes on the Isle of Wight, an island off the south of England. There, they could escape the watchful eye of those who insisted that all the colonists take the oath of supremacy before embarking for the New World. Finally, they all embarked together from Cowes on their long journey into the future of Catholicism in British America on November 22, 1633. Their immediate destination was the Canary Islands and then onto Barbados, where they replenished their supplies.

While on the voyage, Fr. Andrew White wrote a tract that had become a classic because it was an authoritative eyewitness account of the significant happenings of the voyage. In this work, Father White gave a detailed account of the journey from their embarkation from London, including the first months after disembarking in Maryland. It was completed in April of 1634 and published in London in July 1634.[733] As the title suggested, *Relatio* was

---

and Stanley Leathes (Cambridge: Cambridge University Press, 1903), 31.

[729] Menard and Carr, "The Lords Baltimore," 168.

[730] Dolan, *The American Catholic Experience*, 73; Ahlstrom, *Religious History*, 406; Thomas J. Campbell, *The Jesuits, 1534–1921: A History of the Jesuits from Its Foundation to the Present Time* (New York: Encyclopedia Press, 1921), 339.

[731] Fr. Timothy Hayes is in parentheses because not all historians mention him as one of the original Jesuits. However, it is interesting that he appears on a list of the early Jesuits in the "Catalogue of Early Jesuits in Maryland" in Rev. William P. Treacy's *Old Catholic Maryland and Its Early Jesuit Missionaries* (13, 167). Cf. Dolan, *The American Catholic Ex*perience, 73. When Dolan gives the count of the number of those original passengers on the *Ark* and the *Dove*, he does not mention Father Hayes.

[732] Hanley, *Their Rights and Liberties*, 79; Edward S. Schwegler, "The *Ark* and the *Dove*," in *Columbus* (Special Collections: Georgetown University Library, Washington DC, March 1934).

[733] Father White's first *Relatio itineris in Marylandiam*, cited in Hughes's *Documents*,

published also for further advertisement–a planned second voyage–which was why it was returned so quickly and published.

Robert Emmett Curran, in his study of seventeenth-century Jesuit missionary spirituality, commented on Father White's *Relatio*, saying, "[Father White] had a keen eye for natural detail as well as a deep faith in God's abiding blessings on their venture."[734] It can be determined from his writings that Father Andrew White was a pious man always calling on God's presence along with all the saints. For example, upon embarking, Father White wrote in his *Relatio*, "[W]e placed the principal parts of the ship under the protection of God, of His holy Mother, of St Ignatius and of all the Angels of Maryland."[735]

Then Father White made specific note of their stop at Barbados, the nearest port after crossing the ocean, where they stayed from the third to the twenty-fourth of January 1634. While there for supplies, Father White and his companions toured several of the Caribbean islands. Marking this visit to these islands, Father White stated the following in his *Relatio*:

> [We] stopped there ten days, being invited to do so in a friendly way by the English Governor and two Catholic captains. The Governor of the French colony on the same island treated me with the most marked kindness.[736]

They saw a number of Irish Catholics who had been banished into bondage from the Virginia colony onto Saint Kitts and Montserrat near Barbados because they were Catholics.

---

no.1 (1:94–107), was originally written in Latin and was a special report sent to his superior general. The English translation of this original work was *A Relation of the Successe-full Beginnings of the Lord Baltimore's Plantation in Mary-Land. Being an Extract of Certaine Letters Written from Thence, by Some of the Adventurers, to Their Friends in England. To which Is Added, The Conditions of Plantation Propounded by His Lordship for the Second Voyage Intended This Present Yeere* (1634). His second version was "A Brief Relation of the Voyage unto Maryland," cited in *Woodstock Letters*, I (1872: 12–24, 71–80, 145–55), and referred to in Hughes's *Texts* (1:275). The version of this text used in this thesis is Fr. Andrew White, *Relatio itineris in Marylandiam: Declaratio coloniae domini baronis de Baltimore, excerpta ex diversis litteris missionorum ad anno 1635, ad annum 1638*, ed. E. A. Dalrymple (Baltimore: Maryland Historical Society; Fund Publications, 1874).

[734] Curran, *American Jesuit Spirituality*, 48.

[735] White, *Relatio*, 1634.

[736] Andrew White, "Relations," in Henry Foley, SJ, *Records of the English Province of the Society of Jesus. Historic Facts Illustrative of the Labours and Sufferings of Its Members in the Sixteenth and Seventeenth Centuries*, 8 vols. (London: Burns and Oates, 1877–1883), 3:339; Campbell, *The Jesuits*, 307.

> By noone we came before Monserrat. The inhabitants of
> Monserrat are Irishmen, who were banished by the English of
> Virginia, on account of their professing the Catholic faith.[737]

What was significant about this visit was their encounter with several groups of slaves of Irish descent. The Jesuit historian Thomas J. Campbell reflected on the tour Father White made of Saint Kitts and Monserrat in his survey history of the Jesuits. Regarding the situation of slaves on Saint Kitts and Montserrat, Campbell said the following:

> For people of Irish blood these islands, especially Saint
> Kitts and Montserrat, are of a thrilling interest. On both of
> them were found numbers of exiled Irish Catholics held as
> slaves. As early as 1634 Father White on his way to Maryland
> saw them at Saint Kitts.[738]

This experience inevitably would have a long-range influence on Father White's attitude against bondage. It was probably this experience that grounded his own resistance to slavery.

Continuing en route to the colonial setting in Maryland, Father White told of their arrival on February 27, 1634, in Virginia. Leonard had letters for John Harvey, the governor of Virginia, from King Charles I. Expecting the worse, they thought it necessary to visit their neighbor colony. They met the governor and various settlers, including William Claiborne, to learn something about

---

[737] This is a reference to an experience of Father White that he records in "Father Andrew White's Briefe Relation" in *Calvert Papers*, Fund Publication no. 35, 3, 37.

[738] Campbell, *The Jesuits*, 307. This text was taken from Father White's "Relation of the Voyage of Maryland." It would be important to note that Campbell gave statistics on Irish slavery later at the time of the Puritan Revolution, Cromwell's reign in England from early 1640 to the mid-1650s.

Campbell spoke of Irish slaves in Jamaica brought there after Cromwell took the island. Campbell spoke of the Irish boys and girls sent to Jamaica as slaves–"one thousand Irish girls and a like number of Irish boys were sent there" (*The Jesuits*, 308).

Abbot Emerson Smith also reported that Irish were slaves not only in the Caribbean but also in the colonies. Cf. Abbot Emerson Smith, *Colonists in Bondage: White Servitude and Convict Labor in America, 1607–1776* (Chapel Hill: University of North Carolina Press, 1947), 163.

To substantiate this, cf. James S. Olson, *Catholic Immigrants in America* (Chicago: Nelson-Hall, 1987), 17. According to Olson, Cromwell had engaged in "genocidal campaigns" into Ireland, "destroying the economy and reducing the Irish population by more than a third in only eleven years" (*Catholic Immigrants in America*, 17–18).

the area they were to settle. William Claiborne warned them that the natives were planning for war. Father White recorded in *Relatio*,

> At this time Captaine Claiborne was there from whome we understood the Indians were all in armes to resist vs, haveing heard that six Spanish ships were a comeing to destroy them all the rumor was most like to have begunne from himself, we had the kings letters, and my Lord treasurers to the governors which made him show to vs the best vsage, the place affoed with p-mise to furnish vs with all manner of Provisions for our Plantation though much against his Councells will.[739]

The new colonists continued their voyage by navigating the Potomac River to Maryland. They arrived on March 5, 1634, on Blackiston's Island, renamed by them Saint Clements Island, in Maryland.[740] Leonard Calvert and some of his leadership and Father Altham went with Capt. Henry Fleet as an interpreter to speak to the Indians about their gaining land for settlement. Father White was left behind on the island to take care of those left behind and to repair his loss of linen upon the arrival in the colony.[741]

Unlike the earlier colonial ventures, Marylanders by their actions gave clear evidence that they had no plans to enslave the local native peoples, the Piscataway and others. They made a visit to the chief of the Piscataway, an Algonquian Indian tribe, for example, to negotiate a peaceful settlement with the Indians for their lands. The Indians, at first, hid, but then the chief with five hundred braves met the colonists, who soothed their anger by their gentleness and signs of friendship and by the gifts they offered.

> The Maryland leaders made a conscious effort to avoid conflicts with the–local Indians that might lead to warfare such as the Jamestown settlements had faced.[742]

---

[739] *Calvert Papers*, 3, 38.

[740] Cf. Andrews, *The Founding of Maryland*, 58–63; Shea, *History of the Catholic Church*, 41–44; Menard and Carr, "Lords Baltimore," 170–2.

[741] *Woodstock Letters*, 40:181; Foley, *Records*, 3:351–54.

[742] Menard and Carr, "Lords Baltimore," 187. This referred to the venture of Sir Walter Raleigh between the years 1584 and 1590, in which he acquired and sought to establish the territory of Virginia and North Carolina, and the whole settlement ended up being wiped out. Quinn, "Introduction: Prelude to Maryland," 16–17 (cf. *supra*, p. 200).

Each of them spoke as friends, explaining their mission. The military and the leadership of the colony spoke of peace. Father Altham spoke of his mission to administer spiritual matters and, in sign language, gave his first catechism class.[743] Then Father Altham returned with Leonard Calvert and arrived on March 25, 1634, whereupon they erected a huge white cross, and Father White became the first English-speaking priest to offer Mass in the New World.[744] Within a few days, they went in search of a place to build the first city and discovered on the Saint Marys River about six miles upstream a small farming tribe called Yaocomico. It was here that Leonard Calvert wished to set up Saint Marys City. Menard and Carr cited a letter of Leonard Calvert, the governor of the Maryland colony, to Sir Richard Lechford, a colleague in England:

> We have seated ourselves within one half mile of the river [a reference to Saint Marys River], within a pallizado of one hundred and twentie yeards square with four sides . . . we have mounted one peece of ordnance and placed six murderers in parts most convenient; a fortification (we thinke) sufficient to defend against any such weake enemies as we have reason to expect here.[745]

Fr. Andrew White also described the geography of the area where the settlers landed in his second *Relatio* (1635), the one after the first year of the settlement. Father described it in this way:

> [It is] a very commodious situation for a Towne, in regard the land is good, the ayre wholesome and plesant, the river affords a safe harvour for ships of any burthem, and a very bould shoare; fresh water and wood there is in great plenty, and the place so naturally fortified, as with little difficulties it will be defended from any enemy.[746]

---

[743] *Woodstock Letters*, 40:181.

[744] Menard and Carr, "Lords Baltimore," 171.

[745] Menard and Carr, "Lords Baltimore," 184. In footnote 25 on page 214, the authors make reference to Fund Publication no. 35, 21; *Calvert Papers*, no. 3, 25. According to Menard and Carr, the "pallizado" was a "ditched, banked, and palisaded enclosure of the strong point or 'fort'" (186); see "fortification" in Newman, *The Flowering of the Maryland Palatinate*, 16, 41, 44, 175.

[746] Fr. Andrew White, "A Relation of Maryland," in *Narrative of Early Maryland, 1633–1684*, ed. Clayton Colman Hall (New York, 1910; repr. 1967), 73.

Unlike the reports from many of the other settlers from Europe, this group of English gentlemen adventurers–instead of taking the land from the Indians–offered to purchase it. James Axtell said that Leonard Calvert "'bought' thirty miles of ground and a village from the Yicomicos, the local natives."[747] For the natives, money was not the usual means whereby one purchased goods or property. So Calvert purchased the property by bartering with a supply of farming tools and cloth and the help from his settlers on how to use the hoes and hatchets. So on March 27, 1634, the official Maryland expedition was now settled.

Axtell, in talking about that "sale," said that the Indians made out well in the deal for the property. Also, he continued by saying that the Yaocomico received them so well because they probably needed the Marylanders to protect them from another warlike tribe, the Susquehannocks, who roamed from Pennsylvania down to Maryland.[748]

Current restoration of the early Maryland settlement, archeological evidence, and various experts on the period confirmed the fact that, like its predecessor colonies (Massachusetts Bay and Virginia), the first thing the colonizers did was to build a fort.

> [The] fort was thought to be necessary as protection against the Indians–not only those nearby, but also the Susquehannocks and marauding bands of Iroquois from the north. The governor [Leonard Calvert] was aware from his meetings with his Indian neighbors that only a few years previously a band of such invading "Senecas" has massacred the inhabitants of nearby Moyoane, a Piscataway village that had existed for at least three hundred years.[749]

They lived in the fort, but within days of their settling into Saint Marys City, the colonists found an excellent relationship with the Indians. There was no evidence that they lived in the fort very long.

There was harmony that existed from the beginning. They hunted in the woods together and shared whatever they brought back. The women, settlers, and natives exchanged skills. The settlers learned the various arts

---

[747] James Axtell, "White Legend: The Jesuit Missions in Maryland," *Maryland Historical Magazine* 81 (Spring 1986): 1-7, 2. Unlike the other two British colonial settlements, the Maryland settlers sought some agreed upon exchange for occupying the territory. Nevertheless, this too seemed to be a questionable maneuver just to occupy the land.

[748] Axtell, "White Legend," 2.

[749] Menard and Carr, "Lords Baltimore," 186.

from the natives that were important in their new situation, while the natives learned weaving and spinning from the settler women. "This was the nature of the relationship between the colonists and the aborigines until in 1638 when [William] Claiborne began his activities."[750] The statement was a direct reference to the disruption of the harmony that originally existed between the settlers and the natives. Claiborne spawned dissention between the natives and the settlers of the Maryland colony, which as we shall see later resulted in the invasion of the colony by Claiborne and Puritan traders.

3.2.7. THE ECONOMY OF THE COLONY AND THE JESUIT MISSION

There were two ways the colonists made a living; they either inhabited and planted or inhabited and traded. The former traded to supply the deficiency of the necessities of life precipitated by the level of crop failure. For example, Thomas Cornwallis was one who inhabited and traded.[751] In a letter to Cecil Calvert, the second Lord Baltimore, Cornwallis declared that he was not in the colony "to plant the stinking weed of America, and as he could not dig and was ashamed to beg. He would pack up and go back to England, unless he were allowed to trade."[752] To trade, one had to have a license, and they were taxed. These restrictions were necessary to control the potential excesses in trading known to be taking place in the other colonies.

The adventurers sometimes had thousands of acres, but they "could not yield more corn or tobacco than the few acres each man could clear with axe and grub, or cultivate with spade or hoe."[753] The workers on the land were those many servants brought over by the adventurers. These servants had to be supported sometimes for as long as three or four years, depending on the terms of their indenture. So to get the necessities of life, they had to engage in trading with the natives. "The Indians sold beaver and corn to the settlers for cloth, axes, and hoes. On the other hand the settlers bought goods which they

---

[750] *Woodstock Letters*, 9 (1880): 169–70.

[751] Thomas Cornwallis of London and of Burnham Thorpe, County Norfolk, was one of the original investors in the Maryland venture. He was appointed one of the commissioners to Leonard Calvert, governor of the Maryland colony, on the voyage; and after landing, he was made a councilor. "[He] was engaged in not only trade with the Indians in beaver and com, but as a merchant he sold essentials to the early settlers by imports from England and the Continent" (Newman, *The Flowering of the Maryland Palatinate*, 188–89).

[752] Thomas Cornwallis to Cecilius, Lord Baltimore, April 16, 1638, *Calvert Papers*, no. 1, 172, 174–75.

[753] Joseph Zwinge, SJ, "Our Fathers in the Colonization of Maryland," in *Woodstock Letters*, 36:84.

needed for the Indian trade from the merchants of England or Virginia, paying for them with beaver and tobacco."[754] So the colonists traded their crops with the Indians and neighboring colonies to make their living.

Because they spent most of their time in missionary work, the Jesuits could not grow their own crops. However, the sixty or so men they had to support could grow crops for them. The Jesuits also traded for some of the necessities of life and for those who called on them for charity. They paid a tenth in taxes to Leonard Calvert, the governor of the colony. An issue arose regarding the trading on the part of the Jesuits, which at that time was not normally permitted by the order. In this instance, the Jesuit general did not admonish the priests for the practice but advised restraint.

> The F.F. [fathers] wrote to Fr. Prov[l] and he to Fr. Gen. about the necessity of trade, as there was no money in the Colony. He [the general] wrote that he could not reprove it as it was necessary, but it must be done with moderation.[755]

The Jesuits acquired property for the manors (ministry centers) in the same manner as the other adventurers, from land grants based on the number of people they transported and who were a part of their household. Five large manorial estates (Saint Inigoes Manor, Newtown, Saint Thomas Manor, Cedar Point Neck, White Marsh, and Bohemia) were established.[756] Out of these centers, they fostered the church life of the colonists as well as the natives. Over and above his missionary work among the Indians and the colonists, Father White with his companions also sought to establish a college at Saint Marys City.[757]

In the beginning, according to the first conditions of plantation (1633), the Jesuits were given two thousand acres for their use, like all the other adventurers of the Maryland colony. Father White transported twenty-six people initially (1634). During the next four years (1634–1638), he had another twenty-eight transported and in 1639 another twenty.[758]

---

[754] Zwinge, "Our Fathers," 36:84.

[755] Zwinge, "Our Fathers," 36:85.

[756] Joseph Zwinge, SJ, "Jesuit Farms in Maryland," in *Woodstock Letters*, vol. XXXIX (1910): 374–82, 374.

[757] Ahlstrom, *Religious History*, 1:411.

[758] It would be important to point out that the manorial system was in line with the palatine statute of the Maryland charter, stipulated by Cecil Calvert, second Lord Baltimore–the proprietor of the colony–and executed by Leonard Calvert, the governor of the colony. It had been stated that the first conditions of plantation (1633) (cf. *supra*, p. 218) established the initial holdings of each of the original investors. The Jesuits (Fr. Andrew White, specifically) were reported by Fr.

In an effort not to single out a particular religious group or interest, the Maryland charter did not permit the Jesuit order to hold property in mortmain. Mortmain was an inalienable possession of lands or buildings or other gifts by religious or ecclesiastical institution granted by the charter. Therefore, they were permitted to hold property based only on the land grant given to all the original investors as presented in the first conditions of plantation (1633). This also meant that the Jesuits were not supported by Cecil, Lord Baltimore, the way religion had been supported in the Newfoundland colony.

Nevertheless, the religious life of the people did not suffer in any way because of this. There was some advantage to this in that the Jesuits produced for themselves, making use of the manorial system in which they had over sixty men and thousands of acres of land for planting crops. As had been noted, there was an astonishing similarity between the Jesuit missions in Paraguay and the manorial system or farms that were established in the Maryland colony.

The Jesuit missionaries under the direction of Fr. Andrew White participated in the economy of the colony according to what was cited above. There, it was called the Jesuit social policy. It can be seen most clearly in the various worldwide Jesuit missions but specifically in Paraguay, where it was called the *reducciόne*.[759] The Paraguayan reductions existed between 1610 and 1768.[760] The Jesuits established and maintained these mission towns in southern Latin America in the territory of the Chaco and Guarani peoples.[761]

Thomas Copley (for more on Copley, see *infra*, p. 256) to have transported at least sixty persons to the province. The Jesuits were one of the largest landholders of all the adventurers. Colman Hall, ed., "Annual Letter of the Society of Jesus, 1641," in *Narratives of Early Maryland, 1633–1684* (New York, 1910; reprinted in 1967), 118; Hughes, *Text*, 1:244–52; Patents, 1:17, 18, 20, 25, 37, MSS, Hall of Records, Annapolis, MD; Menard and Carr, "Lords Baltimore," 167–215, note 15, 213; Newman, *The Flowering of the Maryland Palatinate*, 61–67.

[759] Cf. Father Andrew, *supra*, p. 226.

[760] For further background on the Jesuit missions in Paraguay, confer with the works listed in footnote 175.

[761] The territory of the seventeenth-century Paraguayan reductions extended 650 Ian from north to south and 600 Ian from east to west. The territory comprised present-day Paraguay, northeastern Argentina, and Uruguay. It also included the territory to the north known as the Viceroyalty of Peru. The Viceroyalty of Peru incorporated large parts of Bolivia and the Brazilian province of Paraná and Rio Grande do Sul. The viceroyalty was the civil boundary established by Spain, whose center of administration was at Asunción (Graham, 13–14; also, cf. P. Caraman, *The Lost Paradise: An Account of the Jesuits in Paraguay, 16071768* (London: Sidgwick & Jackson, 1975), 14.

The native peoples came into these towns for their protection, education, and conversion.[762]

The word *reduction* is a transliteration of the Spanish word *reducciône*. Its root is *reducer*, which in the seventeenth century means to gather into mission settlements.[763] The Latin is *re* and *ducir* (*reduco, reducere*). It means "to lead back, to lead out, to restore to righteousness, to save" and is translated as follows: *aldeia* in Brazilian, *reduçoes* in Portuguese.[764]

The Jesuits in Paraguay developed the technique whereby they kept their missions in geographical isolation and independent of the European settlers. This element of the Jesuit social policy was probably one of the issues that led to the land controversy in the Maryland colony. Father White was probably attempting to establish this type of isolation, and at the point of the land controversy, it became the most significant regarding the reception of the Jesuits in the colony.

The structure of the *reducciône* was unlike the encomienda-*doctrina* system, which was forced onto the people. The encomienda process violently took the natives from their natural habitat into towns under their control.[765] Attacking the fiber of the existing native societies, the system neglected the care and education of the natives, forcing them to live in abominable conditions. There were even reports of torture. Through the encomienda process, the conquerors were ruthless in their pillaging and confiscating of natural resources.[766]

There was an interrelationship between education and the economy of the reduction.[767] Previous tribal customs of the Guarani and the gospel ideals were the basis of a communal economy. The missions were centers of agricultural and craft industries in which the natives freely contributed their labor for

---

[762] Graham, *Vanished Arcadia*, 13–14; Caraman, *Lost Paradise*, 14; cf. also Latourette, *History of the Christianity*, 3:154–56.

[763] McNaspy, *Lost Cities of Paraguay*, 8–9.

[764] Campbell, *The Jesuits*, 302.

[765] Tiebesar, 5:331; Latourette, *History of the Christianity*, 3:92; Campbell, *The Jesuits*, 300.

[766] Hanke, *Spanish Struggle*, 19–20; Neill, 145. To dispel the horror of the encomienda system, the Jesuits countermanded with their more inclusive and humane social policy by making themselves known as the "protectors" of the natives, even against the conquistadores. They sought to concretize the papal bull of Paul III of 1537, which condemned, as a serious crime, anyone who enslaved the natives of South America. Jesuits, even at this early period, protested to the Crown the enslavement of natives. For the first time, they applied for royal protection and received it; thereupon, the colonists were outraged and cut off Jesuit food supplies to force a change in their social policy (Campbell, *The Jesuits*, 300).

[767] Caraman, *Lost Paradise*, 116–30.

the benefit of the community.[768] The priests set up the reductions based on a combination of communal and private ownership of the land and all it produced. The agriculture and the crafts were communal, while each family owned their own gardens and a horse and cow.[769] Work was limited to eight hours per day, and salaries involved payment in food, clothes, and homes.[770] No person went lacking for any reason.

The Jesuits established an integrated economic network that was so productive that it placed them beyond competition with other colonials. Though the structure of this system was communal, they had an extensive capital base. Because of its expanse, it had broad connections and a credit market among the Spaniards in Latin America and in Spain.[771] This capital provided a strong base that undergirded the wider Jesuit missionary work in Paraguay and in other parts of Latin America. The Jesuits were also the recipients of large bequests, and the Crown exempted them from the tax burden because of their missionary status.

They made use of their colleges and institutions to market the products of their broad agricultural holdings.[772] This eliminated the middleman, which added to the efficiency and thus to their success. They exported products that were in demand all over Europe during the seventeenth century, for example, *Ilex paraguariensis* or yerba maté, called Jesuit tea. Another economic resource was cattle raising for hides.

As we had seen, there was evidence that Father White was familiar with the *reducciône*. He had studied in Spain during the time the Jesuits were heavily engaged in Paraguay. It was very likely that Father White was probably trying to establish a similar type of approach to the native in the Maryland colony.

---

[768] Nicholas P. Cushner, "'Palaces in the Desert': The Jesuits of Paraguay, 1607–1768," *America* 138, no. 5 (February 11, 1978): 94–95. There were stories and rumors that the Jesuits owned and operated gold mines on the reductions, that the reductions were almost a cover-up for the mining. Cushner said that the two authors Furlong and Marner provided strong evidence to discount the fact of such mines. Cushner added, "[T]hese mines existed only in the fevered imaginations of Europeans who could conceive of wealth only in terms of precious metals coming from the mines of the New World." But according to Cushner, it was the efficiency of the administration of the reductions by the Indians that produced the so-called wealth of the Jesuits.

[769] Storni, 12:166.

[770] Mourre, 3386.

[771] Cushner, 95; cf. Storni, 166, which states, "Domestic industries were encouraged and their products as well as agricultural surpluses were sold by the Jesuits to the outside world to procure any items needed in the mission economy."

[772] Cushner, 94.

He must have thought that the palatinate had given them privileges in this direction.[773]

According to Emmett Curran, it was the spirituality of the Jesuits that was the driving force of Fr. Andrew White and his companions.[774] They relied almost totally on the *Exercises* of Ignatius for spiritual sustenance. This Jesuit missionary spirit seemed to strongly underpin the activities of Father White and his companions as they served in Maryland. Fr. Andrew White and Fr. John Altham and Bro. Thomas Gervase busied themselves with establishing the mission, securing a place for work among the settlers, and trying to make inroads among the natives. Father White recorded in *Relatio* (1634) the experiences of the settlers' living in the wigwams among the Indians while their houses were being built. He referred to his living with the natives in an Algonquin longhouse, the house of the chief. Ives, in his history of Maryland, said that it was "to this wigwam of an Indian chieftain in the primitive village of St. Mary's in 1634, [that] the Roman Catholic Church in the United States can trace its juridical beginnings."[775] The Protestants also held their own religious service.[776]

Because of the small number of Jesuits, their missionary efforts to the native peoples were limited as late as 1638. Another problem during this early period was the prohibition by John Lewger, secretary of state of Maryland, of Jesuits living among the Indians. He feared the natives would transmit disease and be hostile toward the settlers and the priests. There were reports that a trader had been killed and that the Indians were against the English. But when it was learned that what they feared was unfounded, they were permitted to go in the following year.[777]

It was likely that the Indians, as in other colonies, may have been exploited by the traders. But the Maryland colony did not involve themselves in an antagonistic relationship with the native people. Father Poulton, the new superior, lived in the mission in Saint Marys while Fr. John Altham lived on Kent Island, where Claiborne had his trading post; Father White went among the Piscataway, where he was received by the *tayac*, Kittamaquund. The *tayac*, as the chief in the Piscataway people were called, was someone whom Father White baptized, hoping to sway most of his tribe to the Catholic faith. As it

---

[773] See *supra* for Father White's background among the theoreticians of Spanish missionary activities at Saint Alban's at Valladolid and Saint Hermenegild at Seville, where he had both studied and taught.

[774] Curran, *American Jesuit Spirituality*, 47.

[775] Ives, *The* Ark *and the* Dove, 129.

[776] Ellis, *American Catholicism*, 24.

[777] Ellis, *American Catholicism*.

happened, only Kittamaquund and his family and maybe a few others were baptized.[778]

As was true for Jesuits involved in all the missions, Father White's first task was to learn the language of the native people, and he became the first to "reduce an American Indian language into writing. After preparing a grammar and dictionary, he also translated a catechism."[779] Father White, in all his writings, even his letters that were written and sent back to England, was always opposed to slavery and sensitive to the Indians and treated them with respect. This insight warranted the situating of slavery in colonial Maryland.

3.2.8. SLAVERY IN THE MARYLAND COLONY

We had seen that a major ingredient of the rising of the modern state in the New World was slavery.[780] Though one of the earliest colonies to exact slave laws, it would be vital for this study to examine the issue of slavery and its distinctive character in the Maryland colony. Depending on the period, there were three categories of labor in the Maryland colony: bond servitude (1634–1664), slavery (1664–1805), and wage labor (1805–).[781] As seen above, the Maryland colony was one of the planting colonies and therefore needed a strong labor force. But from its earliest period up to the first slave laws of the general assembly of 1663/4, unlike most of its neighboring colonies who were originally slave bearing, the Marylanders who invested in the colonial venture depended on bond servitude as a labor system.[782] The original bond servants were those who were not wealthy enough to invest in the venture but who desired passage into the New World. Bondage, as we had seen, was the manner in which they paid for their passage. These servants were bonded for at least three or four years, until they were able to buy back their freedom or to work out arrangements with their masters.[783]

---

[778] Axtell, "White Legend," 3; Curran, *American Jesuit Spirituality*, 10.

[779] Ahlstrom, *Religious History*, 411–12. Much appears in the annual letters regarding the mission in the Maryland colony.

[780] The slave industry in British America has been discussed in chapter 1 above. This effort is important, however, to situate slavery in Maryland more specifically. Consider this section within the context of slavery as we have already seen it in chapter 1, "The Slave Industry in British America."

[781] Annual Letters (Georgetown Archives and Special Collections) and Land Records (Maryland Hall of Records); cf. also Peter C. Finn, "The Slaves of the Jesuits in Maryland" (master's dissertation, Georgetown University, Washington DC, 1974), 5–6.

[782] David Brion Davis, *Slavery in Colonial Maryland*.

[783] Menard and Carr, "Lords Baltimore," 205.

As a specific instance of there being no slavery in the Maryland colony during this early period, Fr. Andrew White of the Jesuit missions had in his household Mathias de Sousa, a mulatto who was never referred to as a servant. But we knew that he was a servant from the documentation listing those on the original voyage. The list made the distinction between those who emigrated and those who were transported. Those who emigrated were the adventurers or investors in the colonial venture. Those who were transported were indentured servants until they worked out their indebtedness. The amount of time was usually four years. Mathias de Sousa was listed as transported. Another mulatto by the name of Francisco was one of the original bond servants, brought by Father White in 1634.[784]

Mathias de Sousa served out his term under Fr. Andrew White while working as his close companion. In fact, Mathias de Sousa in 1638 departed the colony compound at Saint Marys City with White to work with him among the Piscataway Indians. White and de Sousa were to work together for about eight years among the Indians, ministering to and teaching them.[785]

Another way Marylanders derived bond servants was through redemption. The redemptioners were those involved in purchasing slaves (redeeming them) from slavery under the terms of bond servitude. In 1638, the Jesuits redeemed four servants from Virginia. It cannot be determined whether these four servants were mulattoes or Negroes because of the number of whites who were bought and sold like "real slaves."[786] That the Jesuits were buying servants just four years after the colony landed suggested that the servants they had transported with the original settlers in the September 1633 expedition had fulfilled the terms of their servitude. These freed servants began a new life but still in relation to the manors to which they had been attached.[787]

Servants, upon fulfilling the terms of servitude, could and sometimes did become indebted again. Mathias de Sousa had more than one stint of servitude. After being a servant with Fr. Andrew White, he incurred another indebtedness. He became indebted to John Lewger, secretary of the Maryland Province, for four months, stemming from his loss of a court case in 1642.

Bond servants, after their term of servitude, were considered settlers; they received their own estates under the terms of the Maryland charter. Upon

---

[784] Liber ABH, folios 65–66. The Jesuits are reputed to have brought along about twenty-six servants in the original voyage. None of them were referred to as slaves, and only Mathias De Sousa and Francisco were referred to as being of African descent.

[785] Liber ABH, folios 65–66.

[786] *Woodstock Letters*, 41:203–4.

[787] Hughes, *Text*, 1:336–37. The Annual Letters of 1638 mentioned that four servants were bought in Virginia. "Alii multi ad fidem conversi sunt cum 4 servis quos in Virginia ad usus necessorios mercati sumus" (*Woodstock Letters*, 41:203–4).

receiving an estate, they also had voting rights in the Maryland General Assembly. In fact, in 1639, De Sousa was recorded as owner of a Justinian Snow estate and also as serving in the Maryland Assembly of March 23, 1641/2. He was listed on the roster of that assembly as Mathias de Sousa, freeholder.[788]

What was interesting was that there was no use of the term *slave* in the literature of the colony from its founding in 1634 until the Maryland Assembly of 1663–1664 when An Act Concerning Negroes and Other Slaves regarding slaves was passed. In Maryland, there were numerous people who were bonded; but up to that point, they were–for the most part–indentured servants.[789] An Act Concerning Negroes and Other Slaves stated,

> Bee itt Enacted by the Right Hon[ble] the Lord Proprietary by the aduice and Consent of the upper and lower house of this present Generall Assembly That all Negroes or other slaues already within the Prouince And all Negroes and other slaues to bee hereafter imported into the Prouince shall serue Durante Vita And all Children born of any Negro or other slaue shall be Slaues as their ffathers were for the terme of their liues. And forasmuch as divers freeborne English women forgettfull of their free Condicon and to the disgrace of our Nation doe intermarry with Negro Slaues by which alsoe diuers suites may arise touching the Issue of such woemen and a great damage doth befall the Masters of such Negroes for preuention whereof for deterring such freeborne women from such shamefull Matches. Bee itt further Enacted by the Authority advise and Consent aforesaid That whatsoever free borne Woman shall inter marry with any slaue from and after the Last day of this present Assembly shall Serue the master os such slaue dureing the life of her husban And that all the Issue of such freeborne woemen soe marryed shall be Slaues as their fathers were And Bee itt further Enacted that all the Issues of English or other freeborne woemen that haue already marryed Negroes shall serve the Masters of their Parents till they be Thirty yeares of age and noe longer.[790]

---

[788] Newman, *The Flowering of the Maryland Palatinate*, 260–61.

[789] It was during the assembly, which lasted from September 15, 1663, to September 6, 1664, that An Act Concerning Negroes and Other Slaves was passed. Thus, the Maryland colony became the first colony to make a law concerning slaves and slavery.

[790] William Hand Browne, ed., *Archives of Maryland: Proceedings and Acts of the General Assembly of Maryland. January 1637/8–September 1664* (Baltimore, Maryland: Maryland Historical Society, 1884), 533.

This document was a significant landmark in the early development of laws concerning slavery and slaveholding and of who was or was not a slave. The law stated that all slaves, Negro and white children of slaves included, would serve "durante vita," for the duration of their lives. As the law stated, this measure was to prevent court proceedings regarding property rights. Specifically, it would block servants from acquiring property as had been the case. Also, it must be noted that the whites who came under this law were probably Catholics who were now proscribed.

The durante vita law made an intriguing distinction between "all Negroes and other slaves," which inferred that there were those other than Negroes who were slaves. The extent of the law defined as slaves in perpetuity white women who intermarried and the children of white women sired by slaves. It was interesting that the law said nothing about the children of white men born of Negro women. Supposedly, the law was a means of preventing freeborn white women from marrying or miscegenating with Negro men.[791] Until the Maryland Assembly of 1663/1664, slavery had not been officially a part of the early Maryland colony.[792] In fact, it was probably the first time that the word *slavery* appears in any British colonial documents. Even in 1664, when An Act Concerning Negroes and Other Slaves did appear, there was a relatively small number of slaves in the Maryland colony.[793] It was not until 1664 that slavery per se actually began in the Maryland colony, and the practice grew at a slow rate.

Substantiating the idea of the slow development of slavery was Maryland's involvement in bond servitude. In discussing the diversity in the Maryland colony and in particular religious diversity, David W. Jordan referred to the composition of the colony regarding slavery. After stating that the majority of the colonists were planters who owned their land, Jordan asserted, "In 1649 the majority of freemen were landowners who usually possessed between one hundred and five hundred acres. Most had accumulated this property after modest beginnings in the colony as indentured servants or free immigrants with little capital." He continued, "Very few individuals of wealth had migrated to Maryland; indeed, an estimated seventy-five to eighty percent of the immigrants arriving before 1685 entered the colony as servants. . . . Servants seemed little removed from landowners, and many officeholders were freedmen of but a few years' duration themselves."[794]

---

[791]   Browne, *Archives of Maryland*, 533.
[792]   Darold D. Wax, "Black Immigrants: The Slave Trade in Colonial Maryland," *Maryland Historical Magazine* 73, no. 1 (March 1978): 30–45.
[793]   Wax, "Black Immigrants," 31.
[794]   David W. Jordan, "'The Miracle of This Age': Maryland's Experiment in Religious Toleration, 1649–1689," *The Historian: A Journal of History* 47, no. 3 (May 1985):

The advancement of individual interests in conjunction with freedom from the restrictions were in conflict with traditional old-world religious values, which in the case of the Jesuits were already the occasion of severe conflict in Spanish America, where the slave trade was already rampant. We saw in chapter 1 how the Spanish Dominicans in the persons of Las Casas (*Brevisimo relación de la destrucción de las Indias*, 1542), Vitoria, and de Soto and the Spanish Jesuits in the persons of Molina and Suarez suffered recrimination when they gained a reputation in the Atlantic world for standing against the enslavement of natives. One of the ways was to put pressure on the Jesuits by controlling their land acquisitions in the Maryland colony. This control resulted in a serious controversy between the Jesuits and the Calvert founders of the Maryland colony. As we shall see in the next section, the outcome was the expropriation of the English Jesuits and thus the banishment of traditional old-world religious values and the ensconcing of a new world order.

3.3. THE STRUGGLE FOR HUMANITY

3.3.1. LAND CONTROVERSY AND THE CONCORDAT OF 1647

As previously argued, many proclaimed the Maryland colonial venture beginning in the seventeenth century to be a great victory for Catholics. However, argued from a completely different perspective, that of a critique of the modern state with its idea of sovereignty, the converse was so.[795] The actual invasion and violent overthrow of the colony with its Jesuit mission in 1644–1646 took place within the context of the land controversy that resulted in the Concordat of 1647. The land controversy can be seen as a devastating blow to the establishment of the Catholic Church in the colony. The approach to understanding the land controversy would be to establish an outline of, or to ground, the clash of cultures that characterized the power struggle of seventeenth-century Maryland between secular and religious forces.

Let us return to the foregoing discussion on sovereignty in the modern state as "bureaucratic rationality." The role of sovereignty in the rise of the modern state meant more than economic control or the questions about who

---

338–59. Also, cf. Aubrey C. Land, Lois Green Carr, and Edward C. Papenfuse, eds., *Law, Society, and Politics in Early Maryland: Proceedings of the First Conference on Maryland History, June 14–15, 1974* (Baltimore and London: Johns Hopkins University Press, 1977).

[795] The rise of the new freedoms gave rise to secular theories that neutralized the meaning of religious values. For a summary of the role of the new freedoms in the undermining of the human spirit at a time when a political economy rooted in slavery and the slave trade was on the rise, see Linden, "Review Symposium," 138–40; see also Linden, "The Founding of the Catholic Church."

was human (New World colonization, slavery, and the slave trade). It had, from its beginning, been characteristic of modernity and the modern nation-state to be an embodiment of rational order. The Maryland colony, by 1647, was being remade into an entity that was subservient to laws based on precepts of reason that had a centralized power base within itself and was resistant to controls from outside itself. No aspect of this new structure could be beyond the planned rationality, especially a religious entity and certainly not the Jesuits.

Therefore, it had become intolerable that any colony based on the old order could stand in the face of the rising new world order; and certainly, the Jesuits would not be allowed to establish missions. Be reminded that the late 1640s was "one of the most critical periods of English, and consequently, of Maryland history. Cecil Lord Baltimore was venturing to advance religious freedom during a period of religious upheaval."[796] Religious freedom was a new reality, which meant, as we had seen, not only a distancing from the religious understanding and practices of the Old World (Catholic countries in Europe), that is, "the union of church and state."[797]

In the modern state, separation of church and state meant something quite the opposite. Separation of church and state was in accordance with the meaning of modernity as abstract rationality and a whole lot more. It was—as seen in chapter 1—a reasoned, planned, or ordered way of viewing or understanding the world buttressed by scientific and philosophical method.

For example, viewed from the "underside of history," the modern state, slavery, and exploitation were associated with the "new" spirit of religious freedom.[798] Religious freedom was the complete failure of the old-world experience of the union between church and state. The new modern state that was aborning lacked grounding in the past. What was observed here in the seventeenth century were the origins of the shift to a new order. Religious freedom was to become the new "religious dynamic" that, according to Jan Shipps, was to supplant "the religious dynamic that for centuries—through formal or informal catechizing—had passed from one generation to the next, a body of unquestioned information about divinity, humanity, the system of right relationships that created the social order, and the nature of experience after death."[799] Religious freedom, as it would be forced on the Jesuits, was

---

[796] Edwin W. Beitzell, "Thomas Copley, Gentleman," *Maryland Historical Magazine* 47, (n.d.): 209–23.

[797] Hanley, *Their Rights and Liberties*, 110.

[798] Gustavo Gutiérrez uses the term *underside of history* to refer to a critical interpretation of changes in the sociohistorical context with a concern for how political, economic, and religious issues affect the lives of those being undermined by various ideologies of oppression. Gutiérrez, *A Theology of Liberation*.

[799] Jan Shipps, *Mormonism* (Urbana and Chicago: University of Illinois Press, 1985), 34; Richard Wentz, "John Williamson Nevin and American Nationalism," *Journal*

the underpinning of the "new religious dynamic." Religious freedom in this sense can be characterized as freedom "from" a particular type of religion that lost its ability to influence the character of exchanges evolving in the rising master-slave society.

The land controversy was generated by political interests that were totally opposed to the existence of Catholics and specifically the Jesuits in the Maryland colony. It was particularly about political and religious issues regarding the ownership of property and the conditions of tenure in a feudal/manorial-type structure. The feudal/manorial structure was the rule of Lord Baltimore's colony with the absolute title to all land being held by the proprietor, his heirs, and successors as granted by the Maryland charter. Thus, only Cecil Lord Baltimore and his resident agent had authority to confer land. Though usually kept very strictly, there was evidence that Lord Baltimore himself sometimes failed to impose on the colony at large. Under the privilege of "rights of service (a personal gift) or for financing the transportation of prospective settlers," such exceptions were frequent.[800] This privilege was not the case for the Jesuits. The rule was forced onto the Jesuits and their property. The level of the conflict engendered by the land controversy would permanently change the social and religious history of the colony.[801]

The principal figures in this controversy were Lord Baltimore himself; Leonard Calvert, governor of the colony; John Lewger, who served as the agent of Cecil Lord Baltimore; Gregory Panzani, a member of the Roman oratory serving as a papal envoy to England on behalf of Pope Urban VIII; Fr. Henry More, the Jesuit provincial in England who signed the Concordat of 1647, mandating the conditions under which the Jesuits could stay in the colony; the Jesuits in the Maryland mission, specifically Fr. Andrew White, Fr. John Gravener (alias Altham), Fr. Thomas Copley,[802] and Bro. Thomas Gervase; and the freemen who were the voting members of the Maryland Assembly, the original adventurers along with freed indentures.

The significance of John Lewger and his role in the land controversy was his ideas regarding the separation of church and state. He had been an Anglican priest and rector in Somersetshire, England, before converting to Roman Catholicism. He was a fellow student of Cecil Calvert at Oxford University. Lewger himself converted to Catholicism and became involved in the Maryland venture. He came to the colony at the same time as Father

---

of the American Academy of Religion.

[800] Newman, *The Flowering of the Maryland Palatinate*, 63.

[801] Hughes, *Text*, 1:349, 399.

[802] Fr. Thomas Copley has been just mentioned above. For more specific details on the role of Fr. Thomas Copley in the establishment of the Maryland colony, cf. *infra*, p. 256.

Copley on November 28, 1637. Upon his arrival in the Maryland colony, he served as secretary of the colony, register of grants of land, collector of the customs, receiver of rents, justice of the peace, commissioner of causes testamentary, surveyor general, and councilor of Gov. Leonard Calvert.[803]

The background of the ideas of John Lewger on the topic of separation of church and state stemmed from his two books, the two-volume set called *Erastus Junior* (1659–1660) and *Erastus Senior* (1662), published well after he had become a Catholic and was involved in the Maryland colony. *Erastianism*, as the ideas of Lewger came to be called, came out of the Anglican Protestant establishment. In this theory of Erastianism, Lewger denied the divine origins of priestly orders and ecclesial jurisdiction. Lewger contended that priestly orders and ecclesial jurisdiction were derived from the Parliament. His book stated it as follows: "The pretensions to divine right; in a solid demonstration by principles, forms of ordination, common laws, acts of parliament, that no bishop, minister, nor presbyter, hath any right or authority to preach, &c., in this nation from Christ, but only from the parliament."[804] The argument was that the constitution of the church was not divine but political, merely a department of state. According to Hughes, this position meant that the church was entirely subject to the state. He asserted that "civil fealty towards the King and religious fidelity towards God were so connected that subjects were bound to follow the dictates of the magistrates; since the Church and State were nothing but two denominations for the same society."[805]

Although John Lewger had become a Catholic to escape what was called the Anglican Protestant establishment, he never lost his anti-Catholic attitude. As it was just expressed, it surfaced again in the Maryland colony as he worked out what ultimately became the groundwork for the theory of the separation of church and state for Lord Baltimore. The Jesuit historian Henry Foley, in telling the story of the demise of the Jesuits under the dictates of Lewger, said that "he [John Lewger] retained much of the leaven of Protestantism: for he still maintained those dogmas so justly offensive to Catholic ears."[806] The very ideas he had sought to escape when he became a Catholic earlier had now become the theory on which he operated. From this time on, Lord Baltimore would no longer see the Jesuits as consultants in matters of religion. Hughes asserted that Lord Baltimore was in the hands of John Lewger for his "theological and legal suggestions and consultations."[807]

---

[803]   Hughes, *Text*, 1:380.
[804]   Hughes, *Text*, 1:351.
[805]   Hughes, *Text*, 1:350–52. Cf. also, Foley, *Records*, 3:364–66.
[806]   Foley, *Records*, 3:364–65.
[807]   Hughes, *Text*, 1:369.

In 1638, John Lewger rendered his argument in a bill for the approval of Cecil Lord Baltimore in what was called "The Cases."[808] The document was a resolution that consisted of twenty statutes that were the importation into the Maryland colony of the British penal laws. "The Cases" of Lewger sought to restrict and subject missionary activity in general and the Jesuits in particular to the state. The subservience to the state was of such a nature that the Jesuits were marked out for "expropriation and banishment," yet they were not permitted to move out of the province.[809]

The following statute was an example of the severity of Lewger's "Cases":

> Whether the exemptions of the Clergy for theyr persons, lands, goods, tenaunts, donestiques, or privileg of Sanctuary to theyr houses, or churches, etc., are due to them of Divine right by immediate grant from Christ to his Church, so that princes beccomming Christians were instantly obliged in conscience to allow, and confirme those exemptions, or at least to permit, and suffer the Church to practise, and enjoy them; or whether they hould them of the free, and voluntary guift, and devotion of pious princes, and states, so that in a Country newly erected, or beccomming Christian, a graunt, or Charter from the prynce thereof of such libertyes, and exemptions is necessary, before the Clergy of such a Country can clayme them, as theyr rights and due in point of conscience; and whether before such a graunt, admittance, or allowance of theyr priviledges, may the state practise contrary to them, without sacriledge or incurring the censures of *Bullae Coenae*?[810]

The twenty statutes, as it would be seen, became the substance of several codes passed by the assembly and then approved by Lord Baltimore.

Now the role of Gregory Panzani was important if for no other reason than the influence he executed in relation to John Lewger. He was sent by the secretary of state of the Vatican, Cardinal Barberini, to England as the papal nuncio of Pope Urban VIII. Panzani never went to the colony but functioned on behalf of the pope as an intermediary between the two parties, Cecil Lord Baltimore and John Lewger on the one hand and the Jesuits in the person of

---

[808] Hughes, *Documents*, vol. 1, pt. 1, no. 11 (1638): 158–61; Stonyhurst College MSS, "Cases," *Anglia*, A, iv. no. 108B, 198–200; Maryland Historical Society: Fund Publication, no. 18, 73–78.

[809] Hughes, *Text*, 1:429.

[810] Hughes, *Documents*, vol. 1, pt. 1, no. 11 (1638): 158–61.

the Jesuit provincial, Fr. Henry More, on the other. Panzani's position favored John Lewger's ideas in that Panzani "endorsed compromise with the State, compromise with Protestantism." Consequently, Panzani in his letters even refused to question the position of Erastianism, which was the basis of John Lewger's thought.[811]

Fr. Thomas Copley (1595–1652), alias Philip Fisher,[812] born in Madrid in 1595, was a Jesuit who had been a close companion of Fr. Andrew White at the planning stage of the colonial settlement of Maryland and the establishment of the Roman Catholic Church in British America. As seen above, Father White was the secretary and counselor to Cecil Lord Baltimore. The role of Fr. Thomas Copley was as minister and procurator of the Jesuit residence at Clerkenwell, where he was in charge of domestic affairs. His role also made it his responsibility to arrange for the establishment of the mission in Maryland. This placed Father Copley in an excellent position to also serve in the preparations for the Maryland venture. He would probably have been on the original journey had there not been concerns on his part about his own alien status. Father Copley's heritage was of a distinguished family of Gaton in England, who owned several estates and claimed the baronies of Welles and of Hoo. His grandfather, along with the whole family, was exiled because of troubles in northern England in 1570. As recusants, the family first went to Leuven and then onto Spain, where the grandfather entered the service of the Spanish monarchy via the intercession of Queen Elizabeth (probably a relative).[813]

Fr. Thomas Copley was, as many recusants of that period who wanted to have a public life back in England and particularly as a Jesuit priest, vulnerable to political recriminations for living back in England. He would be even more unprotected if he went to the colony without seeking to lift the opprobrium. Because he did not want to incur any problems for the colony, Father Copley sought governmental protection and immunity. Father Copley thought his duties and responsibilities in the colony would demand that he seek "the

---

[811] Hughes, *Text*, 1:353; Hughes, *Documents*, vol. 1, pt. 1, no. 10A–W (July 11, 1635–August 25, 1636): 149–158.

[812] Often to skirt troubles with English penal laws against priests and Jesuits specifically, the priests used pseudonyms when missioned to the Maryland colony (e.g., the alias of Fr. Andrew White was Thomas White). Therefore, Thomas Copley was the pseudonym of Fr. Philip Fisher. Cf. "Father Philip Fisher, as he is named in the domestic records of the Society, or Thomas Copley, as he appears in Maryland history" (Hughes, *Text*, 1:365–66). It was interesting to note that, after his being kidnapped and brought back to England with Fr. Andrew White, Copley—when he reentered the Maryland colony in 1648—used the pseudonym of Philip Fisher.

[813] Beitzell, "Thomas Copley, Gentleman," 214.

protection of the King of England as 'an alien born' in order that he might have freedom of action. His petition was granted and a warrant was issued on December 10, 1634, securing to 'Thomas Copley, gentleman, an alien,' the appropriate immunities from persecution."[814]

Father Copley had entered the Jesuits in Leuven between 1611 and 1615 around the time Fr. Andrew White was a part of the teaching staff at the college in Leuven.[815] Father Copley was missioned in early 1637 but did not arrive in the Maryland mission until August 8, 1637, where he served at Saint Inigoes with Fr. Andrew White and the other Jesuits. Father Copley was appointed the second superior of the Maryland Jesuits in 1639, giving him the responsibility of the temporal matters of the mission. This task involved providing for the physical needs of the priests on the mission among the natives and making the mission self-supporting. The problem was that "the colonists were not required or asked to contribute to the support of either the priests or their establishments, which was a severe handicap to the missionary work of the priests."[816]

The early delays of the general of the Jesuits was an effort to secure what the missionaries needed to work as missionaries. According to several thinkers like the historian Thomas Hughes, unlike the other adventurers, the Jesuits were not cooperating with the Calverts in the colonial venture to increase their profits. As missionaries, "they expected that, as they were invited to go over, not for the purpose of helping themselves, but of serving the Indians, the colonists, and thereby Lord Baltimore, the latter gentleman would provide for them accordingly; and, while they attended to absorbing duties of the ministry and of charity, they would be treated on the same terms as the clergy in all Catholic and Protestant countries of Europe."[817]

Father White, in the "Declaratio coloniae" or "Account of the Colony" (1633), which contained the first conditions of plantation, had expressed his interpretation of what the Jesuits expected in return–aid in "extending the Kingdom of Christ. The co-operation of the priests simply operated in the first place as a good advertisement, inducing pious Catholics to go abroad and extend the palatine of Lord Baltimore. It proved also to have meant a good substantial contribution of funds and men from the Fathers involved, as if they too were people going out to help themselves and make a fortune."[818]

By 1638, it was clear to the missionaries that Cecil Lord Baltimore had no intentions of supporting the missionary venture. He had made no provisions

---

[814] Hughes, *Text*, 1:366; Beitzell, "Thomas Copley, Gentleman," 215.

[815] *Woodstock Letters*, vol. XIV, 34; also cf. Hughes, *Text*, 1: 168.

[816] Hughes, *Text*, 1:255–57; Beitzell, "Thomas Copley, Gentleman," 216–17.

[817] Hughes, *Text*, 1:255.

[818] Hughes, *Text*, 1:249–51, 255.

for the missionaries. In a letter to Cecil Lord Baltimore dated February 20, 1638/1639, Fr. Andrew White reminded the proprietor that–in the first conditions of plantation, which Father White himself wrote–the mission of the Jesuits was to preach the gospel, the share in the establishment of a plantation like all the other adventurers. In the 1638/1639 letter, Father White asserted, "Seeing in the Declaration and Conditions of Plantation both share in trade and the land runnes in one and the selfe same tenor, and would bee esteemed so it itt weare brought to any hearing." Father White then stated, "I remember when your Lordship corrected the written copie which I made, I gave your Lordship an occasion uppon the graunt of trade to reflecte whether it weare not fitt to limitt the graunt for tearme of life." It was also in the same letter that Father White grounded his being correct regarding Lord Baltimore's commitment to the Jesuits in the "Declaratio coloniae" (Account of the Colony) or the first conditions of plantation by insinuating that the proprietor was engaging in the swindling of the Jesuits.[819]

Father Copley first appeared in the annals of Maryland when he was listed as one of the Jesuits along with Fathers White and Altham, who was summoned to attend the 1638/1639 session of the Maryland General Assembly.[820] As superior, Father Copley became associated with the Jesuit land controversy. This controversy resulted in the Concordat of 1647. Father

---

[819]   Hughes, *Text*, 1:249–50, fn. 1, 398; *Calvert Papers*, no. 28, i, 209.

[820]   The first Maryland General Assembly was called for March 1635. The 1635 assembly passed an ordinance called the "freemen's code," dictating that they apply the English common law to offenders of serious crimes such as murder and felonies. Lord Baltimore disapproved of the code, and thus began a chain of events that were to forever change the political religious dimension for the Jesuits within the colony. It was uncertain whether the Jesuits attended. They even, at that time, may have made use of the proxy vote. Proxy voting in the assembly would become important as the issue of representation would become tied to ownership of property; eventually, only those who owned property would be permitted to take part in the decisions and laws governing the colony. The Jesuits ultimately absented themselves from the Maryland General Assemblies, and Beitzell cited Copley as giving the following three reasons: clergy were disqualified by canon law and civil law in conjunction with the canons from taking an active part in rendering the death sentence as the assembly often had to do, Jesuit constitutions inhibited their participation in deliberations of a political nature, and they were too busy with their missionary work. Because, as we shall see, the Jesuits were eventually unseated from the assembly, they ended up helpless against the rising tide that was opposed to their continued existence in the colony. *Calvert Papers*, no. 28, 164; Beitzell, "Thomas Copley, Gentleman," 220. For more on the proxy issue, cf. Hanley, *Their Rights and Liberties*, 87, and Susan Rosenfeld Falb, "Proxy Voting in Early Maryland Assemblies," *Maryland Historical Magazine* 73, no.3 (September 1978): 217–25.

Copley fought the Calverts over the obligation of the Jesuits to conform to the proprietor's charter regarding the acquisition of property. He upheld the right of the Jesuits to accept unlimited gifts of land from the Indians. In the dispute, Father Copley sought to save the Jesuit lands from confiscation by Lord Baltimore. The governor Leonard Calvert insisted that the Jesuits acquire land only from the proprietary government at the same ratio of the other adventurers. This controversy was the final straw that ultimately and permanently changed the relationship of the Jesuits to the Maryland venture.

In the land controversy, the claim of Cecil Lord Baltimore was that all colonists, including clergy, were under the common law and that there should be no land held in mortmain in the colony. Use of "the grant of religious freedom meant the separation of the functions of church and state; hence, Lord Baltimore was determined not to allow in his domain the creation of an established church. In this, also, he appears to have had the approval of the Jesuit fathers; but with regard to certain important implications flowing from the application of his broad principle there arose differences of opinion between the civil founder and the Jesuits."[821] The separation of church and state meant that the government was not to interfere in spiritual matters, but all the temporal holdings of individuals or of corporate bodies were to be under his jurisdiction.[822]

The principal claim set forth by Father Copley was what had been expected from the beginning. It was for the "privileges generally accorded to the Church by European governments in those days"; namely, that "the lands be held solely for religious and educational purposes should not be subject to the burden of assessment and taxation."[823] Because others like the governor Leonard Calvert and councilor Thomas Cornwallis often sought special privilege themselves, Beitzell asserted that they were "sympathetic" to the cause of the Jesuits.[824]

Another interesting factor was that the land controversy came at a time that the role of the Maryland Assembly in which those known as the freemen took part in the evolution of a new and independent interpretation of the religious liberty component of the Maryland charter. It was also a time when a purely democratic type of rule, in which every freeman sat in the assembly in person or by proxy, was supplanted by a more representative form. Therefore, the effort to define religious liberty became a severe attack on the Jesuits and Catholics led by John Lewger, secretary of the colony and the president of the Maryland Assembly and the freemen. Henry Foley referred to a letter written

---

[821] Andrews, "The Founding of Maryland," 163.
[822] Andrews, "The Founding of Maryland," 163.
[823] Beitzell, "Thomas Copley, Gentleman," 217.
[824] Beitzell, "Thomas Copley, Gentleman," 217.

by the Jesuit provincial to Rome. The Jesuit provincial Father Blount described the freemen as "composed with few exceptions of heretics" who, in the name of the Lord Baltimore and to secure religious liberty (freedom from traditional or old-world religious influence in the governing of the colony), "enacted laws repugnant to the Catholic faith and ecclesiastical immunities."[825]

The new authority, shaped by the 1638/1639 Maryland Assembly, might be characterized as upholding the "spirit of religious liberty" as stated in the founding documents of the Maryland colony. In the ordinance of 1639, drafted in concise form and passed by the Maryland Assembly, "the Marylander could find all his rights and liberties."[826] Hanley described the developments in the colony as challenging the authority of the proprietor and as securing protection from the political forces of England embodied in Lord Baltimore. Quite contrary to Lord Baltimore's intention, the assembly initiated legislation in opposition to the governor as well. Using the notion that it was to the people's good, Hanley asserted that the freemen of the assembly also sought to get away from how "monarchs arbitrarily barter with the sacred rights of their subjects, and it was one of the hopes of the New World that it would protect its future citizens from this menace."[827] Thus, the ordinance of 1639 stood as testimony to the growth of power of a representative assembly in opposition to what was seen as potential monarchical and religious tyranny. So separation of church and state was a significant component of the ordinance of 1639.

The turn toward a new interpretation of religious freedom can be observed in the following cases that appeared before the 1938/1639 Maryland General Assembly. The assembly decisions were concerning the specific cases of two people faced with serious charges. One was William Lewis, who was in the hire of the Jesuits, and the other was Thomas Smith, who was seen as a traitor because he sided with William Claiborne in the fight for Kent Island, whose boundary was within the Maryland territory.

The incident that led to the charge of treason against William Lewis was the proselytization by Lewis of indentured Protestants who did not have the services of a Protestant minister.[828] As seen above, advocacy for a particular

---

825 Foley, *Records*, 3:365.

826 Hanley, *Their Rights and Liberties*, 4–5, 102–8. One of Lord Baltimore's major concerns was the growing independence of the "gentlemen" or "freemen" in legislating for the good of the colony. This group, consisting of the original adventurers and the employees of Lord Baltimore and Leonard Calvert, had begun to develop a power base between 1635 and 1637. The other party that had begun to develop was led by one of the commissioners, Jerome Hawley, who stood on the side of the clergy. Hughes, *Text*, 1:362.

827 Hanley, *Their Rights and Liberties*, 4.

828 In the proceedings against Lewis, it was argued that he "taketh occasion to call them [Protestants] into his chamber, and there labors with all vehemence, craft,

religion–which had been the major concern of those who objected to a colony founded by Catholics–was strictly forbidden by the Maryland charter and was clarified in the "Instructions," given by Cecil Lord Baltimore to the governor and commissioners of the colony as it embarked on its voyage to America.[829]

In the meantime, William Claiborne–the trader from Virginia who had laid claim to Kent Island, which was in the Maryland territory–was supported by Thomas Smith. When Claiborne lost the case, Thomas Smith was charged with treason, was convicted by the assembly, and was executed. Before his execution, Smith asked to see a clergyperson. The clergyperson was refused entrance by the president of the Maryland Assembly. The assembly voted to disagree with the decision of the president, and Smith was permitted to receive the services of a minister before his execution. Both of these cases heard by the Maryland Assembly, along with the code of 1635 and other acts by the assembly, surfaced both the independent authority of the freemen in the assembly and the assembly's significance in the interpretation of religious liberty in the charter. Both of these newly developing powers of the freemen in the assembly would affect the land controversy with the Jesuits.

The controversy between Lord Baltimore and the Jesuits over property rights, according to Fr. Thomas Hughes, began as early as 1633 before the colony embarked on its trip to British America and lasted until about 1670. In fact, the initial hesitancy of the Jesuit general–mentioned beforehand–was connected to the land issue and to how the Jesuits would be cared for in the colony. The original query concerning the stability of the missionary venture by the Jesuit general before he permitted his priests actually to go to invest in the Maryland colonial venture. His concerns were temporarily resolved with the first conditions of plantation, which were drawn up in the land advertisements of the Maryland colony ("Declaratio coloniae," 1633) and used to encourage immigration.[830]

Land was offered as a bounty to adventurers who would bring over a number of servants into the colony. So many acres were allotted to the adventurer, his wife (if married), and each of his children and so many to each of the servants who were brought over. The Jesuits figured that, because they entered the colony, "under the regular [first] *Conditions of Plantation* [they] were entitled to some 28,000 acres of land and in addition had bought other

---

and subtlety to delude ignorant persons. Servants which are under his charge shall not keep or read what appertains to their religion." *Archives of Maryland*, IV, 35–36.

[829]   Hanley, *Their Rights and Liberties*, 76.

[830]   Hughes, *Documents*, vol. 1, no. 9 (1633): 145–49; Hughes, *Text*, 1:249–53. A summary of the first conditions can also be found in Newman, *The Flowering of the Maryland Palatinate*, 62–63.

land" from the natives.[831] The Jesuits wanted to possess the land given by the Indians to advance their missionary work.

With the second conditions of plantation, as "published at Portsmouth, in England, on the 8th day of August 1636, 1000 acres was to be given to every adventurer who would bring over a number not less than five servants; 100 acres was given for self, wife and each child besides."[832] These second conditions were considered more of a warrant from the proprietary to the governor for "'yearly quitrents of 400lbs. of good wheat' for every 2000 acres as granted upon the [first] *Conditions of Plantation*."[833]

It was being argued by Lewger and thus Lord Baltimore himself that the provisions of both the first and second conditions of plantation were not made for their missionary work because the proprietor owned the land, and everyone

---

[831]   To calculate the holding of the Jesuits, Father Zwinge reviewed the claim of Father Copley. Zwinge stated that, in 1650 (August 25), Father Copley–after he returned to the colony in 1648 from the forced exile of himself and Father White– submitted the following claim to the secretary's office of the Maryland colonial authorities. In this claim, Father Copley presented a list of names of servants who had accompanied Father White, first adventurer into the Maryland Province.

Father Copley asserted that "there is undoubtedly at least 8000 acres due the said White and his successors upon the first adventure into Maryland. And I do further certainly believe much more land to be due to the said Gent. for severall other great Adventures made by them into the Province, whose names I cannot suddenly remember, upon the latter *Conditions* [italics added], for I do avouch first and last the Gent. afores[d] have transported at least 60 persons into this Province." Zwinge stated further, "Father Copley claimed 20,000 acres of land, besides the 8000 acres the FF. already possed." The twenty-eight thousand can be calculated as follows: According to the conditions, the Jesuits had been given townlands not included in the twenty-eight thousand called freehold land (four hundred acres), two thousand for every five persons brought into the colony before 1636, and one thousand acres for every five persons brought in after 1636.

Zwinge concluded that "in 1633, 30 men including Fathers and Brothers came over which gave them 10,000 acres; in 1634 and 1635, 5 men came over, which with the 15 assigned men gave them 10,000 acres; after that 30 men crossed the sea to settle in Maryland, which gave them 6,000 acres, or in all 28,000. Of this large amount the Society retained only the town lands, St. Inigos and St. Thomas Manor, in all about 8000 acres. The rest Father Copley distributed to others." Zwinge, "Our Fathers," 52–53; cf. also Beitzell, "Thomas Copley, Gentleman," 217, and Newman, *The Flowering of the Maryland Palatinate*, 61–67 and 76–82.

[832]   Archbishop John Carroll, "Papers Relating to the Early History of the Maryland Mission: Narrative of the Establishment of the Catholic Religion in Maryland and Pennsylvania," in *Woodstock Letters*, vol. IX, no. 3 (1880) 157–67, 170. A summary of the second conditions can be found in Newman, *The Flowering of the Maryland Palatinate*, 64.

[833]   Hughes, *Text*, 1:253.

paid quitrents for use of the land. Consequently, the Jesuits thought they should receive immunity from those parts of the charter that did not permit them to hold land in mortmain in the province.[834] This question was due to the Jesuits and their operation, the establishment of the Catholic Church in the colony, considered a canonical entity under a bishop or, in their case, the Jesuit general. As individual adventurers, the priests were to be treated no different from other settlers. "They were subject to all the ordinances, taxes, servitudes, and burdens. Also because they were under a bishop or in the Jesuit Order, were disqualified from receiving land, buying it, holding it, under whatever title of religion or charity it might have been offered; and, if actually conveyed, it was to be forfeited to the Proprietary."[835]

Centered on the thought of Lord Baltimore about the Jesuits, influenced by John Lewger's idea of the church receiving its authority from the state, along with the developing interpretation of freedom of religion, the land controversy became a full-blown dispute after the assembly of 1637/1638. The results of that assembly were a series of "acts": "An Oath Attached to the Foregoing Conditions," "The Four Points," and "Assignment or Surrender."[836] The passage of these acts was tantamount to the importation of the English penal laws into the Maryland colony against Catholics in general and the Jesuit priests in particular. All these acts were passed before the invasion and routing of the Maryland colony by the Puritans. Lord Baltimore forced the English provincial to issue them to the Jesuit priests in the colony. With the acceptance and approval of these acts, the Jesuits were stripped of the formal status they previously held in the colony. The strictures of the November 10, 1641, third conditions of plantation were "a violation of the intentions manifested by his

---

[834] To hold in mortmain meant an inalienable possession of land protected by the government for religious purposes.

[835] Hughes, *Text*, 1:430–31

[836] Cf. third conditions of plantation, which was against the tenure of land in mortmain, and "An Oath Attached to the Foregoing Conditions," in which all colonists were to resign all right of possessing land acquired from the Indians except through Lord Baltimore: Hughes, *Documents*, vol.1, pt. 1, no. 12A–B (November 10, 1641), 162–63; Hughes, *Text*, 1:499–501, 1:501–5. "Four Points" declared that the Jesuits could not engage in trade with the Indians without license for such from the proprietary, no one could purchase or make use of any land from any Indians, the Jesuits were not exempt from laws duly legislated by the freemen and approved by the proprietary, and all causes—even those usually heard in ecclesiastical courts—were to be withdrawn from the ecclesiastical forum and were to be heard by one authorized by the Lord Baltimore: Hughes, *Documents*, vol.1, no. 15 (1641): 166–68; Hughes, *Text*, 1:431, 506–13. "Assignment or Surrender" asserts that the Jesuits must surrender church and Jesuit rights and lands already received from the Indians to the proprietary with no recompense: Hughes, *Documents*, vol. 1, no. 21 (1642), 190–1; Hughes, *Text*, 1:431, 529–31. Cf. also Foley, *Records*, 3:364–67.

father," George Lord Baltimore, in the original charter. George Lord Baltimore "had provided for just the opposite in the Maryland charter by excluding the Statutes of Mortmain."[837]

Despite the acts of the Maryland Assembly against them, the Jesuits continued to seek immunity from property restrictions. This generated an intense conflict between the Jesuits and Lord Baltimore for about thirty years after the acts of the 1638 Maryland Assembly, especially regarding issue of immunity from the confiscation of church property mentioned in its Act for Church Liberties. In a letter to Lord Baltimore, "[Father] Copley told Baltimore that he was greatly distressed that while immunities were referred to in the *Act for Church Liberties* in his code, no specific provision was made to free the clergy from civil courts nor to do the same for laymen who were employed residents on church land."[838] The act left out the term *immunities*, suggesting that there was no notion of a union between church and state comparable to what existed in Europe, particularly in Spain. Father Copley claimed that the land given them by the natives was "church property," and with a bull of the church (*Bulla Coenae*), they ought to be allowed to keep it and not have to pay taxes on it. The bull stated that confiscation of church property was punishable by excommunication. According to Lord Baltimore, however, the Jesuits–regardless of the ecclesiastical bull designed to prevent the arbitrary confiscation of church property–did not have legal right to their land. The various ecclesiastical laws would eventually determine the status of the Jesuits, "interpreting canon law, and even limiting the application of Papal Bulls."[839]

The land controversy was decided by Cecil Lord Baltimore and on his own behalf. The Jesuits were only permitted to keep the land that came with their original grant (eight thousand acres). The "Old World" policy of the union of church and state, especially in Catholic countries, was not to be implemented in the Maryland colony. In fact, using the very notion of the separation of church and state, Lord Baltimore in 1641 made the decision that was the exact opposite of what the Jesuits had expected. The Jesuit historian Thomas Hanley asserted, "Baltimore did reflect more of the Old World than the New in his code, but he made it forcefully clear that he did not accept [Father] Copley's suggestion that a union of church and state found with accompanying practices in Catholic countries should be enforced in Maryland."[840]

It was precisely in the aforementioned conflict that the clash of cultures or the religious conflict took place. Hanley made the claim that Lord Baltimore

---

[837] Hughes, *Text*, 1:431.

[838] Hanley, *Their Rights and Liberties*, 109; cf. *Calvert Papers*, no. 18, 158–59.

[839] Hughes, *Text*, 1:430.

[840] Hanley, *Their Rights and Liberties*, 110.

was in the tradition of Thomas More and Pope Gelasius. However, it must be noted that the fundamental principle of the new state by the seventeenth century had already become a religion in and of itself. (It had become a civil religion based on reason and representative of the conquest and exploitation of the New World). Its principal consequence was the elimination of the influence of traditional religion on the activities of the modern state.

The Concordat of 1647, passed after the Puritan invasion (1644–1646), mirrored the strictures of the earlier acts. However, the concordat was an even more significant document in the dispute between the Lord Baltimore and the Jesuits.[841] It completely changed the requirements for Jesuits who came to the missions in British America. The Jesuit provincial was forced by Cecil Lord Baltimore through the concordat to issue mandatory restrictions on the colonial church and on the Jesuits.

The concordat comprised a combination of the issues in the dispute of the proprietary and the Jesuits. Unlike most concordats, this one was unilateral. It was drafted by Cecil Lord Baltimore and given to the Jesuit provincial, who was forced to sign it. The concordat conceded to the dictates of the aforementioned acts as well as rendered "new obligations" to be assumed by the missionaries.

Most telling was that the Jesuit provincial was forced to sign away basic rights of his priests, was "personal immunity from arbitrary coercion."[842] "On receiving the slightest intimation from Baltimore or his heirs, and without being accorded the right to ask the reason why, the Provincial was to remove, as the clause had it, the 'one or more of our Society' proscribed by the said Baltimore; and, on failure of the Provincial to effect the deportation within one year, the Calverts, that is, Cecil and his heirs, should be at liberty to use the violence, which the gentleman, unabashed, proceeds to describe in the said paragraph."[843] After being coerced to sign the concordat, the Jesuit general ordered the Jesuits to obey the proprietary. Therefore, the concordat might be described as the document whereby traditional religion, under the guise of religious freedom, became subjected to secular law.

As in the former acts, the Jesuits were not free from obligation of any of the laws. However, in the concordat, a new emphasis was that the freemen in the assembly could vote to withdraw property from clergy if they violated any of the laws regarding "civil contributions, taxes, servitudes, and burdens, whether real or personal."[844] Likewise, the Jesuits were deprived of civic franchises,

---

[841]   Concordat of 1647: Hughes, *Documents*, vol. 1, no. 22 (1647?), 191–96; Hughes, *Text*, 1:430–33, 534, 544.

[842]   Hughes, *Text*, 1:534.

[843]   Hughes, *Text*, 1:534; Cf. Hughes, *Documents*, vol. 1, no. 22, 50.

[844]   Hughes, *Text*, 1:430.

which meant that they were barred from voting in the assembly. It must be noted that enfranchisement was determined by status in the assembly. The Jesuits "were disqualified from receiving land, buying it, holding it, under whatever title of religion or charity it might have been offered; and if actually conveyed, it was to be forfeited to the Proprietary."[845]

Lord Baltimore not only insisted on feudal dependency in terms of the land but he also relegated the Jesuits to being not much more than functionaries. Even their administration of the sacraments was under the scrutiny of the proprietary. Priests were to be inspected and approved of by the legitimate civil authorities. If they did not meet with the approval of the civil authorities, they were to be given L20 sterling and deported.[846] The insistence of Lord Baltimore on forcing Catholic out of the colony was further enforced when the fourth conditions of plantation was issued by the proprietor from London on June 20, 1648. These fourth conditions revoked all previous conditions, and as it confirmed the expropriation of Catholics, including its priests, it also included provisions for Dutch, Italian, and French merchants. All were required to take the oath of fidelity to His Lordship.[847] In reference to the Jesuits and land grants of organized bodies, a statute stated, "Corporations Societies Fraternities Guilds and Bodies Politick as well as Spiritual as Temporal . . . in their own name or Right on in the name or names or right of any other Person or Persons . . . 'without special permission from the Lord Proprietary were prohibited from the future execution of land grants."[848] During the ensuing years, there were other such conditions as well as laws from the assembly that maintained the same approach of keeping religious entities, even the Anglican Church, subservient to the modern state and its designs.

The outcome of the restriction of the Jesuits left them in a difficult position to become as self-sufficient as other adventurers. In fact, unless they accepted the terms of the concordat and the new compromises, they were held bound to the land and were forced to minister to both natives and colonists while in hiding. The Jesuits, who were the principal confidants and coauthors of the original Maryland colony, had become pariahs because of their old-world Catholic background and the influences of a social policy that, by the mid-seventeenth century, had begun to run afoul in the New World. The expropriation of the Jesuits and consequently of the church itself and its enforced subservience laid the groundwork for the kind of disregard of the traditional religious understanding that led to the invasion of the colony by the Puritans (1644–1646).

---

[845] Hughes, *Text*, 1:430–31.
[846] Hughes, *Text*, 1:432.
[847] Newman, *The Flowering of the Maryland Palatinate*, 65.
[848] Newman, *The Flowering of the Maryland Palatinate*, 66.

3.3.2. THE PURITAN INVASION (1644–1646)

The Puritan invasion between 1644 and 1646 must not have come as a surprise to the Calverts or to the Jesuits. The position of the freemen and the efforts of Cecil Lord Baltimore to maintain control of the colony did not hold. The influence of the Puritans and other Protestants in the assembly took advantage of the distance of Lord Baltimore from the colony. It shall be seen that an unstable situation developed rapidly. The attacks began in early 1644. By 1645, the priests were excised from the colony completely, and the Calverts themselves were forced out of the colony.

Even though some of the neighboring British colonies were hostile toward the Maryland settlers, life within Maryland had been relatively peaceful until the acts or ordinances of the Maryland Assembly in 1638. In fact, "it turned out, through no fault of theirs, that the only neighbors whose friendship they could cultivate were the Indians."[849] This statement characterized almost the first twelve years of the life of this Catholic colony. For instance, when the governor tried to begin trading with Massachusetts, it ended up in conflict. In March 1642, the Virginia colony passed the Act against Catholics and Priests. Things had become critical again in England for Catholics, and Ellis pointed out that eleven priests had been executed.[850] He went on to say that Virginia replicated the situation in England by themselves, attacking the priests and Catholics of Maryland. This act basically said that Virginia would no longer even give succor to Catholics who sought refuge in their colony.

The Act against Catholics and Priests was followed up in 1643 with the beginnings of disruption in the Maryland colony.[851] Catholics and their priests had become even more proscribed by Virginians. Virginia had always had a strong hostility toward Maryland and Calvert's vision. For example, we mentioned previously how George Calvert was treated in 1629, when he came looking for support in finding a new territory to settle.

One of the villains in the movement of hostility toward Catholics was William Claiborne. He had been a problem for Lord Baltimore since 1629 and now had started the uprisings in the colony. William Claiborne had been a member of the Virginia Governor's Council earlier and used his influence to establish a trading post on Kent Island, which had caused so much trouble for the Marylanders. Claiborne had a deep hatred of Catholics, and he was against their being settled in Maryland so near to Virginia. From as early as

---

[849]   Andrews, *The Founding of Maryland*, 133.
[850]   John Tracy Ellis, ed., *Documents of American Catholic History* (Milwaukee: Bruce Publishing Company, 1956), 113.
[851]   Ellis, *Catholics in Colonial America*, 335.

1638, the baron had tried to get jurisdiction over the land on Kent Island, which Claiborne obtained from the Indians.

Father White, in his *Relatio*, called William Claiborne and Henry Fleet the chief enemies of the colony and provided evidence of worsening conditions for himself and the colony's Catholics. There was evidence that, after talking with Claiborne, even Henry Fleet–who had earlier assisted the Marylanders– revolted against the colonists and cooperated with Claiborne in spreading rumors among the Indians and incensing them against the Catholics.[852]

Then in 1645, the colony was attacked by a "party of 'rowdies' or marauders led by William Claiborne with Richard Ingle, a Puritan trader from New England. The invaders arrived on the vessel *Reformation*, captured and burned Saint Marys City, and plundered and destroyed the houses and chapels of the missionaries.[853] Even the governor, Leonard Calvert, and his family were forced to flee the Maryland colony. This was documented in an annual letter (1645) to the Jesuit general, which made reference to the abduction of a Jesuit and a companion (probably Leonard Calvert) along with others (probably Leonard Calvert's family).[854]

> At that time [1646] there were in the neighborhood certain soldiers, unjust plunderers, Englishmen indeed by firth, of the heterodox faith, who coming the year before with a fleet, had invaded with arms almost the entire colony, had plundered, burnt, and finally, having abducted the priests and driven the Governor himself into exile, had reduced it [the colony] to a miserable servitude.[855]

There were six missionaries in Maryland at the time of the invasion. Sometime in late 1645 or early 1646, Fr. Andrew White and Fr. Thomas Copley were kidnapped and brought back to England in chains to be hanged for being "returned priests." It was an act of treason for a priest, once he left, to ever return to England.[856] The result, as mentioned before, was that both Fathers White and Copley were able to convince the court that they were back in England against their wills. Even so, they were sent to prison with the sentence of death hanging over them. Father White was reported to have spent three years in prison before he was released and banished from England into Belgium. Initially, Father White sought to return to the Maryland colony,

---

852   *Calvert Papers*, 3:40–41.
853   Campbell, *The Jesuits*, 339–40.
854   Foley, *Records*, 3:320–400, 387.
855   Author uncertain in year 1670, *Calvert Papers*, 7:94–95.
856   Hughes, *Text*, 2:11.

but the Jesuit provincial thought that it was probably too dangerous for him. The provincial also thought that Father White, who was experiencing waning health, had become too old to withstand the rigors of colonial missionary life. At age sixty-seven, Father White slipped back into England, where he lived secretly, ministering to Catholics on the underground in south of the country until he died on December 27, 1656.

There were no priests in the Maryland colony during 1647, and when they did return in 1648, it was in the person of Father Copley. The Jesuits during this period often were in hiding.[857] They were unable to occupy the land they had acquired from the Indians because of the Concordat of 1647 and were seriously restricted in their activities. At this point, Father Copley still continued to pursue the land that rightfully belonged to the Jesuits.

Meanwhile, there was evidence that the Puritans' goal was to completely rid Maryland of its priests. During the Puritan invasion, three other missionary priests who were in the colony escaped into Virginia. There was some evidence that one other priest, Fr. Roger Rigbie, was also kidnapped at the time Fathers White and Copley were kidnapped and brought back to England. But it seemed that Father Rigbie was returned to the Maryland colony, where along with his two companions, Fr. Bernard Hartwell and Fr. John Cooper, he was taken as a prisoner to Virginia. In 1646, Fathers Rigbie, Hartwell, and Cooper were reported to have died "of unspecified causes; their superiors had no doubts that the cause was the murderous 'cruelty of heretics.'"[858] T. Hughes referred to what happened when he said,

> We have averted already to the suspiciousness of this circumstance that three young Jesuit priests should have died in the same year while they were practically in the hands of enemies.[859]

The Maryland colony was under siege for two years, between February 15, 1644, and August 5, 1646. Leonard Calvert, during that time, sought refuge among the English Catholics in the Virginia colony. In 1645, he—with the support of Sir William Berkeley, the Royalist governor of Virginia of the English Catholics (Anglican) and thus also anti-Puritan—pulled together a

---

[857]   Rev. William P. Treacy, SJ, *Old Catholic Maryland and Its Early Jesuit Missionaries* (Swedesboro, New Jersey: St. Joseph's Rectory, 1889), 168.

[858]   Axtell, "White Legend," 5.

[859]   Hughes speculated that these priests died of hardship or by violence they experienced at the hands of Puritans who had brought them into Virginia. Hughes, *Text*, 1:562–64, 2:11; Archives of the Propaganda Fide, Calendar, Series FV, SOCG, 12 (1653–1663): 71rv–72rv.

small army in Virginia and went to war against Ingle and Claiborne to drive them out of Maryland. But this was short lived. While Leonard Calvert was still in exile, on July 30, 1646, he appointed Capt. Edward Hill from Checakone, Virginia–who was a Protestant–to be interim governor. It was not until the autumn of 1646 that order was restored to the colony, and he regained his seat as governor. Except for William Claiborne and Richard Ingle, Leonard Calvert went about pardoning most of the rebels.

It was thought that Gov. Leonard Calvert died on June 11, 1647, from wounds he incurred in the skirmish with the Puritan invaders. On his deathbed, Leonard Calvert appointed anti-Puritan and Catholic Thomas Greene to be governor. On June 20, 1647, the once interim governor Edward Hill made a plea to be governor instead of Greene, warranted by his having been governor while Leonard Calvert was in exile. But the appointment of Thomas Greene as the new governor was upheld.[860]

Despite the success of Thomas Greene as governor, in August 1648, Cecil Lord Baltimore–forced by political expediency–appointed a Puritan by the name of William Stone to be governor, and Thomas Greene was named lieutenant governor. Puritan merchants under the leadership of Oliver Cromwell had revolted against the English Crown and was to gain control of the Port of London and of Parliament. At the same time, Dutch merchants dominated trade in the Chesapeake in Maryland.[861] There also was growing Puritan, anti-Catholic spirit in the colony. Stone was a Puritan who immediately named five other Puritans as his councilors. Cecil Lord Baltimore thought that this new appointment of Puritans would curtail some of the hostility toward Catholics. It, however, worked in reverse. To the detriment of Catholics, an increasing number of Puritans began to gain power in the colony. From then on, the Maryland colony was forced to give up its "catholic" character.

In the meantime, the Massachusetts Bay colony was expelling anyone suspected of being a Catholic. The General Court of the Massachusetts Bay Colony expressed its position against Catholics in a formal act. Likewise, it passed another law, the New England Act against Jesuit Priests (1647). This law barred all Jesuits from entering the New England and New York colonies. If a Jesuit priest was discovered, he was warned and then banished; if he returned, he was to be executed. The Jesuits were only let back into the colonies under the dictates of the Concordat of 1647. The results of these tragic

---

860   Newman, *The Flowering of the Maryland Palatinate*, 144–46.

861   [William Claiborne?], "Virginia and Maryland, or the Lord Baltamore's [*sic*]. Printed Case and Uncased Answered (1655)," in Hall, *Narratives*, 228–30. Cited in J. Frederick Fausz, "The Secular Context of Religious Toleration in Maryland," in Loyola College in Maryland and St. Mary's College of Maryland Lecture Series 1983–1984 on the History of Religious Toleration in Maryland, 14.

events in which the Protestants undermined the original Maryland charter was a different, more submissive Jesuit spirit.

The concessions of Cecil Lord Baltimore led to the Maryland colony becoming a haven or sanctuary for Dutch and Puritan merchant-traders and other disgruntled refugees from the Virginia colony. At this point, the Catholics who stood opposed to the dictates of the Puritan merchant class were banned. A process of dehumanization continued with the establishment of the Act Concerning Religion. This dehumanizing anti-Catholic spirit was to perjure and be the spirit of things up to the ratification of the Constitution of the United States in 1791.

The merchant class, rooted in notions of religious freedom, ultimately left Catholics almost totally disenfranchised and undermined. With the merchant class in power in 1649, a way was prepared for the enactment of the Act Concerning Religion, which then, as we shall see, resulted in 1654 in the complete overthrow of the Calverts and the repeal of the act.

The next section shall be an outline type of chronicling the complex ebb and flow of the later stages of the struggle for humanity of Catholics in the Maryland colony (1649–1791). Although this late colonial period of Maryland warrants more intense reflection, providing only the highlights will serve our purpose. Such an approach is adequate because it is reveals the trends and developments of the dehumanization process while exposing some of the contradictions of religious freedom. What such an outline approach is meant to express is that the religious conflict underpinning the development of religious freedom is a vehicle for the establishment of the modern state. The story we have been telling, as mentioned before, makes use of the Ricoeurian hermeneutics of historical consciousness to provide a specific example in the English-speaking world of the conquest of modernity over five hundred years, culminating in the undermining of a particular type of religion. The main point of this chapter has been to concretize this conquest of modernity whose rational construct expresses itself in egoistic self-interest despite whom it might destroy.

Now let us go another step to show that religious liberty is but a stage in the dehumanization process. This coming of age of modernity in the Maryland colony has led to the commodification of both religion and economic interests. This next section will confirm that the struggle of Catholics for a legitimate place in the society has become subsumed by the drive of the modern nation-state to survive, making everything subservient to itself.

3.3.3. RELIGIOUS LIBERTY AS A STAGE IN THE DEHUMANIZATION PROCESS

The social, political, economic, and religious problems in England led to a civil war in 1642. The result was the execution of Charles I on January 30, 1649, and the aforementioned rise to power of the Puritan leader Oliver Cromwell as dictator of England and the establishment of the Long Parliament. At this time, because of his relationship to the king, Cecil Lord Baltimore's royal protection was gone, and the overall continued success of the Maryland colonial venture was in jeopardy. Again, as already asserted above, William Stone–who was a Puritan–was appointed governor by Cecil Lord Baltimore to save face in the presence of the growing influence of Puritan merchant-traders, to lessen the attacks of critics, and to ward off total rejection of the patent by the Crown due to Puritan influences in the British Parliament.

After appointing Stone, Cecil Lord Baltimore tried to prevent Puritan attacks on Catholics and Anglicans by submitting to the assembly for approval sixteen new laws, among which was a specific one called the Act Concerning Religion. According to the Maryland historian J. Frederick Fausz, the key elements for protection against the Puritans was the demand by Cecil Lord Baltimore that an official oath be taken to be "'true and faithful' to the Proprietor" and to promise "not by my self nor any Person directly or indirectly trouble, molest, or discountenance any Person whatsoever in the said Province professing to believe in Jesus Christ, and in particular no Roman Catholick for or in respect of this or her Religion nor in his or her free exercise thereof . . . [as long as] they be not unfaithful to his said Lordship or molest or Conspire against the Civil Government Established here under him."[862]

Therefore, on April 21, 1649, Maryland became the first colony to offer "religious freedom." The Maryland General Assembly met between the second and twenty-first of April 1649 and passed an amended version of Lord Baltimore's Act Concerning Religion with the substance of his petition standing; namely, that no person should "be in any ways troubled, molested,

---

[862] J. Frederick Fausz, "The Secular Context of Religious Toleration in Maryland, 1620–1660," in Lectures on the History of Religious Toleration in Maryland (Maryland Humanities Council, Inc., Loyola College in Maryland and Saint Mary's College of Maryland: 1983–1984), 5–22, 14–15. *Archives of Maryland*, III, 210, 214. Other significant works on religious toleration are David W. Jordan, "'The Miracle of This Age:' Maryland's Experiment in Religious Toleration, 1649–1689," *The Historian: A Journal of History* 47, no. 3 (May 1985): 338–59; John D. Krugler, "Lord Baltimore, Roman Catholics, and Toleration: Religious Policy in Maryland during the Early Catholic Years, 1634–1649," *Catholic Historical Review* 65 (January 1979): 49–75; Lois Green Carr and David William Jordan, *Maryland's Revolution of Government: 1689–1692* (Ithaca and London: Cornell University Press, 1974).

or discountenanced for or in respect of his or her religion."[863] This act of toleration was an effort on the part of Cecil Lord Baltimore that served as expediency. However, the Act Concerning Religion benefited everyone in the colony but Catholics, who—as we had said—held to traditional old-world values. As we had presented in another article, the original Catholics—especially the Jesuits—and their descendants had religious and political ties to Europe, from which the new colonial leadership sought a clean break. "So, in this process, religious toleration, which was to be enshrined in the Constitution of the United States, was anything but tolerant toward Catholics," both in the Maryland colony and elsewhere.[864]

Consequently, the Act Concerning Religion provided freedom for all religious entities except Catholics. Thomas Hanley concurred with this position when he said, "the Puritan-tinged Toleration Act of 1649 [was not] representative of the Catholics, who had lost their dominant position in the assembly by that time."[865] Hanley then argued that the Act Concerning Religion can be understood only in terms of the ordinance of 1639, which incorporated "Cases" of John Lewger, whose intention was the separation of church and state as mentioned earlier.[866]

The Act Concerning Religion was repealed in 1654, after the Puritan Revolution in England and another assault on the colony by the growing influence of the Puritans in colonial Maryland. The execution of Charles I in England by the Puritans and the coming to power of Oliver Cromwell prompted the overthrow of Lord Baltimore and his regime and the repealing of the Act Concerning Religion. This action definitively removed the Calverts from the colony, banned all Catholics and their public worship, and established status for the Puritan traders. Even though the Calverts would gain control again between 1658 and 1660 when the Stuarts ascended the throne in England, the Puritan regime continued a process of disenfranchising Catholics. Between 1660 and 1689, after the restoration, Gerald P. Fogarty stated that—even though Lord Baltimore was not restored to complete control of the Maryland colony— "Catholics reverted to their previous status . . . they built most of their few public churches."[867]

With the Glorious Revolution of 1688–1689 and the accession of the king and queen William and Mary to the British Crown, the Maryland charter of George and Cecil Lord Baltimore was abrogated. At that time, the charter was managed by Charles Calvert, who succeeded his father, Cecil, when he died on

---

[863] *Archives of Maryland,* III, 210, 214.
[864] Linden, "Review Symposium," 139.
[865] Hanley, *Their Rights and Liberties,* 123.
[866] Hanley, *Their Rights and Liberties,* 123.
[867] Fogarty, "Property and Religious Liberty," 583.

November 30, 1675. Charles Lord Baltimore was the first of the proprietors to be resident in the colony. He was also the first Protestant Calvert to become proprietor.

In the meantime, between 1692 and 1702, laws were passed to establish the Anglican church. Maryland became a royal province that diminished some of the control of the Puritans but installed the English church, which then forced Catholics to live again under a severe penal code. This meant that avowed Catholics were not permitted to own property, hold office, or vote and could only worship secretly. There existed what Theodore Maynard described as a Protestant supremacy that did not tolerate the coexistence of Roman Catholicism.[868]

The forced and enforced acquiescence of the citizens of the Maryland colony, especially of Catholics, to the modern state and its politics evolved through a period of more than one hundred years. Throughout this period, the Protestant proprietor had little regard for Catholics as had the Calvert ancestors. Therefore, Catholics–in an effort to survive–were coerced into following the dictates of the modern state. For example, bond servitude had ended in the 1660s, and Catholics–like other adventurers, including the Jesuits–had become slaveholders. Under the guise of religious freedom, a new religious dynamic was being created. As exhibited in the following instances, even the Jesuit priests were coerced ideologically to join in the discourse for religious freedom. Fr. Gerald Fogarty referred to Fr. Peter Atwood and Fr. George Hunter specifically.

According to Fogarty, Fr. Peter Atwood, SJ (1682–1734)–in a manuscript called "Liberty and Property or the Beauty of Maryland Displayed," in a context of dwindling rights (Catholic disenfranchisement by penal codes)– delineated two principal issues of the early eighteenth century in Maryland. They were "whether Catholics had the right to vote and hold office and whether Maryland itself was subject to English stature law."[869] He said that Cecil Lord Baltimore linked civil rights to the right of property ownership. Even though he held that "the right to religion was prior to property, religious freedom was 'fundamental,' and perpetual law of Maryland on which rested the enjoyment of all other rights and privileges, including the right to property."[870]

---

[868] Theodore Maynard, *The Catholic Church and the American Idea* (New York: Appleton-Century-Crofts, Inc., 1953), 11.

[869] Fogarty, "Property and Religious Liberty," 587.

[870] Peter Atwood, "Liberty and Property or the Beauty of Maryland Displayed," *United States Catholic Historical Magazine* II (1889–1890): 237–63; Fogarty, "Property and Religious Liberty," 573–600, 587–88; 587; also, see the original document in the hand of Fr. Peter Atwood, "Liberty and Property," Georgetown University Special Collections, Georgetown University Library, Washington DC.

Fogarty said that, as Atwood recounted the history of said liberties, he recalled that Cecil Lord Baltimore, "in order to encourage others to transport themselves thither [to Maryland], he soon publishes a declaration, throughout all England and other ye King's dominions, that whosoever of his, Majesty's subjects would go and settle in Maryland, should not only have a considerable Tract of land granted unto them gratis, but should there enjoy all Rights and Priviledges equally and without distinction."[871]

Thus, Father Atwood–Fogarty suggested–by stressing religious liberty as an individual right, forced it into the private realm. Accordingly, Atwood also formally connected religious liberty to property, and Fogarty added that Atwood was thus connecting the possession of religious freedom to buying and selling for profits and prosperity. Fogarty asserted that "Atwood premised his interpretation of the Maryland tradition on the principle that religious toleration was the 'fundamental law' of Maryland. From that was derived the right of all colonists to their property. Conversely, no one could be deprived of either his property or a right accruing to it simply because of religious allegiance; recognition of property rights guaranteed one the freedom necessary to live out one's religious convictions."[872] Father Atwood's conclusion was that legislation must be based on representation and thus the right to vote and that the Maryland colony was independent of the British Parliament and its penal code.[873]

However, Gerald Fogarty reminded us that, in the face of Father Atwood's arguments, the Catholic struggle for a place in the modern state during the 1740s and 1750s was responded to by more anti-Catholic laws passed by the lower house of the Maryland Assembly. Fogarty added that the lower house sought to limit further the privileges of Catholics as well as the confiscation of the property of the Jesuits. The upper house of the assembly, on the other hand, rejected the lower house laws because, as a body, they represented the interests of the proprietor and the landed gentry. These laws were tampering with the basic right of property.[874]

Another figure highlighted by Gerald Fogarty during this period before the War of Independence was Fr. George Hunter (1713–1779). Father Hunter was the Jesuit superior of the Maryland mission during the late 1750s who pled the cause of Catholics. His reflection was similar to that of Fr. Peter Atwood. Fr. George Hunter engaged in a discourse regarding the 1756 Act for Granting a Supply of Forty Thousand Pounds for His Majesty's Service. This law, passed by both houses, imposed a tax on the land and charged Catholics

---

[871] Atwood, "Liberty and Property," 238.
[872] Fogarty, "Property and Religious Liberty," 591–92.
[873] Atwood, "Liberty and Property," 253–63.
[874] Fogarty, "Property and Religious Liberty," 593.

double the amount charged to everyone else. Father Hunter engaged in a dispute against the double taxation of Catholics. According to Fogarty, Father Hunter explained that "the double tax was a breach of a promise."[875] Father Hunter argued as follows:

> Notwithstanding all the hardships and restraints the Roman Catholics were laid under by these several Penal Laws, contrary to the solemn promises made to their ancestors, which induced them to quit their native soil in order to settle in that new Colony, and secure to their prosperity a peaceable, quiet habitation, in the free exercise of their religion at the expense of their lives and fortunes; they patiently submitted to all whilst allowed the exercise of their religion, though deprived of many means of advancing their fortunes common to their fellow subjects.[876]

Fogarty noted how Father Hunter stressed that the prior anti-Catholic laws, though unjust, had never had the force of disenfranchising. This was not completely so because, if we would recall, the Jesuits had been partially disenfranchised as early as 1647. None of Father Hunter's efforts to have the act of 1756 revoked were successful.

Also of significance was the Antilon–First Citizen debate beginning in January of 1773, the year of the suppression of the Jesuits. The historical context for this debate was one of accommodation by the Catholics of Maryland (like the Carrolls, who by this time were "passing for American"), who were seriously being disenfranchised. The debate took place in the *Maryland Gazette*. Daniel Dulany Jr. was a lawyer and scholar of colonial Maryland. Charles Carroll of Carrollton was the leading Catholic figure in Maryland at the beginning of the revolutionary era. Both Dulany and Carroll used the pseudonyms "Antilon" and "First Citizen" respectively.[877] Under the auspices of constitutional issues, they raised the same questions as the two earlier figures; the questions about the excessive taxing and disenfranchising of Catholics surfaced again in the letters. Not surprising, however, and of

---

[875] Fogarty, "Property and Religious Liberty," 596.

[876] George Hunter, "A Short Account of the State and Condition of the Roman Catholics in the Province of Maryland, Collected from Authentic Copies of the Provincial Records and Other Undoubted Testimonies," in *Woodstock Letters*, X (1881): 15–16. Cf. Fogarty, "Property and Religious Liberty," 596.

[877] Peter S. Onuf, ed., *Maryland and the Empire, 1773: The Antilon–First Citizen Letters* (Baltimore and London: Johns Hopkins University Press, 1974).

greatest significance were the arguments regarding the constitutional nature of sovereignty in the modern state.

Peter S. Onuf, in his introduction to the letters between Dulany and Carroll, stressed the importance of sovereignty as essential to the constitutional context of the debate. Onuf cited the following thinkers to demonstrate the significance of sovereignty as an issue. He wrote, "Sovereignty was the single most important abstraction of politics in the entire *revolutionary* [emphasis added] era."[878] In an effort to give an even more specific designation to the idea of sovereignty, Onuf cited F. H. Hinsley, who said that "[m]odern sovereignty theory avoids the identification of sovereignty with a particular branch of government, or even with government as a whole. Sovereignty is the principle of association in a polity, the mutuality of state–(the government) and community. So long as the relations between the community and state continue to require regulation–there will be need for the concept of sovereignty, which authorizes and justifies the regulation authority."[879] Thus, sovereignty was not a reference to an absolute sovereignty as exercised by the king- or crown-in-parliament or government. The sovereignty that was evolving in America was, as Onuf asserted, a sovereignty as abstraction.

Overall, as the new age progressed, Fogarty said that Catholics found themselves at the hub of the principal constitutional issues: "no taxation without representation, no laws passed without the consent of the governed, and no parliamentary jurisdiction over the colonies."[880] Catholics were the standard bearers for limited government, and they linked ownership of property to civil rights, and both were secured because of religious freedom. All these positions upheld the rising ideas about sovereignty and the idea of the modern state. Read from the critical perspective we had attempted in this chapter, it can be said that Catholics had moved from being the victims of freedom to prospering from the deprivation of others of freedom through ownership of property and the holding of slaves as a way of increasing their prosperity.

According to John Tracy Ellis in his work entitled *Perspectives in American Catholicism*, Catholics laid the theoretical groundwork for the idea of the separation of church and state along with the principle of equal and universal religious toleration for those of all faiths.[881] Ellis put this problematic in perspective when he wrote,

---

[878] Onuf, *Maryland and the Empire*, 5; Gordon Wood, *Creation of the American Republic, 1776–1787* (Chapel Hill: University of North Carolina Press, 1969), 345.

[879] Onuf, *Maryland and the Empire*, 6–7; F. H. Hinsley, *Sovereignty* (London: Watts, 1966), 235.

[880] Fogarty, "Property and Religious Liberty," 599.

[881] John Tracy Ellis, *Perspectives in American Catholicism*, Benedictine Studies

> The Catholic . . . has been able to associate with the total American experience in a way that would have been unthinkable for many European[s] and Latin American[s]. Washington, Lincoln, and Theodore Roosevelt, for example, are his heroes in a way that Bismark, Cavour, and Clemenceau could never be for the Catholic of Germany, Italy, or France.[882]

The Catholic devotion to America and Americans was confirmed in the letters sent to (December 1789) and received from George Washington (March 12, 1790) on the occasion of his inauguration as president of the United States. In the letter of the Catholics to Washington, they testified to their joy at his election to the presidency; they talked about his character of justice and truth and expressed gratitude for his public service to the nation. George Washington, on the other hand, upheld Catholics in general, praised them for their zeal, spoke of the beneficial effects of Catholics' promoting the welfare of all, declared his wishes for their success, and concluded with a prayer for the future happiness of all Catholics.[883]

3.3.4. CONTEMPORARY IMPLICATIONS AND FUTURE CHALLENGES

We are at the end of a five-hundred-year period in history, an era of geographical expansion that is radically being transmuted into expansion into cyberspace or *inner space*. This bygone era can be characterized by the confiscation of the natural resources from native peoples around the world, by trafficking in human life, by industrialism and materialism, and by capitalism, colonialism, and imperialism. The new age will be dominated by *virtual reality* radically controlled by managed technology.

In *Political and Social Essays*, Ricoeur uses prophetic language that suggests radical shifts more serious than experienced during the sixties. Ricoeur has been envisioning what "*others have since begun to construct; namely, the managerial estate, i.e., the postcapitalist society* [emphasis added]."[884]

(Baltimore and Dublin: Helicon Press, 1963), 5.

[882] Ellis, *Perspectives in American Catholicism*, 58.

[883] Peter Guilday, *The Life and Times of John Carroll: Archbishop of Baltimore (1735–1815)* (New York: Encyclopedia Press, 1922), 363.

[884] The following authors, some of whom I will present in the last chapter, also envision a managerial estate or postcapitalist society: Robert B. Reich, *The Work of Nations: Preparing Ourselves for Twenty-First Century Capitalism* (New York: Alfred A. Knopf, 1992); Peter F. Drucker, *The Post-Capitalist Society* (New York: Harper Business, 1993); Peter F. Drucker, *The New Realities: In Government and Politics/In Economics and Business/In Society and World View* (New York: Harper & Row, 1989);

As we shall see, the evolving managerial estate or post-capitalist society can be defined as the development of a global society beyond natural national/international allegiances.[885] The new global order, managed by science and technology, will promote changes from a nation-state to organizations sponsored by international world governments, which will jeopardize the integrity of the human person.

The technocrat, the one who is skilled in reason-based scientific skills, has already eliminated the need for a God. The technocrat is the dominant figure who will manage all future human transactions. The role of the technocrat is to make all natural and human resources beneficial, serving the dominance in this period of radical transition. Therefore, just as these constructs of the rational mind became beneficial to the wealthy merchant bankers and traders, so too will the artificial intelligence replace the human mind.

Religion was transformed into what might be described as a commercial cult propagating expansion. The rise of the modern state, initially theocratic, enthroned a new kind of God, the god of money, and human relations were elitist in nature–based on a radically new belief that there were those who were saved and those who were unsaved, the elect and unelect–supported by an adjusted Christianity. The hallmark of the modern state and its economic principles insisted on a covenant with religion whereby God was not to enter into human transactions. God was called on only in the event of a crisis or to bless commercial transactions. Keeping this covenant gave rise in North America to the attack on Catholics, the extermination of native peoples, and the beginnings of the African slave trade.

With the transition from the monopoly of the god of money to the god of science and technology and the managerial estate, the human being is being redefined. A new age is dawning worse than the first, an age of total dehumanization and despiritualization of the human being, in which we see not only that God has created us and left us to ourselves, the mental

---

James Burnham, *The Managerial Revolution: What Is Happening in the World* (New York: John Day Company, Inc., 1941); Peter L. Berger, *A Far Glory: The Quest for Faith in an Age of Credulity* (New York: Free Press, 1992);

Allan Bloom, *Closing of the American Mind: Higher Education Has Failed Democracy and Impoverished the Souls of Today's Students* (New York, London, and Toronto: Simon & Schuster Inc., 1987); E. D. Hirsch Jr., *Cultural Literacy: What Every American Needs to Know,* updated with appendix and expanded by E. D. Hirsch Jr., Joseph Kett, and James Trefil (New York: A Division of Random House, 1988; Houghton Mifflin Company, 1987); and Harold Bloom, *The American Religion: The Emergence of the Post-Christian Nation* (New York: Simon & Schuster, 1992).

[885] Confer with what Paul Ricoeur says regarding "the emergence of a single, world-wide civilization"; cf. *supra*, pp.1–2 and footnotes 2–3.

construct of Deism, but also that we see an attempt to deny completely the existence of a divine or spiritual principle operating in the human being or in the world. Consequently, we are facing the threat of unprecedented new oppression. A few examples include the attempt to create life in the laboratory; effecting bizarre changes in the gene pool constitutes, in this age, a new slave block for the buying and selling of human beings. By experimentation in human reproduction through biological and genetic engineering and by the international control of social, economic, and human development through the growing managerial estate, we face not only the confirmation of black slavery but also the creation of a new type of slave market. Mental capacity now distinguishes the saved from the unsaved. Those established as not having minds become the victims of scientific experimentation and are used in developing methods for the perfection of the human species (*technological eugenics*). With the possibility of nuclear annihilation, we all face what is worse than the decimation of the native peoples during Western expansion.

Thus, this subject would be significant because we would give a new interpretation to the story of the founding of the Catholic Church in the British colonies, of the Negroes and natives and the ethos enslaved them, and especially of the role of Fr. Andrew White in the founding of the Maryland colony. Instead of adapting to the new economic principles, Father White–in the spirit of the Jesuits of the sixteenth and seventeenth centuries–resisted and made efforts to establish a constructive alternative based on Christian principles. They understood that the natives, the first Catholics from Europe, and African natives all belonged to the one community regardless of their beliefs or their ethnic background. It should be remembered that, simultaneous with the shutting down of Father White and the Jesuits in the southern Maryland colony and their being kidnapped and returned to England, slave traders were to become masters of the new territories. Instead of social values rooted in traditional Catholic principles, the developing slave system peopled by the kidnapping of Irish girls, the capture of African males, and the destruction of natives began to emerge. There was a continuous clash between Catholic principles and the capitalist spirit of Calvinism with its destructive values.[886] The roots of church practices in early southern Maryland can be symbolized in the person of Father White. His missionary spirit set the church apart from the rising spirit of capitalism, which was to become visibly associated with slavery and slave trading.

---

[886] Capitalism, according to Max Weber, is not pursuit of gain simply; it is "identical with the pursuit of profit, and forever *renewed* profit, by means of continuous, rational, capitalistic enterprise" (*The Protestant Ethic and the Spirit of Capitalism*, 16–18; cf. Weber, *The Protestant Ethic and the Spirit of Capitalism*, 98–128).

CONCLUSION

In this chapter, we have told the story of the establishment of the Maryland colony from the space of our current society. For an understanding of the use of this "untold" story, recall the theories of Fernand Braudel concerning the *longue durée*. In the case of earliest colonization theory and its being rooted in "the feudal law and institutions," it can be argued that the events in the foundation of the eastern North America function as quasi actors, quasi-plots, or conjunctures in the rise of the Atlantic world with its accompanying political economy. Likewise, the rise of the Maryland colony is but a conjuncture, even though an extremely powerful one, concerning the slow, imperceptible development of a plot. Interpreting these events as part of the *longue durée* unmasks the relative autonomy of the feudal system overseas (e.g., the enslaving and killing of the natives and the Africans), even though it will eventually include the advice and consent of the settler population (e.g., the Maryland Assembly) as well as in matters of securing a place for native peoples (e.g., the Jesuit reductions of Latin America and the Maryland colony of eastern North America). These stories are the subplots, quasi-plots, or conjunctures of the long time span history and not history of heroic, privileged individuals (to use Braudel's terminology); geographical locations count–but it is, at the same time, something that is part of a semiplot (to use Ricoeur's terminology).

Regardless of how noble their efforts in the establishment of a feudal/ manorial palatinate, the original founders were destined to fail. In the early seventeenth century, the Maryland colony with its unique social policies sought to provide a solution for much of the religious strife of their English homeland. They were interested in a society that would allow them to practice religion without persecution. With the Calverts, Fr. Andrew White–a Jesuit priest, cofounder and historian for the colony–and his companions, steeped in the humanistic understanding of the state, worked for its establishment in the Maryland colony. The concept of shared responsibility prevailed as Father White worked energetically with fellow English settlers; with Mathias de Sousa, a black from the Canary Islands; and with Indians alike.

The original charter (1632) of the Maryland colony, however, existed only a short twelve years between 1634 and 1646, when warring parties raided the colony. At this point, a major revolution to overhaul the colony was initiated. To the degree that those under the original charter yielded to or accommodated themselves to the rising Puritan class, they were able to continue to exist in the colony. Leonard Calvert, the governor of the colony, was forced out of the colony into Virginia. Fathers White and Copley were kidnapped and brought back to England in chains to be hanged, but instead, they were imprisoned and later banished. Several other priests were killed. "The conquerors *had* become the conquered" (emphasis added).[887]

Such was the experience for the Catholics of Maryland from the time they were overrun in 1646. Cecil Lord Baltimore capitulated to the growing Puritan influence. In 1649, the Act Concerning Religion of the Puritan-dominated Maryland General Assembly was passed, in which everyone except Catholics were tolerated in the colony. By 1654, the final stage of the revolution meant that the colony was finally organized as a nation-state with Puritan leadership. Eventually, Maryland became one of the earliest colonies to have slave laws (the Maryland General Assembly's Act Concerning Negroes and Other Slaves, 1663/4).

In light of these events, the Jesuit missionary work in Maryland can be compared with their missionary work in various other places; it would be considered minuscule. The converts were few, and the accomplishments were small. They did not have the kind of support enjoyed by fellow Jesuits who were missionaries in colonies and in lands populated by Catholics. For example, James Axtell wrote about the difference between the Jesuits in Maryland and the Jesuit mission in French Canada. The French Canadian venture took place in a Catholic atmosphere where there was little political opposition, whereas the Maryland venture tried to take shape and to survive in a hostile atmosphere.[888]

All of Axtell's points of distinction had been noted, but the most impressive message he communicated was not so much the positive information on the French missions. What was most challenging was what Axtell did not say. Nowhere was it stated that Father White's struggle involved more than ensuring that colonists could have the comforts of their church in a foreign situation and the teaching and baptizing of the natives (the latter being a protection against slave traders).

In the first chapter, we presented the background for what took place in the founding of the Maryland colony. In this second chapter, we sought to ground the evolution of the science-based bureaucratic rationality called the modern nation-state. In this chapter, we saw how Father Andrew White and his companions and, in the end, even the Calverts were caught up in a clash of cultures: traditional religious and political values versus the rising modern nation-state with its radically new politics and its merchant-trader economics, including slavery and the slave trade. Therefore, our presentation of the crushing of the Maryland colony was not just a recording of historical events. It was a paradigm for understanding the Atlantic world in which the

---

[887]   Dolan, *The American Catholic Experience*, 73.
[888]   Axtell, White Legend," 5–6.

modern state, with its ideologies of oppression, became the dominant force from the seventeenth century onward.

This chapter has not been just the telling of an event-by-event story of the Maryland colony and the interaction between Protestants and Catholics. It has been the slow-moving (*longue durée*) grounding of the political and religious forces that have created the Atlantic world. Disclosing the events of the untold stories centered on the establishment of the Maryland colony not only unmasks the past of Catholics in the United States but also reveals the roots of the clash of those political and religious expressions of modernity and the dehumanization process. The task inevitably has led to greater insight into the trends, developments, and future challenges related to the religious wars characteristic of the opening up of the Atlantic world. The following are theoretical presuppositions out of which this narrative evolved:

1. The motive for immigration to the British colonies was religious as well as entrepreneurial. It was religious in the sense that Puritan New England established an elitist theocracy, and the English church in Virginia established a state religion. It was entrepreneurial in that their intent was to profit by engaging in land speculation and the exploitation of the native peoples and the natural resources. They often warred against the native peoples to take the land.

2. The Maryland colony was truly *catholic* in its foundation, with salvation and survival encompassing all people. They accepted the native peoples as human beings like themselves, unlike the founders of other settlements. Contrary to what happened in the other British colonial settlements, they bartered for the land, and all interaction with the natives was conducted in peace. The settlers of the Maryland colony within weeks began to live among the native peoples as friends.

3. The first settlers of the Maryland colony, along with the Jesuits, were opposed to production for profit; to trading in general, especially slavery; and to slave trading.

4. Catholics became the victims of slavery either by themselves being forced into slavery or by persecution when they refused to accommodate the new economics of slavery.

These presuppositions grow out of a study of the attack on Catholics in the colony.

The study of the events surrounding the Calverts and the Jesuit priest Fr. Andrew White and his companions exposes a contradiction in the dominant belief. These events say that the idea of religious toleration and Christian fellowship has not applied to everyone. In other words, it is impossible to reconcile the persecution of Catholics, the killing of Jesuit priests, the kidnapping of Father White and his companions, their being brought back to England in chains to be hanged, and their ultimately being enslaved with the commonly held ideals of the modern state; namely, "liberty and equality." These are all critical issues regarding Catholics of early Maryland, whose elimination has been the repression of significant history of the victims of westward expansion. This discovery counters the dominant view that heralds a history in the United States of "freedom for all" and "religious toleration."

The history of the rise of the United States can hardly be separated from its roots in southern Maryland, where Catholics were attacked and undermined because of their resistance to the rising political economy based on trading. Because of the threat they were to the colonial venture, Catholics were denied the freedoms accorded to others. Catholics, at the dawning of U.S. freedoms, stood on the downside of the rising political economy.

The founding of the Maryland colony has taken place in the midst of tremendous paradigm shifts, culminating in the rise of modernity and the modern nation-state. Western expansion and the rise of money, the Protestant Revolution, and the Renaissance with its attendant new philosophical expression, the Enlightenment, have undergirded these shifts. In conclusion, the theory of this chapter has been that there is a direct connection between the religious/cultural clash of seventeenth-century Maryland and the rise of modernity. The latter has its starting point in the former.

GENERAL CONCLUSION

O UR ATTEMPT IN this work had been to understand the prevailing aristocracy in the New World with its newly developing capitalist economy of slavery and slave trading as a legacy of the modern state. The British colonies Maryland, Virginia, and New England were only major protagonists in a quasi-plot centered on the role of modernity in the rise of the Atlantic world. Thus, these settlers were the descendants of people who had protection their interests as a goal. They created a world that was a disparate entity among themselves and disparate from their past. These settlers found unity in religion only when ministers stirred the courage of their men with prayer before they were about to go into war to protect their economic interests against the Indians and later when they fought against England itself to solidify their "freedom."

More specifically, this piece of the unfolding history of colonial Maryland reveals the overlapping struggle for salvation and survival on the part of Irish Catholics, Africans, and native Americans–then and now. The decimation of Native Americans, the introduction of the slave trade, and slavery in perpetuity for the nonwhite offspring of chattel slaves demonstrate the urgency for further scientific research on the continuing war against slavery and slave trading in the United States.

So rather than joining those who herald Catholics as contributing to Western freedoms or those who castigate them as the first slavers of the colonial period, the purpose of this dissertation has been to relate their true beginnings as a struggle for survival. Not only will this approach exculpate

Catholics of the onus of being the initiators of slavery but this work has also been an attempt to disclose that the Catholics in the colonies and its priests at this stage have found themselves victim of the rising modern nation-state. This purpose has necessitated the uncovering and the taking of a new look at the historical data of early seventeenth-century Maryland. Using the Ricoeurian notion of the hermeneutics of historical consciousness as a way of redescribing this story, we have developed a new interpretation. The Ricoeurian theory of history has provided the paradigm, the background, and the context for the analysis of the modern state.

The founders of the Maryland colony and with them Father White, who established the church, were frustrated by the more than one hundred years of religious conflict and "trafficking" in human life that they inherited. The merchants had already expanded to the East. But the overland trade routes had closed down with the rise of the Ottoman Empire. So they sought to renew their profits based on what could be derived from the resources to the West, native peoples and their lands as well as slavery. It was this period in history that laid the foundation for and conferred a spirit of exploitation and dehumanization on the colonies in North America.

Contrary to these forces, we demonstrated that the foundation of the Maryland colony in 1634–with its charter that was inclusive of all religious beliefs and that carried a belief that all people were human–was an attempt at solving the long history of conflict. Their vision was undermined in 1646 as the colony was overrun by a Puritan revolution that sought to vitiate the Maryland idea. Ultimately, the Puritan invasion set in motion in Maryland what was eventually to be exclusively a trip up the high road of profits, power, and privilege for the few. The net impact of these reforms resulted in the compromise of the Christian spirit, which accompanied the rise of chattel slavery and slave trading. In 1689, the second stage of this process to undermine a vision was completed with the transport of the Glorious Revolution from England to the colonies.

By 1770s, Marylanders saw that their solution would be further undermined and destroyed as their very citizenship was questioned; they were seen as "papists" who had no rights, not even the right to own property. As Jay Dolan wrote in reference to this Catholic colonial experience, "The conquerors had become the conquered." As they conformed to the conditions of compromise or were persecuted, they adapted themselves to the merchants and their trading practices. From this point on, true freedom meant freedom to take part in the commercial practices of the elite. The choice was to vie for the profits of the slave merchants rather than to resist them as the early Catholics had done. If anyone dared resist, they would be punished. Thus, the compromise of the Maryland Catholics had consequently left them unable to distinguish themselves from the perpetrators of 250 years of the most brutal decimation and enslavement the world had ever known.

The newly evolving society after the ratification of the Constitution of the United States providing for the separation of church and state even more firmly undermined the vision of the early Marylanders. Our theory was that the Catholics in Maryland struggled against the dehumanization process and were attacked and ultimately either became victims themselves of slavery or were forced to accommodate themselves to the economy of slavery and slave trading. This hypothesis had guided us through this study and can be the starting point for future study of the clash between religion and the newly rising modern state the United States.

This is a study of the results of the collusion between economic and anti-Christian religious forces arrayed against the traditional religious order. Such "new" religious forces are Christian in ideals only while its practice results in the experienced contradictions of the dehumanization process.

BIBLIOGRAPHY

A. BOOKS AND ARTICLES BY PAUL RICOEUR

History and Truth. Edited by John Wild. Translated by Charles A. Kelbley. Northwestern University Studies in Phenomenology and Existential Philosophy. Evanston, IL: Northwestern University Press, 1965.

"From Existentialism to the Philosophy of Language." Appendix to *The Rule of Metaphor. Criterion* 10, no. 3 (Spring 1971).

Political and Social Essays. Edited by David and Joseph Bien Stewart. Athens, OH: Ohio University Press, 1974.

The Conflict of Interpretations. Edited by Don Ihde. Northwestern University Studies in Phenomenology and Existential Philosophy. Evanston, IL: Northwestern University Press, 1974.

"On Biblical Hermeneutics." *Semeia* 4 (Fall 1975): 23–148.

Interpretation and Theory: Discourse and the Surplus of Meaning. Fort Worth: Texas Christian University Press, 1976.

The Rule of Metaphor. Translated by Robert Czerny and Kathleen McLaughlin. Toronto: University of Toronto Press, 1977.

Main Trends in Philosophy. New York: Holmes & Meier Publishers, Inc., 1978.

"Imagination in Discourse and in Action." In *Analecta Husserliana*, 7, edited by A.-T. Tymieniecka, 3–22. Dordrecht, Boston, and London: D. Reidel Publishing Company, 1978.

The Philosophy of Paul Ricoeur: An Anthology of His Work. Edited by Charles E. and David Stewart Reagan. Boston: Beacon Press, 1978.

"My Relation to the History of Philosophy." *The Iliff Review* 35, no. 3 (Fall 1978): 5–12.

"The Narrative Function." *Semeia* 13 (1978): 177–202.

"Philosophical Hermeneutics and Biblical Hermeneutics." Pittsburgh: Pickwick Press, 1978, 321–39.

"Ideology and Utopia as Cultural Imagination." Edited by Donald M. Borchert and David Stewart. Athens: Ohio University Press, 1979, 107–25.

The Contribution of French Historiography to the Theory of History. Oxford: Clarendon Press, 1980.

Hermeneutics and the Human Sciences. Edited and translated by John B. Thompson. New York: Press Syndicate of the University of Cambridge, 1981.

"On Interpretation." In *Philosophy in France Today*, edited by A. Montefiore. Cambridge: Cambridge University Press, 1983.

Time and Narrative. Translated by Kathleen McLaughlin and David Pellauer. Vol. 1. Chicago and London: University of Chicago Press, 1984. Original *Temps et Récit.* Paris: Editions du Seuil, 1983.

The Reality of the Historical Past. The Aquinas Lecture 1984. Milwaukee: Marquette University Press, 1984.

Du texte a l'action. Essais d'herméneutique II. Collection of articles in *Esprit.* Paris: Éditions du Seuil, 1986.

Lectures on Ideology and Utopia. Edited by George H. Taylor. New York: Columbia University Press, 1986.

"Life: A Story in Search of a Narrative." *Facts and Values. Philosophical Reflection from Western and Non-Western Perspectives.* Edited by M. C. Doeser and Kraay. Dordrecht: Martinus Nijhoff, 1986.

"The Fragility of Political Language." *Philosophy Today* 31 (Spring 1987): 35–44.

"Rhetoric-Poetics-Hermeneutics." Edited by Michel Meyer. Dordrecht: Kluwer Academic Publishers, 1989, 137–97.

Soi-même comme un autre. Paris: Éditions du Seuil, 1990.

Lectures 1. Autour du politique. Collection la Couleur des ideas. Paris: Éditions du Seuil, 1991.

From Text to Action: Essays in Hermeneutics II. Translated by Kathleen Blarney and John B. Thompson. Evanston, IL: Northwestern University Press, 1991.

B. BOOKS AND ARTICLES ABOUT PAUL RICOEUR

Carr, David. "Life and the Narrator's Art." In *Hermeneutics and Deconstruction*, edited by H. Silverman and D. Ihde. Albany: State University of New York Press, 1985.

–––. *Time, Narrative, and History.* Bloomington/Indianapolis: Indiana University Press, 1986.

Encyclopaedia Universalis France, 1985. *Universalia: Les événements, les hommes, les problémes en* 1984, 1985, s.v. "Paul Ricoeur" by Jean Greisch.

Ihde, Don. *Hermeneutic Phenomenology: The Philosophy of Paul Ricoeur.* Evanston, IL: Northwestern University Press, 1971.

Joy, Morny. "Time and Narrative I." *Religious Studies Review* 1, no.1 (July/ October 1986): 247–51.

Kearney, Richard. "Dialogues with Paul Ricoeur." Manchester, UK; Dover, NH: Manchester University Press, 1984, 15–46.

–––. "The Creativity of Language." Manchester, UK; Dover, NH: Manchester University Press, 1984, 17–36.

–––. "Myth as the Bearer of Possible Worlds." Manchester, UK; Dover, NH: Manchester University Press, 1984, 36–45.

Kellner, Hans. "As Real as It Gets: Ricoeur and Narrativity." *Philosophy Today* 34 (Fall 1990): 229–42.

Kemp, T. Peter, and David Rasmussen, eds. *The Narrative Path: The Later Works of Paul Ricoeur*. Cambridge, London: MIT Press, 1988.

Kepnes, Steven D. "Time and Narrative II." *Religious Studies Review* 1, no.1 (July/ October 1986): 251–54.

Klemm, David E. *The Hermeneutical Theory of Paul Ricoeur: A Constructive Analysis*. London and Toronto: Associated University Presses, 1983.

Spielgelberg, Herbert, in collaboration with Karl Schuhmann. "Paul Ricoeur and Some Associates." In *The Phenomenological Movement: A Historical Introduction*. 3rd ed., 585–611. The Hague, Boston, and London: Martinus Nijhoff Publishers, 1982.

Stewart, David. "The Christian and Politics: Reflections on Power in the Thought of Paul Ricoeur." *Journal of Religion* 52, no.1 (January 1972): 56–83.

Surber, Jere Paul. "Ricoeur and the Dialectics of Interpretation." 13–25.

C. BOOKS AND ARTICLES RELEVANT TO HERMENEUTICS

Bleicher, Josef. *Contemporary Hermeneutics: Hermeneutics as Method, Philosophy and Critique*. London: Routledge & Kegan Paul, 1980.

Encyclopedia of Religion. 1987 ed., s.v. "Hermeneutics."

Geertz, Clifford. *The Interpretation of Cultures*. New York: Basic Books, Inc., 1973.

Long, Charles H. *Significations: Signs, Symbols, and Images in the Interpretation of Religion*. Philadelphia: Fortress Press, 1986.

Long, Charles H. "Towards a Post-Colonial Method in the Study of Religion." *Religious Studies News, Spotlight on Teaching* 10, no.2 (May 1995): 4–5.

Madison, G. B. *The Hermeneutics of Postmodernity*. Bloomington/Indianapolis, IN: Indiana University Press, 1988.

Thompson, John B. *Critical Hermeneutics: A Study in the Thought of Paul Ricoeur and Jurgen Habermas*. New York: Press Syndicate of the University of Cambridge, 1981.

Blumenthal, David R. "Ontological and Liberation Theology: Two Modes of Religious Reflection." *Religious Studies Review* 15, no. 2 (April 1989): 122–25.

Bourgeois, Patrick L., and Frank Schalow. "Hermeneutics of Existence: Conflict and Resolution." *Philosophy Today* 31 (Spring 1987): 45–53.

Rahner, Karl, ed. *Encyclopedia of Theology: The Concise Sacramentum Mundi*. 1975 ed., s.v. "Hermeneutics" by Karl Lebmann.

D. BOOKS AND ARTICLES RELEVANT TO METHODOLOGY

Gates, Henry Lewis. "The Voice of the Text." In *Clark Library Lectures*, edited by Richard Popkin, 193–210. Leiden: E. J. Brill, 1988.

Gutiérrez, Gustavo. *The Power of the Poor in History*. Translated by Robert R. Barr. Maryknoll, NY: Orbis Books, 1983, 1984.

Marrou, Henri-Irénée. *The Meaning of History*. Translated by Robert J. Olsen. Montreal and Paris: Palm Publishers; Editions du Seuil, 1966, 1959.

Tracy, David. *Analogical Imagination*. London: SCM Press Ltd., 1981.

E. GENERAL REFERENCE WORKS

Cross, F. L., ed. *The Oxford Dictionary of the Christian Church.* 2nd ed. London, New York, and Oxford: Oxford University Press, 1957, 1958, 1974, 1977, 1978, 1983, 1984, 1985.

Flew, Anthony, ed. *A Dictionary of Philosophy.* 2nd ed. New York: St. Martin's Press, 1979.

Hammond, N. G. L., and H. H. Scullard, eds. *The Oxford Classical Dictionary.* Oxford: Clarendon Press, 1979.

Hastings, James, ed. *Encyclopedia of Religion and Ethics.* Edinburgh and New York: T&T Clark; Charles Scribner's Sons, 1920.

New Catholic Encyclopedia, The. 15 vols. with supplements. New York: McGraw-Hill Book Company, 1979.

New Encyclopedia Britannica, The. 30 vols. 1975 ed. Chicago; London, Toronto, Geneva, Sydney, Tokyo, Manila, Seoul, and Johannesburg: Benton, 1943.

Patrick, David, and Francis Hindes Groome, eds. *Chambers's Biographical Dictionary.* Philadelphia, London, and Edinburgh: J. B. Lippincott Company; W. & R. Chambers, Ltd., 1902.

Reid, Daniel G., Robert D. Lindner, Bruce L. Shelly, Harry S. Stout, eds. *Dictionary of Christianity in America.* Downers Grove, IL: InterVarsity Press, 1990.

Roth, C., and G. Wigoder, eds. *Encyclopaedia Judaica.* 16 vols. Jerusalem: Encyclopaedia Judaica Publishers, 1971.

Runes, Dagobert D., ed. *Dictionary of Philosophy.* Savage, MD: Littlefield, Adams Quality Paperbacks, 1983.

Software Toolworks Illustrated Encyclopedia (TM), The. Grolier Electronic Publishing, Inc., 1991.

Wiener, Philip P., ed. *Dictionary of the History of Ideas: Studies of Selected Pivotal Ideas.* New York: Charles Scribner's Sons, 1974.

F. DOCUMENTS, DOCUMENTARIES, DISSERTATIONS, MANUSCRIPTS, THESES, AND SPEECHES

A History of Black Presence in London. Documentary. London: Greater London Council, County Hall, 1986.

Bishops of the Second Plenary Council. Pastoral Letter. *The Emancipated Slaves.* Baltimore: Second Plenary Council, 1866.

Bishops of the Tenth Provincial Council. Pastoral Letter. *Our Colored Brethren.* Baltimore: Tenth Provincial Council, 1869.

Book One: Roots of Racism. Documentary. London: Institute of Race Relations, 1982.

Book Three: How Racism Came to Britain. Documentary. London: Institute of Race Relations, 1985.

Book Two: Patterns of Racism. Documentary. London: Institute of Race Relations, 1982.

Brockhage, Joseph D., STL. "Francis Patrick Kenrick's Opinion on Slavery." PhD diss., Catholic University of America Studies in Sacred Theology, Catholic University of America, 1955.

Browne, William Hand, et al., eds. *Archives of Maryland: Proceedings and Acts of the General Assembly of Maryland.* Baltimore: Historical Society of Maryland, 1883–.

Duncan, Richard R., compiler. "Master's Theses and Doctoral Dissertations n Maryland History." *Maryland Historical Magazine* 80 (1985): 261–76.

"Eighteenth Century Slave Advertisements." *Journal of Negro History.* N.p., n.d.

Finn, Peter C. "The Slaves of the Jesuits in Maryland." MA thesis, Georgetown University, 1974.

Garvey, Marcus. *Speeches Delivered by Marcus Garvey at Royal Albert Hall.* June 6, 1928.

General Court and Court of Appeals of Maryland. Document. "Mary Butler(a) against Adam Craig." Charles County, Maryland, 1787.

Graham, Michael, SJ. "A Neste of Jesuits: Religion, Rebellion, and the Paranoid Style in Early Maryland." Manuscript. N.d.

Hall, Clayton Colman, ed. "Narratives of Early Maryland, 1633–1684." *Original Narratives of Early American History*, edited by Franklin Jameson, PhD. Reproduced under the auspices of the American Historical Association. New York: Charles Scribner's Sons, 1910.

Huggins, Willis N. "The Contribution of the Catholic Church to the Progress of the Negro in the United States." PhD diss., Fordham University, 1932.

Humphrey, Robert L., and Mary Elizabeth Cambers. *Ancient Washington: American Indian Cultures of the Potomac Valley.* George Washington University Studies, no.6. Washington DC: George Washington University Press, January 1977.

Keane, James Patrick. "The Status of Catholics in Maryland, 1689–1760." MA thesis, Catholic University of America, 1950.

Mazique, Jewell C. "The Role of the Church in the Establishment of Slavery and Segregation in the United States." Unpublished manuscript, Wesley Theology Seminary, 1959.

McKenna, Horace, SJ. "History of the Church and Society in Southern Maryland." The Rev. Horace McKenna, SJ, Papers, Box 15/Folder 35. Georgetown University Library: Special Collections.

Records of the Office of the Secretary of the Interior Relating to the Suppression of the African Slave Trade and Negro Colonization, 1854–72. Pamphlet. Washington: National Archives, 1961.

Stone, Garry Wheeler. "Fur Traders and Field Hands: Blacks in Manorial Maryland, 1634–1644." Special Collections, Georgetown University, 1984.

G. BOOKS AND ARTICLES RELEVANT TO GENERAL HISTORY

Appleby, Joyce Oldham. *Economic Thought and Ideology in Seventeenth Century England*. Princeton: Princeton University Press, 1978.

Ahlstrom, Sydney E. *A Religious History of the American People*. 2 vols. Garden City, NY: Image Books, 1972.

Andrews, Charles M. *The Colonial Period of American History*. New Haven and London: Yale University Press.

Barr, Stringfellow. *The Pilgrimage of Western Man*. 2ⁿᵈ ed., 1962. Philadelphia and New York: J. B. Lippincott Company, 1949.

Barraclough, Geoffrey. *History in a Changing World*. Norman, OK: University of Oklahoma Press, 1955.

Bokenkotter, Thomas. *A Concise History of the Catholic Church*. Garden City, NY: Image Books, 1979.

Boorstin, Daniel J. *The Americans: The Colonial Experience*. New York: Vintage Books, 1958.

Burman, Edward. *The World before Columbus 1100–1492*. London: W. H. Allen and Co., 1989.

Campbell, Thomas J. *The Jesuits, 1534–1921: A History of the Society of Jesus from Its Foundation to the Present Time*. New York: Encyclopedia Press, 1921.

Canny, Nicholas, and Anthony Pagden, eds. *Colonial Identity in the Atlantic World, 1500–1800*. Princeton, NJ: Princeton University Press, 1987.

Churchill, Winston S. *A History of the English-Speaking Peoples*. New York: Dodd, Mead, and Company; Doubleday and Company, Inc., Image Books, 1959, 1975.

Curran, Francis X. *Major Trends in American Church History*. New York: American Press, 1946.

Daniel-Rops, Henri. *The Church in the Eighteenth Century*. Translated by John Warrington. Garden City, NY: Image Books, 1966.

Dobree, Bonamy. *English Revolts*. London: Herbert Joseph Ltd., 1937.

Ellis, John Tracy. *American Catholicism: The Chicago History of American Civilization*. Edited by Daniel J. Boorstin. Chicago: University of Chicago Press, 1956.

Ellis, John Tracy, ed. *Documents of American History*. Milwaukee: Bruce Publishing Company, 1956.

———. *Perspectives in American Catholicism*. Dublin: Helicon Press, 1963.

Ewen, E. L'Estrange. *Lotteries and Sweepstakes: An Historical Legal and Ethical Survey of Their Introduction, Suppression and Reestablishment in the British Isles*. London: Heath Cranton, 1932.

Garraghan, Gilbert J. *The Jesuits of the Middle United States*. New York: American Press, 1938.

Gaustad, Edwin Scott. *A Religious History of America*. New York, Evanston, San Francisco, and London: Harper & Row, 1966.

Greene, Jack P. *Settlements to Society: 1584–1763*. Edited by David Donald. New York: McGraw-Hill Book Company, 1966.

Hales, E. E. Y. *The Catholic Church in the Modern World: A Survey from the French Revolution to the Present*. Garden City, NY: Hanover House, 1958.

Holmes, J. Derek, and Bernard W. Bickers. *A Short History of the Catholic Church*. New York, Ramsey, NJ: Paulist Press, 1983.

Keating, Geoffrey, David Comyn, and Patrick S. Dinneen, eds. *The History of Ireland*. London: Irish Text Society, 1902–1914.

Kirchner, Walther. *Western Civilization since 1500*. College Outline Series. New York, Evanston, San Francisco, and London: Barnes and Noble Books, 1958.

Latourette, Kenneth Scott. *Three Centuries of Advance, AD 1500–AD 1800*. Vol. 3. *A History of the Expansion of Christianity*. 3 vols. New York and London: Harper and Brothers, 1939.

–––. *A History of Christianity*. Vol. 2, *AD 1500–AD* 1975. New York: Harper & Row, 1953; rev. ed., 1975.

Madariaga, Salvador de. *The Rise of the Spanish American Empire*. London: Hollis and Carter, 1947.

Manschreck, Clyde L. *A History of Christianity in the World: From Persecution to Uncertainty*. Englewood Cliffs, NJ: Prentice-Hall, Inc., 1974.

Maynard, Theodore. *The Story of American Catholicism*. New York: Macmillan Company, 1960.

McKay, John P., Bennett D. Hill, and John Buckler. *A History of Western Society. From Antiquity of the Enlightenment*, Vol. I. *From Absolutism to the Present*, Vol. II, 2nd ed. Boston: Houghton Mifflin Company, 1983.

Morrison, Samuel Eliot. *The European Discovery of America: The Southern Voyages, AD 1492–1616*. New York: Oxford University Press, 1974.

Neill, Stephen. *A History of Christian Missions*. Edited by Owen Chadwick. The Pelican History of the Church 6. Vol. 6, 2nd ed. New York: Penguin Books, 1964.

Nettels, Curtis P. *The Roots of American Civilization: A History of American Colonial Life*. New York: Appleton-Century-Crofts, 1963.

Noll, Mark A., and Nathan O. Hatch. *Christianity in America. A Handbook*. Icknield Way, Tring, Herts, England; Sutherland, Australia: Lion Publishing; Albatross Books, 1983.

Nye, R. B., and J. E. Morpurgo. *A History of the United States: Vol. I, The Birth of the United States*. 2nd ed. (1964). Harmondsworth, England: Penguin Books Ltd., 1955. Reprint, 1961.

Palmer, R. R., and Joel Colton. *A History of the Modern World*. 3rd ed. New York: Alfred A. Knopf, Inc., 1950.

Perry, Richard L., ed. *Sources of Our Liberties*. New York: Associated College Presses, 1959.

"Revolution Had Limited Goals, Historian Says." *Washington Post*, March 9, 1976.

Sansone, Vincent. "The Expansion of Christianity in the English Colonies of North America." Unpublished manuscript, Church History Seminar, 1986.

Sarles, Frank B., and Charles E. Shedd. *Colonials and Patriots: Historic Places Commemorating Our Forebears, 1700–1783*. Vol. VI, The National Survey of Historic Sites and Buildings. N.p, n.d.

Schoenwald, Richard L., ed. *Nineteenth-Century Thought: The Discovery of Change*. Englewood Cliffs, NJ: Prentice-Hall, Inc., 1965.

Shea, John Gilmary. *The Catholic Church in Colonial Days: The Thirteen Colonies; The Ottawa and Illinois Country; Louisiana; Florida; Texas; New Mexico and Arizona, 1521–1763*. New York: John G. Shea, 1886.

Spalding, John Lancaster. *The Religious Mission of the Irish People and Catholic Colonization*. The American Catholic Tradition Series. New York: Arno Press, 1978.

Sweet, William Warren. *Religion in Colonial America*. New York: Charles Scribner's Sons, 1942.

Ver Steeg, Clarence L., and Richard Hofstadter, eds. *Great Issues in American History: From Settlement to Revolution, 1584–1776*. New York: Vintage Books, 1969.

Wittke, Carl. *We Who Built America: The Saga of the Immigrant*. New Jersey: Prentice-Hall, Inc., 1939.

Woodward, C. Vann. *The Future of the Past*. New York: Oxford University Press, 1989.

H. BOOKS AND ARTICLES RELEVANT TO RELIGION AND POLITICAL REGIME

Babcock, Robert, and Kenneth Thompson, eds. *Religion and Ideology*. Manchester: Manchester University Press in Association with the Open University, 1987.

Baltzell, E. Digby. *Puritan Boston and Quaker Philadelphia: Two Protestant Ethics and the Spirit of Class Authority and Leadership.* New York and London: Free Press; Collier Macmillan Publishers, 1979.

Bautier, Robert-Henri. *The Economic Development of Medieval Europe.* Edited by Geoffrey Barraclough. Translated by Heather Karolyi. San Diego: Harcourt Brace Jovanovich, Inc., 1971.

Bellah, Robert N., and Richard Madsen. *The Good Society.* New York: Vintage Books, 1991.

Bennett, Lerone Jr. *The Shaping of Black America.* New York: Penguin Books, 1969.

Bentwich, Norman. *The Jews in Our Time.* Harmondsworth, Middlesex, Baltimore, Mitcham, and Victoria: Penguin Books Ltd., 1960.

Bieler, Andre. *The Social Humanism of Calvin.* Translated by Paul T. Fuhrmann. Richmond, VA: John Knox Press, 1964.

Bowden, Henry Warner. *American Indians and Christian Missions: Studies in Cultural Conflict.* Edited by Martin E. Marty (Series ed.). Chicago History of American Religion. Chicago and London: University of Chicago Press, 1981.

Brown, Robert McAfee. *The Spirit of Protestantism.* New York: Oxford University Press, Inc., 1961, 1965.

Butterfield, H. "Toleration in Early Modern Times." *Journal of the History of Ideas* 38 (1977): 573–84.

Campbell, A. C., ed. *The Rights of War and Peace.* Washington and London: M. Walter Dunne, 1901.

Chadwick, Owen, ed. *The Reformation.* Vol. 3. The Pelican History of the Church, 6 vols. Harmondsworth, Middlesex, England: Penguin Books, Ltd., 1964, 1966; rev. ed., 1972.

Chatellier, Louis. *The Europe of the Devout: The Catholic Reformation and the Formation of a New Society,* 1987.

Chroust, Anton-Hermann. "Hugo Grotius and the Scholastic Natural Law Tradition." *New Scholasticism* 17, no.2 (April 1943): 101–33.

Clancy, T. H. "Priestly Perseverance in the Old Society of Jesus: The Case of England." *Recusant History* 19, no. 3 (1989): 286–312.

Commager, Henry Steele. "Commager Speaks Out on America." *Sky* 7, no. 5 (May 1978): 35–37.

Dawson, Christopher. *Religion and the Rise of Western Culture: The Classic Study of Medieval Civilization.* Gifford Lectures Delivered in the University of Edinburgh, 1948–1949. Foreword by Archbishop Rembert Weakland. Garden City, NY: Image Books, 1991; Sheed and Ward, Inc., 1950.

–––. *The Gods of Revolution: An Analysis of the French Revolution.* Introduction by Arnold Toynbee.

De Madariaga, Salvador. *The Rise of the Spanish American Empire.* London: Hollis and Carter, 1947.

Eliot. T. S. *The Idea of a Christian Society.* London: Faber and Faber Limited, 1939.

Encyclopedia of Philosophy. 1967 ed., s.v. "Sophists" by G. B. Kerferd.

Gay, Peter, and the editors of Time-Life books. *Great Ages of Man: Age of Enlightenment.* Edited by Leonard Krieger. New York: Time Incorporated, 1966.

Gilbert, Alison, and Richard Maxwell Brown, eds. *Anglo-American Political Relations, 1675–1775.* Twentieth Conference on Early American History. Rutgers University Press, 1966.

Gipson, Lawrence Henry. *The Coming of the Revolution, 1763–1775.* Edited by Henry Steele and Richard B. Morris Commager. The New American Nation Series. New York: Harper and Row, 1954.

Goetzmann, William H., ed. *Colonial Horizon: America in the Sixteenth and Seventeenth Centuries. Interpretive Articles and Documentary Services.* Reading, MA: Addison-Wesley Publishing Co., 1969.

Greene, Evarts Boutell. *Provincial America, 1690–1740*. New York: Frederick Ungar Publishing Co., 1964.

Grotius, Hugo. *The Rights of War and Peace*. Including *Law of Nature and of Nations*. Translated by A. C. Campbell. Introduction by David J. Hill. Washington and London: M. Walter Dunne, 1901.

Hancock, Ralph C. *Calvin and the Foundations of Modern Politics*. Ithaca: Cornell University Press, 1989.

Harkness, Georgia. *John Calvin: The Man and His Ethics*. New York, Nashville: Abingdon "White to Baltimore, February 20, 1638/9." *Maryland Historical Society* 1 (1889): 209. "An Editorial: Hibernians Have Ancient Beginnings." *Catholic Standard* March 12 1987. Press1931.

Harrison, A. W. *Liberal Puritanism*. London: Epworth Press, 1935.

Hatch, Nathan O. *The Democratization of American Christianity*. New Haven: Yale University Press, 1989.

Heimert, Alan. *Religion and the American Mind: From the Great Awakening to the Revolution*. Cambridge, MA: Harvard University Press, 1966.

Heimert, Alan, and Perry Miller, eds. *The Great Awakening Documents Illustrating the Crisis and Its Consequences*. New York: Bobbs-Merrill Company, Inc., 1967.

Helm, Paul. *Calvin and Calvinists*. Edinburgh: Banner of Truth Trust, 1982.

Helps, Sir Arthur. *The Conquerors of the New World and Their Bondsmen: Being a Narrative of the Principal Events which Led to Negro Slavery in the West Indies and America*. Vol. 2. London: William Pickering, 1852.

–––. *The Spanish Conquest of America*. London and New York: n.p., 1900.

Hely, Labbe V. *Etude sur "Le droit de la guerre" de Grotius*. Paris: Imprimerie Jules LeClere, 1875.

Hill, Christopher. *Puritanism and Revolution: Studies in Interpretation of the English Revolution of the Seventeenth Century*. London: Mercury Books, 1958, 1962.

Himy, Armand. *Le Puritanisme*. Paris: Presses Universitaires de France, 1987.

Hobson, J. A. *The War in South Africa: Its Causes and Effects*. New York: Howard Fertig (originally published by George Allen & Urwin, 1900), 1969.

Hood, F. J. "Revolution and Religious Liberty." *Church History* 40 (1971): 170–81.

Howe, David Wait. *The Puritan Republic of Massachusetts Bay*. Bowen: Merriel Co., 1899.

Keesecker, William F., ed. *A Calvin Treasury: Selections from Institutes of the Christian Religion*. New York: Harper and Brothers, n.d.

Keller, Rosemary Skinner. *Georgia Harkness: For Such a Time as This*. Nashville: Abingdon Press, 1992.

Kessler, S. "Locke's Influence on Jefferson's 'Bill for Establishing Religious Freedom.'" *Journal of Church and State* 25 (1983): 231–52.

Kedutan, ichard D., ed. *The Sociology of Religion: A Methodology*. New York and London: Appleton-Century, Inc., 1967.

Krugler, J. D. "Lord Baltimore, Roman Catholics, and Toleration. Religious Policy in Maryland during the Early Catholic Years, 1634–1649." *Church History Review* 65 (1979): 49–75.

Lippy, C. H. "The 1780 Massachusetts Constitution. Religious Establishment or Civil Religion?" *Journal of Church and State* 20 (1978): 533–49.

Luebke, F. C. "Origins of Thomas Jefferson's Anticlericalism." *Church History* 32: 344–56.

MacAlister, Lyle N. *Spain and Portugal in the New World, 1492–1700*. Vol. 3, *Europe and the World in the Age of Expansion*. Minneapolis: University of Minnesota Press, 1984.

Macpherson, C. B. *The Political Theory of Possessive Individualism*. Oxford: Oxford University Press, 1962.

Manuel, Frank E., ed., *The Enlightenment*. New Jersey: Prentice-Hall, Inc., 1965.

Marsden, George M. *Religion and American Culture.* San Diego: Harcourt Brace Jovanovich, 1990.

Means, Philip Ainsworth. *The Spanish Main: Focus of Envy, 1492–1700.* New York and London: Charles Scribner's Sons, 1935.

Moore, Barrington Jr. *Social Origins of Dictatorship and Democracy: Lord and Peasant in the Making of the Modern World.* Boston: Beacon Press, 1966.

Morgan, Edmund S. *The Puritan Dilemma: The Story of John Winthrop.* Edited by Oscar Handlin. Boston, Toronto: Little, Brown and Company, 1958.

–––. *The Puritan Family: Religion and Domestic Relations in Seventeenth Century New England.* New York: Harper Torchbooks, 1944.

Mott, R. J. "Sources of Jefferson's Ecclesiastical View." *Church History* 3: 267–84.

Nettels, Curtis P. *The Roots of American Civilization.* New York: Appleton-Century-Crofts, 1963.

New, John F. *Anglican and Puritan: The Basis of Their Opposition, 1558–1640.* London: Adam and Charles Black, 1964.

New Catholic Encyclopedia, The. 1967 ed., s.v. "Las Casas, Bartolomé de," by André Saint-Lu.

–––. 1967 ed., s.v. "Latin America, Church and the Indian in," by Stafford Poole.

Nieuwenhove, Jacques Van, and Berma Klein Goldewijk, eds. *Popular Religion, Liberation and Contextual Theology.* Translated by Irene Bouman-Smith. Kampen, Netherlands: Uitgeversmaatschappij J. H. KOK, 1991.

Noll, Mark A., Nathan O. Hatch, and George M. Marsden. *The Search for Christian America.* Westchester, IL: Crossway Books, 1983.

Okie, Laird. "Daniel Neal and the 'Puritan Revolution.'" *Church History* 55, no. 4 (1986): 456–67.

Oldham, J. H. *Christianity and the Race Problem.* London: Student Christian Movement, 1926.

Oliver, James, and Christina Scott, eds. *Religion and World History: A Selection from the Works of Christopher Dawson.* Garden City, NY: Image Books, 1975.

Olmstead, Clifton E. *History of Religion in the United States.* Englewood Cliffs, NJ: Prentice Hall, Inc., 1960, 1961, 1962, 1964.

Plato. *Gorgias.* Translated with an introduction by W. C. Helmbold, a Liberal Arts Press book. Indianapolis and New York: Bobbs-Merrill Company, Inc., 1952.

———. *Republic.* Book I. Translated and edited by B. Jowett with an introduction by Louise Ropes Loomis. New York: Walter J. Black, 1942.

Porter, N. *The Educational Systems of the Puritans and Jesuits Compared.* New York: M. W. Dodd, 1851.

Reinhard, Wolfgang. "Reformation, Counter-Reformation, and the Early Modern State: A Reassessment." *Catholic Historical Review* 75, no.3 (July 1989): 383–404.

Reinitz, Richard. *Tensions in American Puritanism.* Edited by Loren Baritz. Problems in American History Series. New York, London, Sydney, and Toronto: John Wiley & Sons, Inc., 1970.

Rhep, I. "The Transformation of Virginia, 1740–1790." *Church History* 33 (1984): 107.

Robertson, James Oliver. *American Myth, American Reality.* New York: Hill & Wang, 1980.

Ruchames, Louis, ed. *Racial Thought in America.* Vol. 1, *Puritans to Abraham.* Boston: University of Massachusetts Press, 1969.

Schaff, D. S. "Bellarmine-Jefferson Legend and the Declaration of Independence." *Church History* II, 8: 239–76.

Schama, Simon. "PBS Storms the Barricades." Part 2. *New York Times Magazine,* September 10, 1989, 50–51.

Scott, James Brown. *The Spanish Origin of International Law: Francisco De Vitoria and His Law of Nations.* Oxford and London: At the Clarendon Press; Humphrey Milford, 1934.

Simpson, Alan. *Puritanism in Old and New England.* Chicago and London: University of Chicago Press, 1955.

Smith, Gary Scott. *The Seeds of Secularization: Calvinism, Culture and Pluralism in America, 1870–1915.* Grand Rapids, MI: Christian University Press, 1985.

Sorel, Albert. *Europe: Under the Old Regime.* Translated by Francis H. Herrick. New York: Harper & Row, 1947.

Stephenson, George M. *The Puritan Heritage.* Westport, CT: Greenwood Press, Publishers, 1952, 1978.

Suárez, Francisco. *On Faith, Hope and Charity.* León and Coimbra, 1621.

Swanson, Guy E. *Religion and Regime: A Sociological Account of the Reformation.* Ann Arbor: University of Michigan Press, 1967.

Tawney, R. H. *Religion and the Rise of Capitalism.* New York and Toronto: New American Library, 1954.

Thompson, D. G. "General Ricci and the Suppression of the Jesuit Order in France, 1760–1764." *Journal of Ecclesiastical History* 37, 3 (1986): 426–41.

Tibesar, A. "The King and the Pope and the Clergy in Colonial Spanish-American Empire." *Catholic Historical Review* 75, 1 (1989): 91–109.

Tocqueville, Alexis de. *The Old Regime and the French Revolution.* Translated by Stuart Gilbert. New York: Doubleday, 1955.

Todd, John M. *Reformation.* London: Darton, Longman & Todd, 1971.

Vitoria, Francisco de. *Comentarios inéditos a la II-II* [of Thomas Aquinas]. 6 vols. "On whether infidels can be compelled to accept the faith." Vol. i, quo. x, art. 7.

Waller, George M., ed. *Puritanism in Early America*. Problems in American Civilization: Readings Selected by the Department of American Studies, Amherst College. Boston: D. C. Heath and Company, 1950.

Walzer, Michael. *The Revolution of the Saints: A Study in the Origins of Radical Politics*. Cambridge: Harvard University Press, 1965.

Watkins, Owen C. *The Puritan Experience*. London: Routledge & Kegan Paul, 1972.

Weber, Max. *The Protestant Ethic and the Spirit of Capitalism: A Classic Study of the Fundamental Relationship between Religion and the Economic and Social Life in Modern Culture*. Translated by Talcott Parsons. Foreword by R. H. Tawney. New York: Charles Scribner's Sons, 1958.

Wertenbaker, Thomas Jefferson. *The Puritan Oligarchy: The Founding of American Civilization*. New York: Grosset & Dunlap, 1947.

Willison, George F. *The Pilgrim Reader: The Story of the Pilgrims as Told by Themselves and Their Contemporaries, Friendly and Unfriendly*. Garden City, NY: Doubleday & Company, 1953.

Wright, Louis B. *Gold, Glory, and the Gospel: The Adventurous Lives and Times of the Renaissance Explorers*. New York: Atheneum, 1970.

Wynter, Sylvia. "New Seville and the Conversion Experience of Bartolome De Las Casas." Part 1. *Jamaica Journal* 17, no.2 (May 1984): 25–32.

Ziff, Larzer. *Puritanism in America: New Culture in a New World*. New York and London: Viking Press; Oxford University Press, 1973.

I. BOOKS AND ARTICLES RELEVANT TO THE HISTORY OF MARYLAND

Andrews, Charles M. *The Colonial Period of American History*. 4 vols. New Haven, CT, 1937.

Andrews, Mathew Page. *The Founding of Maryland*. Baltimore: Williams & Wilkins Company, 1933.

–––. *History of Maryland: Province and State*. Garden City, NY: Doubleday, Doran & Company, Inc., 1929.

Attwood, Peter, SJ. "Liberty and Property" or "The Beauty of Maryland Displayed. Being a Brief and Candid Search and Inquiry into Her Charter. Fundamental Laws and Constitution. By a Lover of His Country." *U.S. Catholic Historical Magazine* (1889–1890). Original handwritten manuscript, Georgetown University Archives: Special Collections, 1680/90.

Aveling, J. *The Jesuits*. New York: Stein and Day Publishers, 1981, 1982.

Axtell, James. "White Legend: The Jesuit Missions in Maryland." *Maryland Historical Magazine*, July 1986, 1–7.

–––. *The Invasion Within: The Context of Cultures in Colonial North America*. New York and Oxford, 1985.

Baltimore Catholic Review. "The Tercentenary of the Founding of Maryland." Supplement. June 15, 1934.

Barnes, Bart. "The Big Dig at St. Marys City." *Washington Post*, August 6, 1972.

Bassett, Bernard, SJ. "Three Men from Maryland." *Jesuit* (Spring 1974).

Beitzel, Edwin Warfield. *The Jesuit Missions of St. Mary's County, Maryland*. Abell, MD: by the author, 1959.

–––. "Newtown Hundred." *Maryland Historical Magazine* 51 (June 1956): 125–39.

–––. "Thomas Copley, Gentleman." *Maryland Historical Magazine* 47 (1952): 209–23.

Blow, Michael, ed. *The American Heritage: History of the Thirteen Colonies*. New York: American Heritage Publishing Co., Inc., Simon and Schuster, Inc., n.d.

Brugger, Robert J. *Maryland: A Middle Temperament, 1634–1980*. Baltimore: Johns Hopkins University Press, 1988.

Burley, Paul S. "Quander Clan Relates Significance of Heritage." *Hilltop*, September 19, 1986.

Carroll of Carrollton, Charles. "Journal of Charles Carroll of Carrollton during His Visit to Canada in 1776, as One of the Commissioners from Congress," with a memoir and notes by Brantz Mayer. Baltimore: printed for the Maryland Historical Society by John Murphy, 1876.

———. "The Negro, a Beast" or "In the Image of God." Georgetown University Archives: Special Collections. St. Louis: American Book and Bible House, 1900.

Carr, Lois Green. "Sources of Political Stability and Upheaval in Seventeenth-Century Maryland." *Maryland Historical Magazine* 79, no. 1 (Spring 1984): 44–70.

Catholic Standard. "The Pious and Noble Purpose." Supplement. June 17, 1982.

Census Index. "Heads of Families-Maryland." 1790.

Charter of Maryland, The. June 20, 1632. Reprint, June 20, 1982.

Clark, Tom. "Keeping the Faith amid the Early New England Colonies." *Sky Magazine*, May 1978.

Curran, Robert Emmett, ed. *American Jesuit Spirituality: The Maryland Tradition, 1634–1900.* Mahwah, NY: Paulist Press, 1988.

Curran, R. Emmett, SJ. "'Splendid Poverty': Jesuit Slaveholding in Maryland, 1805–1838." In *Catholics in the Old South: Essays on Church and Culture*, edited by Randall M. Miller and Jon L. Wakelyn. Macon, GA: Mercer University Press, 1983.

Dolan, Jay P. *The American Catholic Experience: A History from Colonial Times to the Present.* Notre Dame: University of Notre Dame Press, 1992.

Duncan, Richard R., compiler. "Master's Theses and Doctoral Dissertations on Maryland History." *Maryland Historical Magazine* 80, 3 (Fall 1985): 261–76.

Ellis, John Tracy. *American Catholicism.* Edited by Daniel J. Boorstin. Chicago: University of Chicago Press, 1956.

Essary, J. Frederick. *Maryland in National Politics from Charles Carroll to Albert C. Ritchie.* 2nd ed. Baltimore: John Murphy Company, 1915.

Falb, Susan Rosenfeld. "Proxy Voting in Early Maryland Assemblies." *Maryland Historical Magazine* 73, no.3 (September 1978): 217–25.

Fausz, J. Frederick. "'The Seventeenth-Century Experience': An Introduction." *Maryland Historical Magazine* 79, no. 1 (Spring 1984): 3–6.

–––. "Present at the 'Creation': The Chesapeake World that Greeted the Maryland Colonists." *Maryland Historical Magazine* 79, no.1 (Spring 1984): 7–20.

–––. "The Legacy of Toleration." *Country Magazine: Celebrates Maryland's 350th (1634–1984)* (1984).

Fogarty, Gerald P., SJ. "Property and Religious Liberty in Colonial Maryland Catholic Thought." *Catholic Historical Review* 72 (October 1986): 573–600.

Folsom, Franklin. "Colonial Irish Share Their Charm, Wit and Skills with a New Nation." *Sky Magazine*, May 1978.

Garraghan, Gilbert J., SJ. *The Jesuits of the Middle United States.* 3 vols. Chicago: Loyola University Press, 1983.

Hakluyt, Richard. "Selection 1, Arguments for Planting English Colonies in America: Richard Hakluyt, 'A Discourse Concerning Western Planting' (1584)." In *Settlements to Society: 1584–1763. A Documentary History of American Life.* Vol. 1, edited by David Donald and Jack P. Greene. New York: McGraw-Hill Book Company, 1966.

Hanley, Thomas O'Brien. *Their Rights and Liberties: The Beginnings of Religious and Political Freedom in Maryland.* Westminster, Maryland: Newman Press, 1959.

Hargrove, M. *An Argument in the Case of James Sommersett, A Negro, Lately Determined by the Court of King's: Wherein It Is Attempted to Demonstrate the Present Unlawfulness of Domestic Slavery in England to which Is Prefixed A State of the Case.* London: W. Otridge, 1772.

Head, Carolyn. "First Black Family Reunion." *Hilltop*, September 19, 1986.

Henderson, Randi. "St. Clements, Cradle of State." *Baltimore Sun*, December 21, 1977.

Hughes, Thomas, SJ. *History of the Society of Jesus in North America: Colonial and Federal*. Documents, one volume in two parts. London: Longmans, Green & Co., 1908, 1917.

Ives, J. Moss. *The* Ark *and the* Dove: *The Beginnings of Civil and Religious Liberties in America*. London, New York, and Toronto: Longmans, Green, and Co., 1936.

Johnson, Whittington B. "The Origin and Nature of African Slavery in Seventeenth Century Maryland." *Maryland Historical Magazine* 73, no. 3 (September 1978): 236–45.

Johnson, Gerald W. *The Maryland Act of Religious Toleration: An Interpretation*. Including "An Act Concerning Religion," passed April 21, 1649, by the Maryland General Assembly. Annapolis, Maryland: Hall of Records Commission, 1973.

Kelly, Frederic. "A Future Built on the Past." *Sun Magazine*, October 22, 1972.

Klapthor, Margaret Brown, and Paul Dennis Brown. *The History of Charles County Maryland: Tercentenary Year 1958*. N.p., n.d.

Krug, Margaret. "Legends and Visions: Origins of Emmitsburg Church Tied to Indian Lore." *Catholic Review*.

Krugler, John D. "Sir George Calvert's Resignation as Secretary of State and the Founding of Maryland." *Maryland Historical Society* 78 (1973): 239–54.

———. "'With Promise of Liberty in Religion': The Catholic Lords Baltimore and Toleration in Seventeenth-Century Maryland, 1634–1692." *Maryland Historical Magazine* 79, no. 1 (Spring 1984): 21–43.

Lemay, J. A. Leo. *Men of Letters in Colonial Maryland*. Knoxville: University of Tennessee Press, 1972.

Linden Jr., Phillip J. "Part Three: Review Symposium. Stephen Ochs's *Desegregating the Altar: The Josephites and the Struggle for Black Priests, 1871–1960*." *U.S. Catholic Historian* 11, no. 1 (Winter 1993): 138–40.

Liston, Paul F., Mark Zimmermann, and John B. Brady. *The Plundering Time*. Washington DC: Abbeyfeale Press, 1989.

Makofsky, Abraham. "Tradition and Chance in the Lumbee Indian Community of Baltimore." *Maryland Historical Magazine* 75 (1980): 55–71.

Maryland Historical Magazine. "Hammond vs. Heamans." N.d.

–––. "Lord Baltimore's Case." N.d.

–––. "Maryland: A History, 1632–1974." Review of Recent Books, 70: 315–16.

McCabe, James F., CSP. "Church, Slavery, Civil War: Catholics Differed on the Issues but Avoided a North-South Split." *Catholic Review*, July 19, 1974.

McCarthy, Norman. "America's First Catholic Church." *Catholic Standard*, August 4 1983.

–––. "Historic Roots of the Archdiocese of Washington." *Catholic Standard* 39, no. 41 (October 12, 1989): 46–55.

McSherry, James. *History of Maryland*. Edited by Bartlett B. James. Baltimore: Baltimore Book Co., 1904.

Menard, Russell R. "Population, Economy, and Society in Seventeenth-Century Maryland." *Maryland Historical Magazine* 79, no.1 (Spring 1984): 71–92.

Miller, Sammy M. "Free Negroes in the District of Columbia, 1790–1846." Review of Recent Books. *Maryland Historical Magazine* 70: 323–24.

Neill, Edward D. *The Founders of Maryland*. Albany: Joel Musell, 1876.

Newman, Harry Wright. *The Flowering of the Maryland Palatinate*. Baltimore: Genealogical Publishing Co., Inc., 1961.

O'Connell, J. J., OSB. *Catholicity in the Carolinas and Georgia: Leaves of Its History*. Orig. publ. 1878. Reprint, Westminster: Ars Sacra, 1964.

O'Conner, Gov. Herbert, sponsor. *Maryland: A Guide to the Old Line State*. American Guide Series by WPA New York: Oxford University Press, 1940, 1946.

Onuf, Peter S., ed. *Maryland and the Empire, 1773: The Antilon-First Citizen Letters.* Baltimore: Johns Hopkins University Press, 1974.

Phelan, Thomas P. *Catholics in Colonial Days.* New York: P. J. Kenedy & Sons, 1935.

Porter III, Frank W. "A Century of Accommodation: The Nanticoke Indians in Colonial Maryland." *Maryland Historical Magazine* 74 (June 1979): 175–92.

–––. "Behind the Frontier: Indian Survivals in Maryland." *Maryland Historical Society* 75 (1980): 42–54.

Powers, William J. P. "The Beginnings of English Catholic Emigration to the New World." *Records of the American Catholic Historical Society of Philadelphia* XI (March 1929): 15.

Quinn, David B., ed. *Early Maryland in a Wider World.* Detroit: Wayne State University Press, 1982.

Robinson, W. Stitt. "Conflicting Views on Landholding: Lord Baltimore and the Experiences of Colonial Maryland with Native Americans." *Maryland Historical Magazine* 83, no. 2 (Summer 1988): 85–97; Hanover, PA: Sheridan Press.

Schwegler, Edward S. "The *Ark* and the *Dove*: The Story of the Establishment of Religious Liberty in the United States by Its Catholic Free Men of Maryland." *Columbia*, March 1934.

Shehan, Lawrence Cardinal. "The Church of Baltimore and the Blessings of Equal Liberty." *Catholic Review,* July 2, 1976.

Sofio, Tom. "Catholic Indians Convene in Washington." *Criterion* (1982).

"St. Mary's County: Mother County of Maryland." 1634.

Steiner, Bernard C. "New Light on Maryland History from the British Archives." *Maryland Historical Magazine* (n.d.).

Streeter, Sebastian F., ed. "A Relation of Maryland" by Fr. Andrew White in *Papers Relating to the Early History of Maryland.* Baltimore: Fund Publication, 1876.

Verot, Augustine. "A Tract for the Times: Slavery and Abolitionism, Being the Substance of a Sermon Preached in the Church of St. Augustine, 1861." In Michael Gannon, *Rebel Bishop: The Life and Era of Augustin Verot.* Milwaukee: Bruce Publishing Company, 1964.

Washington Post. "Revolution Had Limited Goals Historian Says." March 9, 1976, A14.

Whealy, Mervin B. "'The Revolution Is Not Over': The Annapolis Convention of 1786." *Maryland Historical Magazine* 81, no. 3 (Fall 1986): 228–40.

Whelan, Thomas A. "The Jesuit Missions of St. Mary's County, Maryland." *Maryland Historical Magazine* 56: 211–12.

White, Andrew. *A Relation of Maryland.* Original, September 8, 1635. Reprint, Ann Arbor: University Microfilms, Inc., 1966.

–––. *Relatio itineris in Marylandiam: Declaratio coloniae domini littens missionariorum ab anno 1635, ad annum 1638* and *An Account of the Colony of the Lord Baron of Baltimore: Extracts From Different Letters of Missionaries, From the Year 1635 to the Year 1677.* Edited by E. A. Dalrymple. Baltimore: Maryland Historical Society, Fund Publication, no.7, 1874.

–––. "A Relation of Maryland." Paper Relating to the Early History of Maryland. Baltimore: Fund Publication, 1876.

–––. *A Briefe Relation of the Voyage into Maryland.* Original, May 1634. Reprint from the original by the Maryland Historical Society Fund Publication, no. 35, 1899. Maryland: Maryland Hall of Records, March 25, 1984.

Woodstock Letters. "History of the Society of Jesus in North America, Colonial and Federal," 35:110–18.

WPA, *Maryland.* Sponsored by Gov. Herbert R. O'Conner. New York: Oxford University Press, 1940.

Wroth, Lawrence c., ed. and intro. *A Declaration of the Lord Baltimore's Plantation in Maryland, Wherein Is Set Forth How Englishmen May Become Angels, the King's Dominions Be Extended and the Adventurers Attain Land and Gear, Together with Other Advantages of That Sweet Land.* The John Carter Brown

Library, June 10, 1929. Reprint, Maryland Hall of Records Commission, June 20, 1983.

Zwinge, Joseph, SJ. "Our Fathers in the Colonization of Maryland," *Woodstock Letters* 36:78, 92.

———. "The Jesuit Farms in Maryland." *Woodstock Letters* 39:374–82; 40:65–77, 180–99; 41:53–77, 195–222, 275–91; 42:1–13, 137–50, 194–200; 43:83–89, 336–52.

J. BOOKS AND ARTICLES RELEVANT TO RACE, RACISM, AND RACIALISM

Biddiss, Michael D. *Father of Racist Ideology: The Social and Political Thought of Count Gobineau.* London: Weidenfeld and Nicolson, 1970.

Bowen, J. W. "Who Are We? Africans, Afro-Americans, Colored People, Negroes or American Negroes." *Voice of the Negro* 3, 77 (1906): 31–36.

Boxer, C. R. *Race Relations in the Portuguese Colonial Empire, 1415–1825.* Oxford: Clarendon Press, 1963.

Braxton, Edward K. "Would African Americans Still Be a Minority Group." *In a Word* 7, 7 (July 1989): 2–3.

Brooks, Roy L. *Rethinking the American Race Problem.* Berkeley: University of California Press, 1990.

Cone, James H. "Speaking the Truth: Ecumenism, Liberation, and Black Theology," 51–60. Grand Rapids, MI: William B. Eerdmans Publishing Company, 1983.

Cox, Oliver Cromwell. *Caste, Class, and Race: A Study in Social Dynamics.* New York and London: Modern Reader Paperbacks.

Fehrenbacher, Don E. *The Dred Scott Case–Its Significance in American Law and Politics.* New York: Oxford University Press, 1978.

Fields, Barbara J. "Ideology and Race in American History." Essay, 143–77.

Frazier, E. Franklin. *The Negro Family in the United States*. Chicago: University of Chicago Press.

Garvey, Marcus. "The Case of the Negro for International Racial Adjustment, before the English People." Speech. Royal Albert Hall, London, England, June 6, 1928.

Gillard, John T., SSJ. *The Catholic Church and the American Negro: Being an Investigation of the Past and Present Activities of the Catholic Church in Behalf of the 12,000,000 Negroes in the United States, with an Examination of the Difficulties which Affect the Work of the Colored Missions*. Baltimore: St. Joseph Society Press, 1929.

Hargrave, Francis. *The Case of James Sommersett, a Negro*. London, 1772.

Kolevzon, Edward R. *The Afro-Asian World: A Cultural Understanding*. Boston; Rockleigh, NJ; Atlanta; Dallas; Belmont, CA: Allyn and Bacon, Inc., 1969.

Martin, Tony. *Race First: The Ideological and Organizational Struggles of Marcus Garvey and the Universal Negro Improvement Association*. Contributions to Afro-American and African Studies, no. 19. Westport, CT; London: Greenwood Press.

Miller, Loren. *The Petitioners: The Story of the Supreme Court of the United States and the Negro*. New York: Pantheon Books, 1966.

Montagu, Ahsley. *Man's Most Dangerous Myth: The Fallacy of Race*. Cleveland and New York: World Publishing Company, 1964.

Nation of Islam. *The Secret Relationship between Blacks and Jews*. Chicago: Nation of Islam, 1991.

Portier, William L. "John R. Slattery's Vision for the Evangelization of American Blacks." *Culture of American Catholicism*. Paper presented at the University of Notre Dame, Indiana, October 5, 1985.

Rooney, John. "A Divorce of Sorts." *Millhilliana* 4 (1985): 120–26.

Sowell, Thomas. *The Economics and Politics of Race: An International Perspective*. New York: Quill, 1983.

Swisher, Carl Brent. "Roger B. Taney and the Tenets of Democracy." *Maryland Historical Magazine* 34, no. 3 (September 1939): 207–22.

Whitten Jr., Norman E., and John F. Szwed, eds. *Afro-American Anthropology. Contemporary Perspectives.* New York and London: Free Press; Collier-Macmillan Limited, 1970.

K. BOOKS AND ARTICLES RELEVANT TO SLAVERY SPECIFICALLY

Aristotle. "Politica." In *The Works of Aristotle*, translated by Benjamin Jowett, edited by Sir David Ross. Vol. X, revised ed., I.4, $1254^{a15/a22/b25}$; I.5, 1254; and I.5, 1255^{a1}. Oxford: At The Clarendon Press, 1961.

Augustine. "Epistula 251." *Corpus Scriptorum Ecclesiasticorum Latinorum (CSEL)* 57: 599–600.

Bagú, Serfío. "La economía de la sociedad colonial." *Pensamiento crítico*, no. 27 (1969): 53–61.

Bennett, Lerone, Jr. *Confrontation: Black and White.* Baltimore: Penguin Books Inc., 1965.

––––. *Before the* Mayflower. *A History of Black America: The Classic Account of the Struggles and Triumphs of Black Americans.* 5th ed. Harmondsworth, Middlesex, England: Penguin Books Ltd., 1961, 1962, 1964, 1969, 1982.

––––. *Before the* Mayflower: *A History of the Negro in America, 1619–1962.* Chicago: Johnson Publishing Company, Inc.

Blackburn, Robin. *The Overthrow of Colonial Slavery, 1776–1848.* London and New York: Verso, 1988.

Bontinck, F. "Le rachat d'enfants esclaves dans les rivieres equatoriales (1889–1897)." *Revue africaine de theologie* 11, no. 19 (April 1987): 51–64.

Boxer, C. R. *The Church Militant and Iberian Expansion, 1440–1770.* Baltimore and London: Johns Hopkins University Press, 1978.

––––. *The Dutch in Brazil, 1624–1654.* Oxford: Clarendon Press, 1957.

Brown, Letitia Woods. *Free Negroes in the District of Columbia, 1790–1846.* New York: Oxford University Press, 1972.

Browne, William Hand, ed. *Archives of Maryland: Proceedings and Acts of the General Assembly of Maryland (January 1637–September 1664 and April 1666–June 1676).* Baltimore: Maryland Historical Society, 1883, 1884.

Catterall, Helen Tunnicliff, and James J. Hayden, eds. *Judicial Cases Concerning American Slavery and the Negro: Cases from the Courts of New England, the Middle States, and the District of Columbia.* Vol. IV. With additions by James J. Hyden. New York: Octagon Books, Inc., 1968.

Cobb, Thomas R. R. *An Historical Sketch of Slavery from the Earliest Periods.* Philadelphia and Savannah: T. & J. W. Johnson & Co.; W. Thorne Williams, 1858.

Commanger, Henry Steele. "Commager Speaks Out on America." *Sky* 7, no.5 (May 1978): 35–37.

Corecoran, G. *Saint Augustine on Slavery, Studia Ephemerides Augustinianum* 22. Rome, 1985.

Coupland, Sir Reginald. *The British Anti-Slavery Movement.* London: Frank Cass & Co. Ltd., n.d.

Curtin, Philip D. *The Atlantic Slave Trade: A Census.* 1969 (publisher's data).

–––. *Cross-Cultural Trade in World History.* New York: Press Syndicate of the University of Cambridge, 1984.

–––. *The Rise and Fall of the Plantation Complex: Essays in Atlantic History.* New York: Press Syndicate of the University of Cambridge, 1990.

Daget, Serge, and François Renault. *Les Traites negrieres en Afrique.* Paris: Editions Karthala.

Darity, William A., Jr. "The Class Character of the Black Community: Polarization between the Black Managerial Elite and the Black Underclass." *Black Law Journal* 7, no. 1 (1980).

———. "Mercantilism, Slavery, and the Industrial Revolution." *Research in Political Economy* 5 (1982): 1–21.

———. "The Numbers Game and the Profitability of the British Trade in Slaves." *Journal of Economic History* 45, no. 3 (Sept. 1985): 693–703.

———. "The Political Economy of Uneven Development: From the Slave(ry) Trade to the Managerial Age." Paper presented at the University of Wisconsin. Milwaukee, Wisconsin, May 1991.

———. "Banking on Capital Flight." In *Economic Problems of the 1990s: Europe, the Developing Countries and the United States*, edited by Paul Davidson and J. A. Kregel, 31–40. Edward Elgar, 1991.

Davidson, Basil. *The African Slave Trade: Precolonial History, 1450–1850.* Boston and Toronto: An Atlantic Monthly Press Book, Little, Brown and Company, n.d.

———. *The African Slave Trade. A Revised and Expanded Edition.* Boston and Toronto: Little, Brown and Company, 1961, 1970, 1980.

———. *The African Genius: An Introduction to African Cultural and Social History.* Boston, Toronto, and London: Little, Brown and Company, 1969.

Davis, David Brion. *The Problem of Slavery in Western Culture.* New York and Oxford: Oxford University Press, 1966.

———. "The Continuing Contradiction of Slavery: A Comparison of British America and Latin America." In *The Debate over Slavery: Stanley Elkins and His Critics*, edited by Ann J. Lane. Urbana, Chicago, and London: University of Illinois Press, 1971.

———. *The Problem of Slavery in the Age of Revolution, 1770–1823.* Ithaca: Cornell University Press, 1975.

———. *Slavery and Human Progress.* New York and Oxford: Oxford University Press, 1984.

———. *Slavery in the Colonial Chesapeake (The Foundations of America).* Williamsburg, VA: Colonial Williamsburg Foundation, 1986.

Las Casas, Bartolomé de. *A Short Account of the Destruction of the Indies.* Edited and translated by Nigel Griffin with an introduction by Anthony Pagden. New York: Penguin Books, 1992; original, 1542.

DuBois, W. E. B. *The Suppression of the African Slave-Trade to the United States of America, 1638–1870.* Edited by Philip S. Foner. Black Rediscovery. New York: Dover Publications, Inc., 1970.

Dunn, Richard S. *Sugar and Slaves: The Rise of the Planter Class in the English West Indies, 1624–1713.* New York and London: W. W. Norton & Company, 1972.

Edwards, Paul, and James Walvin. *Black Personalities in the Era of the Slave Trade.* London: Macmillan Press Ltd., 1983.

Elkins, Stanley M. *Slavery. A Problem in American Institutional and Intellectual Life.* Chicago and London: University of Chicago Press, 1959, 1968, 1976.

Feldstein, Stanley. "Memoirs of a Fugitive." Book Review. *New York Times Book Review,* n.d.

Fields, Barbara Jeanne. *Slavery and Freedom on the Middle Ground: Maryland during the Nineteenth Century.* New Haven and London: Yale University Press, 1985.

Finley, Moses I. "Was Greek Civilization Based on Slave Labor?" In Finley, *Slavery in Classical Antiquity: Views and Controversies.* Cambridge: Cambridge University Press, 1960, 61–64.

–––. *Ancient Slavery and Modern Ideology.* New York: Penguin Books, 1980.

Fogel, Robert William, and Stanley L. Engerman. *Time on the Cross: The Economics of American Negro Slavery.* London: Wildwood House, 1974.

Folsom, Franklin. "Colonial Irish Share Their Charm, Wit and Skills with a New Nation." *Sky Magazine* 7, no.5 (May 1978): 31–32.

Franklin, John Hope. *From Slavery to Freedom: A History of Negro Americans.* New York: Alfred A. Knopf, 1947, 1980.

Galenson, David W. *Traders, Planters, and Slaves: Market Behavior in Early English America*. Cambridge: Cambridge University Press, 1986.

Genovese, Eugene D. *The Political Economy of Slavery: Studies in the Economy and Society of the Slave South*. New York: Vintage Books, 1967; original articles, 1961, 1964, 1965.

———. *The World the Slaveholders Made: Two Essays in Interpretation*. New York: Vintage Books, 1971. Originally published by Pantheon Books, 1969.

———. *Roll, Jordan, Roll: The World the Slaves Made*. New York: Vintage Books, 1976. Originally published by Pantheon Books, 1974.

Genovese, Elizabeth Fox, and Eugene D. Genovese. "The Divine Sanction of Social Order: Religious Foundations of the Southern Slaveholders' World View." *Journal of the American Academy of Religion* 55, no. 2 (Summer 1987): 211–33.

Hanke, Lewis. *The Spanish Struggle for Justice in the Conquest of America*. 6th ed. Boston: American Historical Association, 1949. Reprint, Boston: Little, Brown and Company, 1965.

Hayes, III, Floyd W. *A Turbulent Voyage: Readings in African American Studies*. Collegiate Press, 1992.

Hennighausen, Louis P. *The Redemptioners and the German Society of Maryland: A Historical Sketch*. Society for the History of the Germans in Maryland, January 1888.

Hoyland, John S. *The Race Problem and the Teaching of Jesus Christ*. London: Religious Tract Society, n.d.

James, C. L. R. *The Black Jacobins: Toussaint L'Ouverture and the San Domingo Revolution*. New York: Random House, 1963. Reprint and originally published, 1938.

Johnson, Whittington B. "The Origin and Nature of African Slavery in Seventeenth Century Maryland." *Maryland Historical Magazine* 73, no.3 (September 1978): 236–45.

Jordan, Winthrop D. *White over Black: American Attitudes toward the Negro, 1550–1812*. New York and London: W. W. Norton & Company, 1968.

Kastor, Elizabeth. "Toni Morrison and the Terror of Slavery." *International Herald Tribune*, October 7, 1987.

Klein, R. "Die frühe Kirche und die Sklaverei." *Römische Quanalschrift* 80 (1985): 259–83.

———. "Die Sklaverei in de Sicht der Bischöfe Ambrosius und Augustinus." *Forschunger zur antiken Sklaverei*. Stuttgart, 1988, 20.

Kulikoff, Allan. *Tobacco and Slaves: The Development of Southern Cultures in the Chesapeake, 1680–1800*. Institute of Early American History and Culture of Williamsburg, Virginia. Chapel Hill and London: University of North Carolina Press, 1986.

Landman, Isaac, ed. "West Indies." *The Universal Jewish Encyclopedia* 10 (1943): 507.

Luthin, Reinhard H. "A Discordant Chapter in Lincoln's Administration: The Davis-Blair Controversy." *Maryland Historical Magazine* 39 (n.d.): 25–43.

Maxwell, John Francis. *Slavery and the Catholic Church: The History of Catholic Teaching Concerning the Moral Legitimacy of the Institution of Slavery*. Chichester and London: Barry Rose Publishers, 1975.

Mazique, Jewell R. Crawford. "Aristotle: A Study of His Slave Theory with Both Definite and Presumptive Evidence of Its Impact upon Western Civilization." *Dialogue: Journal of Phi Sigma Tau* 1, no.1 (April 1956): 2335.

Meillassoux, Claude. *Anthropologie de l'esclavage: Le ventre de fer et d'argent*. Paris: Presses Universitaires de France, 1986.

Mendelsohn, Isaac. *Slavery in the Ancient Near East. A Comparative Study of Slavery in Babylonia, Assyria, Syria, and Palestine from the Middle of the Third Millennium to the End of the First Millennium*. Westport Connecticut: Greenwood Press Publishers, 1978. Originally published at London: Oxford University Press, Inc., 1949.

Morgan, Edmund S. *American Slavery-American Freedom: The Ordeal of Colonial Virginia*. New York: W. W. Norton & Company, Inc., 1975.

–––. "Slavery and Freedom: The American Paradox." *Journal of American History* 59, no. 1 (June 1972): 5–29.

Morgan, James. *Slavery in the United States: Four Views*. Jefferson, North Carolina; London: McFarland & Company, Inc., 1985.

Newenham, Thomas. "Newenham and Others on the State of Ireland." *Edinburgh Review or Critical Journal* 12 (July 1808): 336–55.

New Catholic Encyclopedia. 1979 ed., s.v. "Slavery (History of)" by Charles Verlinden.

–––. 1979 ed., s.v. "Encomienda-Doctrina System in Spanish America" by A. S. Tiebesar.

New Encyclopedia Britannica, The. 1975 ed., s.v. "Slavery, Serfdom, and Forced Labour."

Nye, R. B., and J. E. Anorpurgo. *On Slavery: A History of the United States*. Harmondsworth, Middlesex, England: Penguin Books, Ltd., 1955, 1961.

Phillips, Ulrich B. *American Negro Slavery: A Survey of the Supply, Employment and Control of Negro Labor as Determined by the Plantation Regime*. Foreword by Eugene D. Genovese. Baton Rouge: Louisiana State University Press, 1966, 1989. Originally published by D. Appleton and Company, 1918.

Pickering, William. *The Conquerors of the New World and Their Bondsmen. Being a Narrative of the Principal Events which Led to Negro Slavery in the West Indies and America*.

Miami: Mnemosyne Publishing Co., Inc., 1852.

Poole, Stafford, CM, and Douglas Slawson, CM. *Church and Slave in Perry County, Missouri, 1818–1865*. Studies in American Religion, vol. 22. Lewiston, NY; Queenston, Ontario, Canada: Edwin Mellen Press, 1986.

Rice, Madeleine Hooke. *American Catholic Opinion in the Slavery Controversy.* New York and London: Columbia University Press; P. S. King & Staples, Ltd., 1944.

Rodney, Walter. *How Europe Underdeveloped Africa.* London: Bogle L'Ouverture, 1972.

Rose, Willie Lee, ed. *A Documentary History of Slavery in North America.* Commentary by Willie Lee Rose. New York and London: Oxford University Press, 1976.

Rostovtzeff, Michael I. *Rome.* Translated by J. D. Duff. Edited by Elias J. Bickerman. New York: Oxford University Press, 1960.

–––. *Out of the Past of Greece and Rome.* New York: Bilbo and Tannen, 1971.

–––. *The Social and Economic History of the Hellenistic World.* 3 vols. Oxford: At the Clarendon Press, 1941. Reissued 1986.

Ruchames, Louis, ed. *Racial Thought in America: From the Puritans to Abraham Lincoln.* University of Massachusetts Press, 1969.

Semmes, Raphael. "Vignettes of Maryland History from the Society's Collection of Broadsides." *Maryland Historical Magazine* 39, no.2 (June 1944): 95–121.

Shell, Robert. "Religion and Slavery in South Africa from Dort to the Trek."

Smith, Abbot Emerson. *Colonists in Bondage: White Servitude and Convict Labor in America, 1607–1776.* New York: Norton Library; W. W. Norton & Company, Inc., 1947.

Sobel, Mechal. *The World They Made Together: Black and White Values in Eighteenth-Century Virginia.* Princeton: Princeton University Press, 1987.

Stampp, Kenneth. *The Peculiar Institution: Slavery in the Anti-Bellum South.* New York: Vintage Books; Alfred A. Knopf, Inc., 1956.

Stuckey, Sterling. *Slave Culture: Nationalist Theory and the Foundations of Black America.* New York and Oxford: Oxford University Press, 1987

Tannenbaum, Frank. *Slave and Citizen: The Negro in the Americas*. New York: Vintage Books. Originally published by Alfred A. Knopf, Inc., 1946.

Thomas, J. A. C. *Textbook of Roman Law*. Amsterdam, New York, and Oxford: North-Holland Publishing Company, 1976.

Tremain, Mary. *Slavery in the District of Columbia: The Policy of Congress and the Struggle for Abolition*. New York: Negro Universities Press.

Washington, Joseph R., Jr. *Anti-Blackness in English Religion, 1500–1800*. Texts and Studies in Religion, vol. 19. Lewiston: Edwin Mellen Press, 1984.

Wax, Darold D. "Black Immigrants: The Slave Trade in Colonial Maryland." *Maryland Historical Magazine* 73, no.1 (March 1978): 30–45.

Wesley, John. *Thoughts upon Slavery*. 1774.

Westermann, William L. "Between Slavery and Freedom." *American Historical Review* 50 (January 1945): 213–16.

–––. *The Slave Systems of Greek and Roman Antiquity*. Philadelphia: 1955.

Williams, Eric. *Capitalism and Slavery*. Introduction by D. W. Brogan. London: Andre Deutsch Limited, 1964. Originally published by Eric Williams, 1944.

Wittke, Carl. *We Who Built America: The Saga of the Immigrant*. Press of Western Reserve University, n.d.

Woodward, C. Vann. *American Counterpoint. Slavery and Racism in the North/ South Dialogue*. Oxford: Oxford University Press, 1983. Original, Boston: Little Brown & Company, 1971.

Wrong, Dennis H. "Slavery: Theory and Practice." *Book Week* 21 (August 1966): 2, 12.

L. BOOKS AND ARTICLES RELEVANT TO CATHOLICISM IN COLONIAL AMERICA

Bartlett, Charles. "Lockean Individualism–An Outworn Ideology?" *Washington Star*, December 8, 1975, A1.

Concilii Plenarii Baltimorensis III. *Acta et decreta*. Baltimore: Concillii Plenarii Baltimorenesis, 1886.

Delaplaine, Edward S. "Chief Justice Roger B. Taney–His Career at the Frederick Bar." *Maryland Historical Magazine* 13 (1918): 109–14.

Ellis, John Tracy. *Catholics in Colonial America*. Benedictine Studies, vol. 5. Dublin and Baltimore: Helicon Press, 1965.

–––. *Perspective in American Catholicism*. Benedictine Studies, vol. 5. Baltimore and Dublin: Helicon Press, Inc., 1963.

Greene, Evarts Boutell. *Provincial America, 1690–1740*. New York: Frederick Ungar Publishing Co., 1905, 1964.

Greene, Jack P. *Settlements to Society, 1585–1763. A Documentary History of American Life*. Edited by Gen. David Donald. New York, St. Louis, San Francisco, Toronto, London, and Sydney: McGraw-Hill Book Company, 1966.

Gross, W. H. "The Missions for the Colored People." Sermon. Third Plenary Council of Baltimore. Savannah, Georgia, 1884.

Guilday, Peter. *A History of the Councils of Baltimore, 1791–1884*. New York: Macmillan Company, 1932.

Gutman, Judith Mara. *The Colonial Venture: An Autobiography of the American Colonies from Their Beginnings to 1763*. New York and London: Basic Books, Inc., n.d.

Maynard, Theodore. *The Catholic Church and the American Idea*. New York: Appleton-Century-Crofts, Inc., 1953.

Nuesse, Celestine Joseph. *The Social Thought of American Catholics, 1634–1829*. PhD diss. Washington DC: Catholic University of America Press, 1945.

Onuf, Peter S., ed. *Maryland and the Empire, 1773. The Antilon-First Citizen Letters*. Baltimore and London: Johns Hopkins University Press, 1974.

Spencer, Richard Henry. "Hon. Daniel Dulany, 1722–1797 (The Younger)." *Maryland Historical Magazine* 13 (1918): 143–60.

Williams, Michael. *The Maryland Idea.* Unpublished manuscript. Georgetown Archives: Special Collections, Georgetown University, Washington DC, n.d.

M. BOOKS AND ARTICLES RELEVANT TO JESUITS

Clancy, Thomas H. "The First Generation of English Jesuits." *Archivum historicum Societatis Iesu* 57 (1988): 137–62.

Foley, Henry, SJ. *Records of the English Province of the Society of Jesus. Historic Facts Illustrative of the Labours and Sufferings of Its Members in the Sixteenth and Seventeenth Centuries.* 8 vols. London: Burns and Oates, 1877–1883.

Lover of His Country. *Liberty and Property or the Beauty of Maryland Displayed.*

Moore, James T. *Indian and Jesuit: A Seventeenth-Century Encounter.* Loyola University Press, 1982.

Treacy, William P. *Old Catholic Maryland and Its Early Jesuit Missionaries.* Swedesboro, NJ: St. Joseph's Rectory, 1889.

N. BOOKS AND ARTICLES RELEVANT TO JUDAISM

Alstat, Rabbi Philip R. "Inspired Founders: Spirit of July Fourth Traced to Biblical Story of Birth of the Jewish Nation." *Jewish Week–American Examiner* (June 28–July 11, 1973): 10.

Churchill, Winston S. *The New World: A History of the English-Speaking Peoples.* New York: Dodd, Mead & Company, 1959.

———. 1971 ed. S.v. "Amsterdam" by Israel Adler.

———. 1971 ed. S.v. "Lopez, Aaron," by Stanley F. Chyet.

———. 1971 ed. S.v. "Marrano" by Martin A. Cohen.

———. 1971 ed., S.v. "Marrano Diaspora" by Martin A. Cohen.

———. 1971 ed. S.v. "New Christians" by Martin A. Cohen.

Landman, Isaac. *The Universal Jewish Encyclopedia*. Edited by Isaac Landman. New York, 1943.

Liebman, Seymour B. "Argentine Jewry: A Historical Perspective." *Midstream* (January 1975): 59–66.

Nation of Islam. *The Secret Relationship between Blacks and Jews*. Vol. 1. Boston: Historical Research Department, Nation of Islam, 1991.

Newman, Louis Israel. *Jewish Influence on Christian Reform Movements*. New York: AMS Press, Inc., 1966.

Sanders, Ronald. "Who Did Discover America." *Midstream* (August–September 1971): 9–21.

Weyl, Nathaniel. *The Jew in American Politics*. New Rochelle. NY: Arlington House, n.d.

Wright, Louis B. *Gold, Glory, and the Gospel: The Adventurous Lives and Times of the Renaissance Explorers*. New York: Atheneum, 1970.

Wylen, Stephen M. *Settings of Silver: An Introduction to Judaism*. New York: Paulist Press, 1989.

O. BOOKS AND ARTICLES RELEVANT TO THE MODERN STATE

Adams, Brooks. "1955." In *The Law of Civilization and Decay*. New York: Vintage Books, 1896, 1924, 1943.

Machiavelli, Niccolò. *The Prince*. Translated and edited by Robert M. Adams. New York: W. W. Norton & Company, 1977.

Adas, Michael. *Machines as the Measure of Men: Science, Technology, and Ideologies of Western Dominance*. Cornell Studies in Comparative History. Edited by George Fredrickson and Theda Skocpol. Ithaca: Cornell University Press, 1989.

Anderson, James, ed. *The Rise of the Modern State*. Atlantic Highlands, NJ: Humanities Press International, Inc., 1986.

Aquinas, Thomas. *Summa theologica*. Complete English edition in 5 vols. Translated by Fathers of the English Dominican Province. Westminster: Christian Classics. Reprinted in 1981 under license granted by Benziger Brothers, Inc.

Arendt, Hannah. *Condition de l'homme moderne* [The Human Condition]. 1988.

Bauman, Z. *Intimations of Postmodernity*. London and New York: Routledge, 1992.

Beard, Charles A. *An Economic Interpretation of the Constitution of the United States*. New York and London: Free Press; Collier-MacMillan Limited, 1913.

Bellah, Robert, Richard Madsen, William M. Sullivan, Ann Swidler, and Steven M. Tipton. *Habits of the Heart: Individualism and Commitment in American Life*. New York and Cambridge: Perennial Library; Harper & Row, 1985.

–––. *The Good Society*. New York: Vintage Books, 1991.

Bloch, Marc. *Feudal Society*. Chicago: University of Chicago Press, 1961.

Bücher, Karl. *Industrial Evolution*. New York: Holt, 1901.

Chambers Biographical Dictionary. 1902 ed. S.v. "Machiavelli, Niccolò di Bernardo Dei."

Chodorov, Frank. *The Rise and Fall of Society: An Essay on the Economic Forces that Underlie Social Institutions*. New York: Devin-Adair Company, 1959.

Claessen, H. J. M., and P. Skalnik. *The Early State*. The Hague: Mouton, 1978.

Commager, Henry Steele. *The Empire of Reason: How Europe Imagined and America Realized the Enlightenment*. New York and Toronto: Oxford University Press, 1977.

–––. "Commager Speaks Out on America." *Sky Magazine* (May 1978).

De Schrijver, Georges. "The Paradigm Shift in Third World Theologies of Liberation: From Socio-economic Analysis to Cultural Analysis.

Assessment and Status of the Question." Liberation Theology Symposium, KU Leuven, November 1996.

Dictionary of Christianity in America. S.v. "Civil Religion" by Robert D. Linder. Downers Grove, IL: InterVarsity Press, 1990.

–––. S.v. "Church and State, Separation of" by James E. Wood. Downers Grove, IL: InterVarsity Press, 1990.

Dworkin, Ronald. *Taking Rights Seriously.* Cambridge, MA: Harvard University Press, 1977, 1978.

Eisenstadt, S. N. *The Political Systems of Empires.* Glencoe: Free Press, 1963.

Findlay, J. N. *Hegel: A Reexamination.* London and New York: George Allen & Unwin Ltd.; Humanities Press, Inc., 1958.

Fowler, Thomas. *Locke.* Makers of Literature. Edited by John Morley. New York: A. L. Fowle Publisher, n.d.

Friedrich, Carl J., ed. *The Philosophy of Kant.* New York: Modern Library, 1949.

Gay, Peter. *The Enlightenment: An Interpretation. The Rise of Modern Paganism.* New York and London: Alfred A. Knopf, 1966; W. W. Norton & Company, 1977.

Giddens, Anthony. *Capitalism and Modern Social Theory: An Analysis of the Writings of Marx, Durkheim and Max Weber.* Cambridge, London, New York, Melbourne, and Sydney: Cambridge University Press, 1971.

–––. *A Contemporary Critique of Historical Materialism.* Houndmills, Basingstoke, Hampshire, and London: Macmillan Press Ltd., 1981.

–––. *The Constitution of Society.* Cambridge: Polity Press, 1984.

–––. *The Nation-State and Violence: Volume Two of A Contemporary Critique of Historical Materialism.* Cambridge: Polity Press, 1985.

Ginsberg, Benjamin. *The Fatal Embrace: Jews and the State.* Chicago and London: University of Chicago Press, 1993.

Gleizes, Albert. *Life and Death of the Christian West.* Translated by Aristide Messinesi. London: Dennis Dobson Limited, 1947.

Hamilton, Bernice. *Political Thought in Sixteenth-Century Spain: A Study of the Political Ideas of Vitoria, de Soto, Suarez, and Molina.* Oxford: At the Clarendon Press, 1963.

Jones, W. T. *A History of Western Philosophy: Hobbes to Hume.* 2nd ed. San Diego, New York, Chicago, Austin, Washington DC, London, Sydney, Tokyo, and Toronto: Harcourt Brace Jovanovich, 1952.

Hegel, Georg Wilhelm Friedrich. *Philosophy of Right.* Translated by T. M. Knox. London: Oxford University Press, 1952.

Lane, Frederic C. "The Economic Meaning of War and Protection." In *Venice and History.* Baltimore: Johns Hopkins Press, 1966.

Levy, Leonard. *Jefferson and Civil Liberties.* Cambridge: Harvard University Press, 1963.

Locke, John. *Essays on the Law of Nature.* Translated and edited by W. von Leyden. Oxford: At the Clarendon Press, 1954. Original, 1660.

–––. *Treatise of Civil Government and an Essay Concerning Toleration.* Edited by Charles L. Sherman. New York and London: D. Appleton-Century Company, Inc., 1937. Original, London, 1690 and 1689, respectively.

–––. *Two Treatises on Government.* A critical and collated edition, edited by Peter Laslett. Cambridge: Cambridge University Press, 1960. Original, London, 1690.

–––. *The Essay Concerning Human Understanding.* 5th ed. Edited by Peter H. Nidditch. Oxford: At the Clarendon Press, 1975. Original, London, 1690.

Machiavelli, Niccolò. *The Prince: A New Translation, Backgrounds, Interpretations, Peripherica.* The Norton Critical Edition. Translated and edited by Robert M. Adams. New York and London: W. W. Norton & Company, 1977.

Manuel, Frank E., ed. *The Enlightenment.* New Jersey: Prentice-Hall, Inc., 1965.

Magdoff, Harry. *The Age of Imperialism: The Economics of U.S. Foreign Policy.* New York and London: Modern Reader Paperbacks, 1969.

McKay, John P., Bennett D. Hill, and John Buckler. *A History of Western Society: From Antiquity to the Enlightenment.* Vol. 1, 2nd ed. Boston, Dallas, Geneva, and London: Houghton Mifflin Company, 1983.

New Encyclopedia Britannica, The. 1975 ed. S.v. "Armed Forces" by Jacques van Doorn.

———. 1975 ed. S.v. "The Enlightenment" by the Editors.

———. 1975 ed. S.v. "Political Economy" by the Editors.

———. 1975 ed. S.v. "Philosophy, History of Western," by Albert W. Levi.

Patterson, Orlando. *Freedom: Freedom in the Making of Western Culture.* New York: Basic Books, 1991.

Paul Edwards, ed., *The Encyclopedia of Philosophy.* S.v. "Locke, John," by James Gordon Clapp. New York: Macmillan Publishing Co., Inc. and Free Press; London: Collier Macmillan Publishers, 1967.

Pleczynski, Z. A., ed. *The State and Civil Society: Studies in Hegel's Political Philosophy.* Cambridge, London, New York, New Rochelle, Melbourne, and Sydney: Cambridge University Press, 1984.

Scruton, Roger. *Kant.* Past Masters Series. Edited by Keith Thomas. Oxford: Oxford University Press, 1982.

Sjoberg, Gideon. *The Preindustrial City.* Glencoe: Free Press, 1960.

Skocpol, Theda. *States and Social Revolutions: A Comparative Analysis of France, Russia, and China.* Cambridge: Cambridge University Press, 1979.

Sombart, Werner. *The Jews and Modern Capitalism.* Translated by M. Epstein. New Brunswick and London: Transaction Books, 1951.

Somerville, John, and Ronald E. Santoni, eds. *Social and Political Philosophy: Readings from Plato and Gandhi.* Garden City, NY: Doubleday & Company, Inc., 1963.

Tawney, R. H. *Religion and the Rise of Capitalism: A Historical Study.* Holland Memorial Lectures, 1922. New York and Toronto: Mentor Books; Harcourt, Brace, & World, Inc., 1954, 1926.

Toulmin, Stephen. *Cosmopolis: The Hidden Agenda of Modernity.* Chicago: University of Chicago Press, 1990.

Wallerstein, Immanuel. *The Modern World-System: Capitalist Agriculture and the Origins of the European World-Economy in the Sixteenth Century.* Studies in Social Discontinuity. New York and London: Academic Press Inc., 1974.

———. *The Modern World System II: Mercantilism and the Consolidation of the European World-Economy, 1600–1750.* Studies in Social Discontinuity. New York: Academic Press Inc., 1980.

Weber, Max. *The Protestant Ethic and the Spirit of Capitalism: A Classic Study of the Fundamental Relationships between Religion and the Economic and Social Life in Modern Culture.* Translated by Talcott Parsons. New York: Charles Scribner's Sons, 1904/5. Reprint, 1920, 1930, 1958.

Wilson, John A. "Egypt through the New Kingdom." In Carl H. Kraeling and Robert M. Adams, *City Invincible.* Chicago: University of Chicago Press, 1960.

Wilson, John F., ed. *Church and State in America.* New York: Greenwood, 1986.

P. BOOKS AND ARTICLES RELEVANT TO POSTCAPITALISM

Barta, Russell. "Work: In Search of New Meanings." *Chicago Studies* 23, no.2 (August 1984): 155–68.

Berger, Peter L. *A Far Glory: The Quest for Faith in an Age of Credulity.* New York: Free Press, 1992.

Bloom, Harold. *The American Religion: The Emergence of the Post-Christian Nation.* New York: Simon & Schuster, 1992.

Burnham, James. *The Managerial Revolution: What Is Happening in the World.* New York: John Day Company, Inc., 1941.

Drucker, Peter F. *The Practice of Management*. New York, Grand Rapids, Philadelphia, St. Louis, San Francisco, London, Singapore, Sydney, Tokyo, and Toronto: Harper & Row, 1954.

–––. *The Age of Discontinuity: Guidelines to Our Changing Society*. New York and Evanston: Harper & Row, 1968.

–––. *The New Realities*. New York, Grand Rapids, Philadelphia, St. Louis, San Francisco, London, Singapore, Sydney, Tokyo, and Toronto, 1989.

–––. *Post-Capitalist Society*. New York: Harper Business, 1993.

Komel, Arniel. "Prosperity Lies in Establishing Global Network." *International Herald Tribune*, October 20, 1987, 1, 7.

Labich, Kenneth. "The Best Cities for Knowledge Workers." *Fortune*, November 15, 1993, 5051 passim.

Maitland, Donald Sir. "Third World Slowly Forging 'Missing Link.'" *International Herald Tribune*, October 20, 1987, 1, 7.

Mbembe, Achille. *Les jeunes et l'ordre politique en Afrique noire*. Chrétiens en liberté/Coll. dirigée par René Luneau. Paris: L'harmattan, 1985.

–––. *Afriques indociles: Christianisme, pouvoir et état en société postcoloniale*. Paris: Éditions Karthala, 1988.

Reich, Robert B. *The Work of Nations: Preparing Ourselves for Twenty-First Century Capitalism*. New York: Alfred A. Knopf, 1991.

Schlesinger, Arthur M., Jr. *The Disuniting of America: Reflections on a Multicultural Society*. New York: W. W. Norton & Company, 1992.

Stewart, Thomas A. "Brainpower. Intellectual Capital Is Becoming Corporate America's Most Valuable Asset and Can Be Its Sharpest Competitive Weapon." *Fortune*, June 3, 1991, 44–46 passim.

Taylor, Mark. *Erring: A Postmodern Theology*. Chicago and London: University of Chicago Press, 1984.